Photoshop® CS3 Workflow

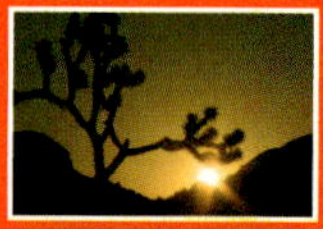
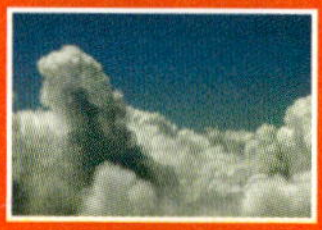
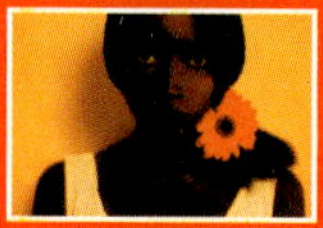
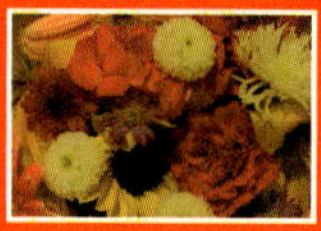
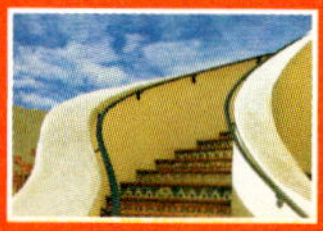

Photoshop® CS3 Workflow

The Digital Photographer's Guide

Tim Grey

WILEY PUBLISHING, INC.

Acquisitions and Development Editor: Pete Gaughan
Technical Editor: Jeff Greene
Production Editor: Debra Banninger
Copy Editor: Kathy Grider-Carlyle
Production Manager: Tim Tate
Vice President and Executive Group Publisher: Richard Swadley
Vice President and Executive Publisher: Joseph B. Wikert
Vice President and Publisher: Neil Edde
Book Designer: Franz Baumhacki
Compositor: Chris Gillespie, Happenstance Type-O-Rama
Proofreader: Rachel Gunn
Indexer: Ted Laux
Anniversary Logo Design: Richard Pacifico
Cover Designer: Ryan Sneed
Cover Photographers: Tim Grey; Michael Tedesco (penguins)

Published simultaneously in Canada

ISBN: 978-0-470-11941-9

Library of Congress Cataloging-in-Publication Data is available from the Publisher.

10 9 8 7 6 5 4 3 2 1

Dear Reader

Thank you for choosing *Photoshop CS3 Workflow.* This book is part of a family of premium quality Sybex graphics books, all written by outstanding authors who combine practical experience with a gift for teaching.

Sybex was founded in 1976. More than thirty years later, we're still committed to producing consistently exceptional books. With each of our graphics titles we're working hard to set a new standard for the industry. From the paper we print on, to the writers and artists we work with, our goal is to bring you the best graphics books available.

I hope you see all that reflected in these pages. I'd be very interested to hear your comments and get your feedback on how we're doing. Feel free to let me know what you think about this or any other Sybex book by sending me an email at nedde@wiley.com, or if you think you've found an error in this book, please visit http://wiley.custhelp.com. Customer feedback is critical to our efforts at Sybex.

Best regards,

NEIL EDDE
Vice President and Publisher
Sybex, an Imprint of Wiley

To Angel: Thank you.

Acknowledgments

Writing a book can be a Herculean effort—especially when you're way behind deadline. Such a project is never a solo effort, even when only one name appears on the cover. I'm very grateful to Pete Gaughan at Sybex Publishing for once again carrying a big stick but wielding it gently to help make sure I actually got all my work done, no matter how far behind schedule I found myself. Very soon Pete and I will work together on a book that starts on schedule and stays on schedule all the way through the project. I promise, Pete. In the meantime, I am often reminded how grateful I am to have the opportunity to work on so many books with Pete.

I am also indebted to Jeff Greene, my friend, co-worker, and frequent technical editor for various books, including this one. He put in many late nights to help make sure this book is as accurate as possible (though I'm convinced his brilliant son Eric actually did most of the work).

I want to thank all of those who have inspired me in one way or another in my life. It would be naive to think I could list them all without forgetting someone, but I'll do my best. Thank you to Miranda, Riley, Angel, Bruce, Susan, Mom, Bob, Heidi, Amy, Tiffanie, Grandma, Greg, Mrs. Shea, Mrs. Pendleton, Mrs. Bower, Mr. Baird, Dan, Peter, John, and Marianne.

And to all the great people I've had the pleasure of meeting at my various workshops, seminars, or other presentations, thank you for your ongoing support. I could try to mention all of you, but I think I'd run out of space and know I'd end up forgetting someone (isn't that right, Marianne?), so I think I better not try. But you know who you are, and I hope you know I appreciate all of you.

Thanks to the photographers who shared their beautiful images with me for this book: Arthur Morris, Matthew Jordan Smith, Alice Cahill, Chris Greene, Gabby Salazar, and Mike Tedesco.

And finally, I'd like to thank all the great people at Sybex who helped make this book possible. Pete Gaughan is at the top of that list. I also want to thank production editor Debbie Banninger, copyeditor Kathy Grider-Carlyle, the compositors at Happenstance Type-O-Rama, and the sales and marketing teams. The entire group at Sybex has been a joy to work with, and I appreciate all the effort they've put forth to help me produce the best books possible.

About the Author

A lifetime of working with computers and a love of photography combine as the perfect passion for Tim Grey. He loves learning as much as he possibly can about digital imaging, and he loves sharing that information even more. He does so through his writing and speaking appearances. He has authored or coauthored over a dozen books on digital imaging for photographers, including *Color Confidence* (Sybex, second edition 2006) and *Lightroom Workflow* (Sybex, 2007). His articles have been published in *Outdoor Photographer*, *PCPhoto*, and *Digital Photo Pro* magazines, among others. He also presents seminars and workshops at a variety of industry trade shows and other venues.

Tim also publishes a regular "Digital Darkroom Questions" e-mail list, where he answers questions related to digital imaging for photographers. To add your e-mail address to his list, visit www.timgrey.com.

Foreword

We're in the midst of a genuine renaissance in photography. Although in the middle of the twentieth century, it seemed that everyone was a photo-enthusiast and basement darkrooms were commonplace, color transparency photography and the proliferation of one-hour labs brought about the demise of the home darkroom. Amateur enthusiast photographers, and even many professionals, migrated away from the do-it-yourself kind of control of earlier years. But now, digital darkrooms and high-resolution digital cameras have brought us back from the laissez faire way of dealing with photographs—press the button and you're done—to an environment where once again the photographer takes complete control over the image from exposure to output.

When I worked in a black-and-white darkroom in school, taking a stack of photo paper and my negatives into that room was like activating a time machine: I would be catapulted hours ahead without necessarily having accomplished anything. My early days learning the digital darkroom did the same thing, except that I also got a sizable dose of frustration to add to the loss of hours. Until my workflow was consistent and efficient, I spent far too much time learning about computers and far too little making my photographs as good as possible.

Workflow is the great buzzword in digital imagery. Everyone wants to know how to establish a good workflow, how other people have set up their workflow, what constitutes an efficient workflow, etc. As photographers, we are concerned about workflow for good reason. Back in the age of film, the workflow was established by the parameters of the medium itself. You exposed the film, sent it to a lab for processing, and made a print or sent the image for prepress. But digital processes don't lend themselves to such a linear progression. Every step in the production of a digital image seems able to take on a new set of possible twists and turns, some of which are productive and some of which are a waste of time.

Although no longer in its infancy, digital imagery is still very much a child on the verge of adolescence. Like that awkward stage of growth and exploration, things are uncertain: there has been no established method to set up a workflow. Photographers have essentially resorted to asking each other, "What do you do?" and then tried to emulate and adopt others' ideas. In *Photoshop CS3 Workflow,* Tim Grey has cut through that trial-and-error system and gives us a methodical and logical means to design an efficient and effective workflow.

Tim Grey has a unique talent for being able to see through the extraneous details and cut right to the core of a problem. As he tackles setting up a workflow, Grey identifies the necessary elements involved and then shows in clear steps how to gain control over those elements to make the problems of workflow disappear into the background.

The best workflow is one that you shouldn't have to think about. We're photographers, not workflow analysts. The real strength of this book is in how it will help any photographer establish a workflow that is simple and doesn't become a distraction. After all, whether you're a pro or an amateur enthusiast, making better images is the goal.

Christopher Robinson
Editor, *Digital Photo Pro*

Contents

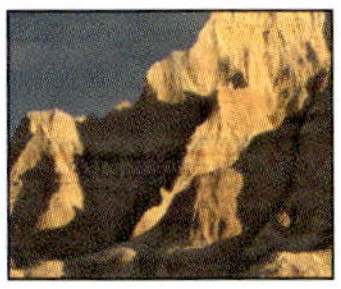

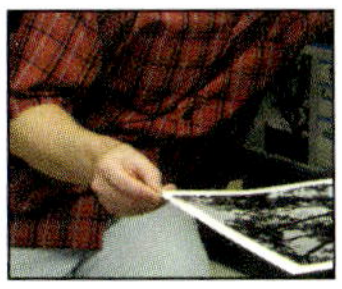

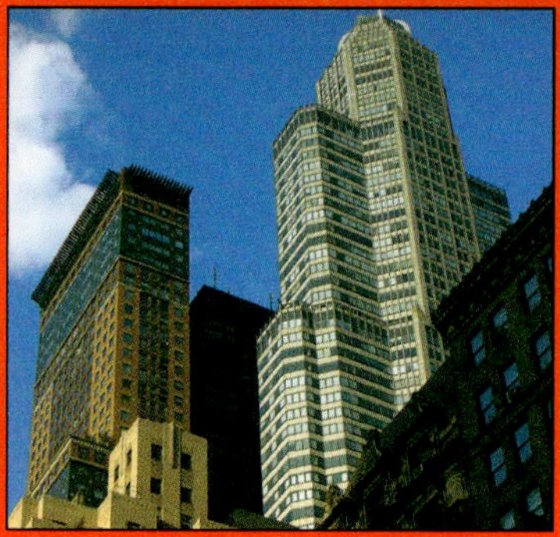

"Following a workflow frees you to think about 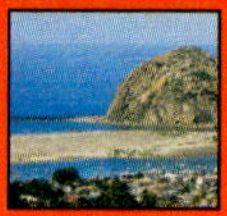 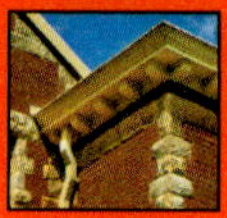  the effect on the image rather than the process."

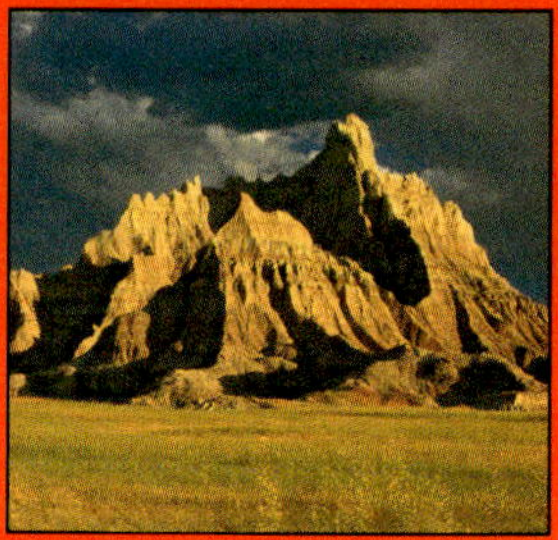

Introduction

Digital photography is an interesting blending of art and technology. It includes the artistic and aesthetic aspects of photography (which itself involves quite a bit of technology) that are so subjective, as well as the finite aspects of digital technology, where everything has very discrete values. This combination allows you to be both very creative and very scientific at the same time.

Although any art form deserves to be exercised with tremendous flexibility, digital technology calls for a certain amount of procedure. To anyone trying to be artistic, procedure is anathema to creativity. And yet, there is much to be gained from following a somewhat systematic workflow.

Following a workflow doesn't eliminate the ability to exercise creativity and subjective decision-making about your photographic images. Instead, I see it as a way to provide structure to your thinking that can actually help you expand the level of creativity you can apply to your images. By having a systematic method for processing your images, you're free to think about the effect on the image rather than the actual process. And just because you have a process doesn't mean it isn't unique or that it can't be revised as the situation warrants it.

In this book, I present a structure you can follow (and modify) when optimizing your images in Photoshop. It isn't designed to be an absolute formula, but rather a guide to help you define a structure for your own workflow. This process works well as a basic flow, but that certainly doesn't mean you should blindly follow the workflow I present exactly as I present it. Instead, think of it as one way to approach the image optimization process, and then fine-tune it to meet your own needs.

Besides wanting to promote a natural flow for making adjustments to images, it is also important to me that detail in the image be preserved and that adjustments are made in a nondestructive manner. As you'll see throughout the book, every adjustment I perform is done on a separate layer, not only keeping the original data safe but also enabling you to revise your adjustments at a later time with no penalty in image quality.

I hope it becomes obvious as you read this book that I am passionate about digital photography and image optimization in Photoshop. My greatest hope is that my passion will be infectious and that you too will grow to be passionate about optimizing your images (if you aren't already).

May you enjoy reading this book as much as I enjoyed writing it; may you enjoy the process of optimizing your own images as much as I do mine; and may the ever-growing possibilities provided by digital imaging make you all the more enthusiastic about photography.

Who Should Use This Book

Photoshop CS3 Workflow really covers the full spectrum of adjustments you'll want to apply to photographic images in Photoshop. As a result, it is appropriate for photographers of all skill levels who would like some guidance in creating the best workflow for image optimization. Beginning users will build a strong foundation and then be able to move on to more advanced topics, while expert users will gain a greater understanding of the issues affecting workflow as well as some new techniques they can use on their images.

This book was written based on Adobe Photoshop CS3, but it's also applicable in large part for users of prior versions of Photoshop (though some new features will obviously not be available). For users of Photoshop Elements, I recommend the book I coauthored with Peter K. Burian, *Photoshop Elements 5 Workflow* (Sybex, 2007), as a great resource for your workflow.

If you're a digital photographer who doesn't feel totally confident that you're getting the most benefit from your image-optimization in Photoshop, this is the book for you.

What's Inside

Chapter 1: Workflow Foundations will help you understand the principles of a good foundation and will get you thinking about your priorities in an image-optimization workflow.

Chapter 2: Download and Sort provides guidance on the process of getting digital captures onto your computer and then sorting and organizing them.

Chapter 3: RAW Conversion shows you how to process your RAW captures to retain maximum detail.

Chapter 4: Rotate and Crop provides the basics of cropping your images as well as rotating them to set the proper orientation or to fix crooked horizons.

Chapter 5: Basic Tone and Color guides you through the basic adjustments that affect tone and color in your images.

Chapter 6: Image Cleanup helps you master the art of repairing damage, dust spots, and flaws in your images to help them look their best.

Chapter 7: Advanced Tonal Adjustments takes things a bit further with tonal adjustments, showing you some of the advanced options available.

Chapter 8: Advanced Color Adjustments offers a look at some of the advanced options available for fine-tuning color in your images.

Chapter 9: Making Selections includes many methods for creating selections, from the basic tools included in Photoshop through some advanced methods.

Chapter 10: Targeted Adjustments lets you put your selections, as well as other techniques, to use so you can apply adjustments to specific areas of your images.

Chapter 11: Creative Adjustments gives you an opportunity to exercise a little creative license with your images by using techniques that go beyond the basic photo optimization.

Chapter 12: Saving Files covers the basics of saving your files to ensure that all the work you've put into the image is retained.

Chapter 13: Workflow Automation will help make your life easier by showing you how to automate repetitive tasks that you need to apply to your images.

Chapter 14: Output Processing finishes up the workflow by discussing how to prepare your images for final output.

Photoshop CS3 Workflow, Online

Some utilities and companion files mentioned in the book are available from Tim Grey's site, www.timgrey.com.

Sybex strives to keep you supplied with the latest tools and information you need for your work. Please check their website at www.sybex.com for additional content and updates that supplement this book. Search for photoshop and workflow (or the book's ISBN 9780470119419) to access the book's update page.

Photoshop® CS3 Workflow

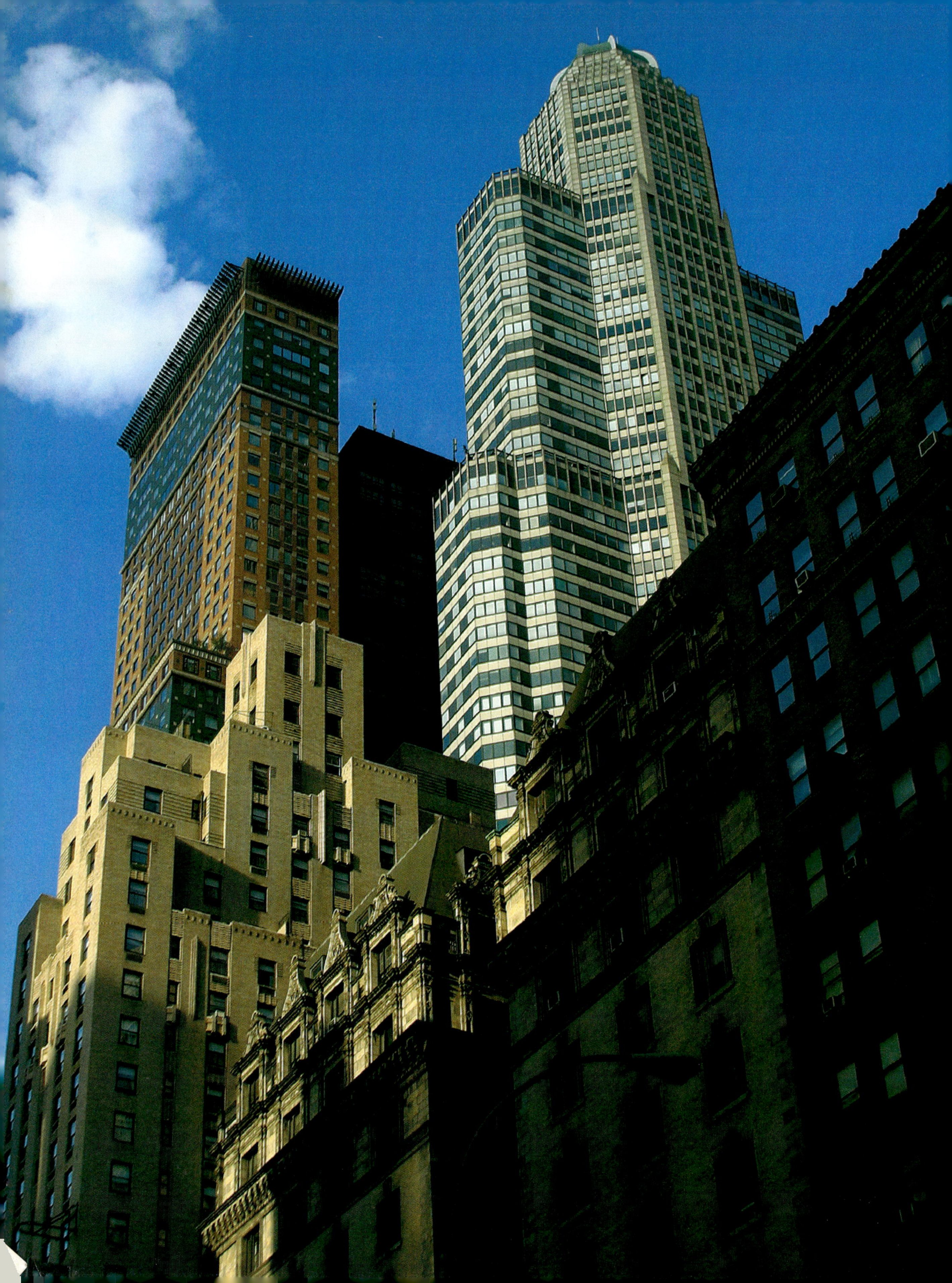

I

Getting Started

Digital photography has opened up a whole new level of control for photographers. Never before has it been so easy to exercise so much control over your photographic images. However, when many photographers start using digital tools, they don't know where to begin. In this section, I'll examine the first steps in establishing and implementing a digital workflow to help you start down the right path to optimizing your photographic images.

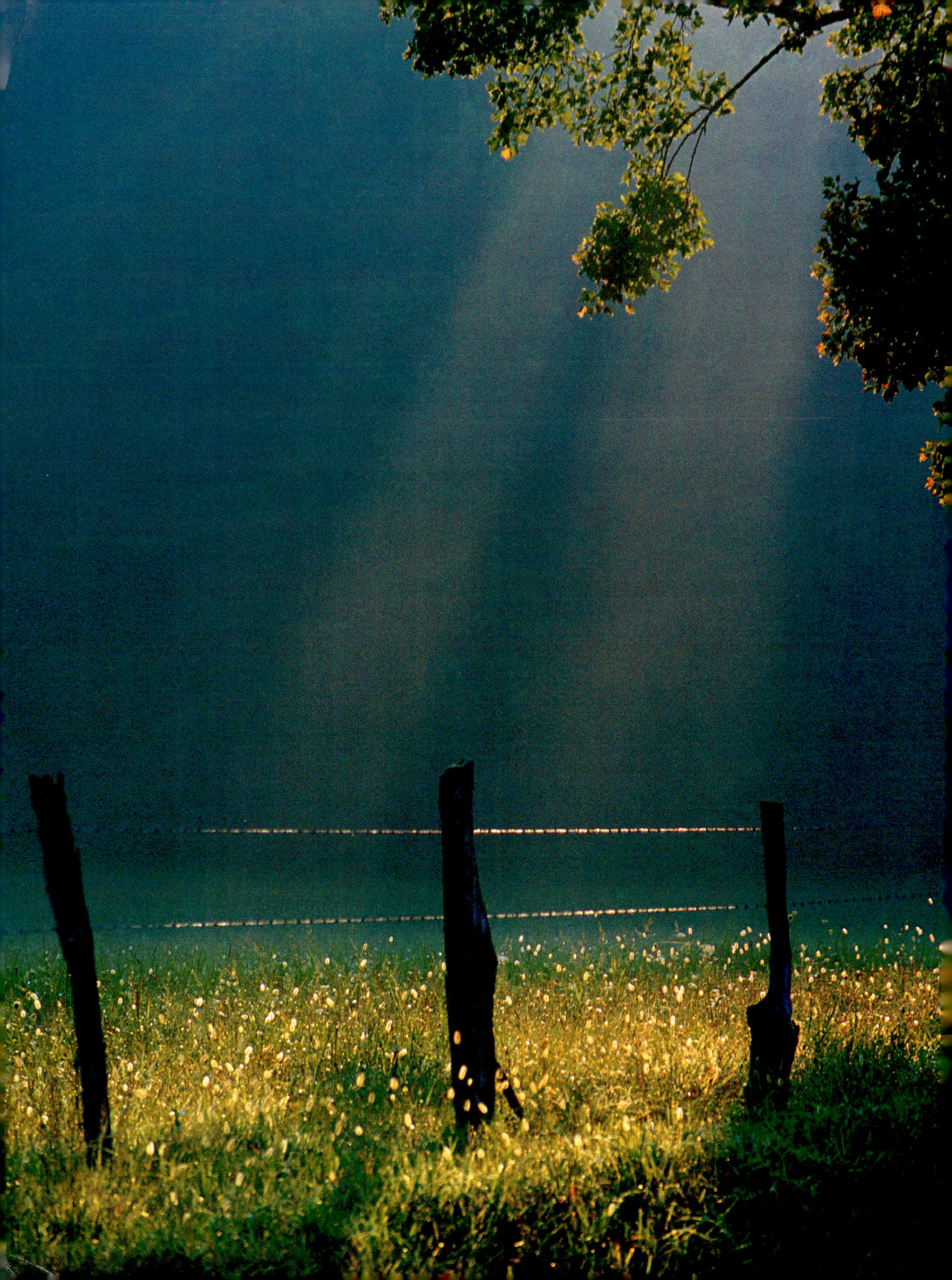

Workflow Foundations

If you've ever worked in a wet darkroom (and believe me, a great many readers of this book probably started with digital and never set foot in a wet darkroom), you know that there is a normal order, or flow, to the work that must be performed to create an image. The paper is exposed from the negative, then slid into the developer where the photograph magically appears, then placed into a stop bath to halt the development process, and finally placed into a fixer to ensure a (relatively) permanent image before the print gets washed and dried. When you're working with pixels in the digital darkroom, there are more options and variables, making an unlimited number of possible paths for optimizing your images. Establishing a workflow provides an efficient method of working on your images to help ensure the highest quality possible.

1

Chapter Contents

The Importance of Workflow

The term *workflow* has become a buzzword in the world of digital imaging, and with good reason. Many photographers feel overwhelmed when they set out to optimize some of their favorite digital captures. Besides not being sure where to begin, they don't know how the process should unfold.

Having a plan for your digital imaging workflow is important not only for making the process more efficient for you, but also for ensuring the best quality in the image. Understanding the benefits of a consistent and optimized workflow will help you appreciate the importance of establishing one.

Quality

For most photographers, the quality of the final image is of paramount importance. The potential quality of the final image is directly determined by the quality of the original capture. So the first step in producing the best images in the digital darkroom is to have the best captures before you even sit down in front of the computer.

After you bring the images into your digital darkroom, a proper workflow helps ensure optimal image quality for professional results. Having a plan for your workflow means you're thinking about the order in which you're performing adjustments and the methods you use to make those adjustments. These are both key factors that affect the quality of the final image, and having a plan focused on optimal quality will give you much better results than adjusting your images in a haphazard fashion.

For example, one of the factors often used to determine overall image quality is the amount of detail visible in the image (Figure 1.1). To ensure minimal detail loss, you can certainly exercise caution when making your adjustments, but a proper workflow will also help achieve this goal.

Note: Quality can be a subjective factor in many images, especially when unique photographic methods or special effects are used. Although the definition of optimal quality can vary by photographer or even by photographic image, your workflow should focus on maintaining the quality and aesthetics of your original image as you captured it, while producing an improvement in the final result.

As you are fine-tuning the workflow you use to optimize your images, consider the effect of the particular methods you're using, as well as the order in which you perform particular tasks, to see if there are things you can do to improve image quality. Throughout this book, I'll be sharing methods for achieving exactly those high-quality results with your digital workflow.

Efficiency

Although image quality tends to be a chief concern for most photographers (as it should be), efficiency is also important. As much as most photographers love working with their images—seeing them transformed from good captures to remarkable images—generally they don't want to sit in front of the computer all day. They'd much rather be out taking new pictures.

By developing a general workflow, you can work much more efficiently. You won't have to stop and think about what the next step is. Although certain images will certainly require extra attention, and at times you will need to try out various techniques before achieving the desired results, an established workflow you are comfortable with will make the work of perfecting your images go relatively quickly.

When giving presentations on digital imaging (see www.timgrey.com for a schedule of upcoming appearances), I may take half an hour to fully discuss the details of one particular adjustment, whereas making the adjustment as part of your normal workflow may require mere seconds or a few minutes at most. However, the time spent understanding how the adjustment works is well worth it. When you're familiar with the tools, you're able to use them much more efficiently. It may take some time for you to fully grasp all the details, but by taking the time to truly understand how the tools work, you'll be much more efficient without compromising the quality of your images.

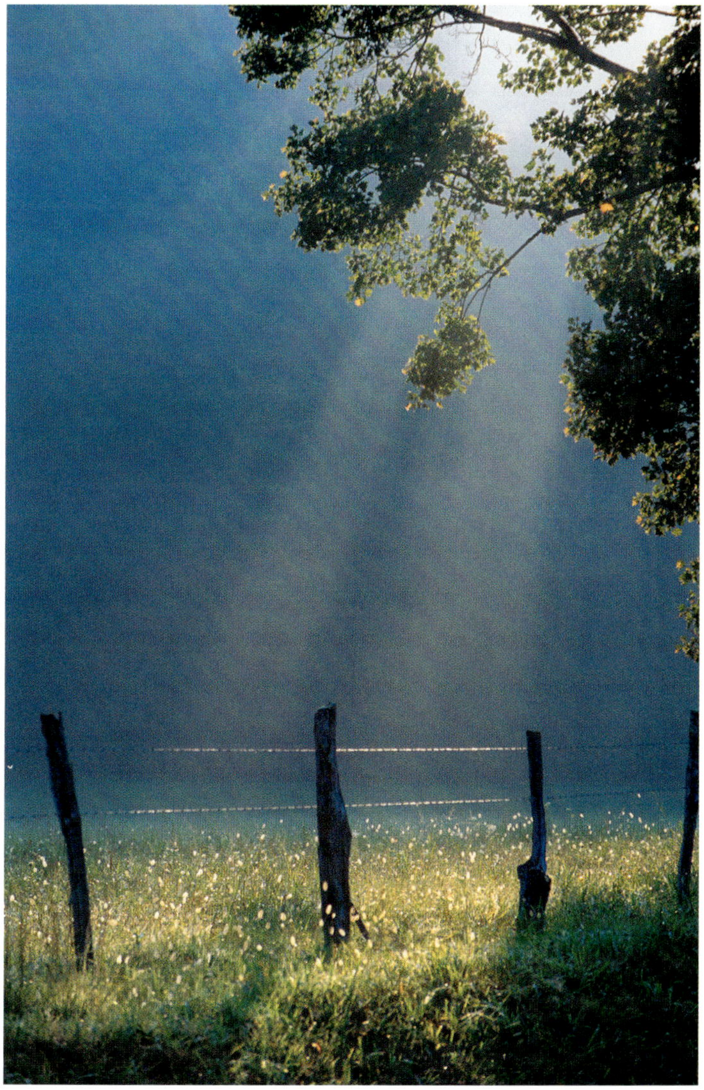

Figure 1.1 Maintaining maximum detail in an image is one of the factors commonly considered to represent good quality, and it is a key concern when the image includes relatively dark shadows. A proper workflow will help you maintain detail and quality in your images. (Photo by Gabby Salazar, www.gabbysalazar.com)

Consistency

Another benefit of a consistent workflow is—no surprise here—consistency. This relates to the two previous topics: by maintaining a consistent workflow, you'll ensure consistent quality in your images and a familiarity that will improve your efficiency. When you find a workflow that works for one image, that workflow (with obvious variations as needed for specific images) will work well for all of your images.

Note: Keep in mind that an established workflow doesn't define absolute rules of what adjustments you must make to all of your images, but rather it provides a roadmap that guides you through the best way to approach your images for optimization.

In effect, if it makes sense to establish a workflow for optimizing your images (and I certainly think it makes a lot of sense), it also makes sense to be consistent in your use of that workflow. In other words, make a plan and stick to it in order to achieve the maximum benefits.

Establishing a Workflow

Because you're reading this book, I'm assuming you already appreciate the value of establishing a workflow for optimizing your digital images. I also assume you aren't completely comfortable with the process you're currently using. As you work your way through this book, that will change.

As you begin creating a workflow that works for you, I strongly recommend making duplicate copies of a couple favorite images that could use some work, and going through the process of experimenting with the adjustments that will form the foundation of your workflow. Because they're just copies of your images, you don't have to worry about whether you produce a good final result, and you can focus on practicing the steps involved and figuring out what works best for you.

Note: Although this chapter is about establishing a workflow for your images, you won't find details of a specific workflow here. That's because this entire book is about the workflow process, and by going through the book in its entirety, you'll learn what steps you need to include in your own workflow, and in what order you'll likely apply them.

Determine Priorities

Your priorities in optimizing your images probably reflect the topics covered in the beginning of this chapter. In particular, you probably want to ensure maximum quality in your images while maintaining efficiency with your workflow. However, you may also have other priorities for your images, which you'll want to consider when fine-tuning your workflow.

The first step in establishing a digital workflow is to think about what is important to you and how you prefer to work. Some of this relates to overall strategies. For example, I strongly recommend using adjustment layers or separate image layers for all adjustments. This approach will be emphasized throughout this book, with a layer-based method for every adjustment presented. Another aspect to consider is the general flow of your adjustments. Do you prefer to clean up dust and other blemishes before you get started, or would you rather move right into tonal adjustments first? This book will present recommendations on what order you should use to make your adjustments, and under which circumstances you should change that order.

Of course, your priorities will depend in large part on the type of work you're doing and the deadline under which you're operating. For example, photojournalists often have speed as their utmost concern. For them, a workflow that focuses on methods to speed up the process of preparing images is optimal. For a nature photographer producing large prints, quality is the greatest concern, even if that means taking considerably longer to process an image. For a given photographer, the optimal workflow may even vary based on the particular project. The key is to define a workflow that meets your typical production needs, but to remain flexible so you can revise your workflow based on changing needs.

One suggestion that may help you determine the basic structure of your workflow is to focus on solving the problem that requires the most significant adjustment first and work your way down from there (Figure 1.2). The specific problem you'd define as the greatest for a given image will obviously be different from one image to the next. Some images will have significant tonal problems because of an error in exposure.

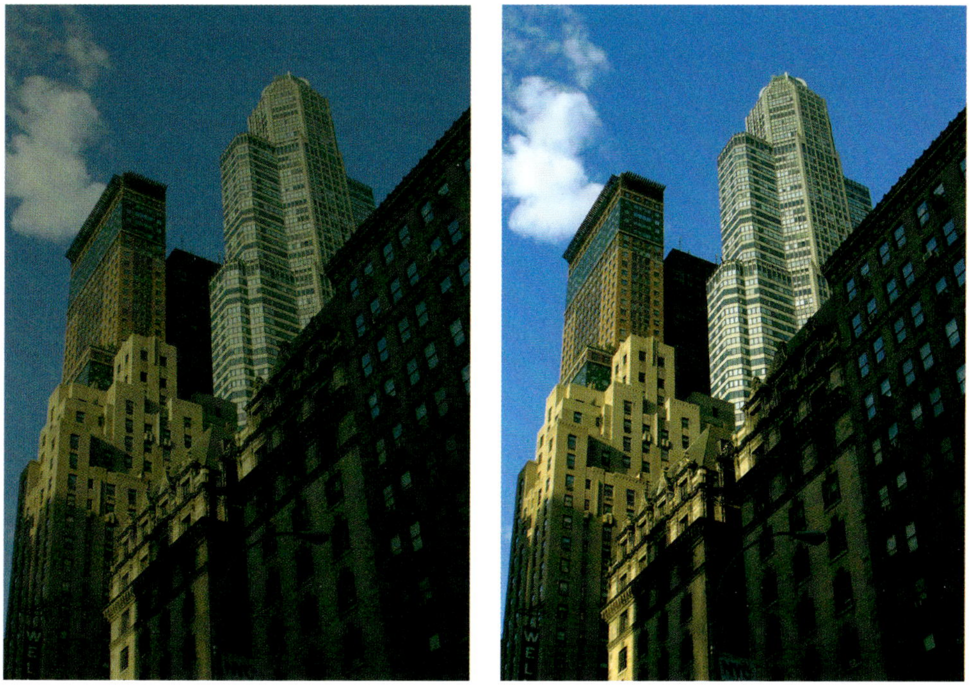

Figure 1.2 For many digital images, the tonal adjustments tend to be the most significant required. Therefore, a typical workflow may include basic tonal adjustments as the first step.

Others will need major color correcting because of lighting issues or a problem with your white balance setting in the digital camera. For scans of older film, the biggest problem may be considerable dust or scratches on the original. In each case, there is a logical order to correcting the image based on prioritizing which problems are of greatest concern.

The most serious problem for each image will vary; however, as you work on more and more images, you'll find that most tend to have a similar order of priorities for problems that need to be fixed. For example, with digital captures I usually find that the color is pretty accurate, so any tonal changes tend to be the most significant adjustments I'll make. For that reason, I usually find that it makes sense to start with broad tonal adjustments, then move on to broad color adjustments, and then move on to fine-tuning adjustments.

All this talk about "problems" may lead you to believe that this book is all about working on your very worst images—or that I'm a terrible photographer! Keep in mind that the problems in an image may be minor. In many cases, you may open an image and feel that it really doesn't need any significant changes. That is the ideal starting point, because such an image allows you to explore how you can make a great photo breathtaking, rather than trying to salvage a bad photo. Even when your original images look great, a proper workflow will help ensure that you produce the absolutely best results possible from every image.

Focus on Results

Although workflow is all about a process, the real purpose of that process is to create the final result (Figure 1.3). Photographers typically capture images because they want to produce beautiful prints or other output to share with as many viewers as possible. We want that final output to be impressive, both because of the content of the image and because of the quality of the final display. As such, it is important that you are thinking about the final result when you're optimizing your images, as well as when you're figuring out your workflow in the first place.

We want to produce the best images possible, and a proper workflow will ensure you are able to maintain that quality throughout the process. However, you should also consider your intent for the final appearance of your images. How you want your images to look at the end of the process can determine the steps you take to adjust the images during that process. For example, if you are preparing an image for a brochure and need it to be a real attention-grabber, you might boost the saturation and kick up the contrast. The same image used for a restaurant menu might need to be toned down for a more subtle appearance. A general workflow will provide the flexibility to adjust the image either way, but the actual process may be different for each.

As you think about the results you are trying to achieve, and the typical order of priorities in producing the best results, you'll get a sense of how you might organize the process of optimizing your images. Give some thought to the order in which you should make your adjustments, and the factors that are particularly important to you when it comes to your images. As you think about these topics, you'll start to get a sense of a workflow that will make sense for you and your images.

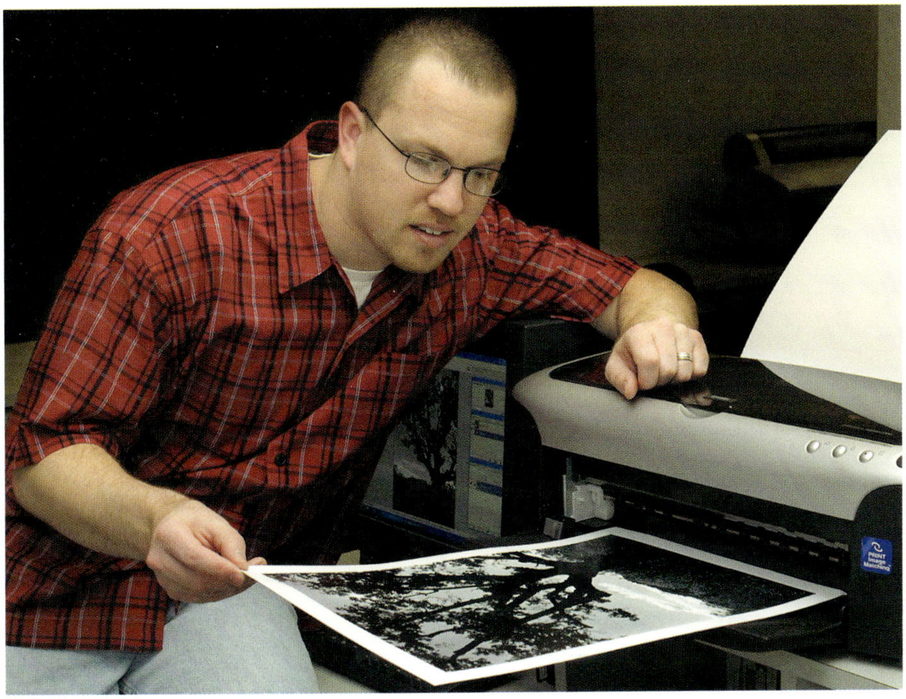

Figure 1.3 For most photographers the ultimate result of their digital workflow is a high-quality print they are proud to display for all to see.

Note: I'd be the last person to suggest you need to write your own manual on how to apply a workflow to your images (especially because this book can guide you through the workflow process). However, it might make sense to write out the basic steps you feel are important as you develop your own workflow. Also, be sure to see the appendix at the back of this book for a workflow guide you can use as you develop your own workflow.

Maintain Flexibility

Another important consideration for your workflow is flexibility. You want to be sure your workflow is making your image-optimization process more efficient, and that it allows you to change your mind about what you want the image to look like.

A Flexible Attitude

One aspect of maintaining flexibility in your workflow is a state of mind. It is important that you don't get caught in the trap of always doing the same things to every image. Each image is unique and deserves to be optimized based on what you judge to be the best result for that particular image. I've known photographers who apply the same adjustments with the same settings in the same order to every single image. This robotic approach to image editing won't demand too much of your time, but it also won't ensure optimal image quality. Some images may be improved by the particular adjustments, while others may be harmed.

Even if you find that certain settings for some adjustments seem to work best for every image, keep in mind that the workflow you establish is a basic guideline for the general order in which you'll perform your adjustments. Don't think of your workflow as a rigid set of rules that dictate what steps should be taken and in what order.

Even after you've established a workflow that helps you achieve exceptional results with your images, don't be afraid to change things around for a particular image. Some images will have unique problems that need to be addressed early in the workflow to maintain high quality. In other situations, you'll simply want to depart from your typical workflow to produce a creative variation (Figure 1.4). Whatever the situation, there are many good reasons to depart from your typical workflow to achieve certain goals. Treat your workflow as a guide for producing the best results with your typical images, but maintain the flexibility to change your process when you feel it will benefit the final result.

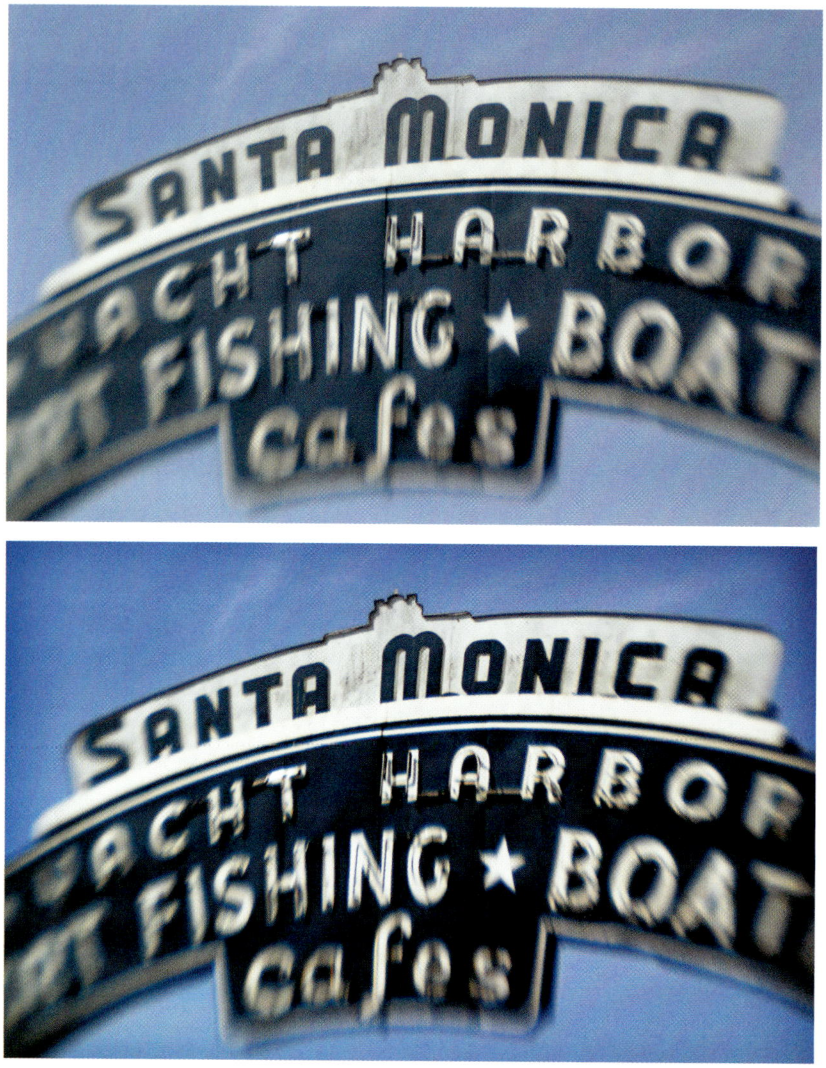

Figure 1.4 Even if you're happy with the way an image has turned out, you may later decide you'd like to stretch the creative limits of that image. Maintaining flexibility with your workflow helps ensure you can always act on your creative ideas.

Layer-Based Workflow

Another aspect of maintaining flexibility is ensuring you'll be able to change your mind and revise the adjustments you've made to an image without reducing the quality of the image or causing an excessive loss of detail. Using layers to optimize your images will ensure you always maintain this flexibility.

I strongly advocate the use of layers for all adjustments to your images (Figure 1.5). The use of layers ensures that the original information in your image is always preserved, provides greater flexibility, and may improve the quality. Throughout this book you'll find techniques for applying many adjustments, all performed with adjustment layers whenever possible. When an adjustment layer doesn't provide the tools needed to achieve a particular change, separate image layers with particular properties will be put to use. As a last resort, when the particular technique doesn't lend itself to using an adjustment layer or empty image layer for the adjustment, a duplicate of the background image layer should be created for purposes of applying the change.

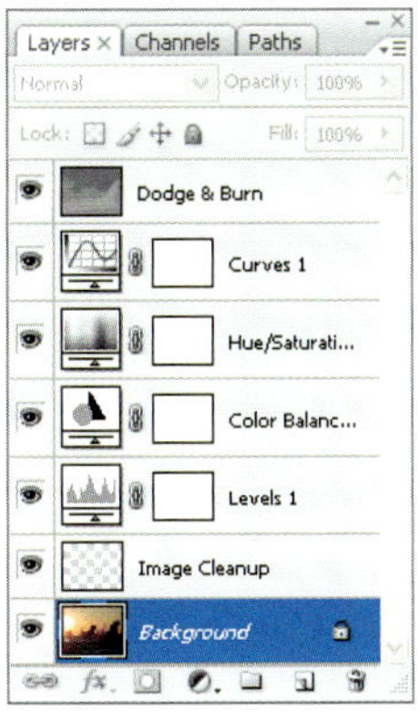

Figure 1.5 By using layers in your workflow, you'll maintain the flexibility to revise the adjustments you've made at any time without risking a loss of detail or quality in the image.

By following this recommendation, you'll ensure that the original image data contained in the background layer is maintained. The result is that you can always return to the image and remove particular adjustments, or fine-tune them if you've changed your mind about the adjustment itself. You may have experienced a situation where you've optimized an image, and then opened it at a later date only to wonder what you were thinking when you made the original adjustments. By working with layers, you can ensure that such situations don't represent a need to compromise the overall quality of the image, but rather represent opportunities to make the image even better than it was the first time you worked on it.

Note: I'll discuss more details of the benefits of adjustment layers in your workflow in Chapter 5, "Basic Tone and Color."

Revising Your Workflow

I think of a digital imaging workflow as a living entity. Not because I have some weird fascination with workflow, but because I realize that your typical workflow will change over time. You need to be comfortable revising your workflow to take advantage of new techniques you learn.

Nothing Is Permanent

A variety of factors may lead you to revise the way you work on your images. For one thing, as you learn new image-editing techniques, you may want to incorporate them into your workflow. As you read more books, take workshops, or just talk to others who are also involved in digital photography, you'll discover new methods that provide more efficient ways to achieve similar results or ways to produce completely new variations of your images.

Because it is simply a guideline for general adjustments, a general workflow provides the flexibility to incorporate new methods into the process of optimizing your images. However, in many cases you may develop a very specific workflow that involves performing specific actions (with variable settings) in a specific order. To ensure you are always able to achieve the best results, be willing to revise your workflow to incorporate new skills as you learn them.

Another factor that can change your workflow is changes in software. With each new version of Photoshop, or with the release (or discovery) of new plug-ins and filters, you'll find ways to add efficiency and creativity to your normal workflow.

The key is to be willing to revise your workflow when appropriate. If you learn a way to make your workflow more efficient or to provide even better results, by all means change your workflow to include such techniques.

Evolving Requirements

As you continue working with your images, you'll likely find that your own requirements will evolve. I consider there to be two general categories for these changing requirements.

The first category represents actual changes to the results you need to produce. For example, if you've been producing only ink-jet prints but now need to be able to prepare your images for offset press output, you may need to revise your workflow to be sure you're producing the best results for that type of output. If you create a website to share your images, you may also need to alter your workflow to include steps for preparing smaller versions of the images as well as thumbnail representations. Whatever the reasons, you'll likely find the requirements placed on your images change over time, and you'll want to be sure your workflow is always ready to meet those demands.

The second category has to do with the likelihood that your standards will get higher with time. If you've been working with digital imaging for any length of time, you can probably relate to this from your own experience. When the first photo ink-jet printers became available, most of us were thrilled with the quality they could provide. However, if you compare that early output to what today's photo ink-jet printers are able to achieve, you'd consider those older models totally inadequate (Figure 1.6). What used to be considered excellent quality is now rated as garbage. As we see what is now possible, what used to be possible is no longer good enough.

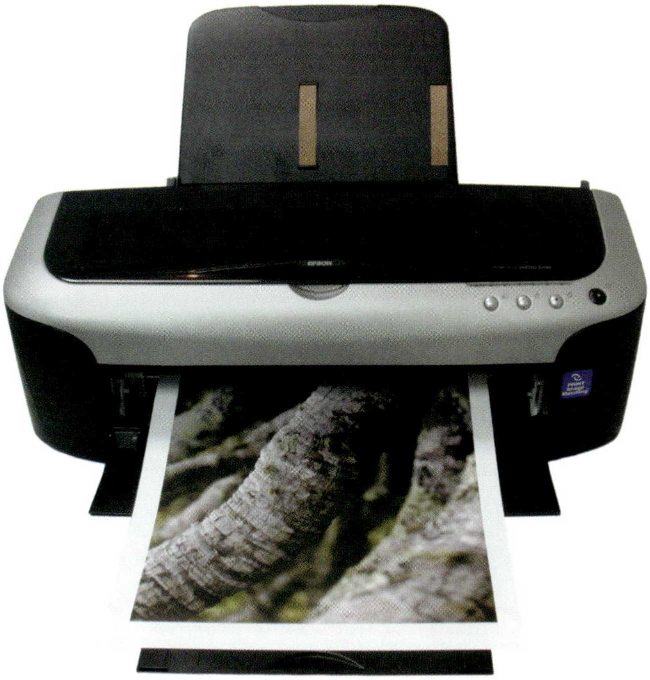

Figure 1.6 Today's photo ink-jet printers produce considerably better quality than those of just a few years ago. Similarly, your capabilities will improve with time, and you may want to revise your workflow over time so you always meet or exceed your own standards.

Similarly, you'll likely find that your own standards increase over time. As you become more skilled in the optimization of your images, you may open older images and wonder how you ever let yourself print them because you know you can do so much better today. As such, your developing skills in image optimization will call for revisions to your overall workflow.

The workflow you use to optimize your images will continue to evolve over time. The most important thing is to actually implement a workflow so it can evolve. Evaluate your images, consider the adjustments that are necessary to achieve the results you desire, and think about a logical way to apply those adjustments that will provide an efficient way to produce consistently high-quality results.

By taking the time to develop such a workflow, you'll ensure that the process is working for you, rather than creating a situation where you are working hard but not producing the consistent quality you desire. With a proper workflow—as you'll find throughout the rest of this book—you'll be able to unleash the great potential of the pixels in your images.

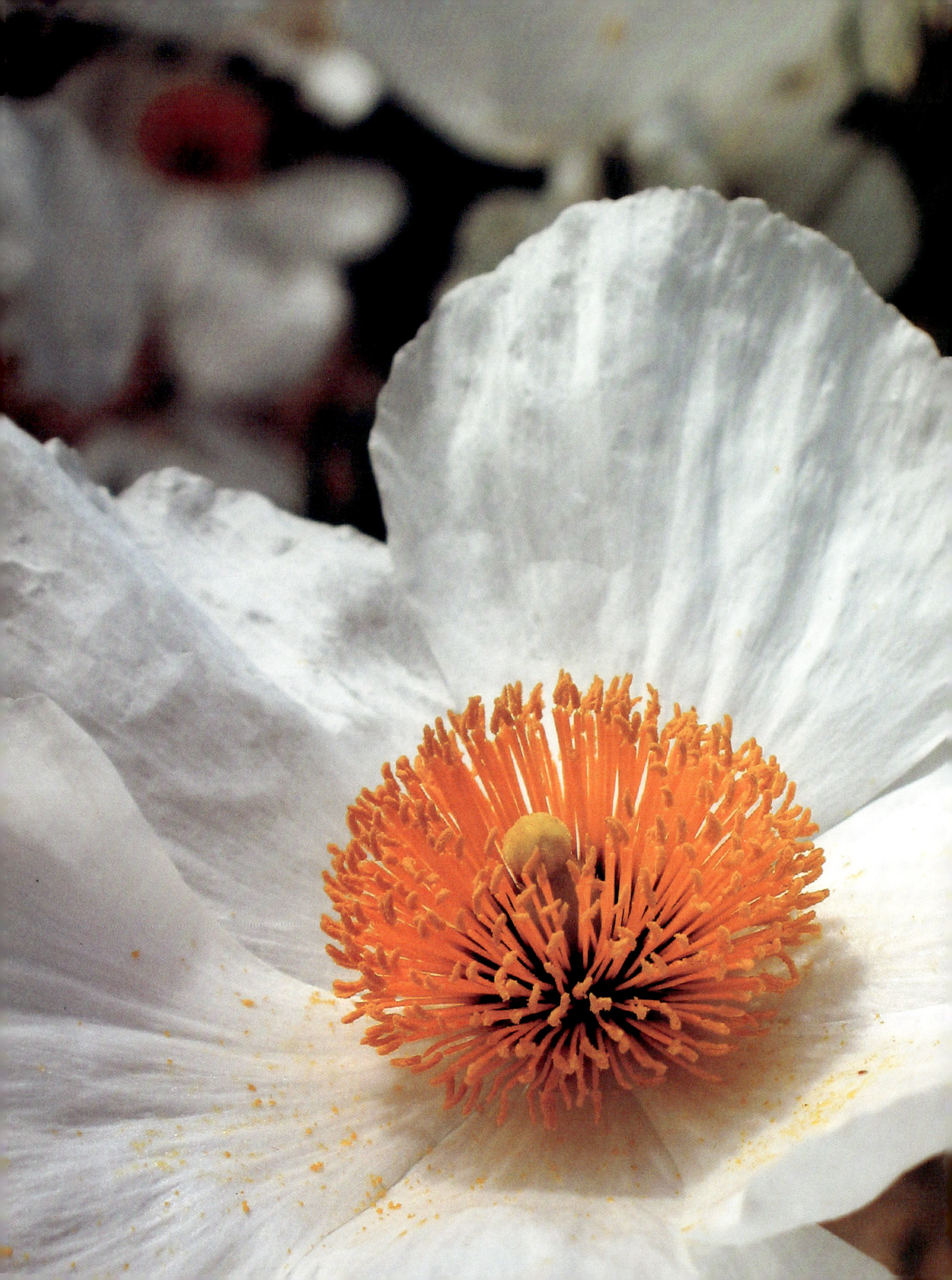

2 Download and Sort

The real workflow for your digital photos starts before the images even reach your computer. Of course, I usually think about the digital workflow as starting before I even press the shutter release button, but the actual workflow of optimizing your images starts with the process of downloading and sorting your images. Proper techniques ensure you'll safeguard your images and keep your growing collection organized.

Chapter Contents

Adobe Bridge

Photoshop includes a tool called Adobe Bridge that enables you to perform a considerable amount of image management (Figure 2.1). It is a photo browser that includes some great features for downloading, sorting, and organizing your images. While there are other tools out there from a variety of companies that enable you to perform many of these tasks, the fact that Bridge is included with Photoshop and provides all the basic features most photographers will need makes it a good solution.

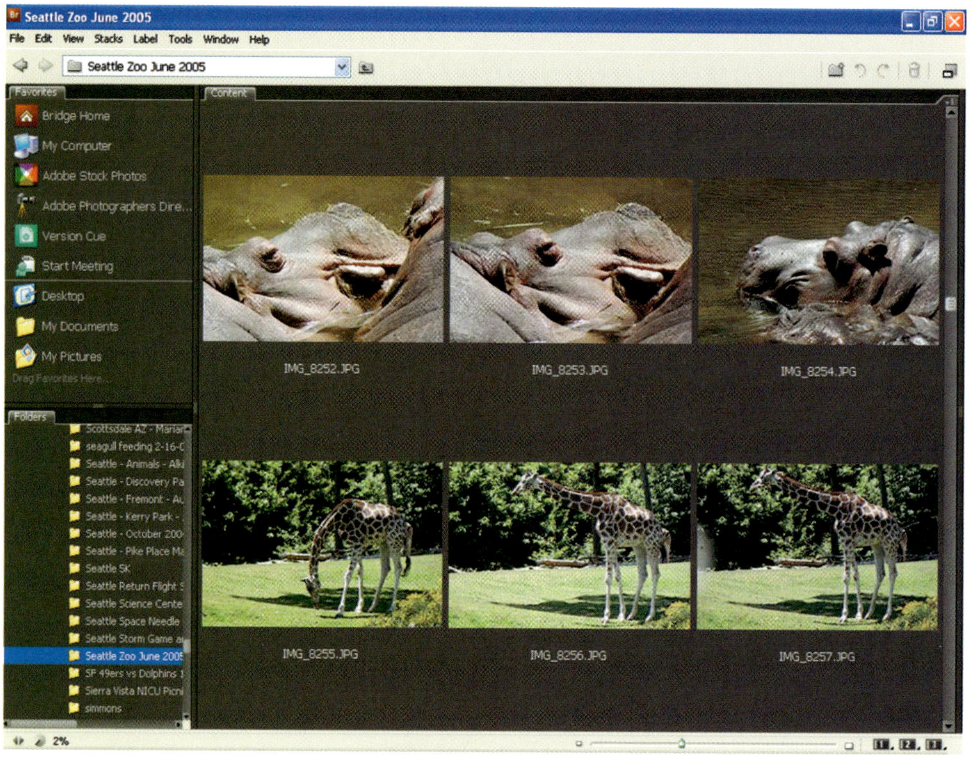

Figure 2.1 Adobe Bridge, which is included with Photoshop, is a tool for managing your images.

Bridge can be accessed from within Photoshop, but it is actually a separate application you can launch by itself, meaning you don't need to have Photoshop running in order to use Bridge. If you already have Photoshop running, you can launch Bridge by selecting File > Browse from the menu or by clicking the Go To Bridge button near the right end of the Options bar.

Preferences

Before you start working with Bridge, it is a good idea to set the preferences to make sure they are set the way you want them. To access the Preferences dialog, select Edit > Preferences from the menu in Bridge (Figure 2.2).

On the left side of the Preferences dialog box is a list of the "pages" available in Preferences. To access options in a particular category, click the name of the page you want to access.

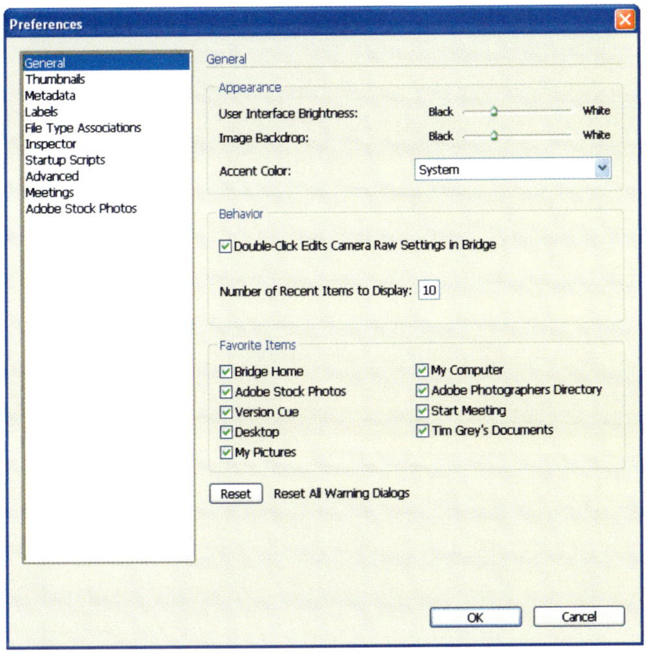

Figure 2.2 The Preferences dialog box contains a variety of settings that affect how Bridge operates.

General

The General page of the Preferences dialog box contains some basic settings that affect the appearance and behavior of Bridge.

The first set of options on the General page relates to the colors used within Bridge. Sliders that allow you to adjust the brightness of the interface (sliding between Black and White) are provided. The User Interface Brightness affects the background color of the general interface areas (such as the background of the Folders panel), and the Image Backdrop slider affects the background color of all areas behind images (such as behind thumbnails and previews). The Accent Color dropdown allows you to set a color for selected items, including images, folders, or other items you're able to select within Bridge. You can select a specific color from the list, or leave it at the default value of System to allow the color settings in your operating system to determine this color.

The first item in the Behavior section is a checkbox called Double-Click Edits Camera Raw Settings in Bridge. When this checkbox is selected, double-clicking on a RAW capture will not open (or switch to) Photoshop, but instead will simply bring up the Camera Raw dialog box. This allows you to adjust the conversion settings for the image without actually launching Photoshop, which can help speed up your workflow. This is helpful when you want to make adjustments to the RAW image but don't actually want to complete the workflow at the same time. The next time you open an image that has been adjusted in this manner, the settings you applied will be retained and used for the RAW conversion (unless you change those settings at that time).

The Number Of Recent Items To Display setting controls how many images will be shown on the list when you select File > Open Recent from the menu. This is a helpful feature that allows you to quickly open recent files without needing to remember where they are. I find 10 is usually adequate, but you can set the value as high as 30 if you like.

The Favorite Items section contains a series of checkboxes that determine what items will be listed in the Favorites panel in Bridge (I'll talk more about this panel later). By default all items in this section are selected. You can tidy up the Favorites panel a bit by removing those you won't use.

The final item on the General page is a button that allows you to Reset All Warning Dialogs. As you work with Bridge, you'll find warning dialog boxes that include a checkbox you can select so that particular warning won't be displayed in the future. If you disable warning messages that you actually do want to see, you can click the Reset button. Keep in mind this will bring back all warning dialog boxes, even those you really don't want to see (it isn't possible to selectively enable specific warnings).

Thumbnails

The next page on the list at the left of the Preferences dialog box is Thumbnails (Figure 2.3). Click this option to view the various settings affecting the display of thumbnail images within Bridge.

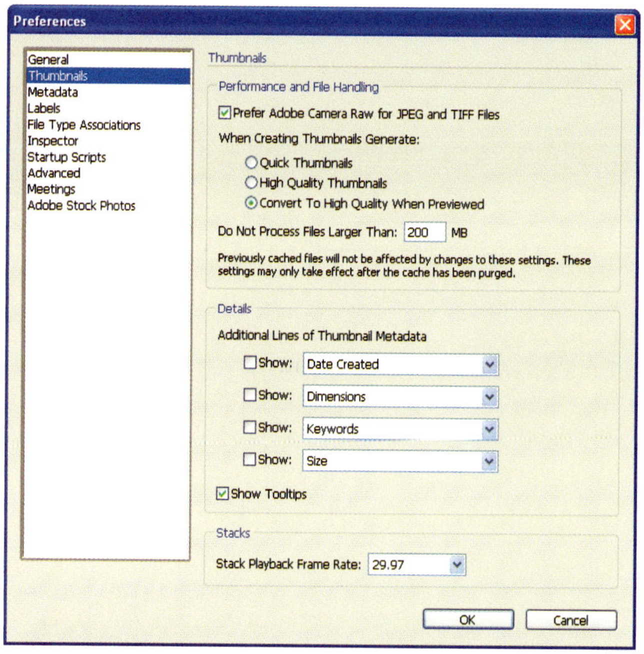

Figure 2.3 The Thumbnails page of the Preferences dialog box includes settings affecting the display of thumbnail images in Bridge.

The first section of the Thumbnails page is Performance and File Handling. The Prefer Adobe Camera Raw For JPEG And TIFF Files option determines how JPEG and TIFF files will be opened. By selecting this option, you'll be able to process these file types with Adobe Camera Raw, providing all the same adjustments for non-RAW images as you can for RAW. I like to keep this option selected because it provides more flexibility for JPEG and TIFF images, and it also creates a more consistent workflow for my images. I only apply modest adjustments to JPEG and TIFF images when using Camera Raw, saving the more detailed adjustments for adjustment layers in Photoshop. I'll discuss the use of Camera Raw in great detail in the next chapter.

The next option allows you to determine how thumbnails will be generated. If you're always in a hurry to see your images and aren't too concerned about the quality of thumbnail images, you can select the first option, Quick Thumbnails. If quality is of paramount concern, even though it means more time will be required to create the thumbnails, you can choose High Quality Thumbnails. I use this option because I want to have the best image quality possible even for thumbnails, and because I don't mind walking away from the computer for a little while to give Bridge time to build the thumbnails for me. The final option, Convert To High Quality When Previewed, is a compromise. It will generate quick thumbnails initially; however, when you actually view a preview image, the thumbnail will be updated to a high quality image.

The last item in this section is a setting that allows you to specify a file size above which Bridge will not generate thumbnails. The default is 200MB, which is probably adequate for most photographers. As you can imagine, processing such large files requires considerable time and can slow Bridge down. Also, if you have a file that large, you probably already know which image it is, as most files won't get that large for most photographers. Of course, if you generate a lot of large images and don't mind the additional time required to generate thumbnails, you can increase this value.

The Details section allows you to specify what information should be displayed with thumbnail images. To enable additional information, select one or more of the Show checkboxes (there are four available) and select the desired information you want from the dropdown to the right of the checkbox. Below these controls is a Show Tooltips checkbox. With this checkbox selected, a box with more details about the image will appear when you hold the mouse over an image for a moment. While this information can be helpful, I find the box a bit distracting, so I prefer to turn this option off and use the metadata panel to view additional details about the image.

The final option on the Thumbnails page allows you to adjust the frame rate used to play the multiple images in an image stack. I leave this at the default value and adjust it from the context menu for stacks as needed.

Metadata

The Metadata page (Figure 2.4) contains a list of all metadata fields available in Bridge. It allows you to control which fields will be displayed on the Metadata panel. I don't find a need to change the defaults; however, if there are extra fields you never reference, or fields excluded by default that you want to see, you can change the checkbox setting for those fields.

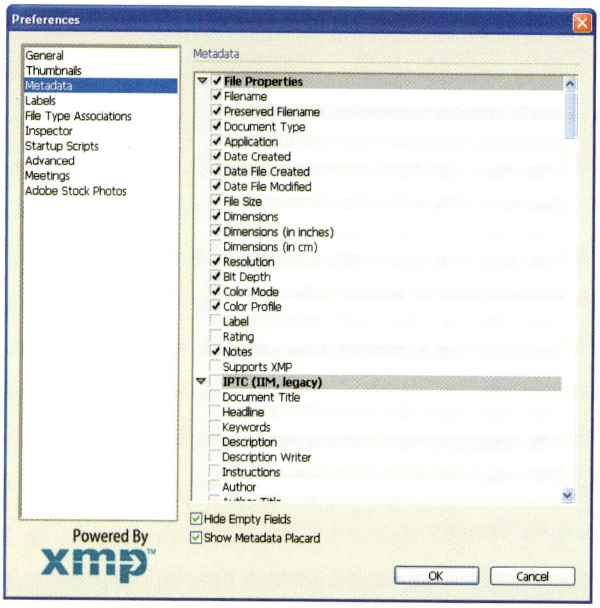

Figure 2.4 The Metadata page allows you to determine which metadata fields will be available in Bridge.

Labels

The Labels page (Figure 2.5) allows you to change settings for the color labels you can apply to your images, which I'll talk about later in this chapter. The first option is a checkbox that determines whether you need to hold the Ctrl/Command key in order to assign a label to an image when using keyboard shortcuts for this purpose. I prefer to require this "extra" key in the keyboard shortcut to help make sure I apply labels only when I really mean to apply them.

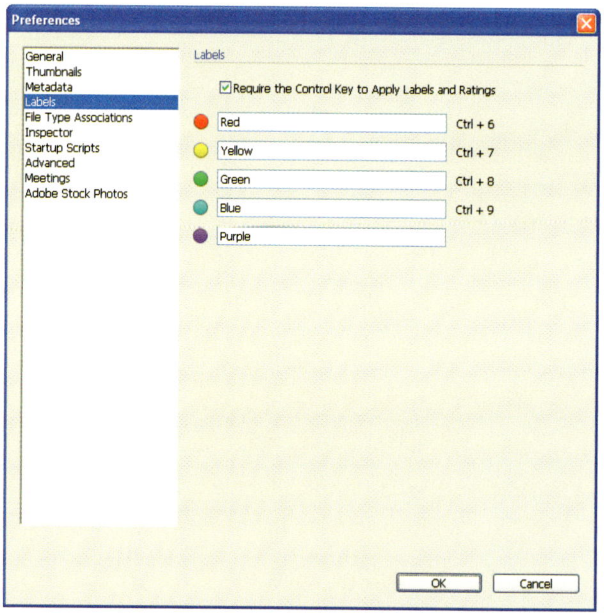

Figure 2.5 The Labels page allows you to change the text related to color labels.

The text boxes below (associated with individual label colors) allow you to specify a name for the label. Only the color actually gets associated with the image, but the text you type here will appear on the menu where you can select the label for specific images. It can, therefore, be helpful to assign values here based on the way you use labels, such as for specific priorities in your workflow or projects on which you are working.

File Type Associations

The File Type Associations page (Figure 2.6) allows you to specify which application should be used to open image types when you open them from Bridge. In most cases, I prefer to use the default settings that will open most image types in Photoshop. If an association gets changed, this is where you can fix it. Of course, if you want a particular image type to open with a different application, you can set that here as well.

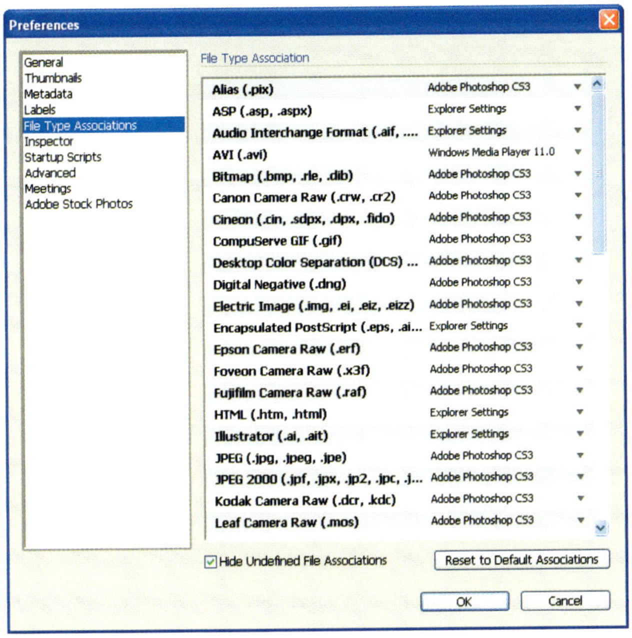

Figure 2.6 The File Type Associations page allows you to specify which application should be used to open files supported by Bridge.

To change the association for a given file type, simply find it on the list and click the dropdown to the right of that file type. From the list, you can choose an application to use, or you can click Browse so you can navigate to a particular application and select it.

A checkbox at the bottom of this page allows you to Hide Undefined File Associations, meaning file types that have the association set to None won't be shown on the list. You can also reset the associations back to their default values by clicking the button at the bottom of the page.

Note: The Inspector page is only applicable to the use of Version Cue, which allows you to manage multiple versions of an image in a workgroup environment and is, therefore, beyond the scope of this book.

Startup Scripts

When Bridge is launched, there are a variety of scripts that get run automatically. Disabling the ones you don't need can improve performance, and you can determine which ones will run on the Startup Scripts page (Figure 2.7). To disable a script, clear its checkbox. For example, I usually disable Adobe Device Central CS3 (because I don't create content to be displayed on mobile devices), Adobe Version Cue (because I don't work in a workgroup environment), Start Meeting (also because I don't work in a workgroup environment), and VersionCueSDKLoader (because I don't work with Version Cue).

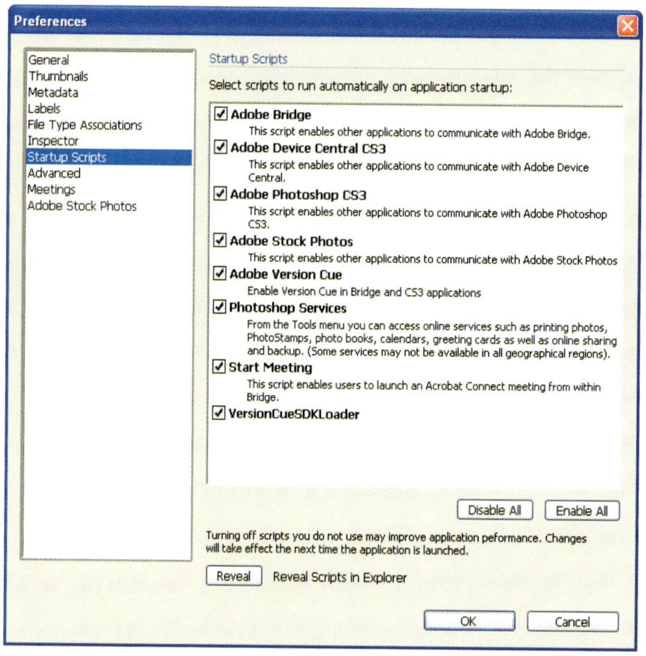

Figure 2.7 The Startup Scripts page allows you to specify which scripts will launch when you start Bridge.

Advanced

The first section of the Advanced page (Figure 2.8) is Miscellaneous, which contains two checkboxes. The first allows you to Enable Color Management in Bridge, which I strongly recommend enabling. Color management is a critical component in a workflow, helping to ensure accurate color throughout the process.

Note: For more information about color management, see my book *Color Confidence* (second edition, Sybex, 2007).

The other checkbox on the Advanced page is Use Software Rendering. Selecting this checkbox will disable hardware acceleration for image rendering. Hardware acceleration is considerably faster, so I don't recommend selecting this checkbox unless you are experiencing problems you think may be related to hardware acceleration (such as frequent crashes).

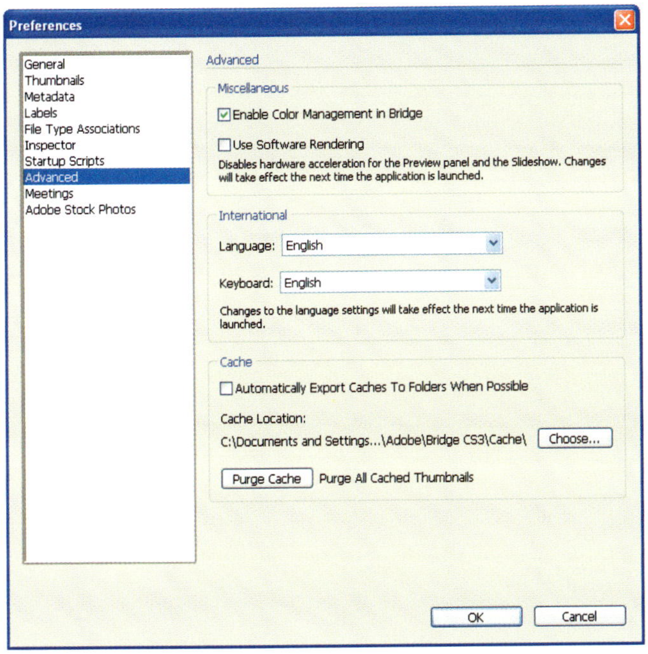

Figure 2.8 The Advanced page includes a variety of advanced settings for Bridge.

Note: The Meetings page is applicable only to workgroup environments and is, therefore, beyond the scope of this book. The Adobe Stock Photos page relates to settings for searching for images from the Adobe stock photography service and, therefore, is not likely to be used by readers of this book who produce their own imagery.

Downloading Photos

Once you've thought about how you want to approach your image downloading, you're ready to start the actual process of downloading your images. Photoshop CS3 now includes the Adobe Photo Downloader utility, which makes it easy to download your images with great flexibility and control.

Adobe Photo Downloader

Photoshop CS3 includes the Adobe Photo Downloader as part of the Bridge browser. It provides a user-friendly method for downloading photos from your digital camera or media cards in a card reader

To get started with the Adobe Photo Downloader, launch Bridge and select File > Get Photos From Camera from the menu. This will bring up the Photo Downloader dialog box (Figure 2.9). Photo Downloader will automatically look for a device as a source of photos on your computer. If it finds one, it will set that as the source and indicate how many images are there for download. It will then display the number of images, total size, and date range (based on capture date) of the images on that source.

If the source is not selected automatically, you can choose it from the dropdown, and if it isn't listed on the dropdown, you can choose "< Refresh List >" to update the list of sources.

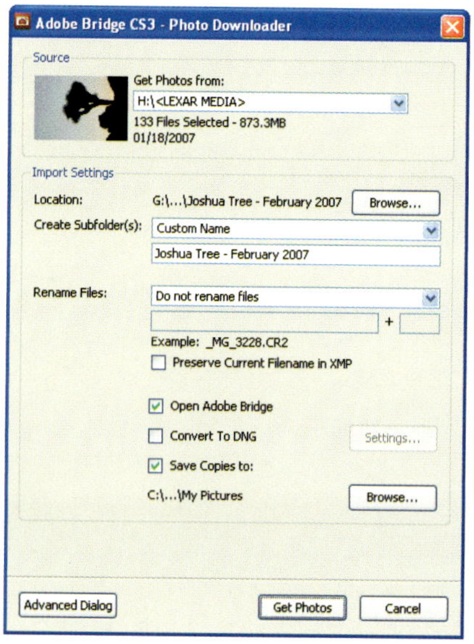

Figure 2.9 Photo Downloader enables you to copy images from your digital media cards.

The Import Settings section of the dialog contains a variety of settings that allow you to specify where you'd like the photos copied and how you'd like them to be processed. The first option is the Location where you'd like to have the photos copied. Click the Browse button to bring up the Browse For Folder dialog box and select (or create) a folder to serve as the primary location for your photos. I strongly recommend that this location be the top-level folder where you store your photos. For example, if you have a "Photos" folder on your hard drive or you store all images on an external hard drive, set that location here.

The next option allows you to create subfolders. At first you might think you really don't want to create subfolders because you want to keep all images from a given photo shoot in a single folder. However, keep in mind that I suggested setting the Location to the top-level folder that contains all the subfolders with your photos. Therefore, I actually use the Create Subfolders option to create the folder that will contain all images from the photo shoot I'm downloading. I select the Custom Name option from the dropdown, which enables a text box where you can enter a name for the shoot, which will be used as the folder name. You can also select one of the options for creating subfolders based on the date.

The next set of controls allows you to rename the files you are downloading. There are a variety of options available from the dropdown based on a combination of dates (today's date or the date the images were captured) and custom text. There is also an option to use the same name as the folder you created above. If you select an option that includes a Custom Name, the text box below will be enabled so you can type a value. This can be helpful for effectively building keywords into the filenames you use for your images. To the right of the text box where you enter a custom name is a box for the sequence number. The default is one; however, if you are adding images with a filename structure that matches one you've used previously, you can set the value to a higher number as needed.

The checkbox below the renaming controls allows you to preserve the original filename in the XMP metadata, so you can always determine what the original filename from the camera was.

The next checkbox is Open Adobe Bridge. If this checkbox is selected, when the download is complete, Bridge will be launched so you can browse those images immediately.

The Convert To DNG checkbox allows you to save your images in the Digital Negative (DNG) format as part of the download process. This option is preferred by many photographers who are concerned about being able to access their proprietary RAW file formats in the future and want to save them in a publicly documented file format. If you select this checkbox, a settings button to the right becomes enabled. Clicking that button will bring up the DNG Conversion Settings dialog box, where you can change how the DNG files are created.

The final checkbox is "Save Copies To," and it will create a backup copy of your images during the download process. I particularly recommend taking advantage of this option if you're traveling away from your primary location and, therefore, aren't able to include these new images in your normal backup process right away. Even if you do have a good backup process that these images will be part of, it is a good idea to copy them to an additional location (such as an external hard drive) during download to help safeguard your images. When you select this checkbox, a Browse button becomes enabled so you can specify the location where you want the copies stored.

When you click the Advanced Dialog button, the Photo Downloader dialog box will expand to a much larger dialog box including thumbnails and other fields (Figure 2.10). Below the Advanced Options settings (the three checkboxes after the renaming controls) will be added an Apply Metadata section. The dropdown at the top of this section allows you to select a metadata template to use. If you use the Tools > Create Metadata Template option in Bridge to create a template with information you want applied to all images, the template will appear on this list. You'll always have the None (don't apply any metadata) and Basic Metadata options. With the Basic Metadata option selected, Author and Copyright fields will be shown below. You can enter information here, and that information will be applied to the metadata of all images as they are downloaded.

The remaining area of the enlarged dialog box is filled with thumbnails of the images on the source media. Besides providing an opportunity to review the images that are being downloaded (which is helpful for confirming you're downloading from the correct card, for example), it also allows you to exclude images from the download if desired. My recommendation is to include all images in the download so you can begin the process of copying the images to your computer, leaving the sorting process for later.

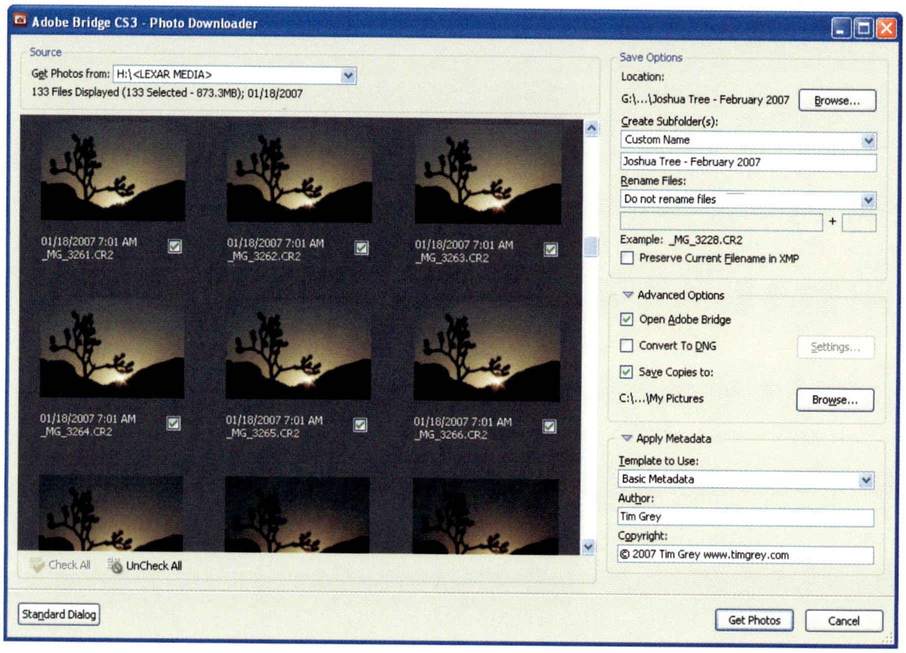

Figure 2.10 The Advanced Dialog button enlarges the Photo Downloader dialog box to include more options, including thumbnail views of all images being downloaded.

Once you've established all the settings you prefer, click Get Photos to start the download process. A dialog box will appear to show you the progress of the download (Figure 2.11). When the download is complete, if you selected the option to open Adobe Bridge, it will be launched and the folder you downloaded images into will be shown. It is a good idea at this point to browse the folder to make sure all images you expected were successfully downloaded.

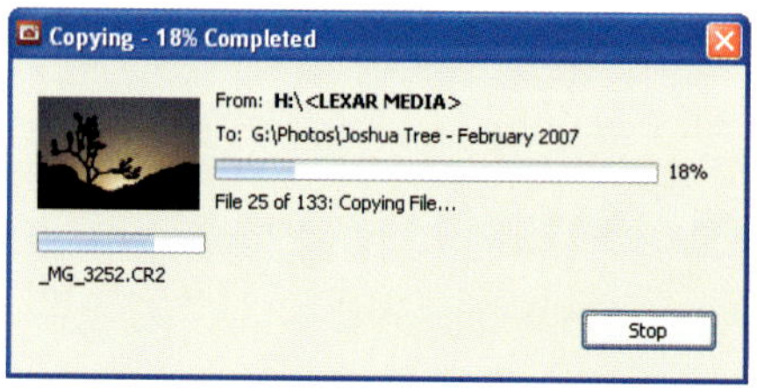

Figure 2.11 A progress dialog box is displayed as images are being downloaded with Photo Downloader.

Note: You might have noticed there is no option in the Photo Downloader to delete the images from your digital media card after download. I see that as a good thing, as I don't recommend deleting until you've confirmed a successful download, and then by reformatting the card in your camera, as discussed later.

Reformatting Digital Media

After you have copied all images from your digital media cards and confirmed that all have been copied safely, you're ready to clear the card so it will be ready for your next photo shoot. Just be sure to safely eject the card or camera within your operating system to avoid potential data problems. I strongly recommend reformatting the cards in your camera rather than deleting or formatting within your operating system. The latter could cause the card to be unusable by the camera until it is reformatted in the camera because of differences in the file system being used. The format option can be accessed from the menu on the LCD display for most cameras.

Note: Reformatting your media card in the camera both erases the images on the card and re-initializes it to help avoid read and write problems.

Formatting the card in the camera erases the images as part of the process, and it is generally faster than any of the other methods for deleting all images from the card. It also re-initializes the card with a new "table of contents." Doing so helps prevent accumulated corruption of the card's file system, helping to ensure you won't experience any read or write problems in the future.

Note: Because the media card serves as an effective backup of the images you downloaded from it, you may want to wait to reformat the card until just before you need it, so you can recover images from it if they are accidentally deleted from your computer. This risk also reinforces the benefit of creating an archival copy of all images immediately after downloading them.

Sorting Images in Bridge

Getting your digital images onto your computer is certainly a start. But as you've probably noticed, those images seem to accumulate quickly, and keeping them organized can be a bit of a chore, especially if you have a backlog of images stored in many folders. When you download your latest images, chances are you want to get started right away working with them. The first step, of course, is to figure out what you have and which images you'd like to start optimizing first.

Light Table Analogy

Most (though certainly not all) photographers who are now capturing images with a digital camera started off with film photography. For those who used slide film, the concept of a light table sorting method is quite clear, and so this has been used countless times as an analogy for sorting digital images.

With slides, the basic process of sorting involved laying out the slides on a light table, starting with an overall review to delete obviously bad images, and then getting a closer look with a loupe to further evaluate those that remained (Figure 2.12). In the process, slides could be grouped based on criteria such as favorites, subject matter, model, or other factors. This allowed the photographer to get organized while working to slim down the number of images. A similar process works quite well when sorting digital images.

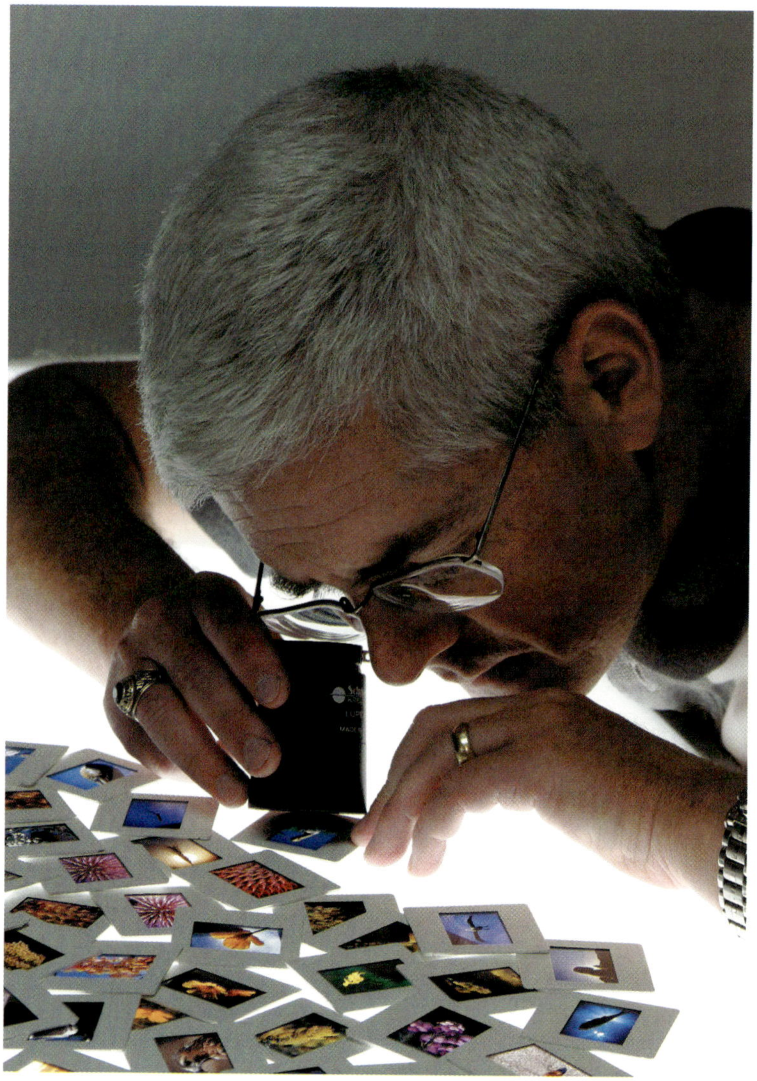

Figure 2.12 A light table provides a good analogy for the process of sorting digital images.

Sorting Strategy

Before you start sorting your images, you'll want to consider a basic strategy for doing so. This will help you work more efficiently, and it will help prevent you from feeling overwhelmed when you have a large number of images to process. I recommend using the following steps as you sort through your images:

1. **Rotate Verticals:** Images captured vertically will appear sideways, making them a little more difficult to evaluate. Rotating them to their proper orientation allows you to review the images as they should appear, without tilting your head or imagining how they will look when rotated.

Note: Some of the latest digital cameras include a sensor to determine when you are capturing an image in the vertical orientation, and automatically flag those images for rotation. Bridge (among other software) will read this flag in the metadata and automatically rotate the image when you open it or view the thumbnail. This eliminates the step of rotating verticals, as it will be done automatically for you.

2. **Discard Bad Images:** Part of sorting through the best images is getting rid of those you know you'll never use. It can sometimes be difficult to get rid of images that didn't turn out well; however, if you want to get better organized, you'll have to take a serious look at the images and decide which you really don't need. I generally recommend going through a two-step process for discarding images, removing the obviously bad images in a first pass and then taking a closer look as you delete images with greater scrutiny. I'll discuss this approach later in this chapter.
3. **Select Keepers:** After you have narrowed the images down to those you definitely want to keep, start deciding which images you'll want to work with for a particular project or simply to print or share with others. You can do this by moving your favorite images into a particular folder, or simply labeling or rating them in much the same way film photographers have marked slides in pages by using a grease pencil.
4. **Organize Images:** You'll want to start organizing the images you're keeping so you'll be better able to locate just the right image whenever you need it. At a basic level, this can mean moving images into categorized folders or renaming the files. More involved strategies can utilize specialized image-management software to provide a higher level of organization, or updating metadata to reflect image details that you want to be able to search on later.

Workspace Setup

With a plan for sorting through your images, you probably feel much more confident about your ability to sort quickly and efficiently. Bridge provides an effective way to perform this task, but the default workspace doesn't provide an ideal setup for browsing your images. Fortunately, a better workspace is just a couple mouse-clicks away.

If you select Window > Workspace from the menu, you'll see a variety of options for different workspaces: Light Table, File Navigator, Metadata Focus, Horizontal Filmstrip, and Vertical Filmstrip. Select each of them in turn to get a sense of what each has to offer. You'll likely find one or two that are particularly good in specific situations. For example, I tend to use File Navigator first to locate the folder containing the images I want to review. Then I'll switch to Light Table workspace to get an overview of the images. Finally, I'll use the Vertical Filmstrip workspace to review the images in more detail (Figure 2.13).

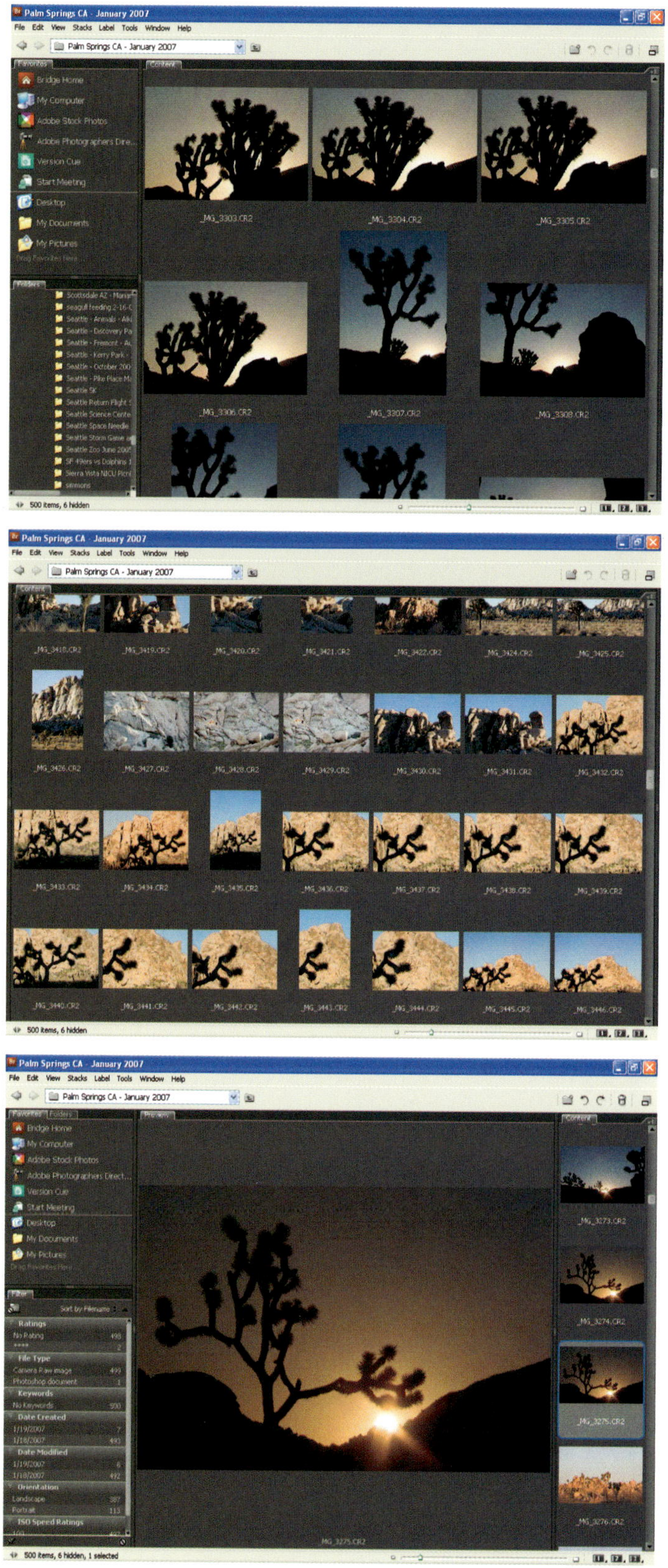

Figure 2.13 I use the File Navigator (top), Light Table (middle), and Vertical Filmstrip (bottom) workspaces most often when working with images.

Bridge provides three shortcut buttons at the bottom-right corner of the window to make it fast and easy to switch between workspaces. To set these buttons to the specific workspaces you use, click and hold your mouse on the button for a moment and choose the desired option. For example, I set the first button to File Navigator, second to Light Table, and third to Vertical Filmstrip. Once you've set the buttons as desired, simply click the appropriate button to switch to the desired workspace.

Light Table

For the first pass of sorting, when you want to get an overall look at the images and start deleting the obviously bad ones, I recommend using the Light Table view.

While you're in this view, you can get an overview of the images and a better sense of exactly what you captured. This is a good opportunity to start thinking about which subjects or particular types of images within the current collection seem to have the most potential. This is also an excellent opportunity to rotate your verticals so they appear with the proper orientation, if Bridge didn't automatically rotate them (which requires that your digital camera support this feature). To rotate images, simply select them and click the appropriate rotation button at the top of the Bridge window (these buttons have circular arrows indicating the direction of rotation).

Note: When you rotate an image in Bridge, only the thumbnail preview is rotated. The actual image isn't rotated until you open it.

You'll also notice at this stage that some images stand out as having particularly bad exposures or other problems that make them candidates for immediate deletion. To remove those images, simply select them and click the trash can button at the top of the Bridge window, press the Delete or Backspace key on your keyboard, or right-click the image and choose Delete from the contextual menu that appears. If you aren't sure whether an image should be deleted just by looking at the thumbnail, don't delete it yet, as you'll have an opportunity to do a more detailed review later. This first stage is a rough edit designed to clean out the collection of images you don't want to waste time scrutinizing.

Filmstrip View and the Loupe

After you've taken an overall look at the images, rotated as needed, and deleted those that you can tell shouldn't be kept just by looking at the thumbnails, you're ready to start taking a closer look and figuring out which should be deleted and which should be included in a particular project or otherwise put to use to share with others. For this type of review, I utilize the Horizontal Filmstrip or Vertical Filmstrip view.

Instead of using your mouse to click the images that you want to view in more detail, I recommend taking a close look at all of the images in your collection. Click the first image on the list (scroll to the top of the list if necessary) and then use the arrow keys on your keyboard to navigate through the images. As you move through the thumbnails, the preview will update based on the currently active image. This gives you a much better idea of the overall composition, exposure accuracy, and image quality, so you can decide whether the image should be deleted or kept. You can also start to get a better idea of which images deserve more attention as you sort through them.

Note: If you select multiple images in Bridge, all of the selected images will appear in the Preview pane, providing a great way of comparing images.

To get an even better sense of the sharpness or other fine-details in the image, you can use the loupe feature. When viewing the image in the Preview panel, you'll notice the mouse pointer is a magnifying glass. Simply click the area of the image you want a closer look at, and a loupe view will appear showing that portion of the image at 100% actual pixel size (Figure 2.14). You can click and drag this view around to get a closer look at different areas of your image.

Note: If you find multiple images that are similar, you can put them into a "stack" to help tidy up the image display. Simply select the group of images, right-click, and choose Stack > Group as Stack from the menu. This will group the images together into a single "stack". You can unstack the images by right-clicking and selecting Stack > Ungroup from Stack.

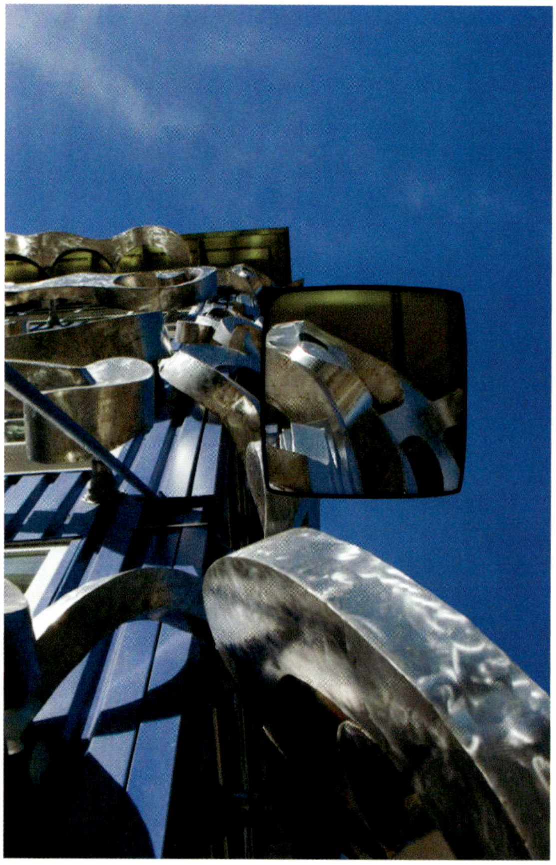

Figure 2.14 The loupe view allows you to get a closer look at specific areas of your image in the Preview panel.

Labels

As you sort through your images, deleting those you know you don't want to keep, you'll start getting an idea of which images you like the best, which you want to include in a particular project, or which you'd like to make a print of as soon as possible. Trying to remember which images are your favorites can be a challenge if you're working with a large number of images at once. The labeling feature in Bridge enables you to mark images with a colored label and then filter the display to show only the images that are labeled, or only those labeled with a specific color.

To label an image, you simply select it and select Label and then the desired color from the menu, or you can right-click on the image and choose a color from the Label menu option. You can also use a keyboard shortcut to label images with some of the key colors by holding Ctrl/Command and then pressing a number: 6 for red, 7 for yellow, 8 for green, and 9 for blue. You can turn off the label by selecting No Label from the Label menu.

Note: If you changed the text associated with the label colors in Preferences, those values will be shown instead of the color name on the menus used for applying a label.

When you label an image, a colored bar appears below the thumbnail (Figure 2.15). This allows you to see at a glance which images you decided were the best based on your review criteria, and you can use the available colors to mark images as being flagged for a particular project or by a particular person.

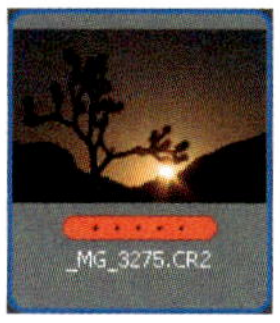

Figure 2.15 When you label an image, a colored bar appears below the thumbnail display.

Of course, just seeing a colored bar below the thumbnail image doesn't quite provide you with a powerful way to review your decisions about the images. However, Bridge provides some additional options to make greater use of the labeling feature (among other metadata applied to the images) through the Filter panel. This panel is included in the Horizontal Filmstrip and Vertical Filmstrip workspaces. It can also be accessed at any time by selecting Window > Filter Panel from the menu.

The Filter panel allows you to click on various image attributes (based on the metadata in the images) to filter the images. You can also sort by various attributes with the dropdown at the top-right, and change the sorting between ascending and descending with a button to the right of that dropdown. In the case of labels, for example, you can click on any of the listed label options (only labels that have actually been assigned to images will be displayed) or the No Label option, so images won't be filtered by label.

Note: Often you'll find that when sorting through a large collection of images, you end up labeling very similar images that didn't show up near each other in the list of images because of the order in which they were captured. This is one of the great things about labeling images because you can identify favorites but then further evaluate that group to determine which images will make the final cut.

If labeling images seems remarkably simple, that's because it is. This simplicity is part of what makes the feature so elegant. You can quickly shift back and forth between similar images, for example, until you decide which is best. Then label one file so you'll know it was your favorite, and you won't need to scrutinize that pair again. You can also use this to sort through images and mark the ones you'd like to utilize for a particular project.

Rating

Labeling allows you to mark images as being selected, and it even enables you to apply some more sophisticated organizing by using different colors for different purposes. However, it doesn't provide a solution that allows you to easily rate the quality or appeal of your images. The Rating option allows you to do exactly that, assigning a value of one to five stars to your images, much like you might rate a movie.

Rating works similarly to labeling but utilizes a star system rather than color codes. To assign a rating, simply select the image (or images) and move your mouse over the row of five dots below the thumbnail (this is the same location where the colored label will appear if you've assigned one to the images). The dots represent the possible star ratings, so click on the first to rate one star, the second to rate two stars, and so on (Figure 2.16). If you have multiple images selected when you click, the rating will be updated to the same value for all of the selected images. You can also remove a rating by clicking to the left of the row of dots.

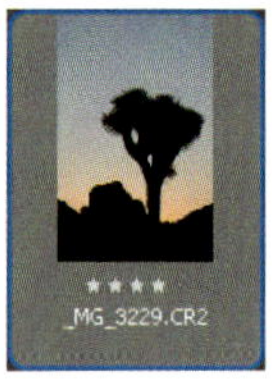

Figure 2.16 When you click in the rating area for a thumbnail image, a star rating will be applied and displayed.

Note: You can hold the Ctrl/Command key and press a number between zero (0) and five (5) to assign a rating to the selected image or images.

When you have assigned a rank to all images that you are considering for your current project, you can sort the images by rating by choosing View > Sort > By Rating. This will cause the images to be sorted by rating, from fewest stars to most stars (Figure 2.17).

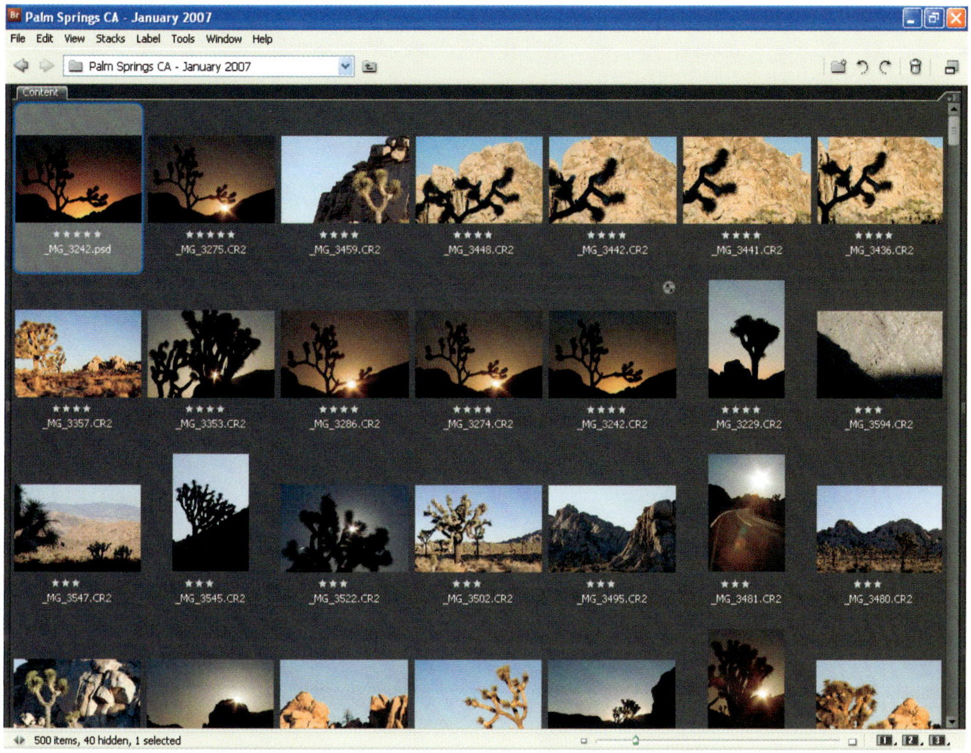

Figure 2.17 Sorting images by rating allows you to sort them in order of priority based on the star rank you have assigned to each image.

Note: You can also change the sorting of images from the Filter panel, as discussed earlier in this chapter.

The rating option in Bridge is a helpful tool for sorting and categorizing images based on how much you like them, making it a great way to filter out your favorite images.

Note: I actually only use the four and five star ratings for my images, on the assumption that any image that would get a lower rating isn't an image I'd use in a project.

Evaluating Images

Although Bridge is an excellent tool for sorting and organizing your images, it doesn't offer the full-zoom review you may want to utilize when making a critical analysis to decide whether an image is worth the effort of putting through your full optimization workflow. To perform the best evaluation, you'll want to open the image in Photoshop and use the many tools for navigation and evaluation to review it.

The various tools for navigation allow you to zoom in and out and move your view around to look at various areas within the image. There are many options, and which works best will depend on how you prefer to work and the particular situation. I recommend getting familiar with all the available options so you can navigate quickly and easily for the most efficient evaluation possible. These skills will also help you throughout the image-optimization workflow.

When you open an image, Photoshop will determine the zoom percentage so that it can display the entire image. This is a perfect feature to allow you to perform an overall evaluation of the image before taking a closer look. How do you like the composition? Do the tonal range and exposure seem appropriate? Is the color accurate? Do you like the image? Are the problems you notice something you can fix easily with minor adjustments in Photoshop?

After you've evaluated the overall image, it is time to take a closer look at various areas of the image and make a more critical evaluation. The navigation tools will allow you to perform just that sort of review.

Zoom Tool

The Zoom tool is the most basic of navigation tools, but it does include some hidden features that can be very helpful. To select the Zoom tool, click its icon (it looks like a magnifying glass) on the Tools palette or press Z on your keyboard.

In the most basic use, after selecting the Zoom tool, you click anywhere in your image to zoom in by one preset percentage level. When you do so, not only will the image be enlarged on the screen, but the point you clicked will become the center of the new display. If you need to zoom out, you can select the minus option on the Options bar or simply hold down the Alt/Option key while you click. When zooming out, the same basic behavior occurs in reverse. The image will zoom out by one level, and the area you clicked on will become the center of the new display.

The capability provides a good way to perform basic zooming on your image. However, the Zoom tool also offers one special capability that makes it incredibly powerful. If you click and drag with the Zoom tool, you'll create a *marquee* (dashed box) on your image. When you release the mouse, the area you dragged the box around will be zoomed to fill the document window (Figure 2.18). This is an excellent way to zoom in on a particular area of your image to give it a closer look.

Another handy hidden feature of the Zoom tool is the ability to quickly go to a 100% view of your image, which is an excellent way to evaluate sharpness and look for small problems such as dust spots within the image. To quickly return the zoom percentage to 100%, simply double-click the Zoom tool's icon on the Tools palette.

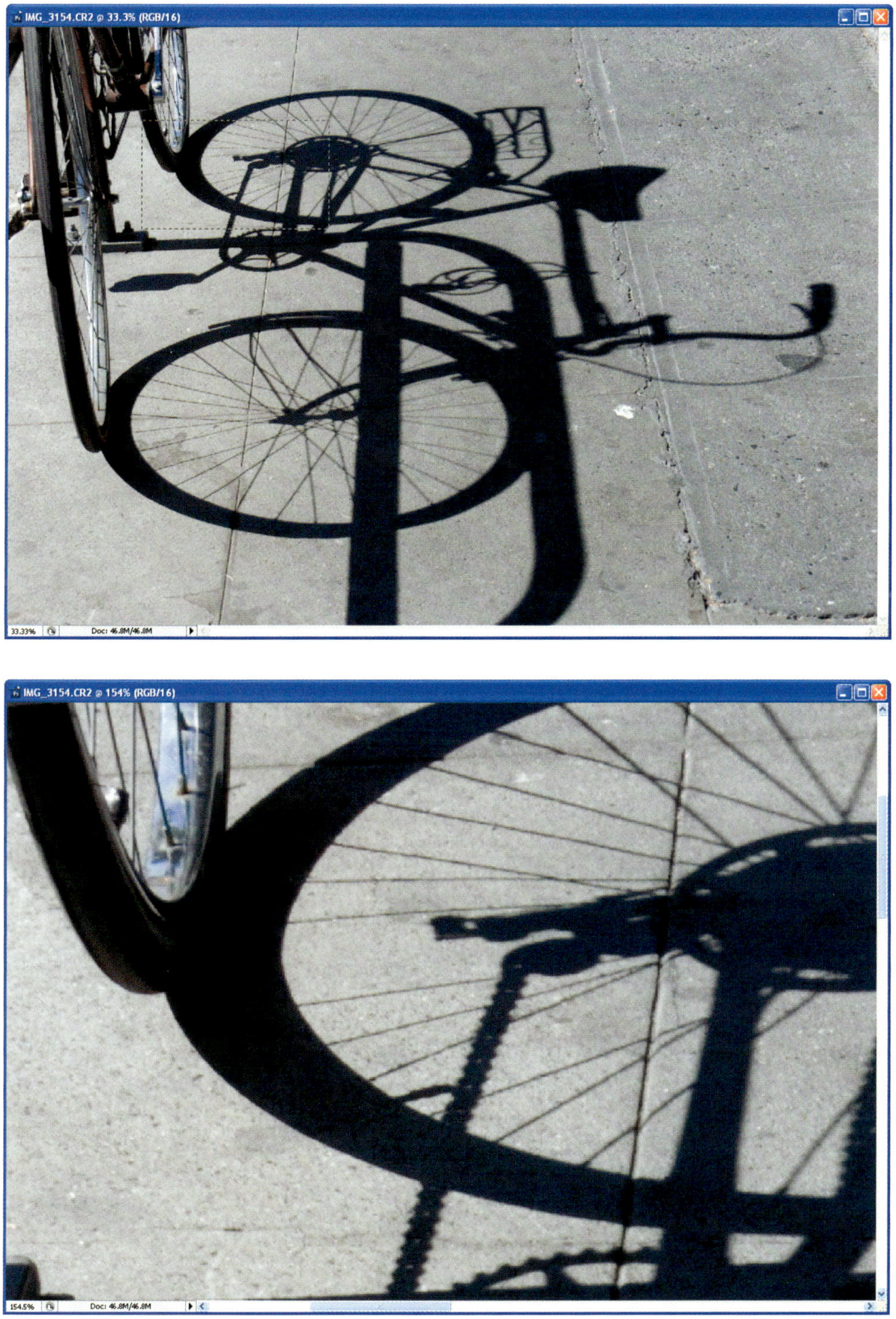

Figure 2.18 Dragging with the Zoom tool defines the area at which you want to take a closer look. (Note the zoom percentage in the title bars.)

Evaluating Sharpness

Determining whether an image is critically sharp is a major aspect of the image review process that leads up to the actual optimization workflow. Many photographers have a difficult time evaluating the sharpness of a digital image displayed on their monitor, especially those who have spent many years evaluating the sharpness of images on film by utilizing a high-powered loupe.

The first step to evaluating sharpness for a given image is to view it at 100% magnification (or Actual Pixels). To do this, you can use the Zoom tool or the keyboard shortcut Ctrl+Alt+0/Command+Option+0. At this magnification, 1 image pixel is represented by 1 monitor pixel. As a result, you are seeing all of the actual pixels within the image for the area that can be seen on the monitor. If you don't have the display set to 100% magnification, the monitor is either using more than 1 pixel to represent each pixel in the image (if the zoom percentage is higher than 100%) or is not showing all pixels for a given area within the image (if the zoom percentage is lower than 100%).

After you are viewing the image at 100% magnification, look to see whether the edges within the subject matter of the image have good contrast. This is the key attribute of an image with crisp focus. Learning to see what a sharp image looks like on a monitor display takes some practice, and the only way to accumulate that practice is to evaluate a large number of images.

Besides simply reviewing the images on your monitor, it can be helpful to first make prints of some of your images, and then compare the printed image (where you'll have an easier time evaluating sharpness) to the image on the monitor at 100% magnification. Comparing these images will give you a better idea of how the monitor display translates into actual image sharpness.

Hand Tool

The Hand tool provides a way to navigate around your image when the magnification is higher than 100% and it spills over the document window. You can think of this tool as behaving the way your own hand would if you were evaluating a large print on a table. Instead of moving your head around to look at different areas of the image, you can simply move the print with your hand. This behavior is mimicked with the Hand tool. You can activate the Hand tool by clicking its icon in the Tools palette or by pressing H on your keyboard.

With the Hand tool active, you can move around within your image by clicking and dragging on the image. The image will move in the direction you drag, with the display being updated in real time so you can watch the image slide around as you move the mouse.

Note: The Hand tool can't move your image around if the image is zoomed out to the extent that you can see the entire image at once.

Another handy trick is to use the Hand tool to quickly display your image at a magnification that allows it to fit within the space available without being obstructed by the palettes (if they are docked to the side of the screen) or to fill the screen display area (if they are not), resizing the image window if necessary. To do so, double-click the Hand tool in the Tools palette. This is a great way to quickly get an overview of the image for evaluating overall composition, tonality, and color.

Navigator Palette

The Navigator palette consolidates many of the features of the Zoom and Hand tools into a single package, and it provides an efficient method for navigating around your image to evaluate various portions of it. If the Navigator palette isn't visible, choose Window > Navigator from the menu to make it active.

The Navigator palette provides a thumbnail preview of the currently active image (Figure 2.19). A red box indicates which portion of the image is being viewed in the document window so you always have a sense of what portion of the image you are looking at. The bottom-left corner of the palette includes a zoom percentage indicator for reference.

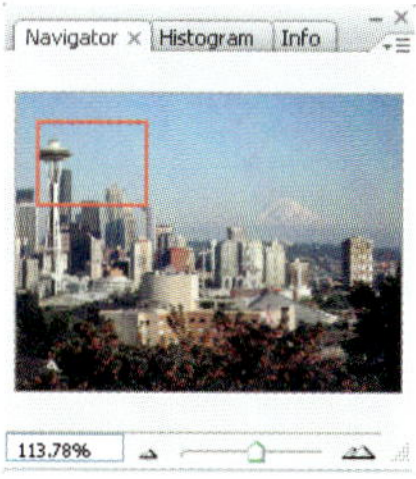

Figure 2.19 The Navigator palette incorporates the basic features of the Zoom and Hand tools into one convenient window, providing an efficient way to navigate around your image.

The zooming features of the Navigator palette are utilized primarily with the slider in the bottom-right corner of the palette window. The "little mountains" button to the left of the slider allows you to zoom out by one preset percentage level each time you click it, similar to Alt+clicking/Option+clicking your image with the Zoom tool. The "big mountains" button to the right of the slider allows you to zoom in by one preset percentage level. You can exercise greater control over the zooming process by adjusting the slider left (to zoom out) or right (to zoom in).

Within the thumbnail display for your image, the red box serves not only as an indicator of which area of the image is currently being viewed, but also as a way to change the view of the image to look at a different area. If you drag the boxed area around within the thumbnail display, the document display will change in real time to reflect the area defined by the box. This is similar to the use of the Hand tool for navigating around your image.

Note: You can't move the red box in the Navigator palette if the entire image is currently visible.

Besides dragging the red box within the Navigator palette, you can also point your mouse to a particular area of the thumbnail and click to center the red box on that spot. This is a great method to use when you want to spot-check various portions of the image. For example, if you're trying to evaluate critical sharpness, you may want to check various areas of the subject and even areas at various distances from the camera to see the effect of depth of field. By simply clicking on various points in the thumbnail of the Navigator palette, you can check multiple areas of the image quickly and easily.

One last trick in the Navigator palette allows you to reproduce the effect of drawing a marquee on your image with the Zoom tool, so you can quickly fill the screen with a particular portion of your image. To do so, hold the Ctrl/Command key and click and drag within the thumbnail display of the Navigator palette to draw a box over the area you want to view. When you release the mouse button, the image will automatically be zoomed and repositioned so the area you drew the box around fills the available space.

The Navigator packs a lot of power into a small palette window and represents an excellent way to navigate around your image as you evaluate it before embarking on your optimization workflow. Getting comfortable with using the Navigator palette will make this process go much more smoothly, and it will give you the sense of being able to look at any portion of your image as needed almost instantly.

Keyboard Shortcuts

For those who love using keyboard shortcuts to speed up their workflow, there are a variety of options for navigating around your images during the evaluation process (as well as during your actual optimization workflow). If you tend to keep one hand on the keyboard as you work, this may be your preferred way to navigate. Even if you prefer to use the mouse as much as possible, remembering a few of these keyboard shortcuts can help improve your workflow by adding to your arsenal of tricks for working with your images. Table 2.1 lists the most common navigational shortcuts.

Table 2.1 Keyboard Shortcuts for Image Navigation

Windows Shortcut	Macintosh Shortcut	Action
H	H	Activates the Hand tool
Z	Z	Activates the Zoom tool
Ctrl++	Command++	Zooms in
Ctrl+–	Command+–	Zooms out
Ctrl+0	Command+0	Zooms document window to fit on screen
Ctrl+Alt+0	Command+Option+0	Zooms to 100% magnification (Actual Pixels)
Spacebar	Spacebar	Temporarily activates the Hand tool regardless of currently active tool
Ctrl+spacebar	Command+spacebar	Temporarily activates the Zoom tool regardless of currently active tool
Ctrl+Alt+spacebar	Command+Option+spacebar	Temporarily activates the Zoom tool in Zoom Out mode regardless of the currently active tool

To zoom in and out on your image, you can hold the Ctrl/Command key and press the plus key (+) to zoom in or minus key (–) to zoom out. This produces the same effect as zooming one level at a time with the Zoom tool, but without changing the center of the view because you aren't clicking on an area of the image when using this keyboard shortcut.

To quickly view the image at 100% magnification (Actual Pixels) for evaluating critical sharpness or other detailed aspects of the image, hold the Ctrl+Alt/Command+Option keys and press the zero (0) key. To get an overall view of the image to evaluate overall composition, tone, and color issues, hold the Ctrl/Command key and press the zero (0) key.

If you want to take advantage of the special capabilities of the Zoom tool, especially the ability to draw a marquee around a particular area of the image and have that portion automatically zoomed to fill the document window, you can hold the Ctrl/Command+spacebar keys to temporarily access the Zoom tool, no matter what tool is currently active. Similarly, you can hold the spacebar at any time to access the Hand tool regardless of which tool is currently active.

Note: In Windows, if you have a checkbox or other control active in a dialog box while trying to hold the spacebar to access the Hand tool, you may not get the behavior you are expecting. This is because the spacebar can be used to toggle such controls. To avoid this, click on an empty area of the dialog box so no control has the focus before using the spacebar as a shortcut key.

As you've seen in this section, there are many options for navigating around your images during the evaluation and optimization processes. Instead of trying to decide which particular methods work best for your needs, make an effort to become familiar with all of them. Doing so will ensure that you have the maximum number of techniques available for any given situation. What you'll likely find is that although you have your favorite methods for navigating around your images, in certain situations other methods are more convenient. By being comfortable with all of the available methods, you'll have maximum flexibility and control when working on your images.

Printing Contact Sheets

After you've sorted through your images and determined those you want to focus your attention on for optimization, you may like to print a contact sheet that includes all or certain of your images both for your own reference and to share with others. Photoshop can build contact sheets automatically from a selection of images and provides excellent control over the output settings.

To start the process, choose File > Automate > Contact Sheet II from the menu. This will bring up the Contact Sheet II dialog box, where you can adjust the various settings to customize the contact sheet you'll be printing (Figure 2.20).

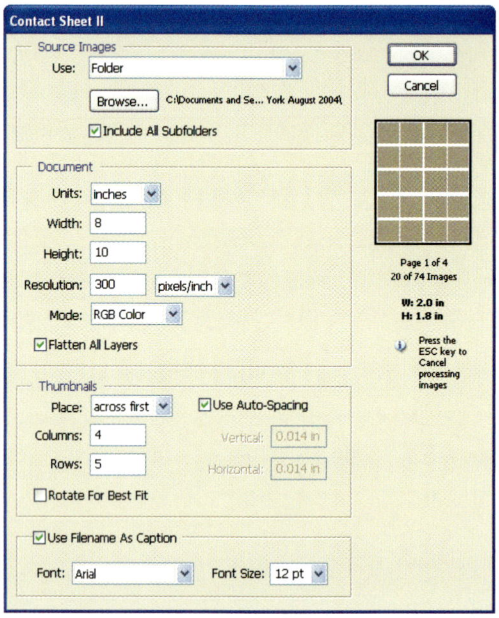

Figure 2.20 The Contact Sheet II automation feature in Photoshop allows you to quickly and easily build contact sheets of your images to share with others.

The Source Images section of the Contact Sheet II dialog box allows you to determine which images will be included in the final contact sheet. Three options are available from the Use popup menu. The Folder option allows you to include all images in a designated folder, which you can set by clicking the Browse (Windows) or Choose (Mac) button. If you select the Include All Subfolders checkbox, all images in all folders within the specified folder will be included. The Current Open Documents option will include in the final contact sheet only those documents that are currently open in Photoshop. Finally, the Selected Images From Bridge option will include all images you have selected within the Bridge window. This last option is a great way of including only labeled images in a contact sheet. This would be accomplished by setting the view to see only labeled files within Bridge, selecting all of them, and then launching the Contact Sheet II automation feature.

The Document section provides options for the page layout of the contact sheet. Set this to a size slightly smaller than the paper size to which you'll be printing. For example, if you'll print to 8.5″×11″ paper, you might set the Width option to 8 and the Height option to 10. Set the Resolution to the desired value for the final output. The default is 72 dpi, but this doesn't produce very good image quality. I recommend setting this value to 300 dpi. The Mode should remain on RGB Color on the assumption you are working with RGB images. You also have the option to Flatten All Layers. I recommend selecting this checkbox so the final document will be a flattened image. Turning off this checkbox provides the opportunity to fine-tune the final layout of your contact sheet after it has been created. However, my feeling is that doing so diminishes the value of using this automated process in the first place.

In the Thumbnails section, you can define how many images should be included on a single page, which in turn determines how small or large the individual thumbnail images will be. You can also decide whether you want the images to be arranged starting across first or down first by choosing the appropriate option from the Place popup menu. The Columns and Rows settings determine the size and quantity of the images on the page, and these values will be based in large part on how the final contact sheet will be used. If it will be used only by you as a general reference, you may be able to fit more on the page with each being smaller, because you are already familiar with the images. If you will be sharing these images with others, you may want to place fewer thumbnails on the page so they can better review the individual images.

The Rotate For Best Fit option in the Thumbnails section will cause images to be rotated as needed. For example, on a layout that favors horizontal images, verticals may be rotated on their side so they can be included at the same size. This provides the advantage of having all images sized the same, but when reviewing such a contact sheet you need to either rotate the page or your head to evaluate the images that were rotated. I prefer to leave this option turned off.

Another option is to Use Auto-Spacing. This will allow Photoshop to automatically determine the spacing between individual images. I recommend leaving this checkbox selected; however, if you prefer to customize the spacing between images, you can deselect the box and then set values for Vertical and Horizontal.

The last section of the Contact Sheet II dialog box includes the option to Use Filename As Caption for the thumbnail images. This is generally a good idea so you can determine exactly which image file on your computer represents a particular image on the contact sheet. With the checkbox selected, you can select a Font and Font Size from the available dropdown lists.

The right side of the Contact Sheet II dialog box includes a preview display of what the layout you've defined will look like, as well as an indication of the number of pages required and the number of images to be included based on your settings. After you've established all your settings, click OK, and Photoshop will process the appropriate images and build your contact sheets. Each page will be a separate document, which you can then save and/or print as needed.

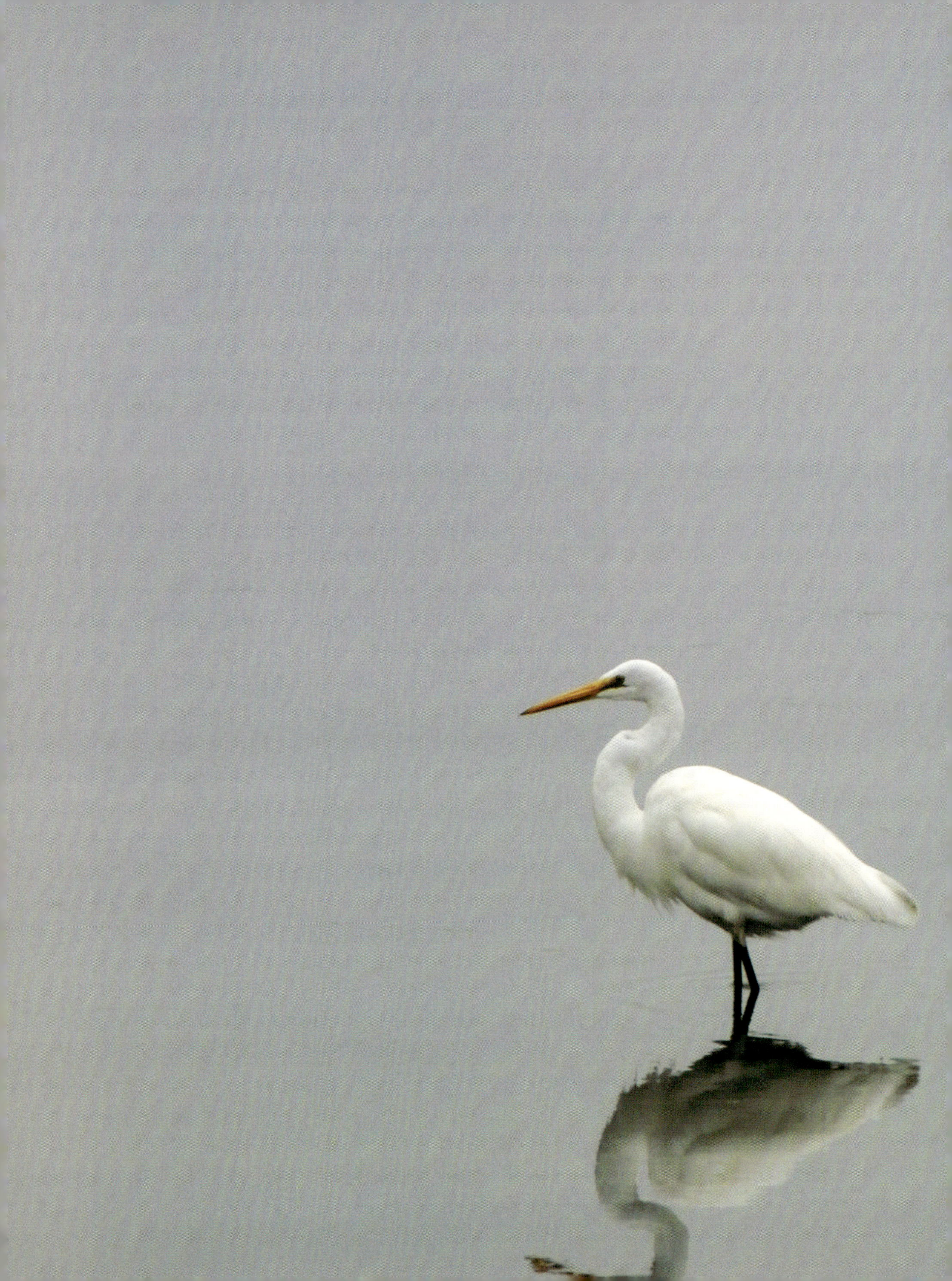

3 RAW Conversion

RAW capture offers many benefits for the digital photographer, and it provides the best opportunity for maximum image quality and detail with a proper RAW conversion. Of course, the advantages of RAW capture come at a price: the step of RAW conversion added to the workflow. Still, when you need optimal quality in your images, the slight reduction in overall workflow efficiency is well worth the benefits you can achieve with RAW capture.

Chapter Contents

Benefits of RAW

Photographers take a lot of steps to ensure the absolute best quality in their images. Using a tripod, employing mirror lockup, selecting lenses with image stabilization or similar technology, and using the lowest ISO setting possible on a digital camera are all examples of such steps. Capturing in the RAW mode offered by many digital cameras is yet another way to help ensure the best image quality.

The quality benefits of RAW capture derive from several factors. Each of these represents a potential benefit to the photographer as well as the quality of the final image.

Note: Remember that although RAW capture offers potential benefits, it still isn't a replacement for using the very best photographic techniques. You still should start with the best photograph possible even when capturing in RAW.

White Balance

Digital cameras introduce the need for photographers to deal with color temperature and white balance. Film photographers have to choose film appropriately balanced for the lighting conditions to be used. However, temperature is a much more significant issue with digital color. The camera needs to compensate for the color of the light, which is measured as a color temperature in degrees Kelvin (Figure 3.1). In a general sense, you can think of this as a way to make a white sheet of paper look neutral no matter what type of lighting is illuminating it. Whether the light source is daylight, fluorescent, incandescent, or flash can have a considerable effect on the color of the light as seen by the camera.

Most digital cameras do an exceptional job of automatically determining the appropriate compensation for the lighting conditions under which you are photographing. For that reason, the Auto setting for white balance can generally be trusted to produce accurate results. With RAW capture, you can trust the Auto setting completely because even if the camera does a poor job, you can correct the image in the RAW conversion with absolutely no penalty in image quality. In fact, adjusting the white balance settings during RAW conversion produces exactly the same effect as if you had used the white balance preset in the camera that matches the color temperature you use during conversion.

Note: Although you can certainly keep your camera set to Auto White Balance when capturing in RAW with the confidence that any errors can be fixed in the RAW conversion, this can slow your workflow. If you'll need to process a large number of images that were captured under similar lighting conditions, you may want to use a custom white balance setting to minimize the effort that will be necessary during the RAW conversion process.

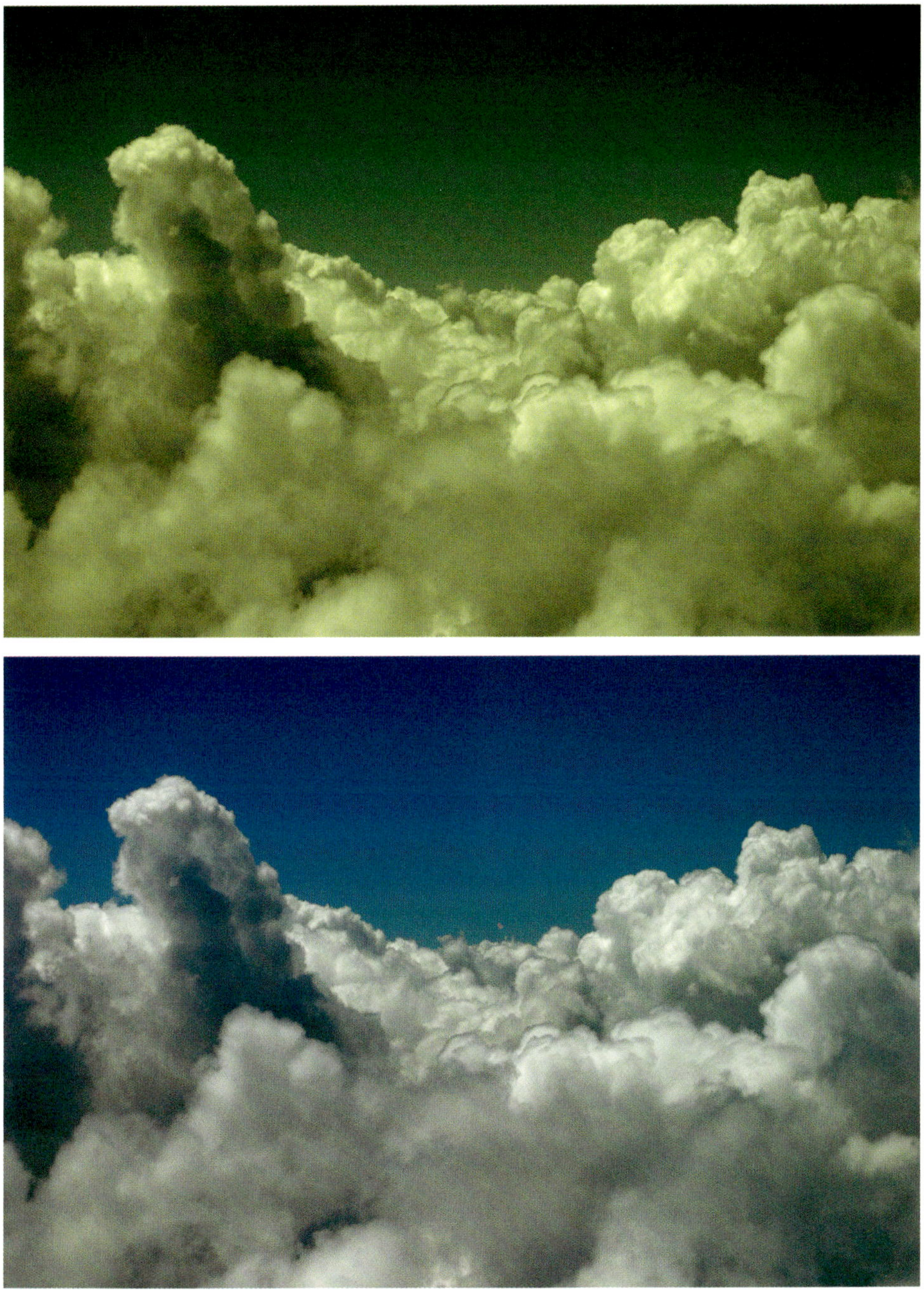

Figure 3.1 Digital cameras need to compensate for the color temperature of the lighting, so that the effect of the color of that light is neutralized in the final image.

Exposure Errors

Because RAW captures are recording the amount of light that reaches the imaging sensor during exposure and aren't being converted immediately to a standard image file format, they offer additional exposure latitude above a JPEG capture. The best digital single lens reflex (SLR) cameras offer about six stops of exposure latitude.

RAW capture adds about three stops of potential latitude. However, it is important to realize that the final image file will still be able to contain only about six stops of latitude. RAW simply offers the ability to extract more detail from the image and make adjustments to recover from exposure errors.

In general, it is possible to compensate for an exposure error of about one stop overexposed or two stops underexposed with RAW capture (Figure 3.2). That doesn't mean you'll always avoid blown highlights if you overexposed by one stop. It also doesn't mean quality will be maintained at the same level as though the exposure were correct at the start. For example, if the exposure is dark and needs to be brightened considerably in the RAW conversion, you'll still have a higher risk of noise and posterization in the darker shadow areas of the image.

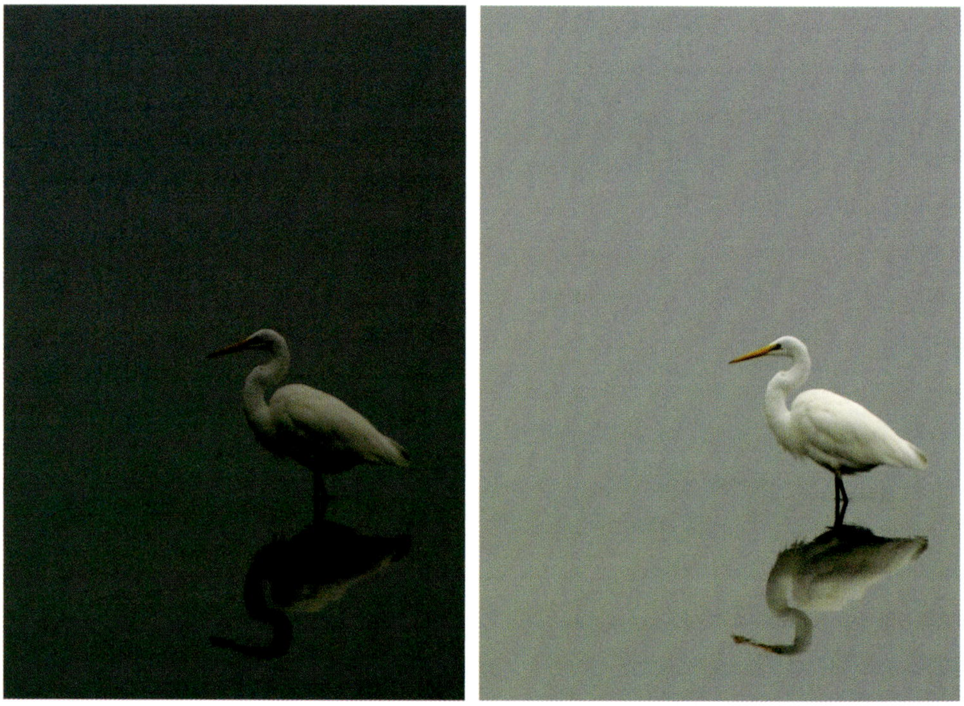

Figure 3.2 RAW capture makes it possible to recover from exposure errors at capture, provided they aren't too extreme.

Note: Just because RAW capture provides greater exposure latitude doesn't mean it offers a panacea for exposure problems. Quality can suffer if you make extreme corrections to RAW captures during the RAW conversion process, so always make an effort to achieve the most accurate exposure possible.

Think of this capability as a way to recover from some exposure mistakes, within reason, as well as a way to fine-tune the exposure after the fact. It won't necessarily save the day with captures that have bad exposures, but it can help make mediocre exposures look exceptional.

High-Bit Data

The final major advantage of RAW capture is that high-bit data (typically 10- or 12-bit data stored in a 16-bit file) is preserved in the capture and can be preserved in the conversion process. This means that more discrete tonal and color values are being recorded and retained in the final image. This is a twofold benefit.

For one thing, the higher bit-depth used for the in-camera analog-to-digital conversion results in more information, so that smooth gradations of tone and color can be maintained. In short, more detail is retained within the image because there are more available values for each pixel. Second, by converting the RAW capture to a high-bit image file, you maintain the benefit of being able to make significant adjustments to the image without risking posterization (Figure 3.3).

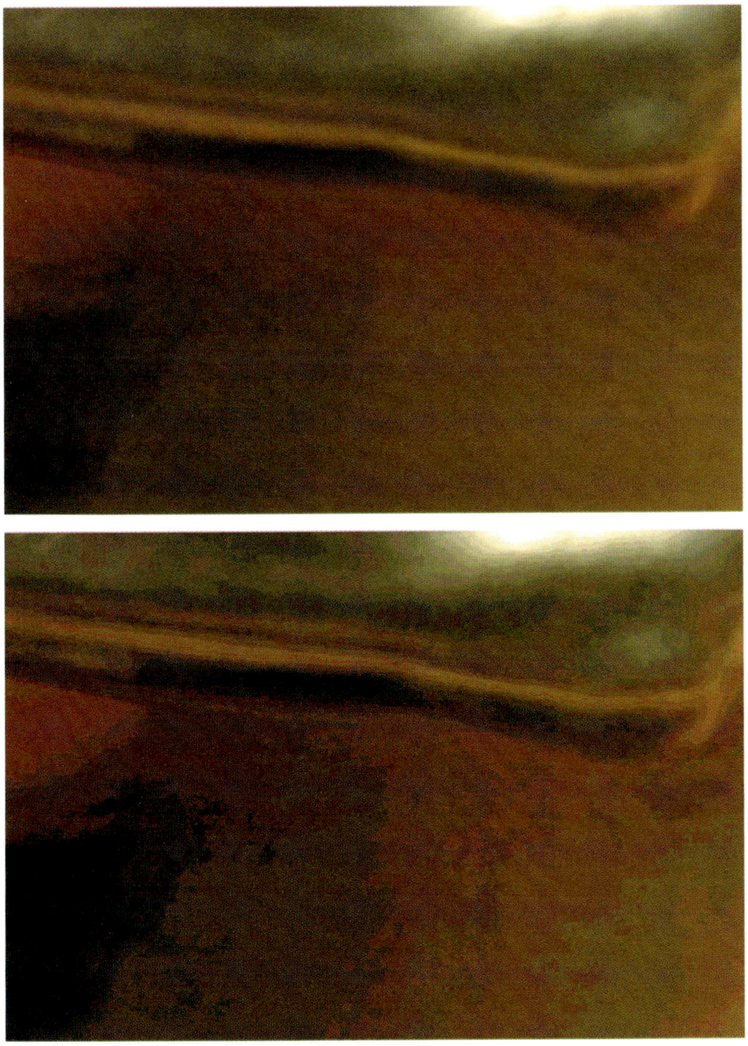

Figure 3.3 The high-bit data of a digital capture helps ensure you don't encounter posterization with your images, even with extreme adjustments. The image on top shows smooth gradations, and the image on the bottom shows posterization.

For images captured with proper exposure, the high-bit advantage is a minor one. However, whenever you need to make significant adjustments to achieve your vision for an image, starting with high-bit data will help you maintain maximum quality throughout the process to the final print.

Higher Image Quality

When you capture in RAW, no image compression is applied, so you are retaining the highest image quality possible. With JPEG, which is the most common alternative to RAW, image compression is always applied to reduce the file size, even when the highest quality option is selected. As a result, there is a risk of *artifacts* (random pixel variations) in the image. Also, because JPEG compression divides the image into blocks of pixels, in some cases a grid pattern may be visible within the image. Capturing in RAW completely eliminates the risk of such artifacts. The price is a larger file size, but the benefits can be significant in some cases in terms of image quality.

Converting with Camera Raw

When your digital camera records in RAW format, it isn't actually creating an image file. Rather, it is creating a data file that contains the information collected by each individual photodiode on the imaging sensor during exposure. This is the reason RAW captures need to be converted in the first place.

Besides enabling you to produce an image file that can be adjusted, the RAW conversion process provides an opportunity to optimize the image. By making careful adjustments in the RAW conversion, you can assure yourself of the best quality possible. However, just because you need to be careful about these adjustments doesn't mean the RAW conversion process can't be incredibly efficient.

Note: If you are using a newly released digital camera, it is possible that Photoshop's Camera Raw plug-in doesn't yet support that model for RAW conversion. However, Adobe provides regular updates to Camera Raw to provide support for new cameras, so watch their website (www.adobe.com) for the latest updates.

Utilizing the Camera Raw plug-in within Photoshop provides a distinct advantage in convenience and workflow efficiency. Bridge (the included file browser) allows you to preview your RAW captures, and starting the conversion process is as simple as opening the RAW file. Furthermore, the Camera Raw interface is designed efficiently to allow you to work quickly when establishing the optimal settings for RAW conversion (Figure 3.4). You can even batch process RAW captures that can be converted with the same settings, such as when the images were all captured under similar lighting conditions.

To get started with Camera Raw, simply open a RAW capture either from the File > Open dialog box or by double-clicking the image thumbnail in Bridge.

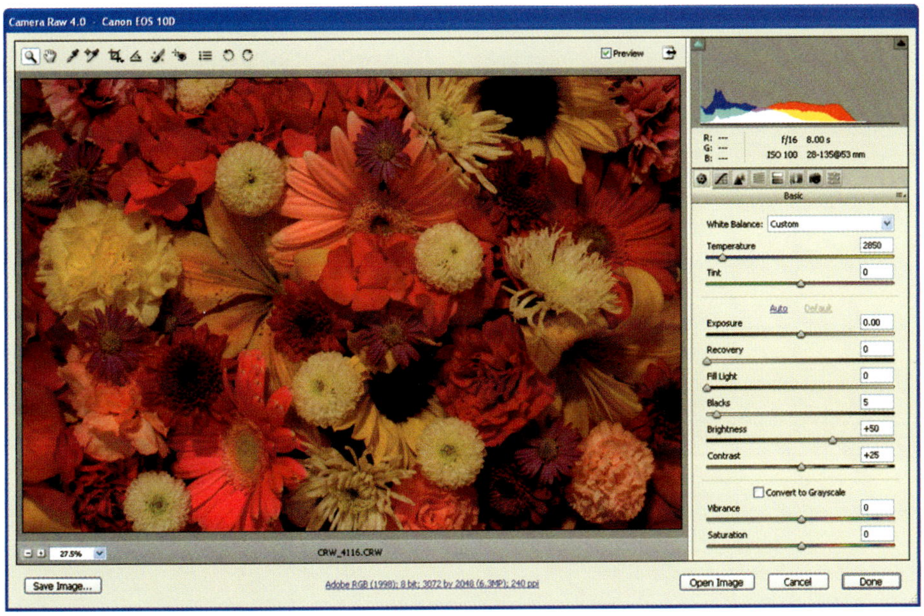

Figure 3.4 The Camera Raw dialog box provides an efficient interface for establishing the optimal settings for RAW conversion.

Camera Raw Settings

The first step I recommend when converting a RAW capture for the first time in Camera Raw is to remove the sharpening that is applied by default. To do so, click the Preferences button on the toolbar in Camera Raw to bring up the Camera Raw Preferences dialog box. Set the Apply Sharpening To dropdown to Preview Images Only (Figure 3.5) and click OK. I strongly recommend doing this for three reasons. First, using a single slider to adjust sharpening doesn't provide nearly the degree of control I'd like to exercise over the sharpening process. Second, the default setting is simply too aggressive and often creates halo artifacts at high-contrast edges within the image. Finally, I prefer not to apply any sharpening until the image is being prepared for final output, as will be discussed in greater detail in Chapter 14, "Output Processing."

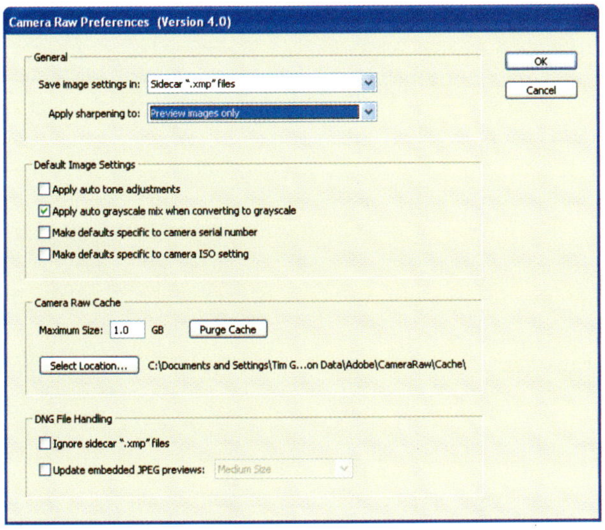

Figure 3.5 By applying sharpening to only image previews in Camera Raw, no sharpening will be applied to your converted images.

In addition to the sharpening setting, you might want to turn on the clipping preview options in the histogram display, so you'll see a color overlay on areas where detail has been lost in the highlights or shadows. I say that you might want to enable this display because you'll also have another option for seeing a clipping preview as I'll discuss later in this chapter. If you want to see a color overlay that identifies areas where clipping has occurred (Figure 3.6), simply click the triangle buttons at the top corners of the histogram display (Figure 3.7). The one on the left toggles the clipping display for shadows and the one on the right toggles the clipping display for highlights. A light gray box appears around the button when the clipping display is turned on.

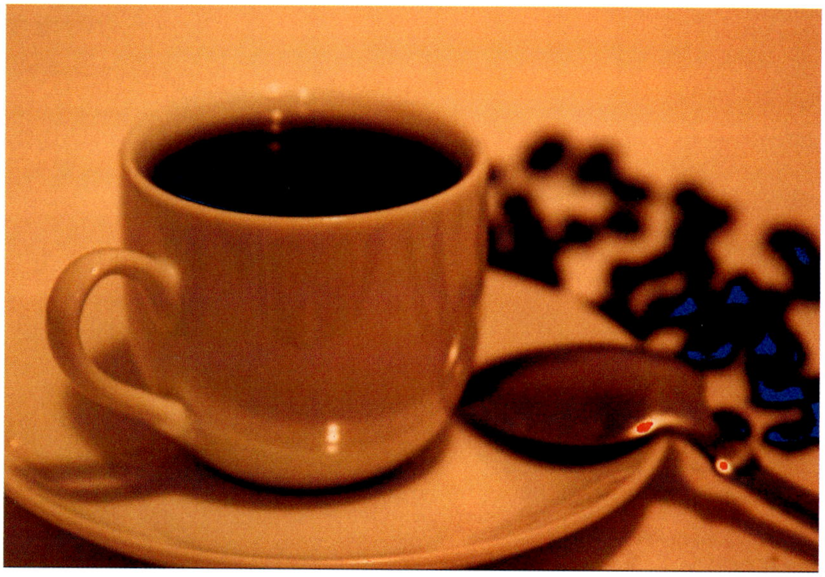

Figure 3.6 The clipping preview display in Camera Raw places a color overlay showing you which areas have lost detail in the shadows or highlights.

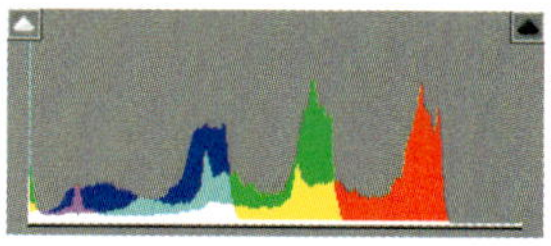

Figure 3.7 You can enable the clipping preview display by clicking the triangular buttons at the top corners of the histogram display.

You also might want to set the Camera Raw dialog box to fill as much space as possible and reserve as much space for the image and controls as possible. The button at the far right of the toolbar (just to the left of the histogram) allows you to toggle between full-screen view and normal view. Simply click the button to toggle.

Toolbar

The toolbar at the top of the Camera Raw dialog box (Figure 3.8) provides a variety of tools for working with your image during the RAW conversion process. Some are very helpful as you're working to establish the best settings for the image in Camera Raw. I tend not to use some of the others in the RAW conversion process.

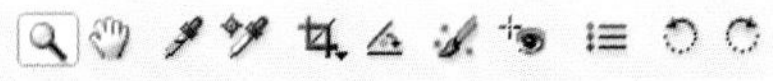

Figure 3.8 The toolbar at the top of the Camera Raw dialog box provides a variety of tools to help you work with your RAW images as you work to optimize the conversion settings.

The first two buttons on the toolbar are the Zoom and Hand tools. These tools function exactly the same as the tools by the same name found within Photoshop. All of the same tricks and keyboard shortcuts are available, so be sure to review these topics in Chapter 2, "Download and Sort," if you're not familiar with them. You can use them to zoom in to get a closer look at any portion of the image you'd like as you're making decisions about the best settings to use for a RAW conversion.

The next two buttons are the White Balance tool and the Color Sampler tool. Both can be used to adjust the color in your image to produce a perfectly neutral value in a specific location. In most cases, I recommend against using these tools. Just because something in your image really was a neutral gray doesn't mean it should appear neutral gray in your image. For the same reason that photographers tend to seek out warm light, such as that found in the early morning and late afternoon hours, you might not want to produce a perfectly neutral color tone in your image. Therefore, in most cases I'll simply work directly with the Temperature and Tint adjustments discussed later in this chapter.

Still, there are situations where these tools can be helpful. If you want to adjust the overall color tint in the image so a specific area of the image is neutral, select the White Balance tool and click on the area in the image you want to make neutral. The Temperature and Tint sliders (discussed later in this chapter) will be adjusted automatically so the pixel you clicked on becomes neutral.

If you want to apply a bit more control to the process, use the Color Sampler tool. Click the button for the tool, and then click in the image to place a color sampler in a spot that you feel should be neutral gray. A new bar will appear showing you the color sampler (you can add up to nine to the image) and the RGB pixel values for the pixel where you placed the sampler. You can then adjust the Temperature and Tint sliders (discussed later) to fine-tune the color. The idea is that you want to make the adjustments so all three values (red, green, and blue) for the desired color sampler have the same value, resulting in a neutral gray. However, you can also "override" that aim based on how the image actually looks. When you're done working with the color samplers, you can click the Clear Samplers button to remove them from the image.

The next four buttons offer adjustments I recommend not applying in Camera Raw. Instead, wait until after you have converted the image and start working through the rest of your workflow. The first of these buttons is the Crop tool, which behaves in an almost identical manner to the Photoshop Crop tool I'll discuss in Chapter 4, "Rotate and Crop."

The next button is the Straighten tool, which allows you to rotate an image quickly and easily to straighten a crooked horizon or otherwise correct the rotation of an image. This tool will both crop and straighten at once. You operate it by simply dragging to define the line that should be perfectly horizontal or vertical. However, as with the Crop tool, I recommend waiting until after the RAW image is converted to use it. I'll show you methods for straightening your image in Chapter 4.

The third of these buttons is the Retouch tool. I definitely don't recommend using this one in Camera Raw, because you'll effectively be altering the original pixel values. You could certainly go back and reconvert the RAW capture if you decide you made a mistake, but it is much better to work on a separate layer for these adjustments in my opinion. I'll show you how to do that in Chapter 6, "Image Cleanup." The same goes for the Red Eye Removal tool. If you need to apply this correction, wait until you get into Photoshop and use the Red Eye tool there.

Camera Raw Preferences

The next button on the toolbar is the Preferences button mentioned at the start of this section. Besides the setting for applying sharpening, there are a few other settings you might want to consider adjusting in the Camera Raw Preferences dialog box. The following settings are available:

Save Image Settings In determines whether the adjustment settings you apply with Camera Raw will be saved in a central database or in a "sidecar" file. I recommend using the sidecar option so the changes will be saved in the same folder as the image (although unfortunately not in the metadata for the RAW file itself). If you use Bridge to copy the file, the sidecar file will go with it automatically. If you use another tool for copying files, be sure to copy both the RAW capture and the XMP sidecar file with the same base filename.

Apply Auto Tone Adjustments will cause Camera Raw to apply a tonal adjustment automatically. You can override these adjustments, but my preference is to never have Camera Raw try to apply an automatic adjustment in the first place. Therefore, I recommend that you not select this checkbox.

Apply Auto Grayscale Mix When Converting to Grayscale determines whether Camera Raw will apply an automatic adjustment when you convert a RAW capture to grayscale within Camera Raw. Because I recommend against using Camera Raw to convert an image to grayscale, this setting isn't really applicable.

Make Defaults Specific to Camera Serial Number allows you to apply different default settings to different cameras of the same serial number. Because cameras of a given model tend to behave very similarly, this option isn't generally necessary. However, there are circumstances where it can be helpful, such as when multiple photographers (with different preferred settings) are using the same copy of Photoshop on the same computer to convert their RAW captures.

Make Defaults Specific to Camera ISO Setting is helpful if you want to apply different settings to captures of different ISO values. This is most helpful when you want to apply different color noise reduction settings for images captured at different ISO settings. In most cases, I prefer to apply the noise reduction settings specifically for each image, so I don't take advantage of this option.

The Camera Raw Cache settings allow you to change the settings for the storage of thumbnail, preview, adjustment, and other information about RAW captures so they can be displayed more quickly. I leave the settings at their defaults, which allows the data to be cached for about 200 images.

The DNG File Handling section provides two options for DNG files, which are obviously only applicable if you save your images in the DNG file format for archival purposes. The first allows you to ignore "sidecar" files, which will cause adjustment settings to be saved within the DNG file. The second allows you to update the embedded JPEG previews in DNG files, with an associated dropdown to select what preview size you want to use.

The final two buttons on the toolbar in Camera Raw are rotation buttons that allow you to rotate your image in 90-degree increments counterclockwise and clockwise, respectively. Most digital cameras provide an automatic rotation feature, so the image will appear with the proper orientation in Camera Raw by default. However, if this doesn't work with your camera and you didn't already rotate the image elsewhere (such as in Bridge), you can apply that rotation here.

White Balance

Note: You can make dependable color adjustments—including White Balance adjustment—only if you are working with a calibrated and profiled monitor display, so be sure to calibrate your monitor on a regular basis.

The adjustments available in Camera Raw are divided into sections, and each section is accessed via a button found below the histogram display. The first section is Basic, which includes basic tonal and color adjustments.

The first set of options in the Basic adjustments relate to White Balance. As its name indicates, the controls in this section allow you to adjust the compensation applied to the image in-camera based on the color of the light illuminating the subject. This can be used to compensate for a shortcoming in the automatic white balance within the camera, or to fine-tune the image to warm it up or otherwise change, in effect, the color of the light used to illuminate the scene.

Note: Although the White Balance presets are the first option on the Adjust tab, I recommend skipping this option (as well as the White Balance tool) and moving directly to the Temperature and Tint sliders discussed later in this section.

White Balance Presets

At the top of the White Balance section is a dropdown list that contains preset options. The default is As Shot, meaning the white balance settings will be set to whatever the camera was set to when the picture was taken. If the camera was set to Auto White Balance, the sliders will reflect the values based on the camera's reading of the light.

In addition to the As Shot setting, additional presets will be listed that match those available within the camera, such as Daylight, Cloudy, Shade, Tungsten, Fluorescent, and others. You'll also notice that Auto is listed as an available preset. It is important to keep in mind that the Auto setting available from the White Balance dropdown does not correspond to the Auto White Balance setting found on your camera. Instead, this setting will tell Camera Raw to evaluate the image and make its own decision about the best settings. It often does a very good job, but it is important to remember it is based on an evaluation of the color values found within the image, not a measurement of the color temperature by the camera.

Finally, at the bottom of the White Balance dropdown is a Custom option. You don't really need to select this directly, because it will be set automatically whenever you adjust the Temperature and Tint sliders.

Although the presets available from the White Balance dropdown provide a quick way to effectively tell Camera Raw what the lighting conditions were at the time of capture, selecting one of these options probably won't produce a perfect result. Because you'll need to adjust the Temperature and Tint sliders for most images anyway, my preference is to leave the dropdown set to the As Shot default setting.

Temperature and Tint Sliders

Note: In CS3, the sliders in Camera Raw now include a visual indication of their effects, such as the blue to yellow gradient shown on the Temperature slider.

The White Balance dropdown and White Balance tool provide the potential to establish good color within the image quickly and easily; however, to me this contradicts the very benefit of RAW capture: the ability to exercise greater control over your images. I strongly recommend skipping the White Balance dropdown and instead starting with the Temperature and Tint sliders. In the vast majority of RAW conversions, you'll probably want to fine-tune these sliders anyway, so it makes sense to start with them and achieve the best results possible in your image.

The Temperature slider allows you to adjust the color temperature of the lighting for which you want to compensate. In theory, that means you simply want to adjust the slider to the color temperature of the lighting under which the image was captured. Of course, chances are you have no idea (or just a general idea) of what that color temperature was. Also, you don't necessarily want to simply compensate for the lighting that was used. Instead, you should take advantage of the capability to fine-tune these adjustments to provide the best image in terms of aesthetics with no penalty in terms of image quality. This will enable you to interpret the image as you desire, rather than simply neutralizing a color cast.

As you get started with the Temperature slider, I recommend moving it between extremes to get a sense of how the adjustment will affect the overall image and to get a preview of what variations might be possible (Figure 3.9). Moving to the left will cool down the image, compensating for "warm" lighting (light with a lower Kelvin temperature), and moving the slider to the right will warm up the image, compensating for "cool" lighting (light with a higher Kelvin temperature). Obviously, either of the extremes isn't likely to be an appropriate choice, but the perspective of those extremes helps you determine which setting is best. After sliding through the extremes, start to settle down on the area that seems to represent the most pleasing color for the image. After you have moved the slider to the point that seems to provide the best color, release the mouse and use the up and down arrow keys on your keyboard to fine-tune the adjustment. This will make it easier to make subtle adjustments as you make a decision about the best look for the image.

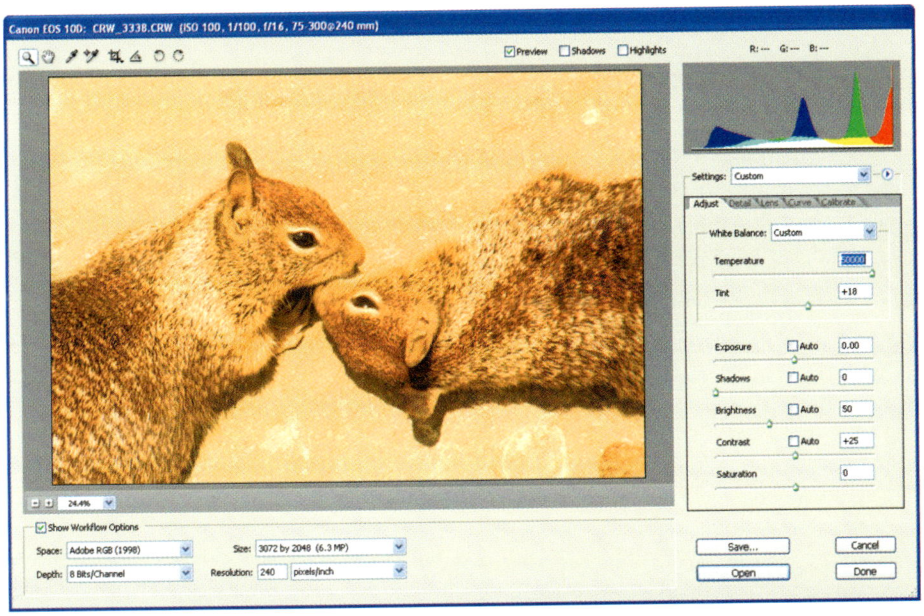

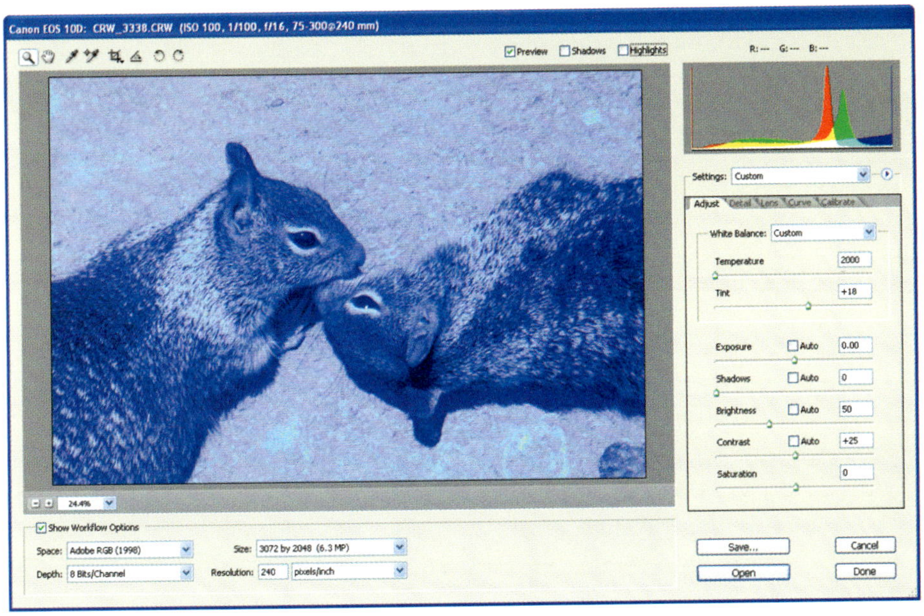

Figure 3.9 Moving the Temperature slider through the extremes to compensate for cool lighting (high Kelvin temperature, top) and warm lighting (low Kelvin temperature, bottom) allows you to get a better sense of how the adjustment will affect the overall image as you settle on a final value.

With the Temperature value established, you can move to the Tint slider. This should be thought of as a tool for fine-tuning the white balance in your image. It effectively adjusts the color balance between green and magenta. As with the Temperature slider, I recommend sliding through the extremes to get a sense of how the image is affected, even though you won't use those extremes for the final setting. Adjust the slider to taste based on the preview image, and then use the arrow keys for fine-tuning, as you did with the Temperature slider.

With both the Temperature and Tint sliders established, the overall color balance of the image should look pretty accurate. Of course, accuracy is in the eye of the beholder here; you may be adjusting the sliders to introduce a desired color cast, as opposed to focusing exclusively on compensating for the color of light that illuminated the scene.

Tonal Adjustments

With the white balance settings established, you're ready to move on to the overall tonal adjustments for the image. When doing so, it is important to keep in mind that the basic goal of tonal adjustments in a RAW conversion should be to optimize dynamic range and ensure maximum detail within the image. In other words you shouldn't be concerned at this point with producing an image that is ready to print because that will be dealt with during the rest of your workflow in Photoshop. Instead, you should be looking to maximize the amount of detail within the image so you have as much flexibility as possible when optimizing the image.

When making tonal adjustments in Camera Raw, the four key controls are Exposure, Recovery, Fill Light, and Blacks. Together these controls allow you to optimize tonal range while maintaining detail, as well as adjusting the overall appearance of the image.

Note: The Auto link above the group of tonal adjustments will cause Photoshop to attempt to automatically set the tonal adjustments. Although this can be helpful for getting started, I recommend simply adjusting the controls manually as described throughout the rest of this section.

Exposure

The Exposure slider allows you to adjust, in effect, the brightness of the image, using as its scale an Exposure Value. In other words, if you adjust the Exposure slider to a +1 value, that is the same as though you had brightened the exposure by one stop in the capture. Likewise, setting the slider to -1 would produce a similar effect to darkening the exposure by one stop in the camera. This would lead most photographers to believe that the Exposure control should be used as a basic brightness adjustment (and would probably make them wonder why there is also a Brightness slider in the same dialog box).

The behavior of the Exposure slider makes it ideal for establishing the white point within your image. By adjusting this slider, you can effectively determine which pixel value within the image should be set to white. This is virtually identical to the behavior of the White Point slider in Levels, as you'll see in Chapter 5, "Basic Tone and Color."

As a general rule, I recommend setting the Exposure slider to maximize the white point for the image without clipping any detail. In other words, use Exposure to brighten the image just to the threshold before you start to lose detail in the highlights. You can watch the histogram display as you adjust the Exposure slider, but it can be a challenge to determine when you've actually started to lose detail. Fortunately, by having the Highlight Clipping option set in the histogram display, you'll have a visual indication when you lose detail in the image. With the checkbox selected, raising the Exposure setting to a value where clipping occurs will cause a red overlay to be shown in those areas. Adjust the Exposure slider to the point just before this overlay starts to appear.

I prefer to use an option with the Exposure slider that provides a bit more detail about any clipping that will occur with the adjustment by utilizing a more powerful clipping preview display. To enable this display, hold the Alt/Option key as you adjust the Exposure slider. When you do so, the image will go completely (or nearly completely) black. As you increase the Exposure value, you'll start to see pixels appear. The color of those pixels indicates the color channels that are losing detail with the current Exposure adjustment, and when the pixels shift to white, it indicates those pixels have indeed gone to pure white. In general, I recommend increasing the Exposure value until you start to see pixels appear, and then moving the slider back to the left until the point just before the pixels start to appear, leaving no pixels visible (except specular highlights).

Although setting the Exposure to make the brightest pixels nearly white works with many images, that doesn't mean it should be adjusted this way for all images. You need to evaluate the image itself to make sure the adjustment is a good one, and refine the adjustment as needed.

Note: If the clipping preview display shows that you have lost detail without an Exposure adjustment, in many cases you may be able to recover that detail by reducing the Exposure setting. For specular highlights (such as reflections from glass or metal), this may not be a significant concern. If the exposure was off by enough, it might not be possible to recover the detail.

Recovery

The Recovery adjustment provides a way for you to recover highlight detail that has been lost based on the Exposure adjustment or in the original capture. As I mentioned in the Exposure section, I recommend adjusting that setting so no detail is lost, which might make it seem that the Recovery adjustment is not necessary. However, it can still be helpful even when no detail has been lost because it can help tone down bright areas that got too bright with the desired Exposure adjustment.

The way I normally work with the Recovery adjustment is to first set the Exposure setting to produce the best result as previously discussed. Then I move the Recovery slider to the right to darken the brightest highlights to help recover detail there.

Note: You can hold the Alt/Option key to get the highlight clipping preview display for the Recovery adjustment, just as you can for the Exposure adjustment.

The other situation where Recovery can be helpful is when the exposure was particularly bright and highlight detail was actually lost in the original capture. In those situations, I'll actually start by increasing the Recovery value before adjusting the Exposure value. Even though Exposure is designed to compensate for a poor exposure, the Recovery adjustment can do a better job of rebuilding lost detail in the image.

Fill Light

The Fill Light adjustment is similar to the Recovery adjustment except that it operates on the shadows instead of highlights in your image. It will brighten up the shadow detail in the image without brightening any pixels that are actually completely black. Move the slider to the right to brighten up shadow areas and reveal more detail. Even if you don't think you'll want to have shadow detail revealed significantly in the final image, I recommend brightening up shadows with the Fill Light adjustment to help maximize the amount of detail in the converted RAW image. You can always increase contrast to darken shadow detail later, but my preference is to start with as much visible detail in the image as possible.

Blacks

The Blacks slider is used for setting the black point in the image, very similar to the behavior of the Black Point slider in the Levels adjustment you'll see in Chapter 5. When you know how to use the Exposure slider, the Blacks slider is suddenly easy to master as well, because it works in virtually the same manner.

As with Exposure, make sure the Shadows Clipping display is enabled with the button in the histogram display. You can then use the Clipping display (which shows up as a blue overlay) while making your Blacks adjustment to see when you lose shadow detail in your image. As discussed for the Exposure adjustment, you can also hold the Alt/Option key to get a more-detailed clipping preview, with the image appearing completely white until pixels are clipped, and then a color (or black) showing where detail has been clipped.

Although it is often beneficial to sacrifice some shadow detail to optimize contrast in an image, I don't recommend giving up this detail during the RAW conversion. Instead, I recommend saving that sort of adjustment for your full workflow in Photoshop. Therefore, the basic process is to adjust the Blacks slider to the right until blue pixels (or any pixel values if you're using the Alt/Option key to see the more detailed clipping preview display) start to appear (Figure 3.10). Then move the slider back to the left until the pixels disappear. This will ensure you have maximized tonal range for the image without clipping detail in the shadows.

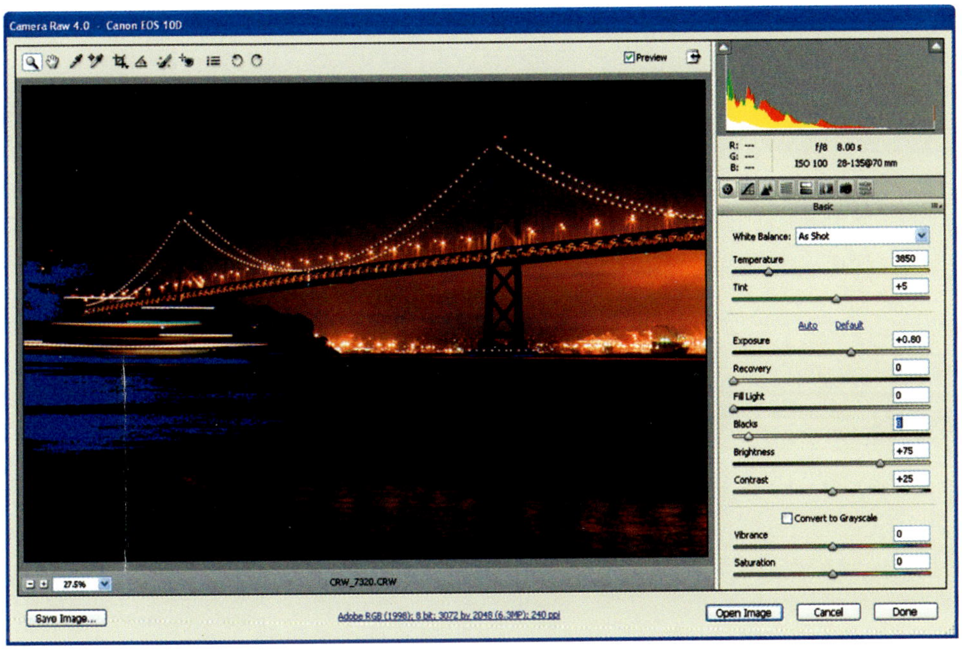

Figure 3.10 The clipping preview for the Blacks slider allows you to accurately establish a setting that optimizes the black point without sacrificing shadow detail.

Note: Even if you don't intend to produce an image with maximum tonal range, I recommend using the preceding procedures outlined for Exposure and Blacks with most images. Doing so will maximize the amount of information in the image. You can always reduce the tonal range with adjustments later, but you can't recover information after the fact unless you reprocess the original RAW capture with different settings.

Brightness

The preceding methods discussed for tonal adjustments will expand the tonal range and detail within your image but may not produce optimal overall brightness. The Brightness slider allows you to correct that problem. You may already be familiar with the Levels adjustment (which will be covered in great detail in Chapter 5), and the Brightness slider is like the Middle Tone slider in Levels. In most cases, you'll find that the tonal adjustments covered previously will enable you to produce a good adjustment, so you won't generally need to use the Brightness adjustment. However, it is a simple way to fine-tune the overall brightness of your image if you find that necessary.

Contrast

Many photographers like to boost the contrast of their images, and in fact many images benefit from an increase in contrast. However, in the case of a RAW conversion, I don't recommend boosting the contrast to the point that the image seems ready to print, simply because it means you are sacrificing too much information in the image at this early stage. Also, you've already established a basic contrast adjustment for the image by adjusting the Exposure and Blacks sliders as outlined earlier. Therefore, I recommend that you not adjust the Contrast slider at all. Doing so will only undo the careful work you did to expand tonal range with the Exposure and Blacks adjustments.

Note: As you're making these tonal adjustments in Camera Raw, if you get to a point where you want to start over, simply click the Default link above this group of sliders to return all of the tonal adjustments to their default values.

Color Adjustments

Below the tonal adjustments in the Basic section for Camera Raw, you'll find some color adjustments. The first is a checkbox to convert the image to grayscale. However, I do not recommend that you use this option. Instead, perform your grayscale conversions using the new Black And White adjustment layer in Photoshop CS3 and discussed in Chapter 11, "Creative Adjustments."

Vibrance

The next color adjustment is the Vibrance slider. This slider is very similar to the Saturation slider, except it produces a more subtle adjustment so you don't have to worry too much about oversaturating the image and producing posterization or artificial colors. It also does an intelligent job of adjusting the colors, producing a less intense effect with skin tones, for example. To increase the vibrance of colors in your image, simply move this slider to the right.

Saturation

The Saturation slider allows you to adjust the intensity of the colors, but it isn't as sophisticated as the Vibrance adjustment. Therefore, I recommend that you not use the Saturation adjustment, instead work with the Vibrance adjustment. If the Vibrance setting doesn't produce a strong enough effect, I still wouldn't use the Saturation slider. Instead, wait until the image is converted and then use an adjustment layer to boost the saturation, as discussed in Chapter 5.

Note: The second section of adjustments is a Tone Curve option. I recommend applying this adjustment as a Curves adjustment rather than in Camera Raw. I'll discuss Curves in detail in Chapter 7, "Advanced Tonal Adjustments."

Detail Adjustments

The preceding settings reflect all the basic adjustments you should need to make to most images. However, in some situations other adjustments can be employed to beneficial effect. They won't apply to every image, but understanding how to use them will help ensure you're able to achieve the best results possible when converting your RAW captures. The third section of adjustments is the Detail options.

Sharpening

As discussed earlier in this chapter, I recommend that you not apply sharpening in Camera Raw. Set the Preferences option so that sharpening is applied only to the preview image, not the final converted image. As a result, there will be no need to adjust the Sharpening setting at all in the Detail section.

Noise Reduction

In some situations, especially with longer exposures or when you use a relatively high ISO setting, you'll find that your digital captures contain a certain amount of noise. This is most often exhibited as a random variation in pixel color values, but it can also show up as variations in tonal values. The variations are on the pixel level, so you'll need to zoom in relatively close to see them. You'll most likely be able to see noise in the shadow areas of your images when it does occur.

Although there are a variety of methods to minimize or eliminate noise in your images after RAW conversion, the Camera Raw dialog box also includes options to help minimize noise. On the Detail tab, you'll find sliders for Luminance and Color Noise Reduction for this purpose.

The Luminance slider allows you to compensate for noise exhibited as tonal variations at the pixel level. This isn't common, but it does occur. When using the Luminance slider, zoom in to a 100% scale (double-click the Zoom tool to change to a 100% view quickly) and view an area of the image that exhibits luminance noise. Then slowly increase the Luminance slider to clear up the noise.

When adjusting Luminance, keep a close eye on various areas of the image. In addition to reducing luminance noise, this adjustment also can produce a softening effect in the image and lead to posterization.

For the more common color noise, the appropriately named Color slider will help (Figure 3.11). The default value is 25, which does minimize a small amount of noise. In general, the Color slider doesn't have a significant effect on sharpness, but it can soften the image slightly when used with a high setting. Use the lowest setting that produces an acceptable reduction in noise within the image. As with Luminance, zoom in at a 100% view while looking at dark shadow areas and other places you can see noise while adjusting the Color slider.

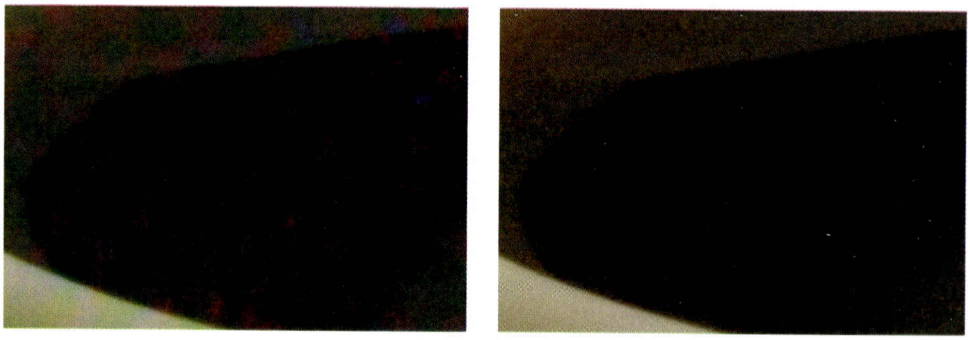

Figure 3.11 The Color slider in Camera Raw allows you to compensate for color noise, which is often found in shadow areas of an image especially when a high ISO setting was used in capture.

Note: The HSL/Grayscale section provides adjustments for fine-tuning individual color values in the image. My recommendation is to apply such adjustments as an adjustment layer after converting the RAW image, as I'll discuss in Chapter 8, "Advanced Color Adjustments."

Note: The adjustments in the Split Toning section are intended for applying a color tone to grayscale images in Camera Raw. My recommendation is to save such a creative adjustment for an adjustment layer in Photoshop after the RAW capture has been converted. I'll discuss this type of adjustment in Chapter 11.

Lens Corrections

The Lens Corrections section provides controls to compensate for problems in your images caused by attributes of the lens used to capture the image. These include adjustments for *chromatic aberration* and *lens vignetting*.

Chromatic Aberration

Chromatic aberration is caused when light of various wavelengths focuses at a different point on the sensor, causing complementary color fringing along high-contrast edges within the image. When you are using high-quality lenses, chromatic aberration is not a common problem. However, with some lenses, particularly wide-angle lenses, it can be an issue. The Chromatic Aberration sliders found on the Lens tab in the Camera Raw dialog box provide a solution.

The two Chromatic Aberration sliders perform the same basic action, but target chromatic aberrations of different colors. The Fix Red/Cyan Fringe slider compensates for red or cyan chromatic aberrations, whereas the Fix Blue/Yellow Fringe slider compensates for blue or yellow chromatic aberrations.

Because the cause of these chromatic aberrations is light of different wavelengths (meaning different colors) being at different focus points when reaching the imaging sensor, the net effect is individual color channels that are out of alignment (either in terms of position or size) from each other. The sliders allow you to adjust the relationship between channels to compensate for chromatic aberration occurring within the image.

At times, it can be difficult to judge exactly what color the chromatic aberrations are. My recommendation is to start by zooming in at a 100% scale and looking at an area of the image that has very high contrast, such as a silhouetted area or a specular highlight. Then slide the sliders to an extreme to give you a better sense of the effect. You should be able to see color halos moving to and fro around the high-contrast edge when you adjust the sliders. Find the slider position that brings the halos to a minimum, both in terms of size and color cast (Figure 3.12).

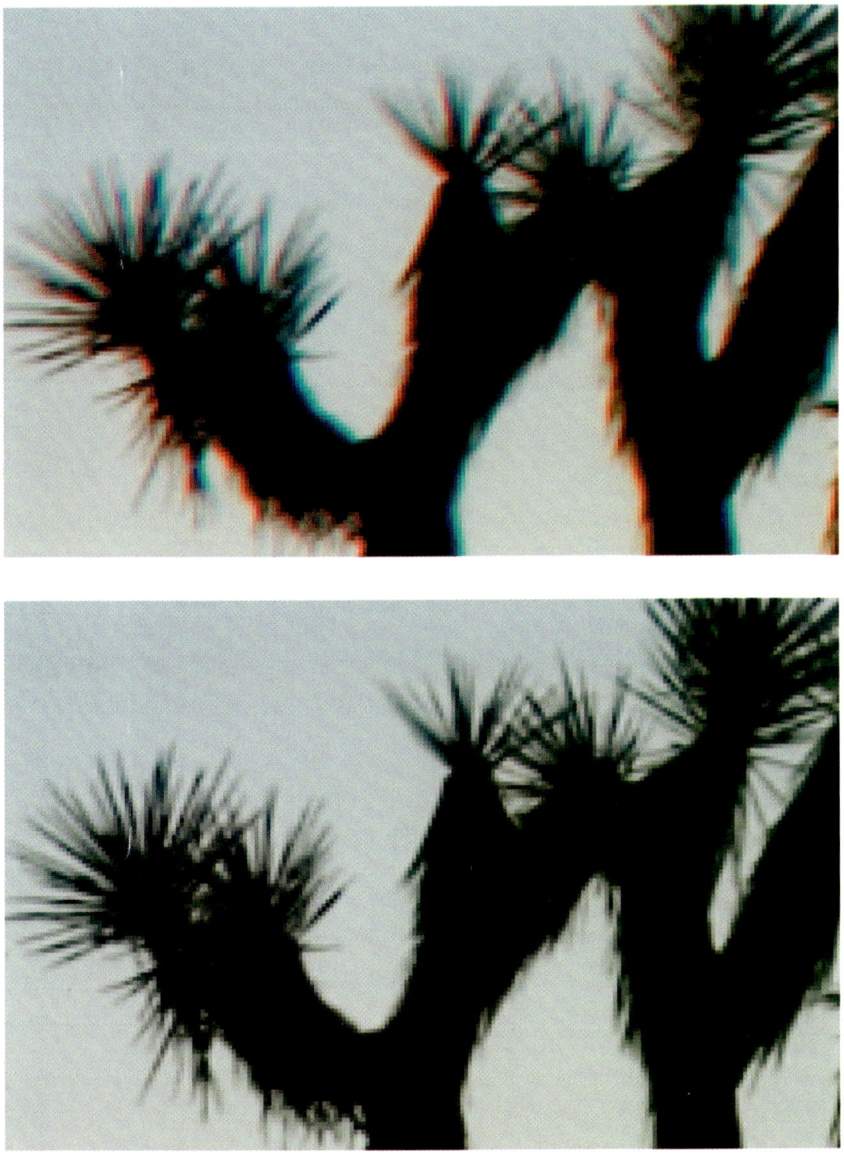

Figure 3.12 The Chromatic Aberration sliders allow you to compensate for color fringing, sometimes seen in images captured using a low-quality or wide-angle lens.

These problems aren't particularly common, but they do occur. Understanding how to resolve these problems in the RAW conversion will prevent you from trying to solve the problem later, when it may be exaggerated by other adjustments you'll be making.

Lens Vignetting

The Lens Vignetting controls found on the Lens tab allow you to compensate for vignetting that occurred in the capture (often the result of light falloff when using a wide-angle lens) or to create vignetting when it didn't occur but was desired. I do recommend using this to remove unwanted vignetting; however, if you're going to apply intentional vignetting, do so in Photoshop rather than in the RAW conversion so it will be easy to revise or remove if you change your mind later.

The Amount slider determines the intensity of the vignette compensation or effect to be applied (Figure 3.13). In effect, it determines how much the corners of the image will be darkened (with a negative value) or lightened (with a positive value). I generally start with this slider to find the amount of compensation required to hide the vignetting that appears in the image.

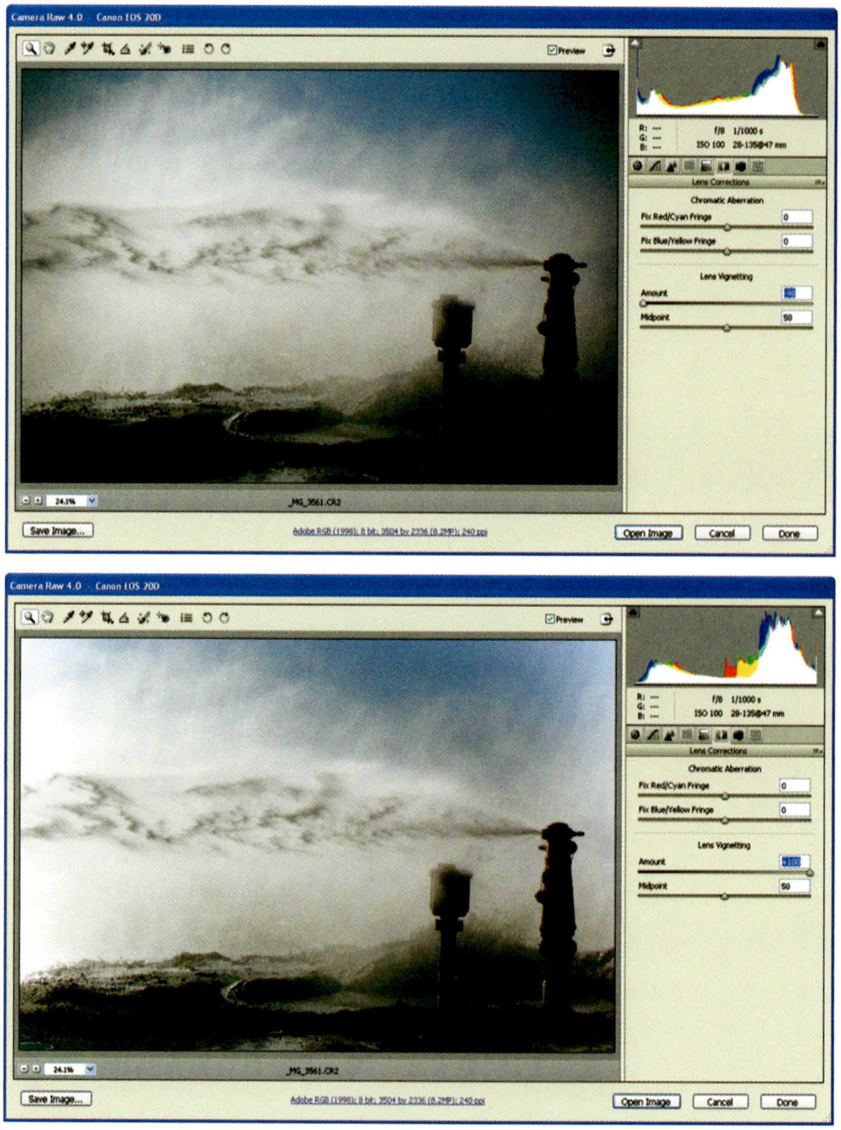

Figure 3.13 The Amount slider allows you to determine how strong the vignetting compensation (or effect) should be. (Photos by Jeffrey M. Greene, ImageWest Photography)

The Midpoint slider determines the size of the area where compensation is needed. Moving the slider to the left will enlarge the area where compensation is applied, and moving the slider to the right will reduce the area (Figure 3.14). Regardless of the settings used, the adjustment will always be tapered so it blends throughout the adjustment area, producing a smooth transition between areas that are adjusted and those that are not.

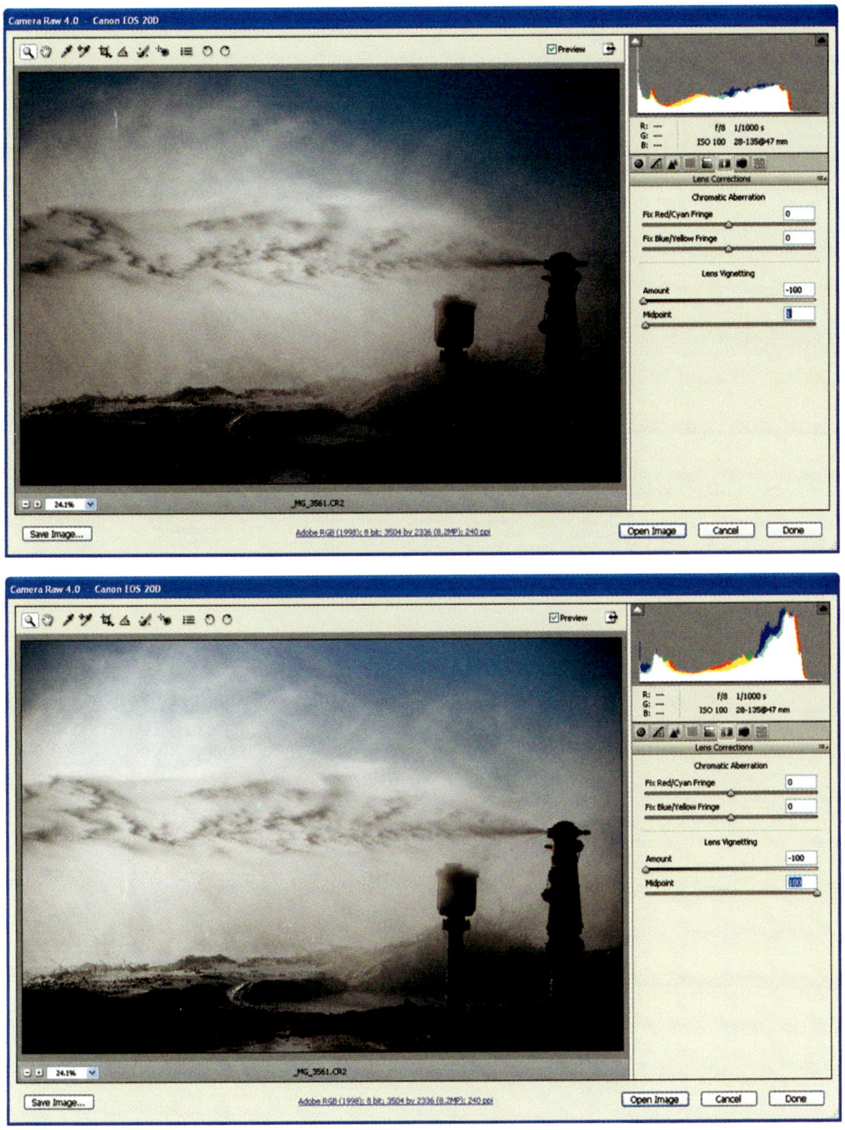

Figure 3.14 The Midpoint slider allows you to set the size of the area affected by the Amount adjustment. (Photos by Jeffrey M. Greene, ImageWest Photography)

Camera Calibration

The colors interpreted by Camera Raw from your RAW captures are based in part on the profiles included within Camera Raw for the cameras it supports. I have found these profiles to be highly accurate and have not seen any situations where they needed to be adjusted. However, if you do feel that Camera Raw is producing unwanted shifts in color when converting images from your camera, the Camera Calibration section provides the flexibility to compensate for that (Figure 3.15).

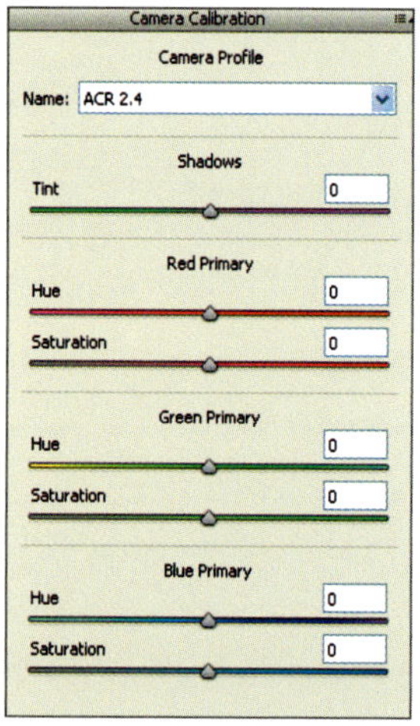

Figure 3.15 The controls on the Calibrate tab allow you to compensate for inaccuracies in the camera profile used by Camera Raw for your particular camera.

The Tint slider adjusts the color values of shadows only, adjusting along a green/magenta axis. This will adjust the color appearance of only the darkest pixels within your images. Use caution when adjusting this slider because the shadow areas of many images are influenced by different light than the rest of the scene, and this can cause confusion as to what is causing the color shift. In most cases, I would say the shift is caused by the natural lighting conditions, not by a problem with your camera profile.

In addition to the Tint slider, there are sliders for hue and saturation for all three color channels (red, green, and blue). The Hue sliders allow you to change the basic color for each of the primary colors. For example, if your reds are showing up a little too magenta, you could use the Red Hue slider to change the color of red for your camera. Likewise, the Saturation sliders for the primary colors affect the intensity of those colors. If you consistently see that greens are oversaturated, for example, you may want to tone down the Green Saturation slider.

If you need to adjust the sliders in the Camera Calibration section, make a note of the settings that produce the best results for your camera. Then open a new RAW capture taken with that camera, and leave all settings at their default values. Adjust the sliders based on the settings you have established, and from the "reveal" menu at the right of the Camera Calibration heading, choose Save New Camera Raw Defaults. This will establish those settings as the default for all images captured with the same camera model.

Note: The final section is Presets, which allows you to select from saved presets to apply to your images in Camera Raw. I don't recommend using presets for your images simply because each image deserves custom adjustments.

Workflow Options

When you've established all the settings to produce the optimal RAW conversion, the only settings that remain are the final output settings. A summary of the settings is displayed below the preview image in the Camera Raw dialog box (Figure 3.16). These general settings don't change the appearance of the image; rather, they are used in the conversion process when the file is finalized as an actual image. To change the settings, click on the summary text to bring up the Workflow Options dialog box (Figure 3.17).

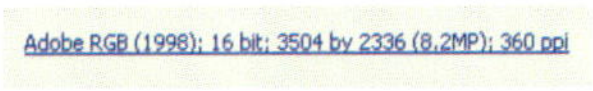

Figure 3.16 The workflow options are displayed in summary below the image in the Camera Raw dialog box.

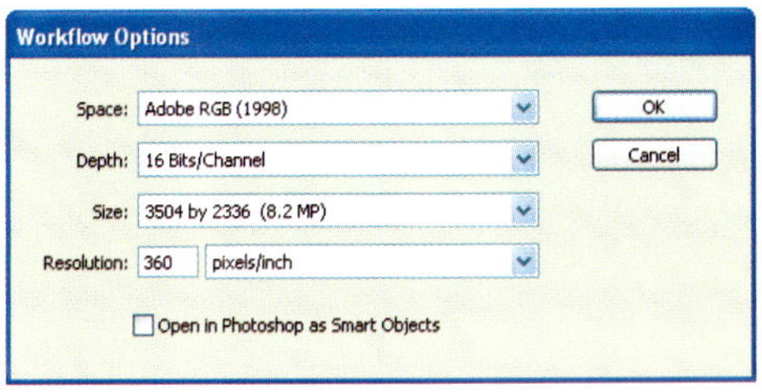

Figure 3.17 The Workflow Options dialog box allows you to adjust the output settings for your image before converting it.

Space

The Space dropdown allows you to select from four basic color-space profiles included with Photoshop. Because you would likely convert the image that results from your RAW conversion to the established working space, it makes sense to use that setting here so the color data doesn't need to be converted a second time. In general, I recommend ProPhoto RGB if you'll maintain a completely high-bit workflow and Adobe RGB (1998) if you'll be working with your images in 8-bit mode.

Depth

The Depth dropdown allows you to select either 8 bits per channel or 16 bits per channel. Because one of the major benefits of RAW capture is that you are able to retain 16-bit data, I strongly recommend choosing the 16 Bits/Channel option. Although a major portion of the adjustments you'll make to the image have been accomplished with Camera Raw, you'll still make more adjustments in Photoshop. By retaining high-bit data, you are maximizing the potential number of colors in the image and will virtually eliminate the risk of posterization.

In short, if the image was worth capturing in RAW to begin with, you should continue to take advantage of every benefit available. Because Photoshop supports adjustment layers and all core features for 16-bit images (since Photoshop CS), there's really no good reason not to keep your image in 16-bit.

Size

The Size option provides various settings for applying interpolation to increase or decrease the size of your image in the RAW conversion process. The potential advantage here is that Camera Raw is already interpolating the individual color channels to calculate full-color information for each pixel because each photodiode on the imaging sensor records values for only a single color, so you can gain a quality advantage by extending the interpolation at this point. If you know you'll be producing large output for a particular image, you may want to interpolate in the RAW conversion to take advantage of the potential benefits.

Resolution

The Resolution setting is provided purely for convenience and will have no effect on the actual pixel dimensions of your image. It exists simply to save you a step in the final output preparation of your image (which will be discussed in Chapter 14). I recommend setting this value to whatever you normally use as an output resolution value. For photo ink-jet output, for example, this should be somewhere between 240 and 360 dpi, and for offset press printing this is usually 300 dpi. Because there is no real effect on the image, you don't need to worry if you aren't sure what value to use; you can always change it later without causing any problems for your image.

Ready to Convert

As you can see, the adjustments you'll need to make within the Camera Raw dialog box are best approached with a logical progression. In general, I see this approach as one of solving the biggest problem with your image first and working your way down. Because the controls are arranged in a way that makes sense for most images, you'll generally just work your way from the top of the Adjust tab to the bottom when adjusting your images.

As you get more comfortable with the adjustments within Camera Raw, you'll find that the process can be quick. Using the techniques described here, you can move from slider to slider in the Basic section quickly without compromising quality. The other settings within the Camera Raw dialog box can generally be left to the settings used for the prior conversion because you will typically use the same general settings for all images you convert.

When all settings have been established for a given image, you can simply click the Open Image button to convert the image. Photoshop will process the conversion within a few seconds, and the image will be ready for you to take through the rest of the optimization process as discussed throughout the rest of this book. If you want to save the resulting image but aren't yet ready to perform the rest of your workflow on this image, click the Save Image button at the bottom-left of the Camera Raw dialog box. This will bring up the Save Options dialog box where you can select where you want to save the image and apply file naming to change the filename. The Format section allows you to choose what type of file you would like to save. I recommend saving as a Photoshop document so you're ready to start performing the other adjustments using adjustment layers discussed in later chapters. The Done button will close the Camera Raw dialog box, but save the settings you've applied so the image will appear as you adjusted it next time you open it in Camera Raw for conversion. Naturally, the Cancel button closes Camera Raw without performing any tasks.

Batch Conversion in Camera RAW

In general, I find that photographers who go to the effort of capturing in RAW mode also want to take a detailed approach to converting their images, working with them one at a time. This is certainly the best way to achieve the very best quality for every image because it ensures that the settings you use are established specifically for the image you are currently converting.

Note: I'll show you how to use the Image Processor to automate the process of converting a group of RAW images in Chapter 13, "Workflow Automation."

However, there are certainly situations where you may want to work with multiple RAW captures at one time to improve your efficiency. This can be particularly helpful when you have a series of images captured under similar conditions that you need to convert quickly. All of the images will probably benefit from very similar settings, so being able to apply the same settings to all, and then fine-tune the settings as needed for each individual image, can be very helpful.

Photoshop makes it incredibly easy to work with multiple images in this manner. To do so, simply open more than one image at a time by selecting multiple RAW captures in the File > Open dialog box or Bridge when opening an image for conversion. When you do so, all of the images will appear in a filmstrip display along the left side of the Camera Raw dialog box (Figure 3.18).

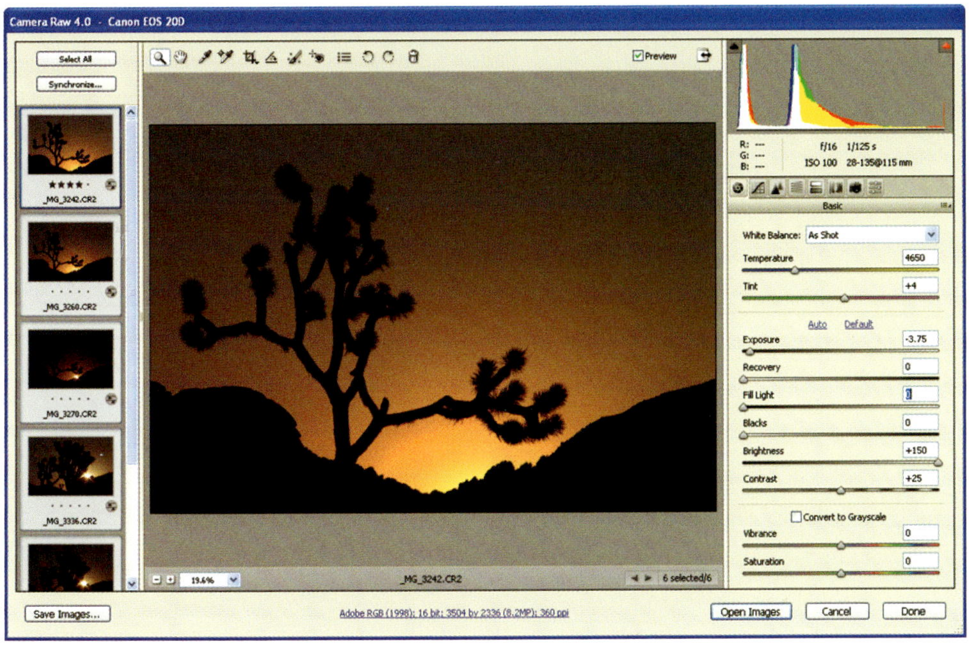

Figure 3.18 The filmstrip view allows you to apply settings to multiple images at once.

The way I approach this task is to first click the Select All button at the top of the filmstrip and adjust the settings in a manner that I think will work for all of the images in the group. Then I click on each image individually to see if any refinement of those settings is necessary, making the necessary changes to the settings.

Note: If you select all the images and click Synchronize, you can select settings from the Synchronize dialog box that you want to apply to all images with the settings taken from the first selected image (the one that appears in the preview). However, my preference is to simply select all the images and adjust the settings directly.

Once you're done adjusting the settings, click Select All again. You can then click Open Images to open all of the images in Photoshop. However, I recommend instead that you click the Save Images button to save all of the images without opening them. If you open too many images in Photoshop at once, you can consume significant amounts of memory, leading to slow performance or even causing Photoshop to freeze up.

Using this option allows you to work with a group of images quickly and easily, without giving up the ability to apply unique adjustments to each image.

Archiving RAW Captures

After you have processed your RAW captures to produce images that are ready to put through your full workflow in Photoshop, you may feel that you no longer need the original RAW capture files. The file you'll save after optimizing your image will become your new master, used as the basis of all prints and other output. However, I strongly recommend that you keep all of your original RAW captures. Just as you wouldn't throw away your original slides just because you have scanned them into the computer, the original RAW captures are still worth saving.

There is a good chance you won't need your original RAW captures later if you did a good job converting and optimizing them, saving them as a new file. However, saving those original captures provides another level of backup, allowing you to reconvert later if you change your mind about how the image should be interpreted or better tools become available for RAW conversion.

When archiving your RAW captures, I recommend keeping the original filenames intact. In fact, I recommend keeping that original filename as part of the filename for the new master image you'll create after you optimize the converted image, so you can always refer to the original RAW capture file easily if needed.

Because you will not need to access the RAW capture files on a regular basis, there's no need to have them taking up space on your hard disk. Instead, you can archive them to CD, DVD, or an external hard disk, and store them in a safe place. Be sure to label the media adequately so that if you do ever need the RAW captures, you'll be able to locate them easily.

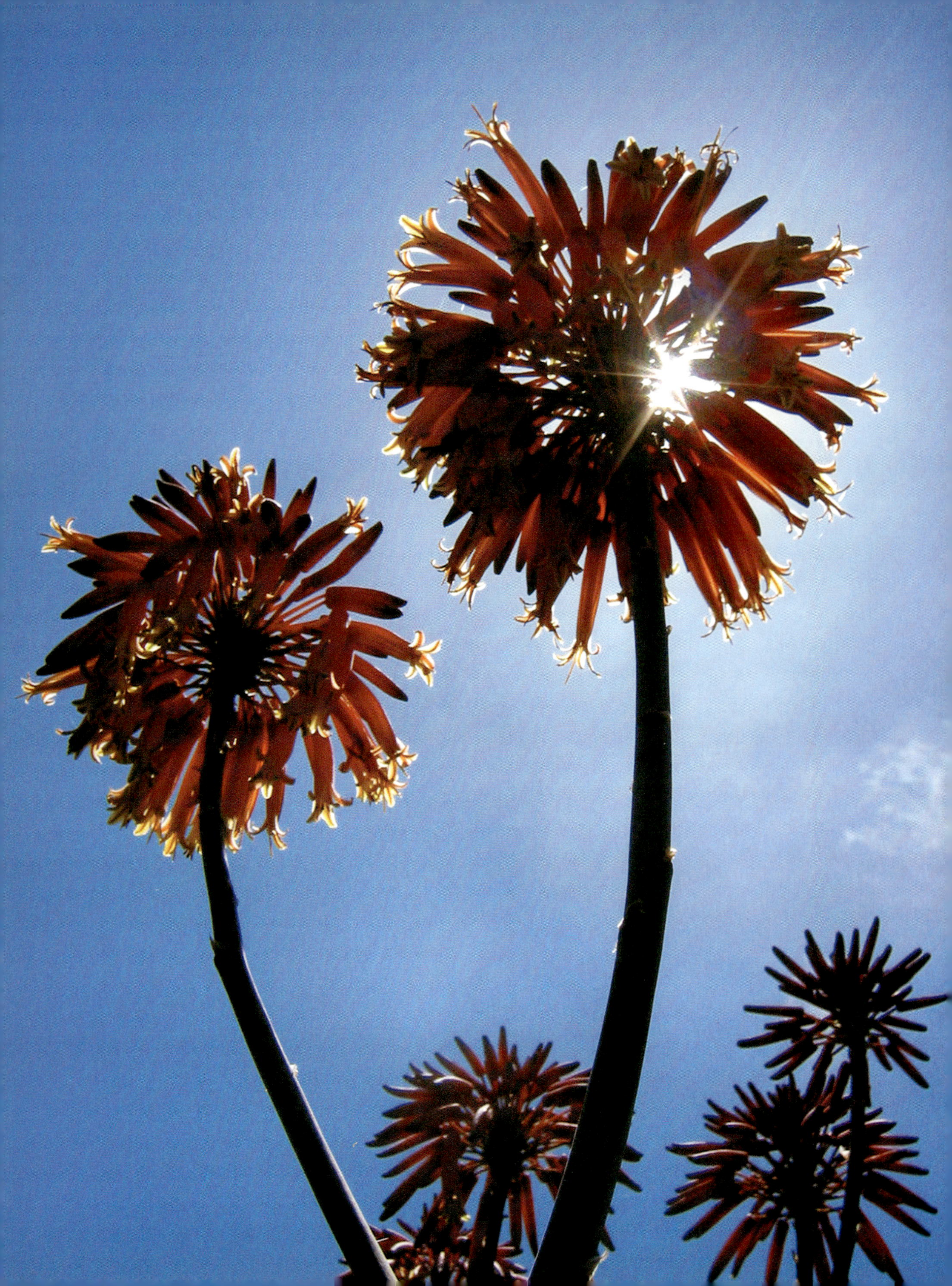

Basic Adjustments

II

In Part I, I covered some of the issues you'll need to deal with before you start the process of optimizing your images. In Part II, I'll cover the basic workflow that is the foundation of optimizing your images. This will provide you with a strong background in the fundamentals, so you'll be ready to move on to more advanced adjustments later in the book.

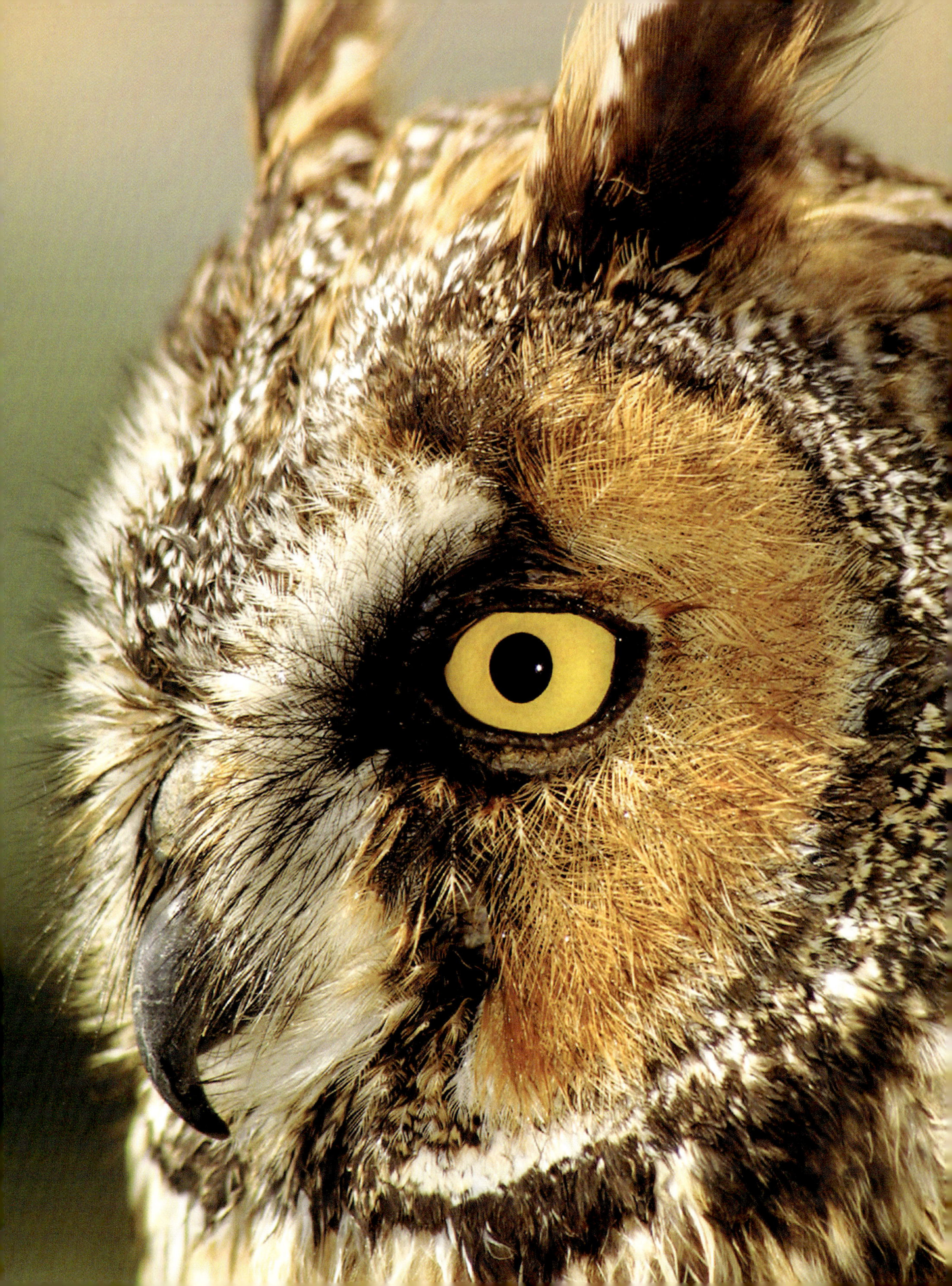

4 Rotate and Crop

Rotation and cropping are methods for correcting the presentation of an image. Rotation ensures the image will be viewed in the proper orientation and that it isn't perceived as being crooked. Cropping removes unwanted peripheral elements that may clutter the image or draw attention away from the intended subject. It makes sense to perform these tasks early in your image-optimization workflow so you'll be making later adjustments based on an accurate view of the image.

Chapter Contents

Basic Rotation

The most basic form of rotation is done in 90-degree increments to correct the orientation of the image. For example, if you forgot to properly rotate the image in your film scanner, or if you are working with a digital camera that doesn't include an automatic rotation capability, you'll need to correct the image yourself.

I recommend performing this basic rotation very early in your workflow simply because it can be challenging to assess tonal and color adjustments in an image when it isn't properly oriented. As soon as I start working on an image, I want to get it properly rotated so I can better evaluate it and, thereby, make better decisions about the adjustments I'd like to make.

Note: Many digital cameras now include a sensor that can detect when you are capturing an image in portrait versus landscape mode; such cameras add a tag to the image's metadata indicating that the image needs to be rotated. Photoshop CS3 will look for this metadata tag and automatically rotate the image appropriately when it is opened.

The first step in performing a basic rotation is to determine which direction the image needs to be rotated and by how much. This is a relatively simple matter of looking at the image and deciding how you'd have to rotate it to turn it "right-side up" (Figure 4.1).

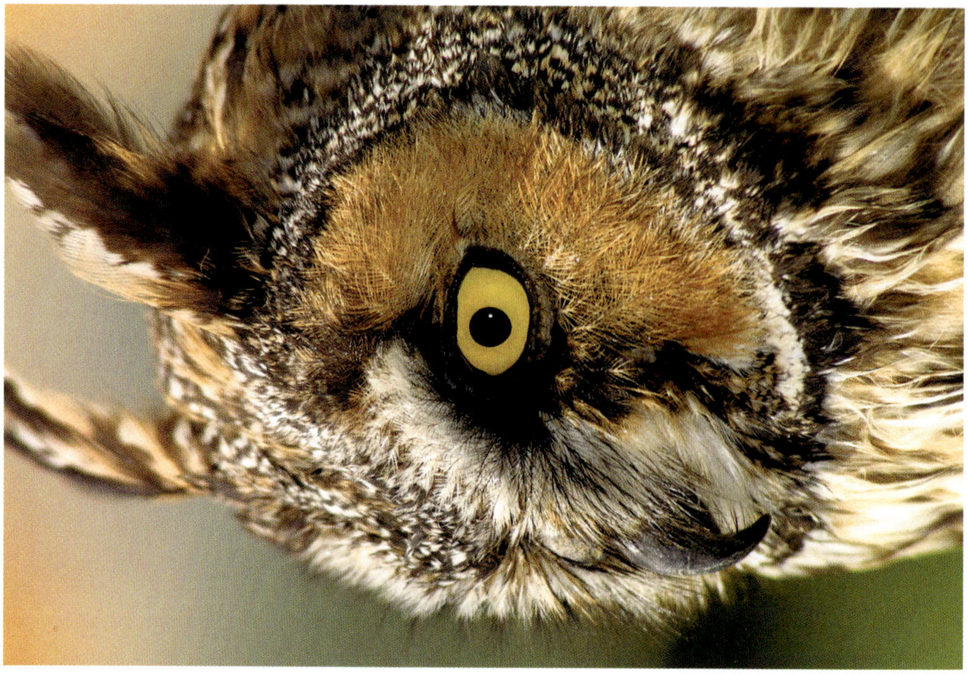

Figure 4.1 When you look at an image that needs to have a basic rotation applied, it is relatively clear in which direction and by how much it needs to be rotated.

Note: Keep in mind that "flipping" an image is not the same as rotating. When you rotate an image, the orientation is changed, but the relationships between objects within the image are not. Flipping creates a mirror image in the direction of the flip, changing the relationships between objects in the image. Flipping should not be substituted for rotation, and it should be done only when you want to produce a mirror image.

After you've determined how an image needs to be rotated, doing so is as easy as selecting the appropriate option from the menu. In Photoshop, the options for basic rotation are found on the Image > Rotate Canvas submenu. There are options to rotate the image 180 degrees (180° on the menu) and 90 degrees clockwise (90°CW) or counterclockwise (90° CCW).

When you select the appropriate option from the menu, the image will be rotated based on that option. At this point the image should be right-side up, in the proper general orientation (Figure 4.2).

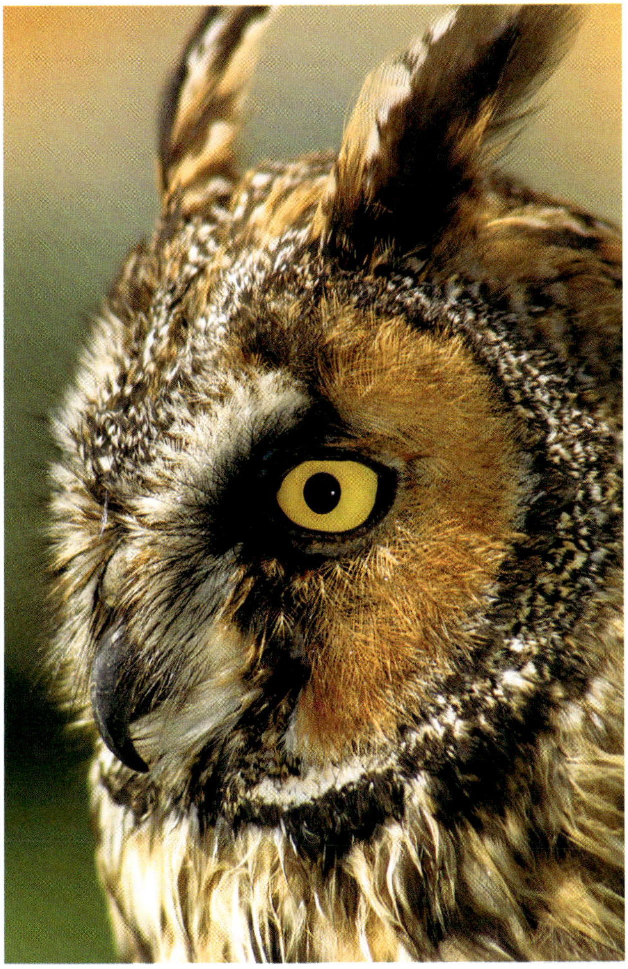

Figure 4.2 When you have applied the proper basic rotation to your image, it should appear in the proper orientation.

Basic Cropping

With the image properly oriented, you can make a more effective evaluation of its composition. In doing so, you may feel that certain areas of the image should be cropped out to strengthen the composition. You may want to eliminate a distracting element, tighten up the overall framing, or change the aspect ratio (relationship between height and width) for aesthetic reasons. For images scanned from film, this is also the point at which you should make sure the entire slide frame has been cropped out, so that only the actual image area is preserved.

I tend to divide cropping into two basic categories. The first is what I call *corrective* cropping, which corrects problems with the image. For example, cropping out the edge of a slide frame of a scanned image would fall into this category. The second category is what I call *artistic* cropping. This changes the artistic or compositional appearance of the image.

Corrective cropping is something that usually can't be avoided. Artistic cropping, on the other hand, is purely subjective. I'll often separate the two of these, so that I'm doing the cropping that must be done first, then applying artistic cropping as a separate process, and focusing more on how I'm changing the interpretation of the image by my choice of cropping.

Note: If you are performing artistic cropping on an image, be absolutely certain you want to eliminate the area being cropped before committing the crop. If you aren't sure, save the artistic cropping for later in your workflow, after you've been able to spend more time with the image. You may find that the areas you wanted to crop earlier suddenly add to the image after applying adjustments throughout your workflow.

For example, I'll start with a corrective cropping to eliminate areas of the image that would be a problem if they were included in the final print (Figure 4.3). If someone was standing right at the edge of the frame in a beautiful landscape shot, or if a bad reflection caused an undesirable glare in one corner of the image, you'd certainly want to exclude that area from the scene.

After cropping to correct problems such as these, you can then move on to artistic cropping. Perhaps you'd like to go so far as to change a horizontal image into a vertical one by cropping most of the sides, or maybe you just need to fine-tune the aspect ratio to emphasize certain elements, such as cropping a little off the top of a landscape scene to emphasize the sweeping horizon. You could also simply focus more attention on the main subject matter by cropping out distracting elements from the peripheral areas of the image.

Cropping is often seen as a minor part of your overall workflow. However, the way you crop an image can have a dramatic effect on its final interpretation. By applying a crop, you are able to move beyond the limitations imposed by the aspect ratio of your film or digital imaging sensor. Making a change to the aspect ratio of your image—presenting something different than the viewer is accustomed to—can add impact to your images. Even when you don't think you need to crop an image, you might spend some time working with the Crop tool to see if there are new ways to present the image that you haven't thought about but that would produce a more aesthetically appealing final result.

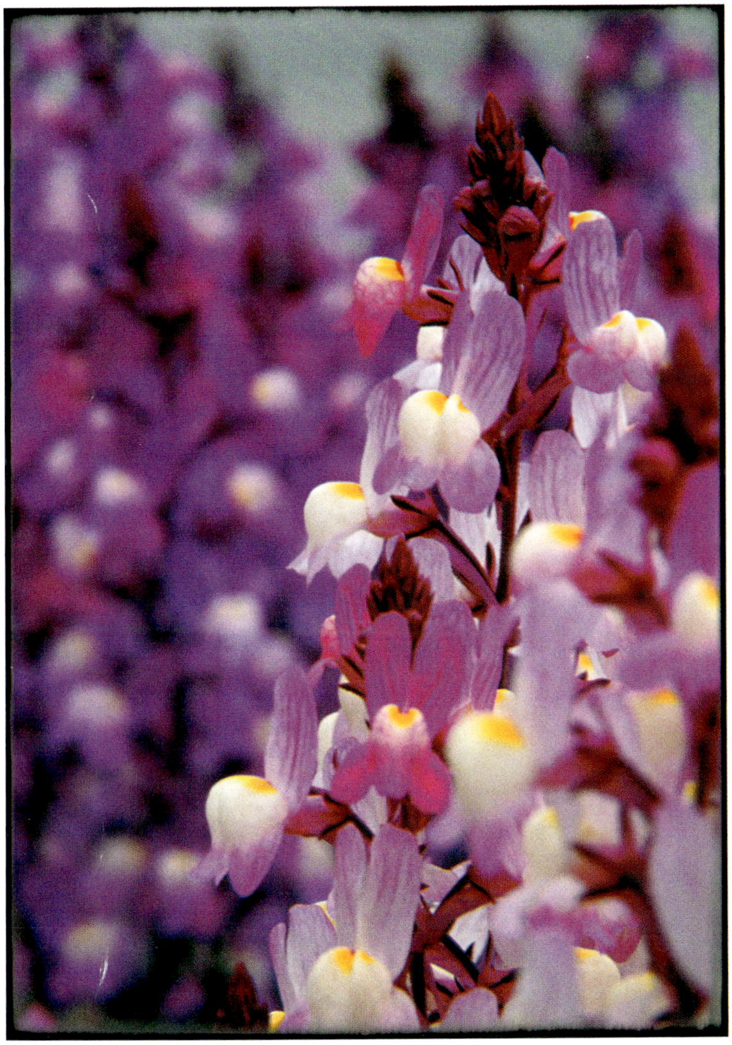

Figure 4.3 When you are working with a film scan, it is important to crop the slide edge from the entire perimeter of the image.

Cropping from a Selection

One of the most straightforward methods of cropping an image is to use a selection as the basis of the crop. Of course, because it is such a simple process, it doesn't offer significant functionality. However, in a variety of situations, starting from a selection is an easy way to crop your image. Creating selections will be covered in extensive detail in Chapter 9, "Making Selections." In the meantime, I'll show you a basic way to create a selection for cropping. When you learn to utilize other selection methods, you can use those for cropping as well.

When using a selection to crop an image, you are defining the outer boundaries of the crop. No matter what the shape of the selection, the final crop will always be to a rectangle. In effect, the cropped image will have outer dimensions defined by the point at which the selection extends farthest in each direction, horizontally and vertically.

The first step is to create a selection that defines the area of the image you want to keep. Start by choosing the Rectangular Marquee tool from the Tools palette. Click and drag on your image to define a rectangular shape, starting in one corner and finishing in the opposite corner (Figure 4.4). The resulting shape should define the area you want to keep, so that only those elements of the image you want to eliminate fall outside the rectangle.

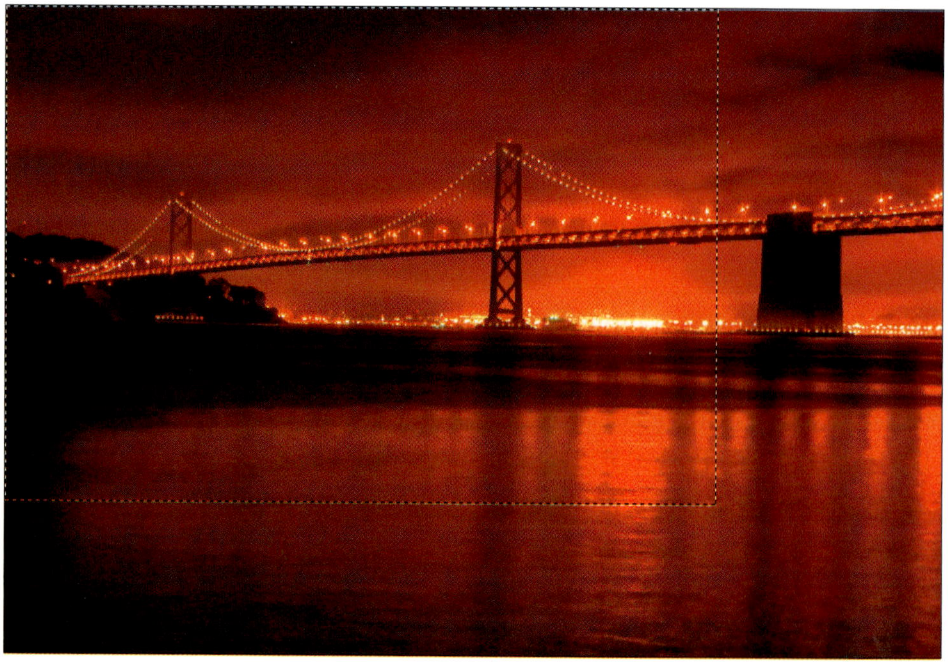

Figure 4.4 The Rectangular Marquee tool can be used to create a selection that defines the area you'd like to crop in an image.

After you have defined a selection within the image, cropping based on that selection can be done by choosing Image > Crop from the menu. This will cause the image to be cropped so the selection defines the new edge of the image. Everything outside that selection edge will be eliminated (Figure 4.5).

Of course, there's no need for the selection to be rectangular just because the cropped image will be. As you'll see in Chapter 9, there are many ways to make selections of a wide variety of shapes, and any of them can be used to create a selection for cropping your image. Just keep in mind that whatever the shape of the selection, the final crop will always be a rectangle that coincides with the outermost points of the selection (Figure 4.6).

It may seem pointless to crop an image by using a selection with a non-rectangular shape when the final crop will be rectangular. However, in certain situations you may find it easier to think about cropping an image by determining the specific areas you want to keep, tracing those areas to produce the selection, and then cropping to match that shape. In other situations, you may create a non-rectangular selection for another purpose and then realize that the selection provides a perfect basis for a crop. The key to remember is that you have a high degree of flexibility when using selections for cropping, so don't feel that you always need to use a rectangular selection.

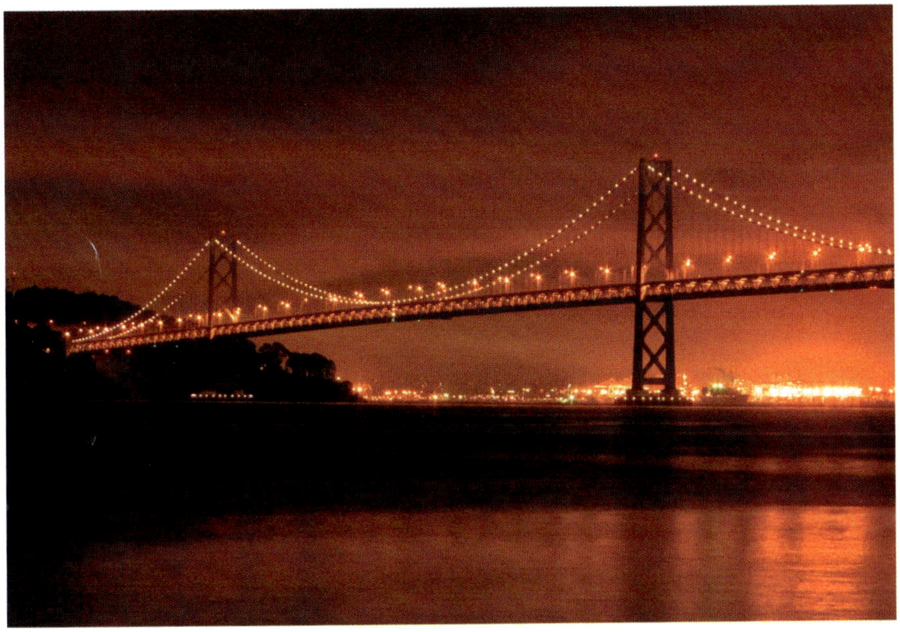

Figure 4.5 After you've defined a selection, you can choose Image > Crop from the menu, and the image will be cropped to the outer edge of your selection.

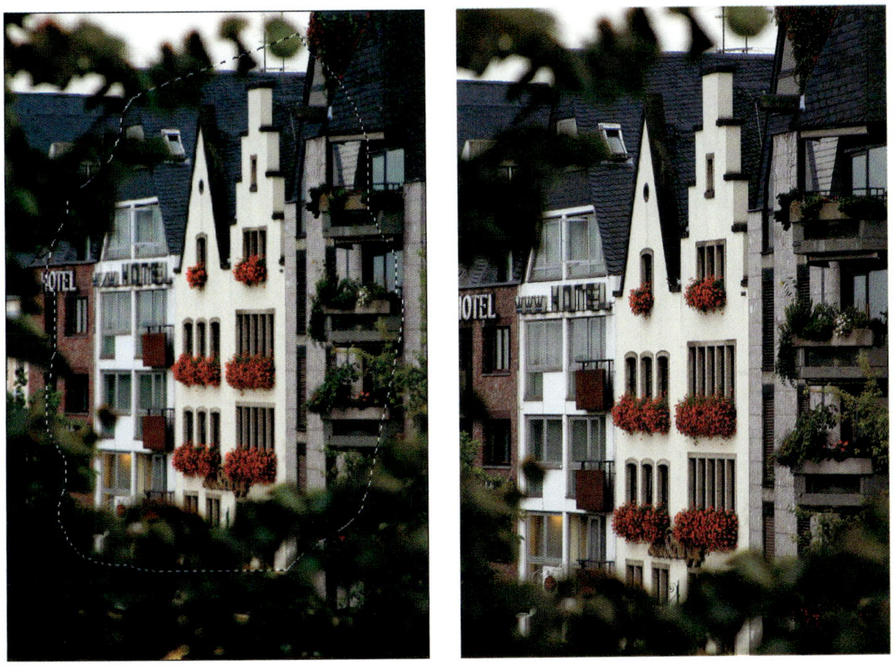

Figure 4.6 You don't need to create a rectangular selection as the basis of a crop, even though the final crop will be rectangular. I've sketched out a selection that simply defines areas I'd like to keep in the image, without following a rectangular shape. (left) After the non-rectangular selection is applied as a crop, the result is a rectangular image that is cropped to the edges of the selection. (right)

Note: You can hold the Shift key while creating a selection with the Rectangular Marquee tool to produce a square selection, which can then be used to crop the image to a perfectly square image area. Chapter 9 will provide you with many more methods for creating selections, all of which can be applied to cropping an image.

Using the Crop Tool

In many cases, cropping from a selection is a preferred method because of its flexibility of allowing you to crop from a selection of any shape (though the resulting crop will still be rectangular). However, the Crop tool is generally the most appropriate choice for most cropping tasks because it is specifically designed for that purpose.

To get started with the Crop tool, select it from the Tools palette or press C. This will change the Options bar to include the settings that are specific to this tool (Figure 4.7). You'll start with a basic crop, so click the Clear button on the Options bar to make sure no sizing options are set. You'll see how to put the other settings to use a little later.

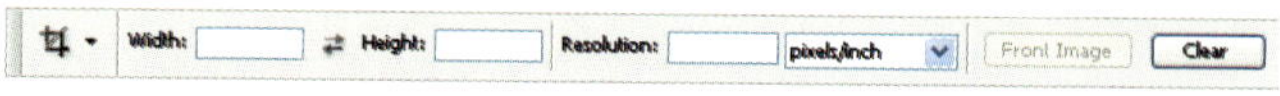

Figure 4.7 When you select the Crop tool, the Options bar will be updated to reflect the options for this tool.

Similar to the use of the Rectangular Marquee tool described in the previous section, you can click and drag across your image with the Crop tool to define the crop area, producing a rectangular box, or marquee, that defines the area to be kept. Anything outside the crop box you define will be removed from the image after you apply the crop.

With the crop box defined, you can adjust the shape of the crop to fine-tune the result you're trying to achieve. At each corner, and at the halfway point of each border line of the crop box, you'll see a small square handle. These handles can be dragged to change the outer dimensions of the crop box. You can also grab any edge of the crop box to drag and resize. If you click and drag one of the handles at the midway point of a border, you'll change the position of that border line only, not affecting the other lines. Dragging a corner handle will change the position of that corner, and thus affect the two lines that intersect at that corner. If you hold the Shift key while adjusting one of the corner handles, you can change the position of that corner without changing the aspect ratio, or relative shape, of the crop.

You may notice that when you have an active crop, the Options bar changes. Most of these controls affect the *shield* that is displayed by default when you are cropping your image. This is the display that darkens the area around the crop, so you can get a better idea of how the image will appear after you apply the crop. The default settings cause the shield to be displayed in black at a 75% opacity. This considerably darkens the area to be discarded in the crop, making it easier to visualize the result (Figure 4.8). However, you can change the settings if you prefer.

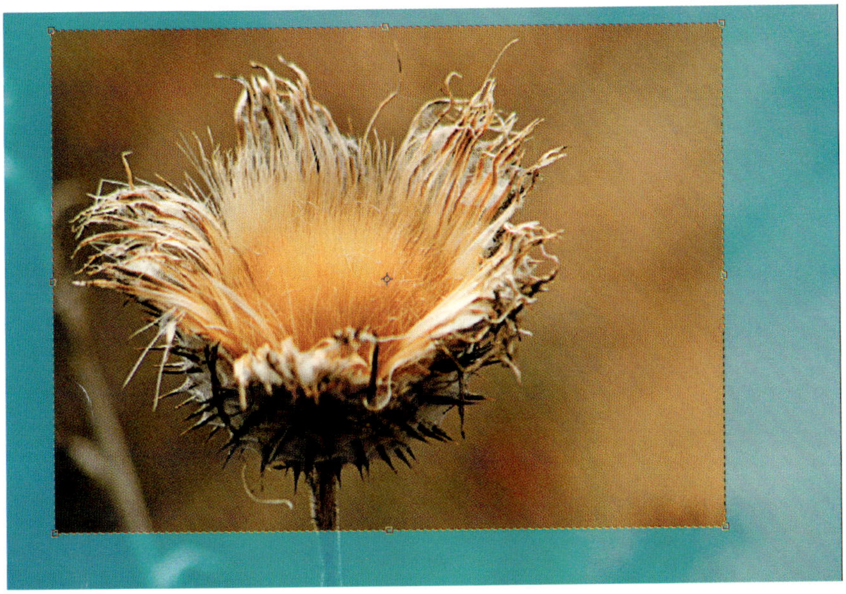

Figure 4.8 The shield for the Crop tool makes it easier to see what the effect of the crop will be on the resulting image.

First, if you prefer not to see the shield, you can deselect the Shield checkbox or press the slash (/) key on your keyboard. Either option serves as a toggle to turn the shield on and off. Although the shield is helpful for visualizing the effect of a crop, it can interfere at times. For example, I sometimes find that it makes it difficult to see exactly where the edge of a crop falls on the image. In those cases, I'll turn it off temporarily to evaluate the image, and then turn it back on to view the overall crop.

Second, it is also possible to change the color or opacity of the shield. The default is a black shield at a 75% opacity. However, you can click the color box on the Options bar to bring up the Color Picker dialog box, and then choose any color you'd like to use for the shield, such as the blue I used in Figure 4.8. For example, for a grayscale image you may find that a black shield blends in too much, in which case you may prefer a colored shield. You can also adjust the Opacity setting as desired to change the degree to which you are able to see the area that is going to be cropped. If you set the Opacity to 100%, you won't see any of the image through the crop shield at all, but instead will have an image that appears to be matted with the selected color as a border. Reducing the Opacity setting will allow you to see a shaded view of the area of the image you are cropping, so you can decide whether you really want to eliminate those areas.

It is important to check the area you are cropping to make sure you're eliminating elements you should, such as the edge of the slide frame in a scan. Also make sure the crop box doesn't extend outside the image area, because that would cause additional pixels to be added around the edge of the image with the background color defined in the Tools palette. I recommend zooming in close to check the corners of your crop, and possibly checking the full perimeter if necessary to ensure you are producing the best crop possible.

Because you are in the middle of a crop process when you check the edges of your crop area, you can't switch to other tools used for navigation. However, keyboard shortcuts provide efficient ways to check the image. The method I prefer is to hold the Ctrl/Command key and the spacebar, which gives you the Zoom tool no matter what tool you're currently using. I then click and drag a box around a corner of the image, defining the area I want to look at more closely, while still holding those keys. This will cause the image to be zoomed in so that area fills the available display area. To return to a view showing the full image, I hold Ctrl/Command and press 0 (the zero key). Repeat this process for each corner of the image to check for appropriate cropping, adjusting the position of the crop box corner as needed. If you want to check the full perimeter of the crop box, you can hold the spacebar after you've zoomed in to activate the Hand tool, which can then be used to drag the image around (by clicking and holding the mouse button and then moving the mouse) while you examine the edge of the crop.

After you have defined the crop for the image as you like it, you're ready to apply that crop. When you have an active crop, clicking the Commit button ✓ on the Options bar will apply the current crop. You can also press Enter/Return on the keyboard, or double-click with the mouse inside the crop box. When you do any of these, the image will be cropped based on the current crop box, with the pixels outside the crop box discarded.

If you decide you don't want to apply the crop, you can click the Cancel button ⦸ or press the Esc key on your keyboard. The crop will not be applied, and the crop box will go away. You can then start over with a new crop or simply move on to using other tools if you decide you don't want to crop the image at all.

Note: If you attempt to switch to another tool or close the image in the middle of a crop, you'll be asked if you want to Crop (apply the current crop), Cancel (go back to what you were doing so you can finish adjusting crop settings), or Don't Crop (switch to the new tool or close the image, canceling the crop).

Crop Size

The Crop tool also provides a variety of options that allow you to specify the aspect ratio of the final crop, as well as the size of the image after cropping. These settings must be established before you create the crop box. So, be sure to apply these settings first, or if you are already in the middle of a crop and realize you need to select a specific size, cancel the crop and set these options before starting the crop process again.

The controls for establishing a specific aspect ratio or image size are quite simple, with values for Width, Height, and Resolution. However, you don't always need to include the Resolution option, and in some cases you may want to exclude it.

When you set a Width and Height value without establishing a Resolution, the image will be cropped to the aspect ratio defined by the Width and Height settings, but the number of pixels within the cropped area won't be changed (no interpolation will be applied). On the other hand, if you do include a value for Resolution in addition to Width and Height, the image will be cropped and resized in one step, so that the cropped image has exactly the dimensions and resolution you specified. This means interpolation will be applied if necessary to change the image to the exact dimensions and resolution you have specified.

> **Note:** The term *interpolation* refers to the process of adding pixels to the image during the process of resizing, effectively filling the gaps between pixels when they are spread out to produce a larger image. The same term is sometimes used for the reverse process, where pixels are removed to reduce the size of an image.

Because setting these values causes the crop to be constrained, when you have values established for Width and Height the crop box you draw will be limited to the specific aspect ratio defined by those values.

For example, if you want to crop an image to an aspect ratio of 1.5:1, which is the aspect ratio of a 35mm frame of film, you could plug in 1.5 for Width and 1 for Height (for a horizontal image) before creating your crop box (Figure 4.9). By leaving the Resolution value blank, only the aspect ratio is being constrained, and the pixels you choose to keep based on the final crop will not be altered. When you click and drag on the image to establish the crop, the shape of the crop box will be determined by the aspect ratio represented by the Width and Height settings you've established. The size isn't limited, and you can make the crop box as big or small as your image will allow. However, no matter what direction you drag the box, the aspect ratio of the crop box will be fixed.

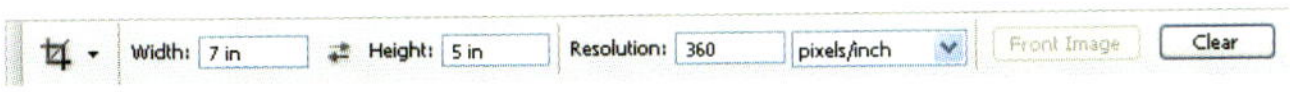

Figure 4.9 The Width, Height, and Resolution settings on the Options bar for the Crop tool provide a way for you to set a specific aspect ratio or final image size for a crop.

Between the Width and Height settings, you'll see a double-arrow icon that, when clicked, will swap those two values. This is handy if, for example, you are creating a collage and want all of the images to be the exact same size, but some are horizontal and some are vertical.

If you want the image after cropping to be a specific size, not just at a set aspect ratio, you'll need to include a value for Resolution. With all three values established, the exact size and resolution of the image after cropping is known, and you can crop and resize in one step. This is a great way to crop an image to fit a specific output size, such as when you need to print an image to fit a particular frame.

> **Note:** Cropping to a specific size or aspect ratio is often done to accommodate the limitations of a frame size or for other reasons related to the final display. If you are cropping out an area only so the image will fit a desired final print size, you may not want to crop it this early in the workflow. Instead, work with a *copy* of your master image. You can then crop to a specific output size without sacrificing anything from your master image.

When cropping to a specific image size, be sure to set the Resolution value to whatever you will be using for the print because the image will be interpolated based on the values you enter. This will be covered in greater detail in Chapter 14, "Output Processing," but when in doubt you can use a Resolution setting of 300 pixels/inch.

Note: When you crop to a specific size and include a Resolution setting, Photoshop will interpolate the resulting image by using the method you have established for Image Interpolation in the General page of the Preferences dialog box. I recommend that you use Bicubic for this setting if you generally make modest enlargements or use Bicubic Smoother if you generally make significant enlargements.

The Options bar also includes two buttons that allow you to adjust the settings for Width, Height, and Resolution. These are the Front Image and Clear buttons, found at the right end of the Options bar when the Crop tool is active. The Clear button clears the values currently entered for Width, Height, and Resolution, resetting the tool back to the default behavior.

The Front Image button allows you to apply the size of one image to the crop settings of another image. As the name indicates, when you click this button, the size and resolution of the currently active image are set as the Width, Height, and Resolution settings for the Crop tool on the Options bar. This is an excellent way to crop and resize multiple images to exactly the same dimensions. For example, if you are creating a collage with multiple images and you want the images to be sized exactly the same, you can crop and resize the first image, and then click Front Image to establish the settings from that image to be used for other images.

Note: Always click the Clear button to empty the Width, Height, and Resolution values after cropping an image to a specific size, so that next time you use the Crop tool you'll be starting with the default behavior.

Perspective

The Options bar for the Crop tool in Photoshop also includes a Perspective checkbox. This allows you to stretch and skew the image to correct perspective problems or to introduce a change in perspective to add a creative twist. This option is most often used to correct perspective errors, such as when your position causes the sides of a building to lean inward, as is often seen when you use a wide-angle lens to capture such an image (Figure 4.10).

Note: The Perspective checkbox is enabled only when you are using the Delete option for the Crop tool on the Options bar. I'll discuss the Hide option later in this chapter.

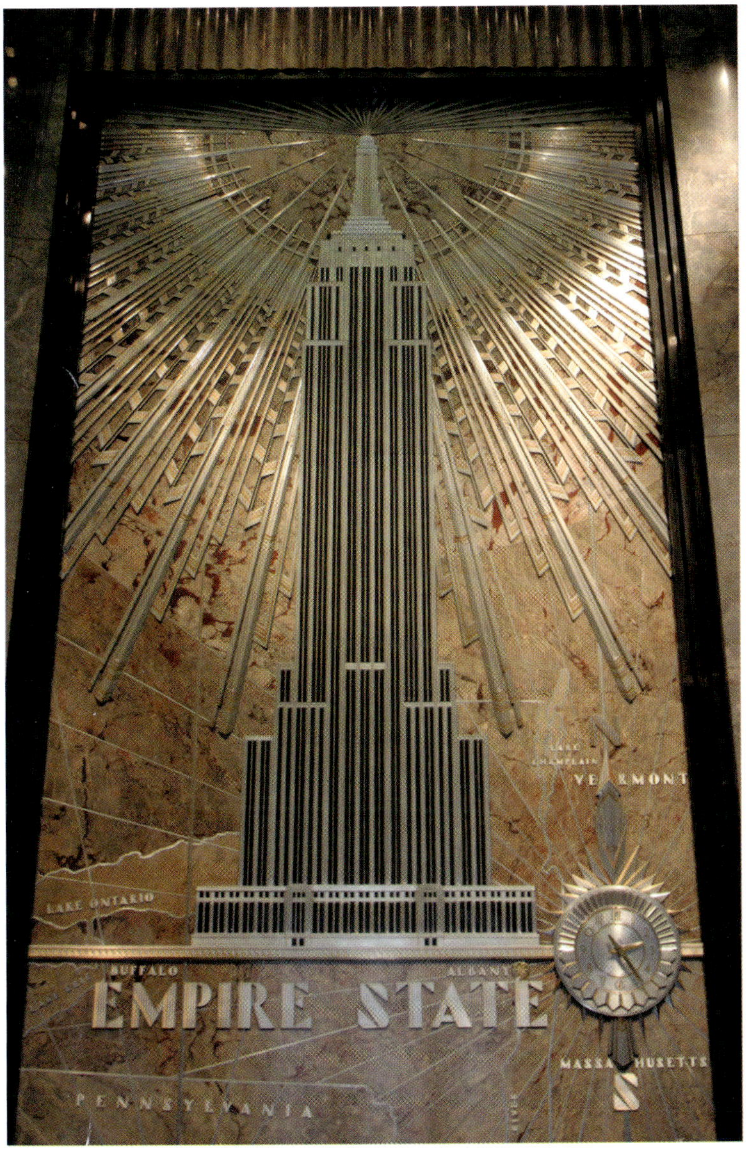

Figure 4.10 When capturing images by looking upward, especially with a wide-angle lens, you'll often see perspective errors that can be distracting.

To get started, create a basic crop with the Crop tool, but don't apply the crop. While the crop is active, you'll see that the Perspective checkbox is available on the Options bar. As you've seen with previous use of the Crop tool, the shape of the crop box is always a rectangle. However, when you select the Perspective checkbox, the box is no longer constrained to a rectangular shape. Instead, you can move any corner of the crop box into any position without changing the position of the others. This allows you to position each of the four corners very precisely to produce the change you want.

Note: If you turn the Perspective checkbox off after enabling it, the corners of the image will revert to a normal rectangle, causing you to lose the relationships between corners you had established using Perspective. Therefore, you shouldn't turn off the checkbox until you're sure you don't want to apply the current perspective adjustment.

Let's consider the example of a photograph of a building, where the outer edges of the building appear to lean inward. If you position each corner of the crop box on a corner of the building and the Perspective checkbox is selected, and you then apply the crop, the image will be cropped and skewed so that each of the corners of the building will be at the corners of the final rectangular image. In the process, the building itself is distorted so it appears with perfectly vertical sides. This gives you an idea of how the tool works. However, applying the effect properly can be a bit more of a challenge because you need to apply the perspective adjustment without cropping too closely to the subject you're trying to correct.

This requires that you judge the appropriate position for each of the corners while keeping them far enough away from the primary subject that the resulting image includes as much of the surrounding area as you'd like to maintain. To make your job easier, you may want to enable the Grid display by choosing View > Show > Grid from the menu. This will display a grid pattern over your image, which you can use to better judge how far each corner of the crop box should be placed from the edges of the subject of your image to ensure the best result.

Note: Another trick for getting the position of each corner correct is to first position each corner exactly on the corners of the object that has the perspective you want to fix. Then drag each corner outward to enlarge the crop area and include more of the image. The shield will stay in position while you are dragging, allowing you to use it as a reference to help ensure you're moving the corner at a 45-degree angle from the starting position by maintaining the same horizontal and vertical distance from that starting position.

So, to put the Perspective option to use, start by creating a basic crop of your image, with the Grid display turned on (Figure 4.11). Then select the Perspective checkbox, and adjust each of the corners of the crop box to a position that causes the lines between each corner to be parallel to the subject you are trying to correct, but far enough away that you are preserving all areas of the image desired. When you have positioned the corners as desired, apply the crop, and the image will be cropped with a perspective adjustment in one step (Figure 4.12).

Note: Getting the best results with the Perspective control of the Crop tool can take practice. If you're not happy with the results you achieve, undo the crop by choosing Edit > Undo from the menu and try again.

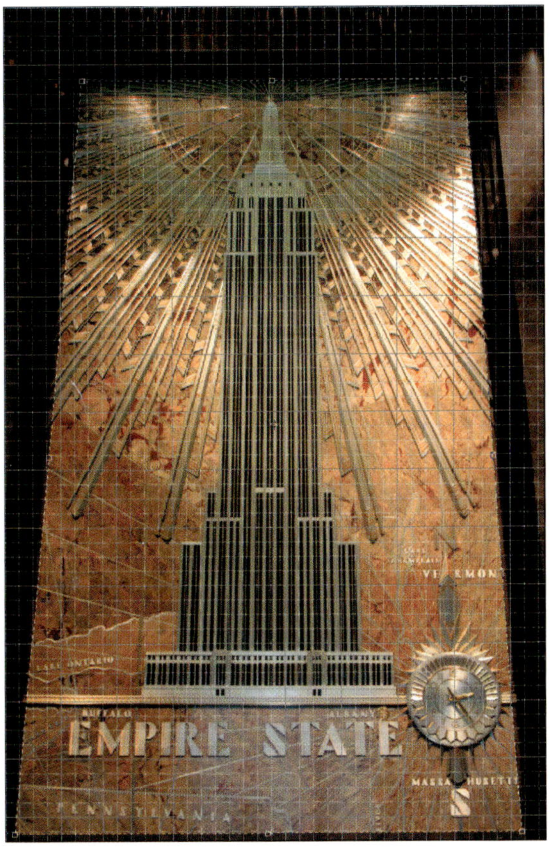

Figure 4.11 Using the Perspective option of the Crop tool, you can apply a crop that will also correct perspective in your image. Turning on the grid display can help you better judge the placement of the corners of the crop box during this process.

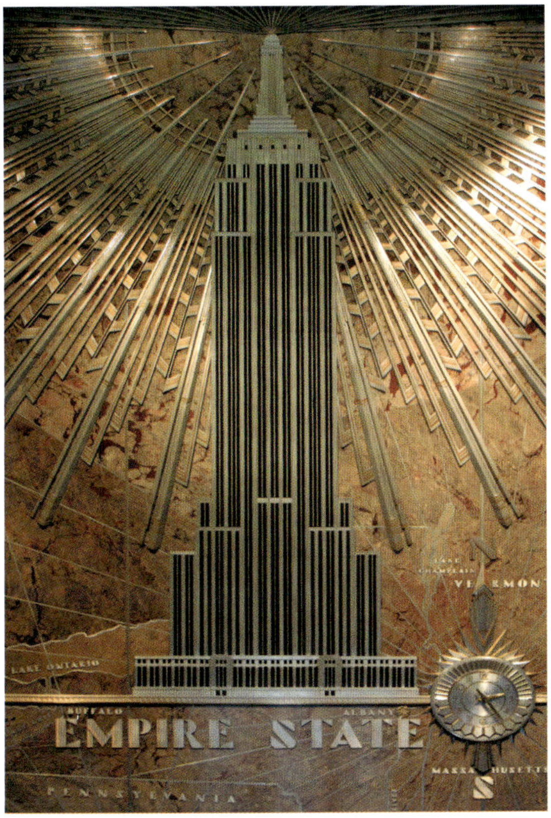

Figure 4.12 After you have established the proper Perspective correction with the Crop tool, Photoshop will skew the image to correct for the distortion.

Nondestructive Cropping

If you want to apply a crop to your image, but you don't feel entirely comfortable making a permanent commitment to the crop, you can take advantage of an option in Photoshop to crop without actually removing pixels. This is accomplished by using the Cropped Area control on the Options bar. The default value is Delete, which causes pixels outside your crop area to be permanently removed. However, you can also choose the Hide option to hide pixels without permanently deleting them.

There are a couple of limitations for the Cropped Area control. The Hide option won't be available if the Perspective checkbox is selected. Also, you can't use the Hide option when you're cropping an image that contains a Background image layer. Virtually every image is going to start with a Background image layer, but you can convert it to a "normal" image layer by simply renaming it. To do so, double-click the thumbnail for the Background image layer on the Layers palette. The New Layer dialog box will appear, providing an option to rename this layer (Figure 4.13). You can simply accept the default settings and click OK.

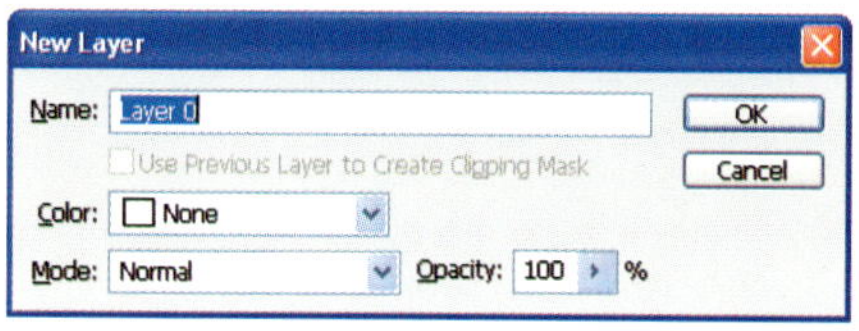

Figure 4.13 When you double-click on the Background image layer, the New Layer dialog box will be displayed. By clicking OK, the Background layer will be converted to a "normal" image layer.

With these conditions met, create a basic crop box by clicking and dragging across the image with the Crop tool. At this point, the Cropped Area option will become enabled so you can choose between the Delete and Hide options. When you choose Hide and apply the crop to your image, the apparent result will be exactly the same as if you had used the default option to Delete pixels. However, the pixels you cropped out haven't been removed from the image. Instead, they are "hiding" outside the new border of your image.

This provides a couple of additional options if you decide later that you don't want the crop to be applied as it was. For one thing, you can select the Move tool from the Tools palette and then click and drag the selected image layer to change which portion of the image is visible. You can think of this as placing a rectangular window over the top of your image, and then moving the image around so that you are able to see different portions of the image at a given time through that window.

The other nice thing about cropping with the Hide option is that the crop isn't permanent. You can restore the entire image at any time by choosing Image > Reveal All from the menu. This will resize the image frame so it matches the outer dimensions of any hidden pixel data. In effect, this restores the image to its appearance before you applied the crop.

Using the Hide option is an excellent way to approach cropping for your master image files when you are pretty sure you want to apply the crop permanently but would prefer to preserve options for later. However, keep in mind that by not deleting the cropped pixels, the file size will be larger than if you had allowed the Crop tool to delete the pixels outside the crop area.

Note: If the image was saved as a JPEG you can't use the Reveal All option, but that shouldn't be an issue because I recommend saving your master image file as a Photoshop PSD or TIFF file.

Arbitrary Rotation

At the beginning of this chapter, I talked about rotating your image in 90-degree increments to correct its overall orientation. However, there will also be times when you want to rotate the image by an arbitrary number of degrees to correct for a crooked horizon or for another object that should be perfectly horizontal or vertical but appears slightly off-kilter (Figure 4.14).

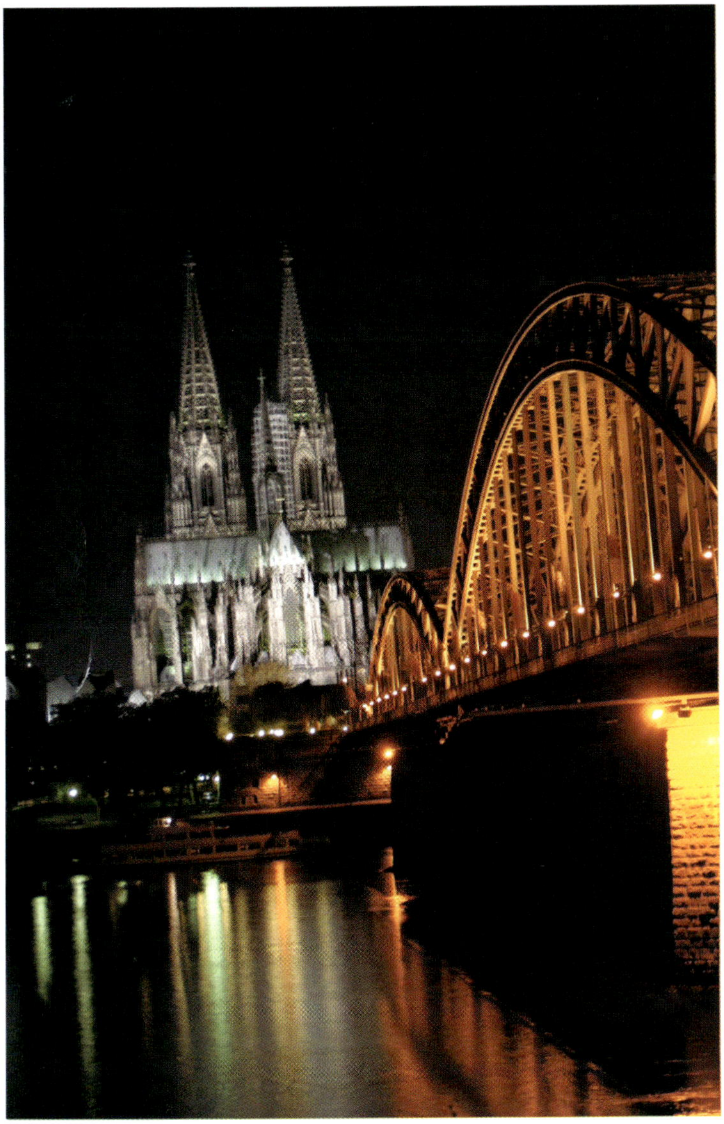

Figure 4.14 When an object that should be horizontal or vertical isn't, you'll need to apply arbitrary rotation to correct the problem.

Whenever you rotate an image by other than 90-degree increments, you will need to crop the image. This is because the resulting image is always a rectangle, and if you have rotated the image by a few degrees, you'll end up with part of the image hanging outside that rectangle and possibly areas within the image rectangle that don't have any actual pixel values (in which case Photoshop will fill these values with the current background color in the Tools palette).

Rotating with the Crop Tool

Because you'll have to crop the image anyway when you apply an arbitrary rotation, it makes sense to use the Crop tool for both the rotation and the cropping. Fortunately, the tool provides exactly that capability.

If you're going to apply an arbitrary rotation to an image, I recommend that you not perform any cropping before doing the combined rotation and crop, so that you have as many pixels to work with as possible when you apply the arbitrary rotation. Using the Crop tool to apply a basic arbitrary rotation is rather easy, and the process starts just as it would for a normal crop. Start by selecting the Crop tool and clicking and dragging on the image to define a basic crop box. To apply a rotation, move the mouse pointer outside the crop box. The mouse pointer will become a double-headed curved arrow. When you click and drag, you'll see that the crop box rotates. This allows you to define the exact angle that the eventual image should be.

Note: The small target icon that appears in the middle of the crop box defines the center of rotation. In most cases, you'll want the center of the crop box to coincide with the center of rotation. However, if you'd like the box to rotate around a different point, you can click and drag this target to a different position.

The best method is to first find something in the image that should be perfectly horizontal or vertical. This may be a horizon line, the edge of a building, or some other object. In some situations, such as a landscape on a hazy day, it may be difficult to see exactly where that line is. However, you'll need to select something within the image to use as your reference line.

With that reference line identified, the next step is to drag one of the edges of the crop box toward that line (Figure 4.15). For vertical objects, you'd move the left or right edge of the box inward, and for horizontal objects, you'd bring in the top or bottom edge. Simply point your mouse to the edge itself or the square handle on the edge, and click and drag inward. Put it relatively close to the reference line, but not right on top of it. If it is right on top of the reference line, evaluating how close they are to being parallel will be difficult. All you really need is for the two lines to be close enough to decide when they are parallel to each other.

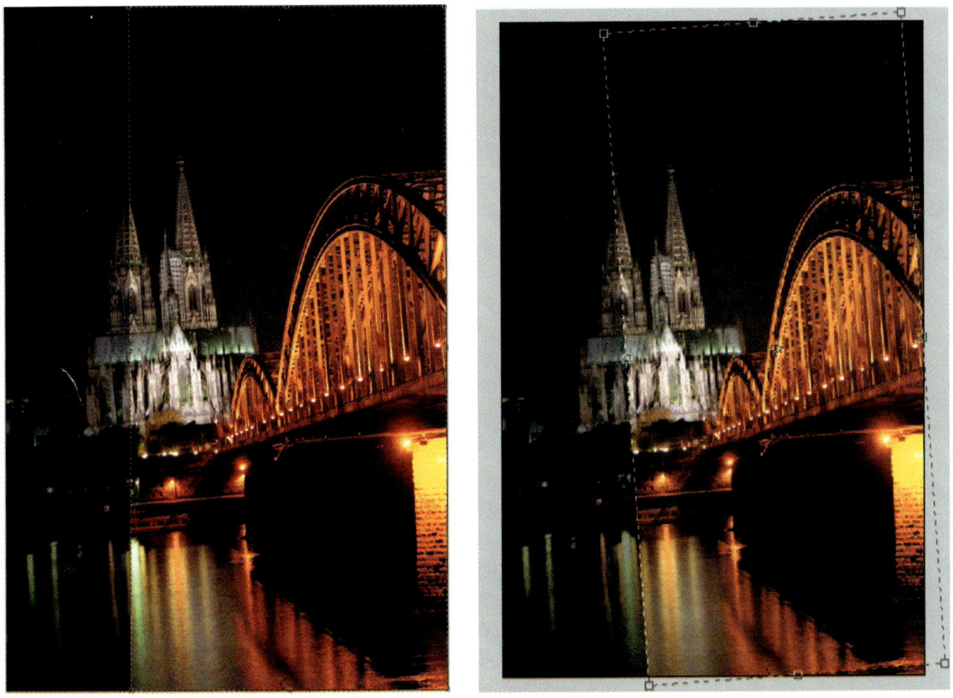

Figure 4.15 The first step in applying arbitrary rotation with the Crop tool is to bring one of the crop box edges in toward your reference line within the image. (left) Rotate the crop box so its edge is parallel with the reference line within the image that should be horizontal or vertical. (right)

With the edge dragged inward near your reference line, move the mouse pointer outside the crop box and click and drag to rotate (as in the second image of Figure 4.15). Rotate the crop box until the edge of the box and your reference line in the image are perfectly parallel. At this point, your angle of rotation is established (Figure 4.16). However, because you brought one of the edges of the crop box inward, you now need to adjust the edges. Also, the rotation may have caused one or more corners of the crop box to move outside the image. Therefore, you need to adjust all four corners so that you are including as much of the image as possible (or as much as is desired) within the crop area and so that all four of the corners are inside the available image area.

After you have established your rotation and corrected your cropping, you'll be ready to apply the crop. When you do so, the image will be automatically cropped and rotated in one step (Figure 4.17).

Note: When cropping and rotating in one step with the Crop tool, you can still use all of the other options, such as those for setting the Width, Height, and Resolution, as discussed earlier in this chapter.

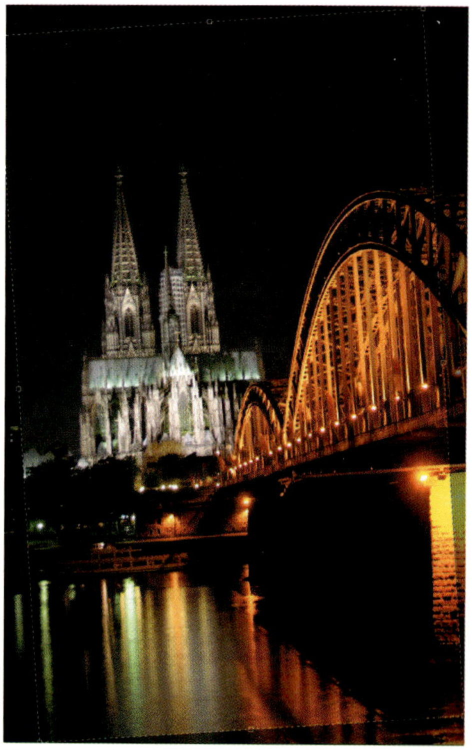

Figure 4.16 After you have rotated the crop box to your reference line, you can adjust all four corners so they are within the image area and the crop can be applied.

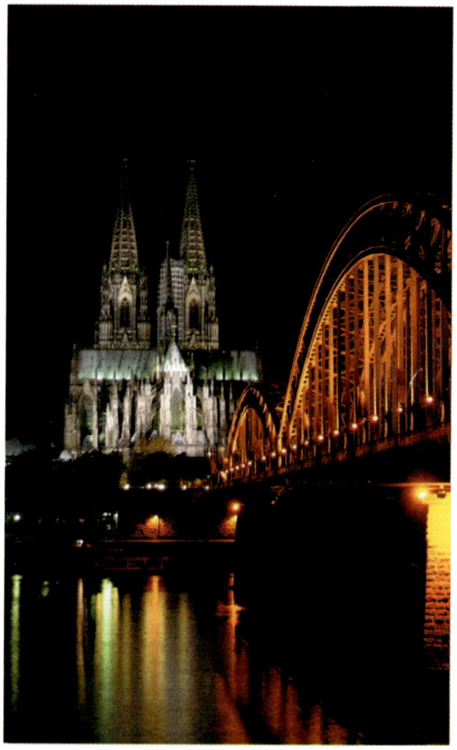

Figure 4.17 When the crop is applied with the crop box rotated, the image will be cropped and rotated in a single step.

Rotating with the Ruler Tool

As much as I love being able to apply cropping and rotation in one step by using the Crop tool, at times it is difficult to critically evaluate how accurate the rotation is when using this tool. In those situations, I utilize the Ruler tool to apply a more accurate rotation, although this method does require that cropping be handled as a separate step from rotation.

Note: In previous versions of Photoshop, the Ruler tool was called the Measure tool.

The Ruler tool allows you to measure a variety of attributes within your image. One of those is the angle, which can then be used to apply an arbitrary rotation to your image. To get started, select the Ruler tool from the Tools palette (it's under the Eyedropper tool; see Figure 4.18).

With the Ruler tool active, click on one point that defines the reference line you want to make perfectly horizontal or vertical, and hold the mouse button down as you drag toward another point on that same line. You don't have to trace the edge of the line, but rather simply hold the mouse button down as you drag and find the right position. When you release the mouse button, the measurement will be made from the point where you first clicked with the mouse to the point where you released the mouse button.

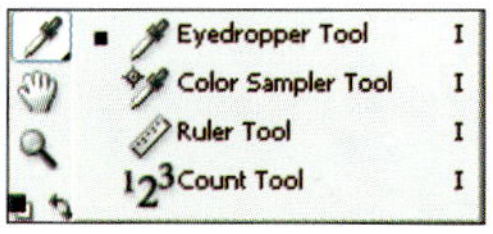

Figure 4.18 The Ruler tool is grouped with the Eyedropper tool on the Tools palette.

Note: If you need to redraw the line created with the Ruler tool, simply click and drag again from a different spot. You can also remove the existing ruler line by clicking the Clear button on the Options bar.

You may notice that the measurements for this line you have created are shown on the Options bar. One of these, labeled *A*, is the angle in degrees defined by your measure line (Figure 4.19). However, you don't have to remember the angle or the direction of rotation, because Photoshop can take care of that for you.

To apply a rotation based on the measure line that you've defined, choose Image > Rotate Canvas > Arbitrary from the menu. The amount of rotation required to make your measure line vertical will be entered in the Rotate Canvas dialog box automatically, and the option for clockwise or counterclockwise rotation will also be selected for you (Figure 4.20). All you need to do is click OK, and the image will be rotated for you automatically, making the line you drew with the Ruler tool perfectly horizontal or vertical as necessary.

After you've applied this rotation, you still need to crop the image to correct for the triangles that are created when the image is rotated to a non-rectangular orientation within a rectangular image frame. To do so, simply apply a standard crop as discussed at the beginning of this chapter, ensuring that only actual image pixels fall within the crop box.

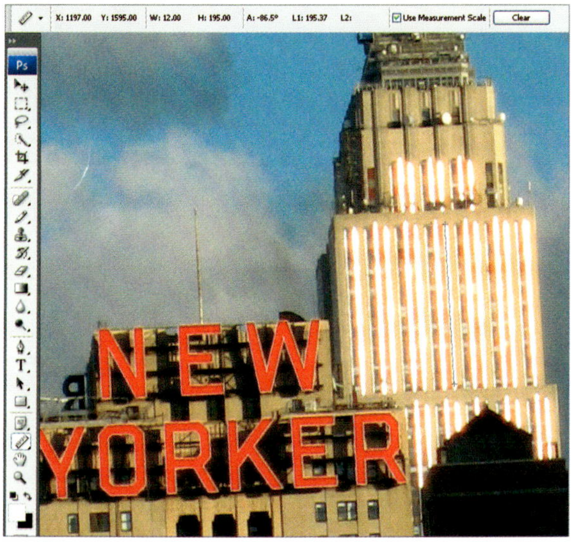

Figure 4.19 When you use the Ruler tool, the angle of the line you create (along with other measurements) is displayed on the Options bar.

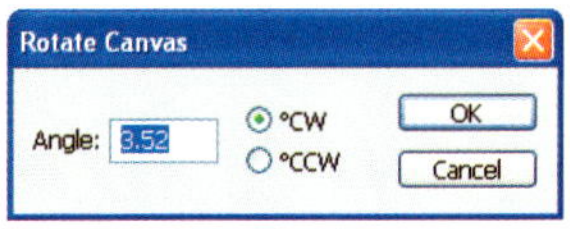

Figure 4.20 When you apply an arbitrary rotation after making a measurement with the Ruler tool, the angle and direction of rotation will be set automatically.

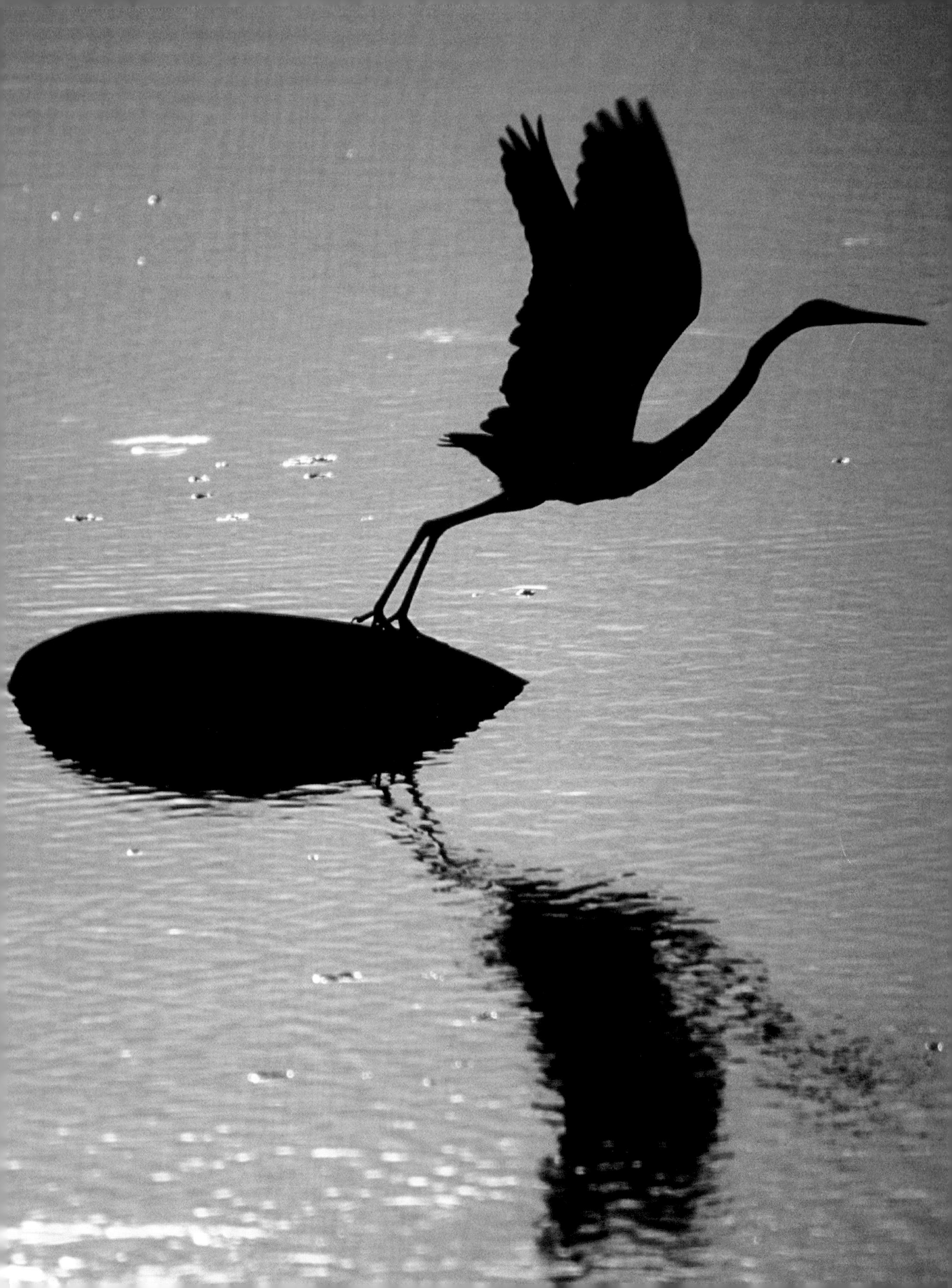

5 Basic Tone and Color

As you start working on the actual adjustments to optimize your images, basic tonal and color adjustments provide the foundation for building the final result. Having a firm understanding of how to apply these basic adjustments will ensure you are working toward the best quality from the beginning. For many images, these may be the only adjustments you need. For other images, these adjustments represent the first step toward producing an image that matches the vision you had when you first clicked the shutter release.

Chapter Contents

Interface Tools for Evaluation

In Chapter 2, "Download and Sort," I presented the navigation tools and explained how they could be used to evaluate your images for sharpness and other image-quality considerations. As you get started with the basic tonal and color adjustments for photographic images, it will be helpful to know about some other methods for evaluating your images so you can make better decisions about specific adjustments and image-quality issues (Figure 5.1).

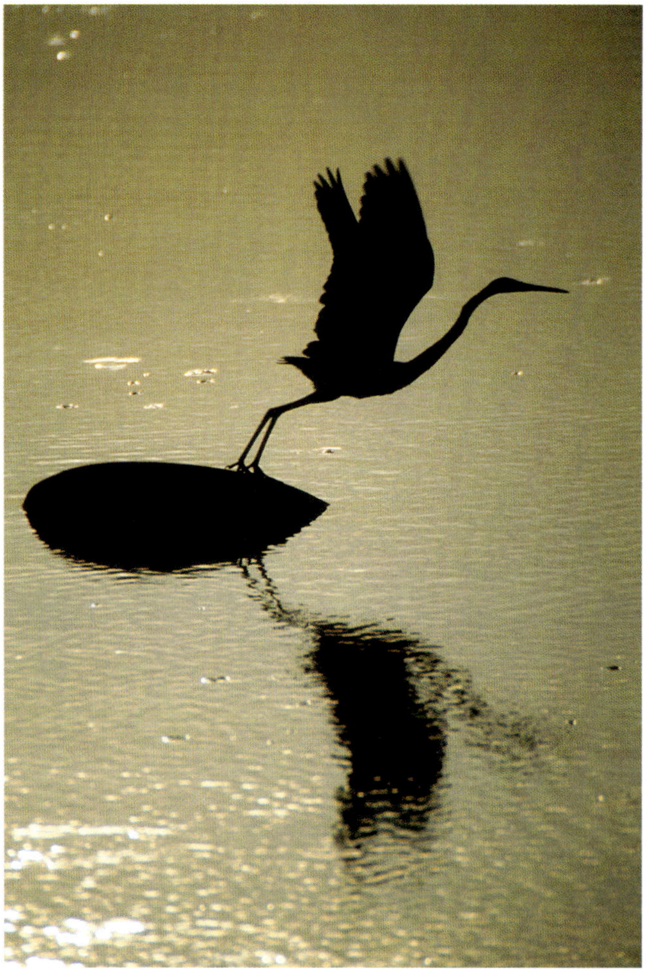

Figure 5.1 Carefully evaluating your image provides the opportunity to ensure that your adjustments result in the image you envisioned, even when tricky lighting conditions create a challenge to achieving the desired result. (Photo by Gabby Salazar)

Evaluate Channels

An image in the RGB color space is defined not by color information directly, but rather by three individual grayscale channels—one each for red, green, and blue. Each of these defines the brightness value for its particular color for each pixel, and the three values combined determine the actual color of each pixel.

You may be tempted to ignore the underlying channel information, focusing your attention instead on the full-color version of the image as you evaluate it. However, looking at the individual channels can help you gain a better understanding of the overall quality of an image.

Each channel contains a grayscale image—a black-and-white version of one of the three color components in your image. To view the channels, you'll first need to make sure the Channels palette is visible (Figure 5.2); if it isn't, choose Window > Channels.

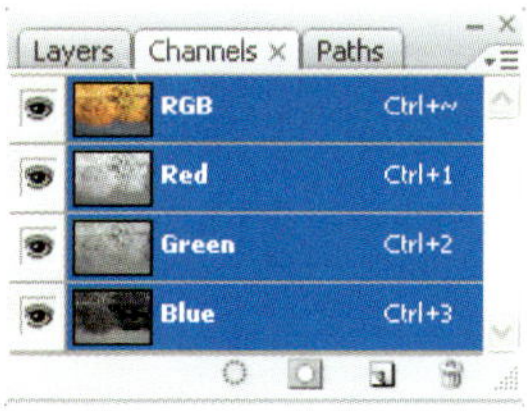

Figure 5.2 The Channels palette allows you to evaluate the individual color channels that make up your image.

To view an individual channel, simply click its thumbnail in the Channels palette. The document display will then be updated so you see only the grayscale information contained in that particular channel (assuming Color Channels in Color is *not* selected in Preferences > Display & Cursors), rather than the full-color version of the image (Figure 5.3).

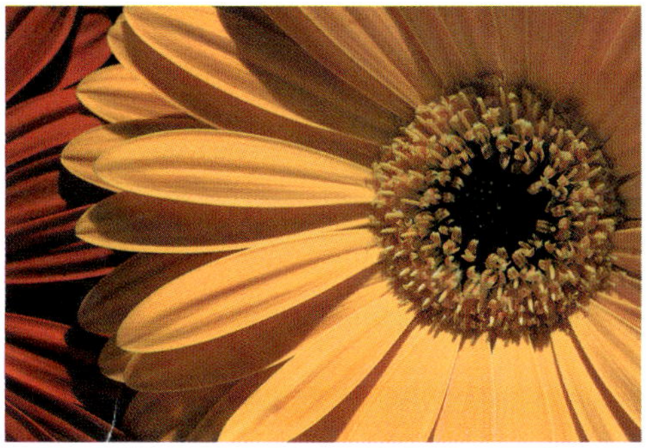

RGB

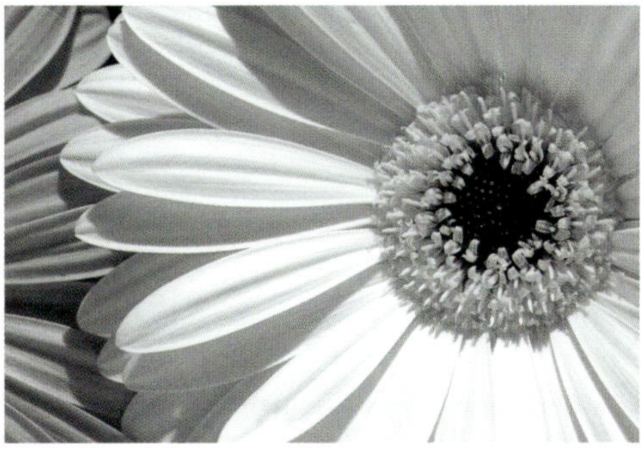

Red channel

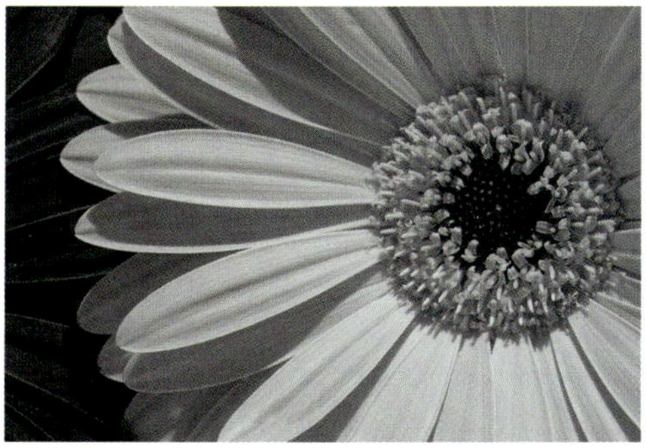

Green channel

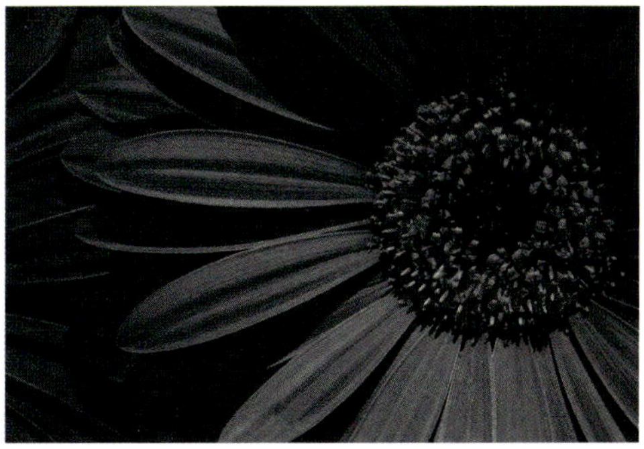

Blue channel

Figure 5.3 Besides looking at the overall color image, reviewing the individual color channels can give you a better idea of image quality.

You can use this grayscale view to evaluate the image for lost detail (much easier to do than when the channels display in color) or for quality problems on a particular channel. Each channel is used to define what color information is available within the image, so for example if there is a loss of detail in the blue channel, you can expect that blue or yellow (the opposite of blue) areas of the image may not have sufficient detail.

This is also a great opportunity to look for noise or other problems that can affect overall image quality. The blue channel is where you'll tend to find the most noise, so taking a close look at it can give you a much better sense of how much overall noise exists within the image. When you are finished evaluating each color channel, click the RGB thumbnail to return to the full-color view of your image.

Evaluating the individual color channels for your image gives you a much better feel for how much detail you've retained, how much color information exists for each color channel, and other issues affecting overall quality. If you have any concerns about the detail or quality of a particular image, a quick review of the individual channels can address those concerns.

Note: For those who like keyboard shortcuts, you can also view the individual channels by holding the Ctrl/Command key and pressing 1 for red, 2 for green, or 3 for blue. To return to the full-color version of the image, press Ctrl/Command plus the tilde key (~). The title bar will indicate which channel you are currently viewing.

Display Full Saturation

If you ever have a difficult time evaluating the overall color in your images, temporarily boosting the saturation to its maximum value can provide a dramatic indication of exactly what colors exist in various areas. Besides exaggerating the colors that obviously exist within the image, this technique often reveals colors you weren't expecting to see. In particular, it can be a great tool for discovering subtle color casts in areas you thought were neutral.

To apply this adjustment, choose Image > Adjustments > Hue/Saturation from the menu. This will bring up the Hue/Saturation dialog box (Figure 5.4), which will be addressed in great detail later in this chapter and in Chapter 8, "Advanced Color Adjustments." Move the Saturation slider all the way to the right, producing a value of +100. This will boost all colors in the image to their maximum saturation. Leave this dialog box open as you evaluate the image, moving it aside if needed by clicking and dragging on the dialog's title bar.

Note: For expediency, we're using a direct adjustment rather than an adjustment layer for this evaluation method. As I'll discuss later in this chapter, I strongly recommend using adjustment layers for all actual adjustments.

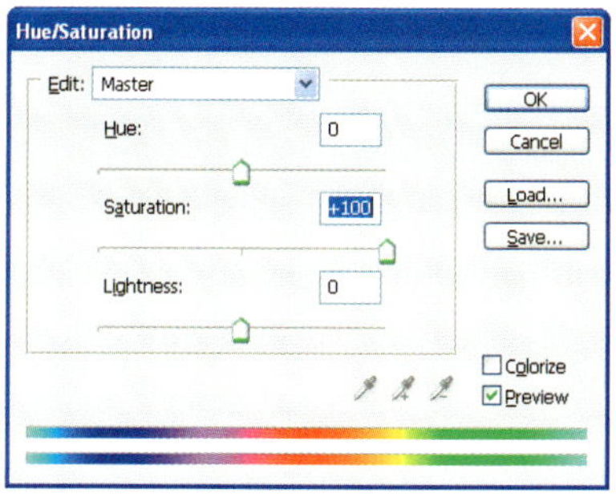

Figure 5.4 The Hue/Saturation dialog box allows you to adjust the saturation of all the hues in your image or of individual hues. To saturate the hues to their maximum potential, move the Saturation slider all the way to the right.

Review the full-saturation display of your image to get a sense of the colors in various areas (Figure 5.5). Pay particular attention to colors you feel don't belong where they appear. Don't worry that the colors temporarily look much worse. Instead, use this as an evaluative tool for making decisions about what color corrections might be necessary later, and what color issues to keep in mind as you work to optimize your images. When you're finished evaluating the image, click Cancel to close the Hue/Saturation dialog box without applying an adjustment to your image.

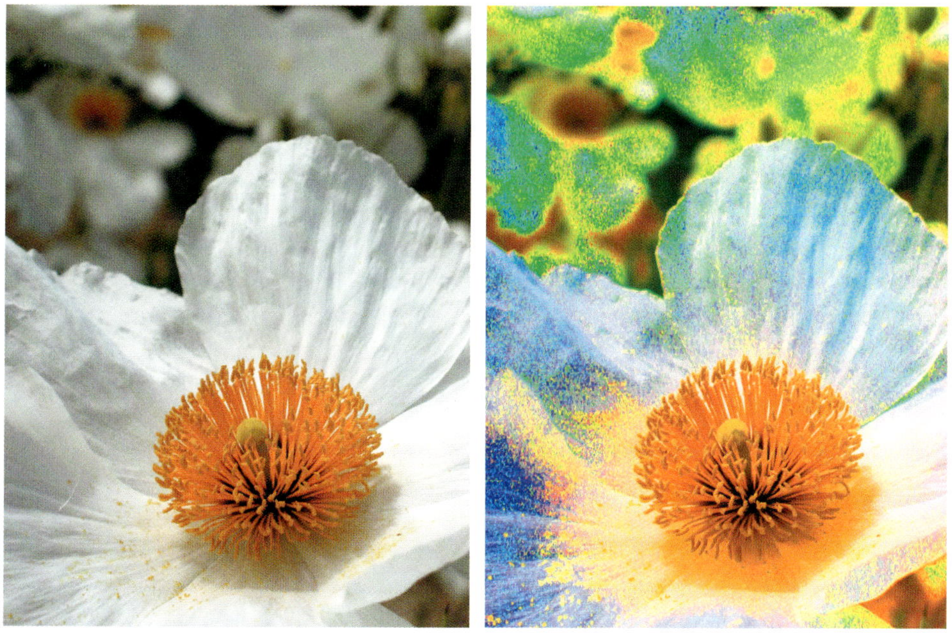

Figure 5.5 By temporarily increasing saturation to the maximum value, you can get a better idea of what color influences can be found in your image.

Prioritizing Adjustments

In any image-optimization workflow, it makes sense to perform the most basic adjustments first and then move on to more advanced adjustments that allow you to exercise better control over your images. Taking this approach tends to simplify the process and allows you to gradually build to more advanced adjustments as needed.

Some images may require only minor adjustment. In those cases, only the basic tools need to be employed. For other images, you may need to pull every trick out of your bag to get the result you are seeking. That doesn't mean you should focus on fixing problem images. In fact, I typically recommend working on only your very best images. The advanced methods, which will be discussed later in this book, are still applicable to those images, allowing you to realize your true vision for them.

Starting the image-optimization workflow with the most basic adjustments also makes sense because that fits well with the typical process of learning to optimize your images. It is normal to start with the basics as you gradually start your trek up the learning curve. With a firm grasp on the basic adjustments you'll want to apply, you can produce pleasing results for the vast majority of your images. As you progress to more advanced techniques, your results will only improve, and you'll be able to better achieve your goals.

In this section and the following ones, I'll be talking about the basic tonal and color adjustments. I often refer to these as the *mini-lab* adjustments because they represent the degree of adjustment you could expect from a good film-processing lab. If the image was captured with proper exposure in the camera, these adjustments may be all you need. More likely, however, you'll want to move beyond these basic adjustments to produce even better results, as I'll discuss in later chapters.

The adjustments are presented here in what I consider to be the most logical order. However, that doesn't mean that this order is right for every image. My general philosophy for performing adjustments is to solve the biggest problem first and then move on from there—in other words, prioritizing the adjustments based on the significance of each adjustment to the final result.

For most images, the tonal adjustment tends to be the most significant. Most digital cameras do an excellent job of capturing accurate color, and saturation tends to be good. Therefore, the standard order for me is tonal adjustment, color balance adjustment, and saturation adjustment.

Note: You should feel comfortable changing the order in which you apply adjustments to your images if the situation warrants it. Focus on solving the most significant problem with your image first and then working onward from there.

If you have an image for which the exposure was very good but the color is a bit off, you should feel perfectly comfortable making your color balance adjustment first before moving on to the tonal adjustments. Although the basic workflow presented in this chapter will work best for the majority of images, you should think of each adjustment as a modular piece of the full workflow. When the situation warrants, you shouldn't hesitate to change the order in which you perform the specific adjustments for your images.

Tonal Adjustments

The broad category of tonal adjustments includes any change in overall brightness or contrast within an image. Even more broadly, this category includes any adjustment that changes the luminosity values of an image, without emphasis on changes to the colors within an image. Tonal adjustments can most certainly affect colors—for example, darkening an image tends to saturate the colors, and brightening makes the colors appear less saturated. However, when making tonal adjustments, your focus is on the brightness and contrast, not the color.

Although there are a virtually unlimited number of methods you could use to perform tonal adjustments, many of which will be covered later in this book, this section focuses on the most basic tonal adjustments.

Brightness/Contrast

The most basic tonal adjustment available in Photoshop is the Brightness/Contrast adjustment (Image > Adjustments > Brightness/Contrast). This dialog box contains only two sliders—one for Brightness and one for Contrast (Figure 5.6).

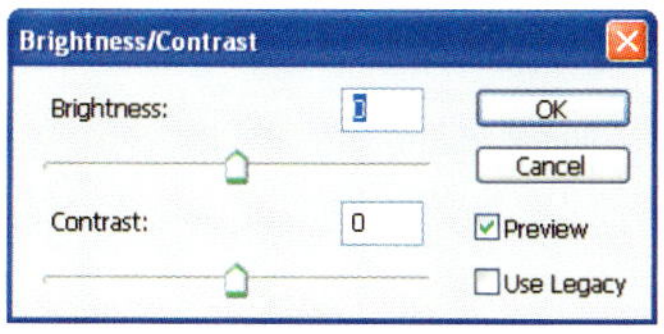

Figure 5.6 The Brightness/Contrast dialog box provides two simple sliders that allow you to easily perform tonal adjustments, but doesn't provide the control necessary to produce the very best results.

Note: With Photoshop CS3, the Brightness/Contrast adjustment has been updated so it will no longer clip highlights or shadows, meaning it won't cause a loss of detail in those areas. This means I no longer need to recommend against the use of this adjustment, and you can feel perfectly comfortable using it if you find it helpful.

The primary limitation of the Brightness/Contrast control is that the contrast adjustment has an equal effect on the shadows and highlights in your image. As you'll see later, other controls such as Levels and Curves allow you to exercise much greater control and are preferred for tonal adjustments. However, the Brightness/Contrast control can still have a place in your workflow. For one thing, it is a good way to get started when you aren't yet familiar with the other options available to you. Also, at times simplicity may be important, either because you are trying to quickly prepare an image for sharing on the Web or via email, or because you are having a difficult time using the more advanced controls on a given image. It is a convenient control to use when an image needs a simple contrast boost (Figure 5.7).

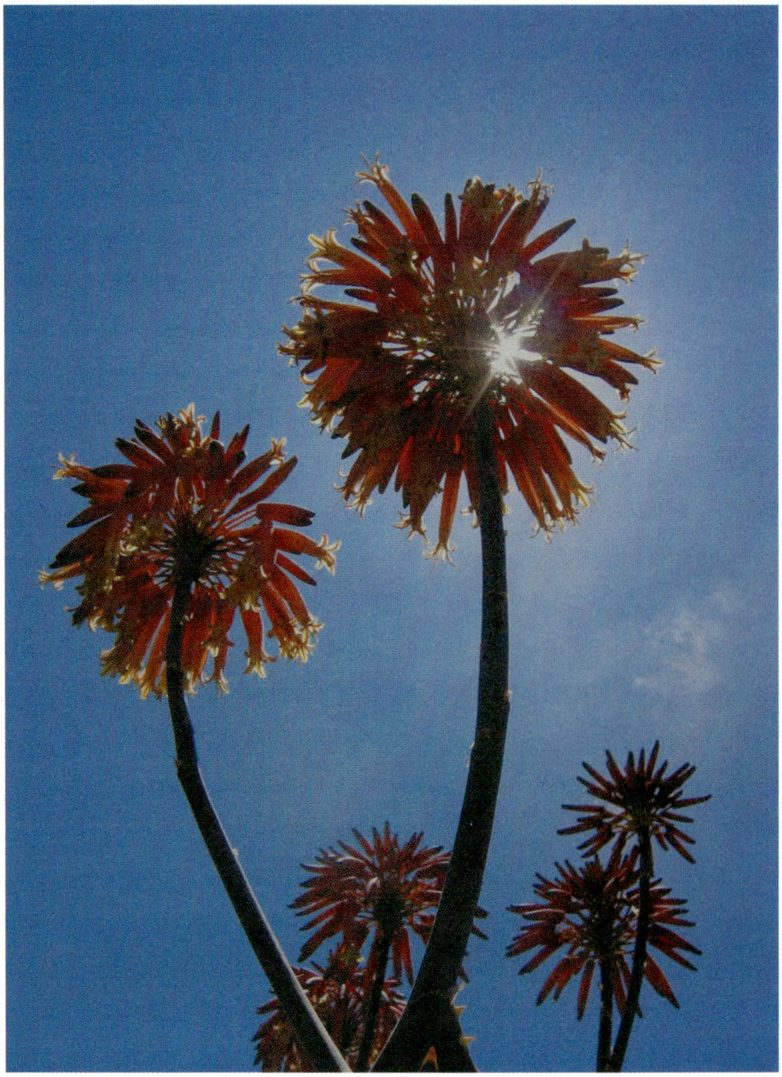

Figure 5.7 When an image requires a simple boost in contrast, the Brightness/Contrast adjustment may provide all the control you need to improve the image.

As you'll see throughout this book, I feel strongly that all adjustments should be performed on a separate layer, rather than adjusting the pixel values in your image directly. *Adjustment layers* are special layers that don't contain pixel data, but instead hold instructions on how the actual pixels in the image should be changed in appearance. Therefore, the first step toward making a Brightness/Contrast adjustment (or any other adjustment for which an adjustment layer is available) is to make an adjustment layer. To do so, click the Create New Fill Or Adjustment Layer button at the bottom of the Layers palette. This is the button with a half-black and half-white circle icon on it. A list of available adjustment layers will then be displayed (Figure 5.8).

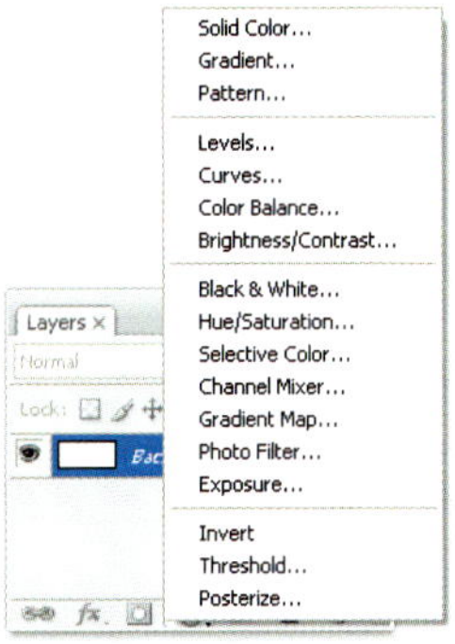

Figure 5.8 Click the Create New Fill Or Adjustment Layer button (the one with the half-black and half-white circle icon) to see a list of available adjustment layer types.

Note: Adjustment layers enable you to provide instructions on how an image should be modified without changing pixel values directly. Using these layers is the preferred method for adjusting your images.

Select the Brightness/Contrast item from the list of available adjustment layers, and the layer will be created. You'll see on the Layers palette that the adjustment layer is placed above the currently active layer. In this case, because you're making the first adjustment on this image, the only layer is the Background layer, so the adjustment layer goes above that. In addition to the new adjustment layer in the Layers palette, the Brightness/Contrast dialog box is displayed (Figure 5.9). You're immediately ready to start making adjustments to the image, comfortable that these adjustments are being handled by an adjustment layer that effectively behaves as a filter over your image, rather than causing changes to the underlying pixel values.

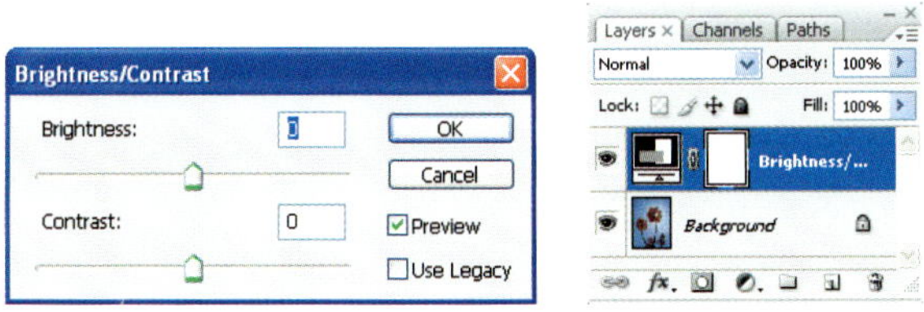

Figure 5.9 The Brightness/Contrast dialog box is displayed when you create a new Brightness/Contrast adjustment layer, allowing you to perform basic tonal adjustments on your image.

The approach I recommend for using Brightness/Contrast is to start with the Contrast slider and then fine-tune with the Brightness slider (Figure 5.10). This is because I consider a good contrast adjustment to be of primary importance. The Brightness slider then becomes something of a fine-tuning control, allowing you to adjust the overall brightness of the image. Make sure the Preview checkbox is selected so you can see the effect of every adjustment in your image as you move the sliders.

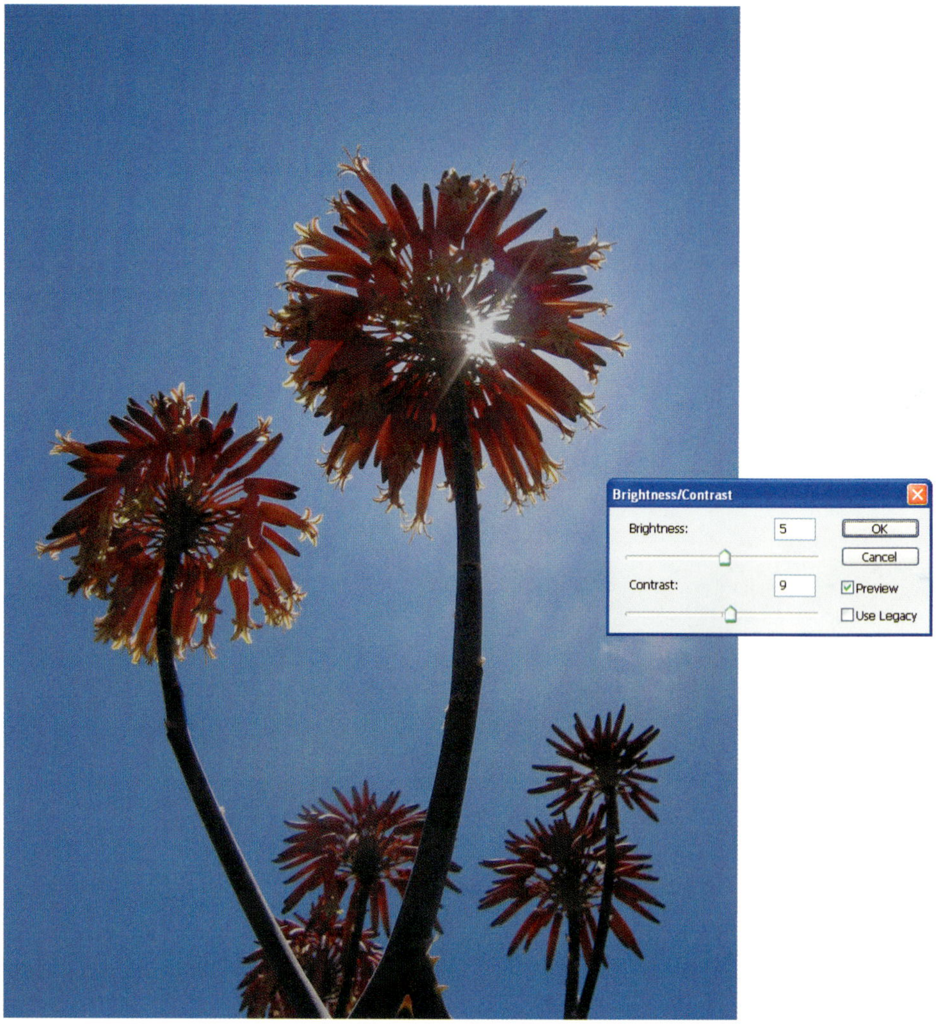

Figure 5.10 A good approach to using Brightness/Contrast is to adjust the Contrast slider to achieve the desired contrast within the image, and then fine-tune using the Brightness slider.

Note: The Brightness/Contrast dialog box includes a Use Legacy checkbox that causes this adjustment to behave as it did in versions prior to Photoshop CS3. I do not recommend using this option unless you need to maintain compatibility for someone else working on the same image on an earlier version of Photoshop, as clipping can occur when you enable this option.

When you're finished fine-tuning the Brightness and Contrast sliders, click OK to apply the changes to this adjustment layer. You're now ready to evaluate the results of your adjustment (Figure 5.11). Although you were able to see the effects of your adjustments as you made them, sometimes it is difficult to make a good evaluation of the final result as you're making minor adjustments to the sliders. Therefore, I recommend that you take an overall look at the image and evaluate it with and without the adjustment you've applied.

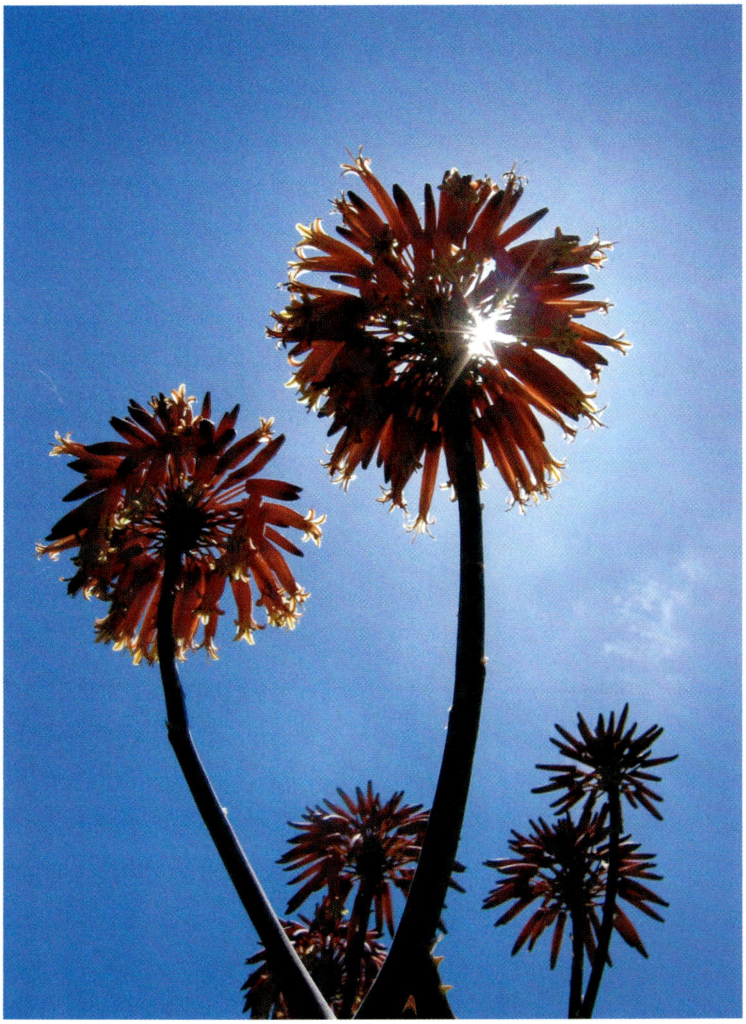

Figure 5.11 Although other adjustment tools provide greater control over the changes you make to your images, Brightness/Contrast does enable you to make good basic adjustments, provided loss of highlight detail doesn't become a problem.

The easiest way to do this is to turn off the visibility of the Brightness/Contrast adjustment layer on the Layers palette. To do so, click the eye icon to the left of the layer. In the case of an adjustment layer, what you're hiding or revealing is the effect of that layer. By toggling the visibility off and on, you can switch between "before" and "after" views of the adjustment. This gives you a greater perspective on the adjustment you've applied to the image, and this context often makes it much easier to make a critical evaluation of the results you've achieved. The hope, of course, is that you like the after version more than the before.

Note: If you are working with a 16-bit image with adjustment layers in Photoshop but need to convert that image to 8-bit, flatten the image first so the adjustment layers will apply to the high-bit data. If you convert to 8 bits per channel without flattening, the adjustment layers will have their adjustments scaled to the 8-bit data, and you'll have lost the benefit of making adjustments in 16-bit.

If at any time you aren't completely happy with the adjustment you've made, whether for the Brightness/Contrast adjustment layer you've created or any other adjustment layer you'll make later, revising the adjustment is remarkably easy. Simply double-click the thumbnail icon on the Layers palette for the adjustment layer you'd like to revise, and the dialog box will be displayed. The sliders and any other controls in the dialog box will be exactly where you left them the last time you clicked OK. You can then change the settings for any of the controls, revising your original adjustment. In fact, you can return to the adjustment layer as often as you like, making an infinite number of revisions, without any concern of cumulative damage to your image. That is because only the final settings count; earlier "versions" don't damage the image because you are applying an adjustment without changing the underlying pixel values in your image.

Benefits of Adjustment Layers

There are many benefits to using adjustment layers rather than adjusting pixel values directly within your image. Among the most significant benefits are the following:

- There is no cumulative loss of image quality when making multiple adjustments because you are effectively applying a filter over your image rather than changing the underlying pixel values.
- You can quickly see a "before" and "after" view of your image by turning off the visibility of any adjustment layer.
- You can revise the adjustment at any time by double-clicking the thumbnail icon for the adjustment layer on the Layers palette, and all the controls will be exactly as you left them the last time you clicked OK in the dialog box for that adjustment layer.
- You can reduce the Opacity of the adjustment layer as a quick way to reduce the effect without changing the actual settings for the adjustment layer.
- You can apply a layer mask to the adjustment layer to target the adjustment to specific areas, as I'll cover in Chapter 10, "Targeted Adjustments."

Levels

The Levels adjustment provides much greater control over tonal adjustments for your images. In many respects, it can be thought of as providing the same overall functionality as Brightness/Contrast, but Levels provides the capability to adjust contrast by independently controlling shadows and highlights within your image.

Of course, this makes Levels sound remarkably easy, which isn't necessarily the conclusion you would draw after looking at the Levels dialog box (Figure 5.12). After you have a better understanding of the basic information presented in this dialog box and of the methods you'll want to utilize for basic tonal adjustments (and even color adjustments by working on individual color channels), you'll feel very comfortable using Levels and will be less likely to decide to revert to Brightness/Contrast.

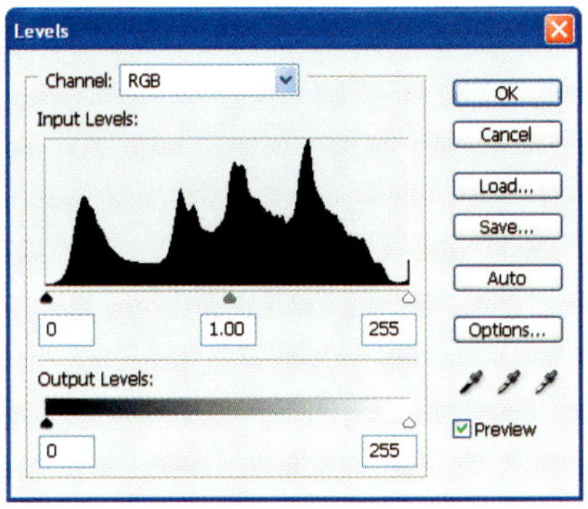

Figure 5.12 The Levels dialog box appears rather complicated; however, after you understand how to utilize this control effectively, you won't feel intimidated. The key controls allow you to adjust the black point (B), middle-tone value (M), and white point (W).

The primary component of the Levels dialog box is a histogram display that charts the distribution of tonal values within your image. The tonal values are represented from black at the extreme left to white at the extreme right. This gradation of tonal values is shown as a gradient bar along the bottom of the histogram chart. The shape of the histogram chart tells you about the distribution of tonal values within the image. For example, histogram data that is shifted toward the left (Figure 5.13) indicates that the image is generally dark. However, that doesn't necessarily tell you anything about the quality of the image; it may simply be a dark scene. Similarly, a brighter image will have a histogram shifted toward the right.

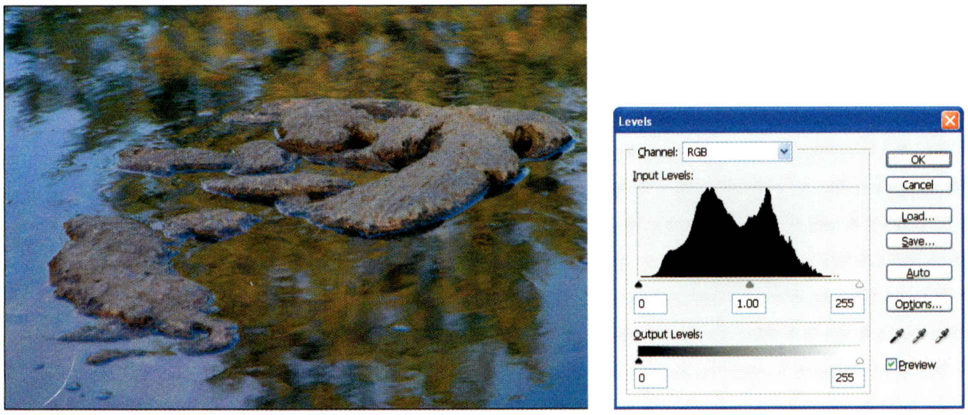

Figure 5.13 A histogram chart that is shifted to the left indicates that the image is relatively dark—but doesn't provide any real information about the quality of the image.

Problem Signs

The key things to watch out for on the histogram are clipping and gapping. *Clipping* is an indication that information has been lost in the highlights or shadows of your image. *Gapping* is represented by gaps in the histogram, and it indicates tonal values that are not represented in your image.

Clipping is indicated on the histogram display by data running off the end of the chart. There are two ways clipping might be displayed. One is as a spike at one end of the chart. This is most commonly seen at the highlight end and is often caused by specular highlights within your image, such as reflections from water, glass, or metal. In other words, it isn't necessarily a major problem within the image, as we don't expect to see detail in such highlights.

The other type of clipping is more likely to represent a problem within your image, especially if it occurs in the highlights. In this type, the data of the histogram gets cut off abruptly at the end of the chart, rather than ending gracefully before the chart ends (Figure 5.14). If you think of the histogram as representing a mountain range, ideally the mountains should gradually drop down to the flatland before the chart ends. If instead the mountains end suddenly in a cliff, detail is lost in the area that would have gradually lowered to the base of the chart. All pixels within the "missing" tonal values have been clipped to the minimum (black) or maximum (white) value at that end of the histogram chart.

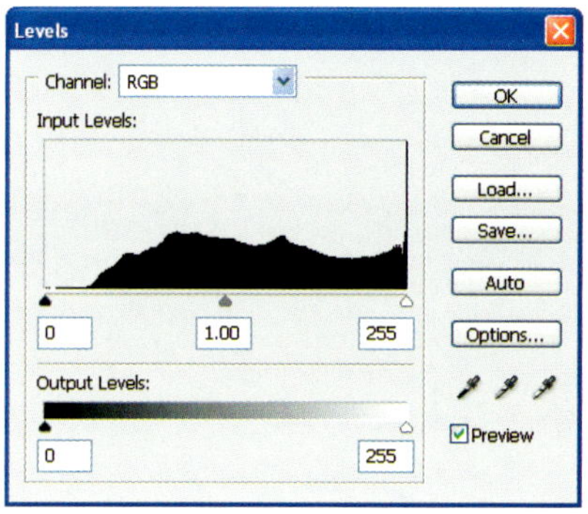

Figure 5.14 Clipping exhibited by an abrupt cutoff of tonal data at the highlight (right) end of the histogram chart indicates a potentially serious loss of detail in your image.

Ideally, your image shouldn't exhibit any clipping when you get started with your adjustments. If it does, it is generally preferred that the clipping occur in the shadows rather than the highlights, as we are usually more forgiving of lost shadow detail in a photographic image than blown highlights. However, you also want to be careful not to produce excessive clipping as you are adjusting contrast with Levels.

Another problem to be aware of is gapping in the histogram (Figure 5.15). You can think of the histogram chart as a bar chart made up of many narrow bars, so that the final result typically looks like a curving data display rather than one composed of individual bars. However, when gapping occurs, you start to see the individual bars that create the data display. Gapping indicates that certain tonal values are not represented by any pixels (or by very few pixels) in the image.

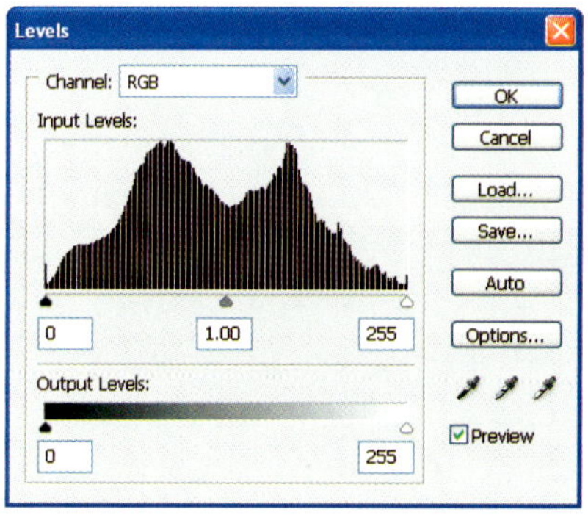

Figure 5.15 Gapping in the histogram indicates that all available tonal values are not represented in the image. When gapping becomes significant enough, the result is a loss of smooth gradations of tone and color in the image, referred to as posterization.

Note: Gaps in the histogram rarely occur for 16-bit files because many more values are available than the 256 represented by the histogram display. Sixteen-bit files have a theoretical maximum of 65,536 tonal values per color channel available, compared to 256 values per channel for an 8-bit file. As a result, 16-bit files can lose a significant number of tonal values without obvious gapping or the posterization of which it can be indicative.

Gaps in the tonal values indicate that smooth and subtle transitions between tones and colors within the image may be compromised. Instead of making a gradual change from one value to another with 10 values in between, for example, the transition may be from one value to another without any transition values between them. This lack of smooth gradations is referred to as *posterization.*

However, gaps in a histogram are not an immediate indication of a serious problem with your image. Minor gaps of only a few pixels wide, representing just a few tonal values, aren't likely to be visible with the human eye. In fact, it isn't until the gaps become relatively extreme (at least 10 tonal values) that they are likely to be visible in the final output. Although gaps certainly indicate a potential problem, they don't define image quality by themselves. If you have significant gapping in an image, use caution not to make extreme adjustments that may worsen the situation, and closely evaluate the final image to ensure there isn't visible posterization.

Basic Levels Adjustments

With a basic understanding of the concepts behind Levels, you're ready to start making an adjustment. To do so, create a new adjustment layer for Levels by clicking the Create New Fill Or Adjustment Layer button on the Layers palette. For most adjustments with Levels, there are only three controls you need to adjust. These are the Black Point, White Point, and Midtone Slider. All three are found directly below the histogram display in the Levels dialog box. The Black Point slider (for shadows) is at the far left, the White Point slider (for highlights) at the far right, and the Midtones slider is between the two. Together these controls allow you to adjust the overall contrast (with the Black Point and White Point sliders) and brightness (with the Midtones slider) of your image with excellent control.

As with the Brightness/Contrast control, I recommend establishing overall contrast before fine-tuning brightness. Therefore, I suggest starting with the Black Point and White Point sliders. They provide contrast adjustment with the ability to vary the amount of adjustment being applied to the shadow and highlight areas of your image. You can, for example, sacrifice more detail in the shadows to improve overall contrast without losing significant highlight detail.

As a general rule, most images benefit from having the brightest pixel value set to white and the darkest pixel value set to black. There are obviously plenty of exceptions to this, but it is a good basic rule. Because we know that the last data point at either end of the histogram chart represents the darkest and brightest pixels, a very basic adjustment could be made by dragging the Black Point and White Point sliders inward to the point where the data begins at each end of the histogram (Figure 5.16).

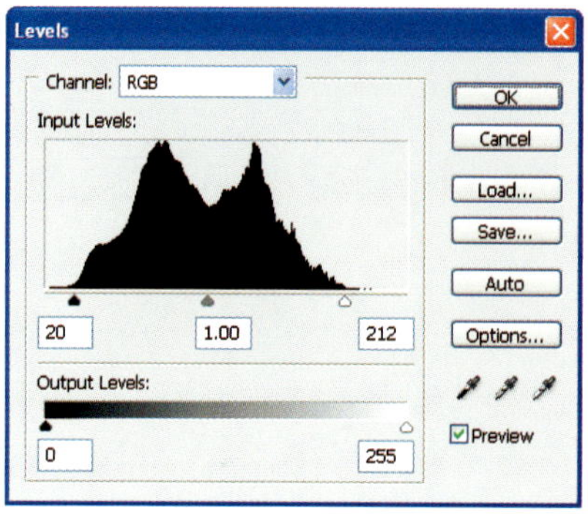

Figure 5.16 A good general approach to setting the black and white points within Levels is to bring the Black Point and White Point sliders inward to the point where the data begins at each end of the histogram chart.

Of course, this is a somewhat arbitrary way to approach an image. Although it will indeed produce good results for most images, it isn't an ideal solution for every one. Photography is very much a visual pursuit, so it makes sense to perform a visual review of the image and decide whether you're happy with the results of the adjustment you've made. You may want to back off the adjustments slightly in some situations to minimize the risk of introducing excessive contrast. In other situations, you may want to bring the sliders in just a bit farther to produce stronger contrast. It is up to you to determine the best adjustment for a particular image.

Note: If you're having trouble making appropriate adjustments, you can hold the Alt/Option key to change the Cancel button to a Reset button in most dialog boxes in Photoshop. If you then click the Reset button, all settings in the dialog box will return to their default values.

After you've established the black and white points for the image, effectively performing a well-controlled contrast adjustment, you are ready to adjust the middle-tone slider. This slider can be thought of as a brightness control. Moving the slider changes which pixel value within the image should be mapped to a middle-gray tonal value, but the result is a brightness shift. This adjustment doesn't have any rule of thumb you can follow in terms of positioning the slider at a particular point along the histogram chart, so you'll need to make a decision based on a visual review of the image.

When you've adjusted all three sliders, you've finished the basic tonal adjustment with Levels. Click OK, and the Levels dialog box will close. As with any other adjustment layer, if you change your mind about the adjustment at a later time, you can simply double-click the thumbnail icon for the Levels adjustment layer on the Layers palette and the dialog box will be displayed, with the sliders positioned exactly as you left them the last time you clicked OK.

Note: The Levels dialog box also includes eyedroppers that allow you to click areas of your image to automatically set the black, white, and neutral values. However, these tools tend to require a hunt-and-peck approach that doesn't allow you to make very accurate adjustments, so I prefer not to use them.

Clipping Preview

Although a basic visual evaluation of your image while making adjustments with Levels is certainly effective, it can be even more helpful to use the clipping preview display available in Levels. This display allows you to see exactly where you are losing detail within your image as you adjust the Black Point and White Point sliders. As a result, you can make a much more informed decision about the settings you'd like to use for these sliders.

When you start with an image that lacks strong contrast (Figure 5.17), and want to maximize the contrast without sacrificing detail in highlights or shadows, the clipping preview display allows you to see exactly where you'll lose detail based on your specific adjustment of the Black Point and White Point sliders.

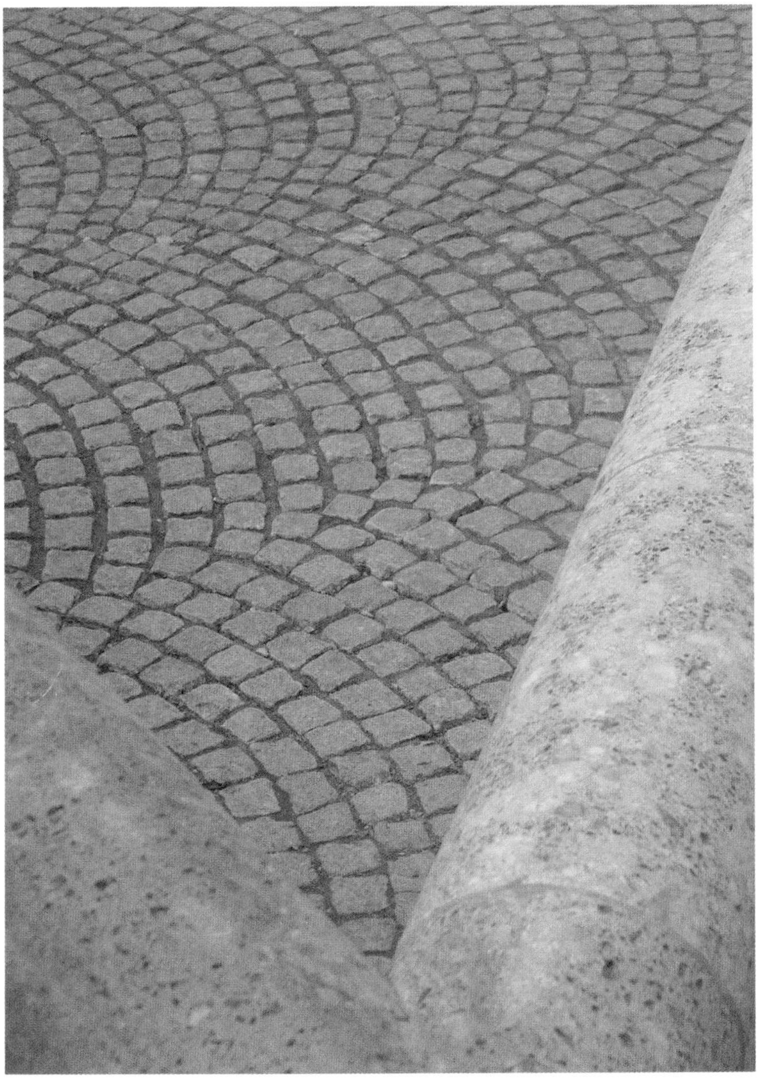

Figure 5.17 In an image, such as this one, that lacks adequate contrast, it is helpful to be able to maximize contrast without sacrificing highlight or shadow detail. The clipping preview feature of Levels provides exactly this solution.

I recommend adjusting the white point first, simply because highlight detail tends to be the more critical adjustment. If you've already created a Levels adjustment layer for the image you're working on, double-click the thumbnail icon for that layer on the Layers palette. Otherwise, create a new Levels adjustment layer.

To enable the clipping preview display, hold the Alt/Option key while you adjust the white point. Your image display will initially change to a completely (or almost completely) black display. This indicates that no pixel values (or very few) are clipped to white without making any adjustment. As you continue to hold the Alt/Option key, slide the White Point slider to the left. More pixels will show up as you move the slider (Figure 5.18). As a general rule, I recommend adjusting the white point until pixels just start showing up in the clipping preview. This is the point where you've maximized contrast and tonal range within the image, while sacrificing minimal highlight detail. Of course, the benefit of the clipping preview display is that you're able to make an informed decision about the amount of detail you are sacrificing to achieve the level of contrast you'd like to see, and that detail's location within the image to achieve the level of contrast you'd like to see in the image.

Note: The color of the pixels that show up in the clipping preview display indicate the color channels that are losing detail within the image. The pixels won't appear as pure white or black in the image until the clipping preview shows those values. However, even if they aren't pure white or black, they are probably very close if any channels are clipping, so you can generally treat such values as though they were indeed white or black.

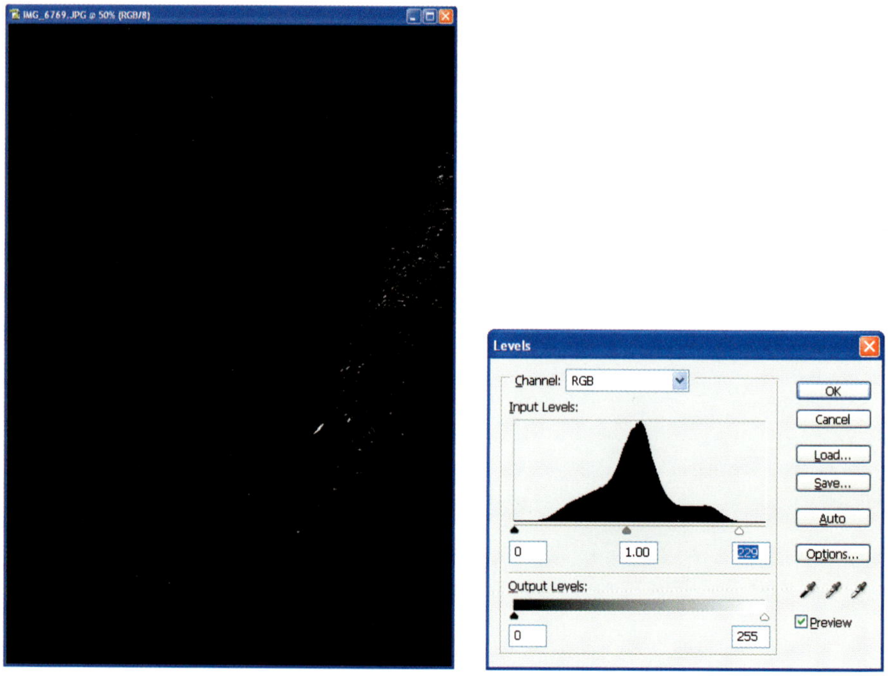

Figure 5.18 By holding down the Alt/Option key while adjusting the White Point slider in Levels, you'll see a clipping preview showing you where in the image you'll lose highlight detail for a given adjustment.

The process for setting the black point is nearly identical: hold the Alt/Option key while adjusting the Black Point slider, and you'll see a similar clipping preview display, except that now it will start completely (or almost completely) white, with pixels showing up to indicate where you're losing shadow detail (Figure 5.19). As discussed previously, you are generally willing to sacrifice more shadow detail as opposed to highlight detail to maximize contrast. The clipping preview allows you to make an informed decision about how much detail you're giving up with a particular adjustment and the location of that detail, so you can better determine the extent to which you can push the black point to produce the desired contrast level.

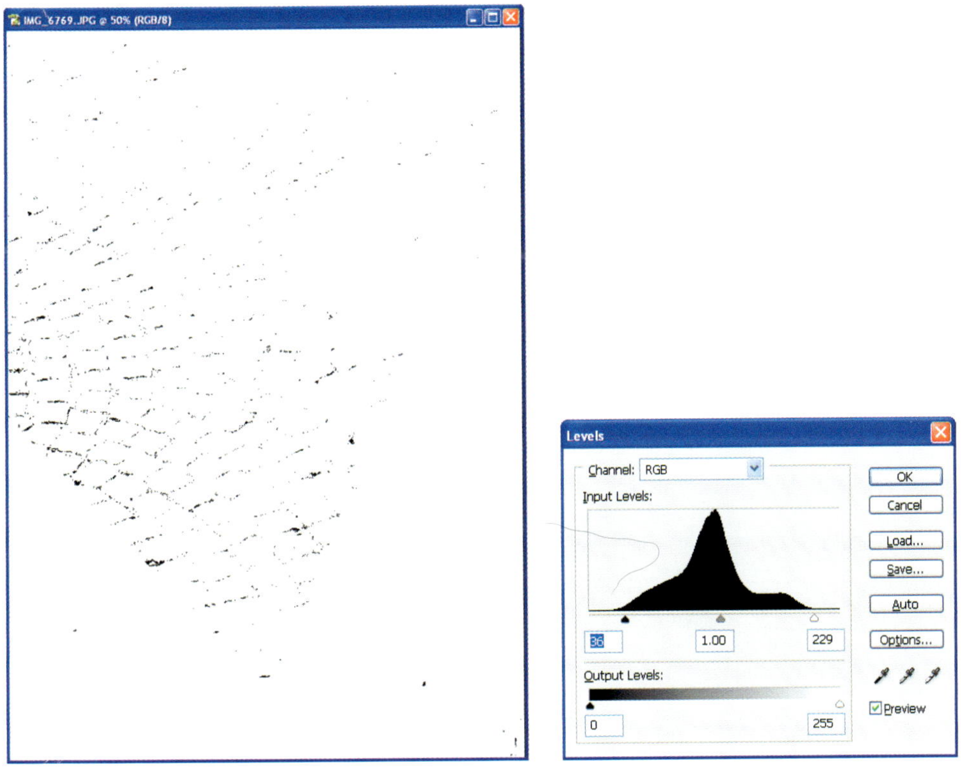

Figure 5.19 While holding down the Alt/Option key and adjusting the Black Point slider in Levels, the clipping preview shows where the image will lose shadow detail for a given adjustment.

After you've adjusted the black and white points by using the clipping preview, you're ready to adjust the Midtone slider for overall brightness. Because this doesn't affect the extreme tonal values within the image, there isn't a clipping preview for the Midtone slider. You'll need to rely on a visual evaluation of the image for this adjustment.

When you're finished with all three of these adjustments, using the clipping preview for the black and white points, you've produced an image with optimal contrast based on your willingness to sacrifice detail to achieve your goals for the image (Figure 5.20).

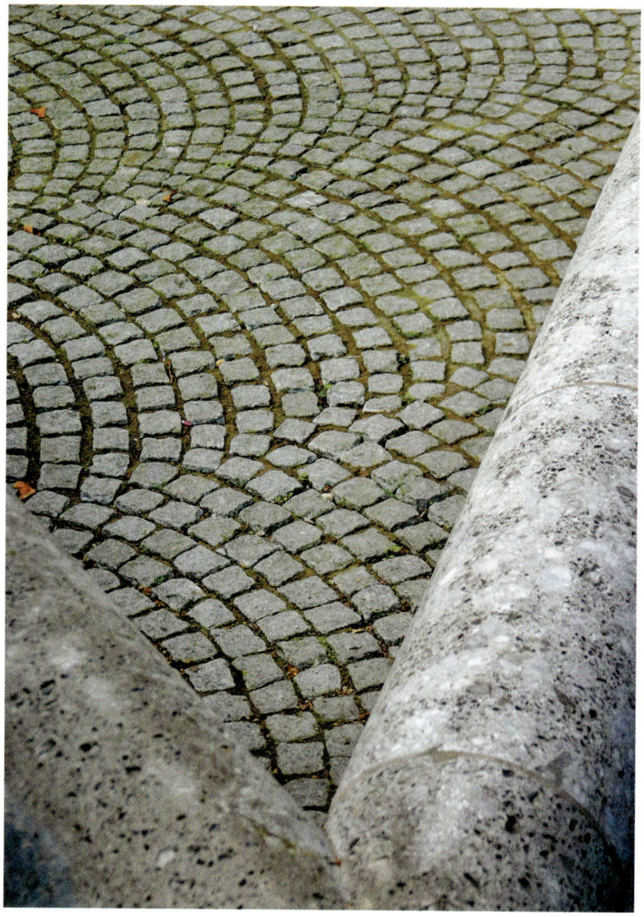

Figure 5.20 After you have adjusted the black and white points by using the clipping preview of Levels, and then fine-tuned the Midtone slider to taste, the result is an image with optimal contrast and with detail lost only where you've decided it was worth sacrificing.

Color Adjustments

After you've optimized the overall tonality of your image, the next step is typically color adjustments. At the most basic level, these include adjusting the color balance to remove any undesired color cast or to introduce one that is desired, and adjusting the saturation of colors within the image to taste.

Color Balance

Color balance adjustments are most often thought of as ways to eliminate an undesirable color cast within an image. In many cases, the goal is to make areas that should be neutral in the image truly neutral. However, this can be a challenging goal. Just because something truly is neutral doesn't mean it should appear as perfectly neutral within your image. For example, if you place an 18% gray card in a scene during sunrise, you can be assured that the gray card won't appear gray. It will be influenced by the warm light of sunrise and will appear with a golden hue.

Instead, I feel the focus of a color balance adjustment should be to eliminate any color influence you don't like and to add a color influence you do like. The result needs to be close to reality to be accepted by those who will view your images, but you do have a fair amount of latitude. Focus on producing the best aesthetic results, and you'll be well on your way to accurate results as well.

The simplest way to make basic color balance adjustments is with the Color Balance dialog box. This dialog box includes three sliders as the primary controls (Figure 5.21). These represent the color axes for each of the three channels that make up your image. As an additional benefit, the sliders are labeled to remind you of the relationships between colors. Colors at opposite ends of a given slider are opposites of each other, and moving the slider in one direction or the other will cause the overall image to be shifted toward that color value.

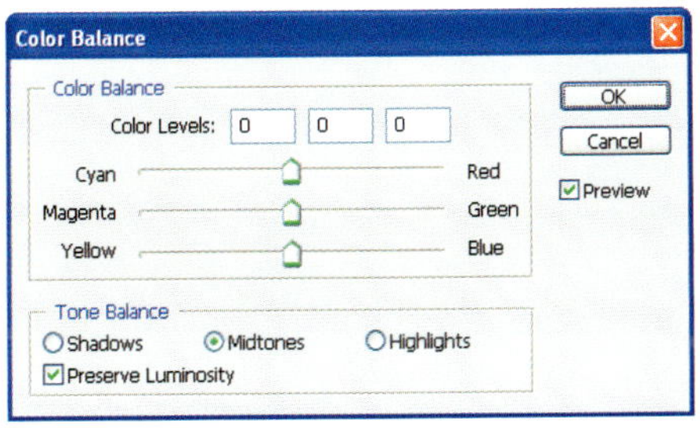

Figure 5.21 The Color Balance dialog box provides sliders for each of the three axes represented by the color channels that comprise an image, and it allows you to adjust the balance for color along each axis.

It is important to keep in mind that when you make a color balance adjustment to your image, you are adjusting all pixel values within the image. Of course, in later chapters you'll look at how to control the adjustments so they affect only certain areas of the image. For now, the key to understand is that just because you are moving a slider between cyan and red doesn't mean you will affect only those pixels within the image that are cyan or red. Rather, all pixels within the image will be shifted toward the color value you choose with the slider.

As with other adjustments, the first step is to create a Color Balance adjustment layer; doing so opens the Color Balance dialog box. I strongly recommend starting with the axis that needs the most significant adjustment. For example, if you have an image with a magenta cast (Figure 5.22), start with the Magenta/Green slider.

When adjusting a given slider, especially if you are not yet comfortable with visualizing the particular adjustment required, I recommend moving the slider through the extremes of its range. Besides helping you get a better sense of where an appropriate color balance exists for a particular slider, this process will also help you develop your skills for understanding how a particular adjustment will affect various color and tonal values within your images. As you move the slider back and forth, starting with the extremes, gradually zero in on the range that seems to provide the most appropriate balance for that channel.

With the slider positioned as accurately as possible with the mouse, you can then take advantage of keyboard shortcuts to fine-tune the adjustment. After you have moved a slider, the text box that holds the final value for that slider will be active. You can then use the up and down arrow keys on your keyboard to adjust the value one unit at a time.

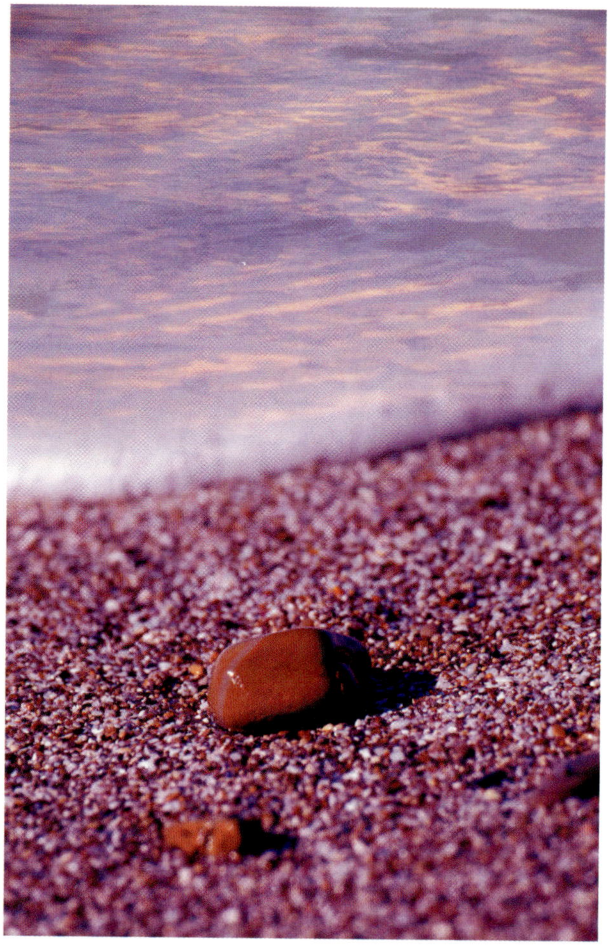

Figure 5.22 If you have an image with a slight magenta cast, the Magenta/Green slider in the Color Balance dialog box should be the first you adjust.

In the case of the sample image with a magenta color cast, your first step would be to shift the color balance toward green by using the Magenta/Green slider (Figure 5.23). This will effectively neutralize the unwanted magenta color cast, producing an image that is relatively neutral with accurate color.

However, just because you have achieved a neutral image with accurate color doesn't mean you are finished with the Color Balance adjustment. In fact, even if you think the image has been adequately corrected with a single slider adjustment, adjust the other two sliders to see if you can produce a better result. Often you'll find that by shifting the other sliders, you'll produce an image with a more pleasing color balance than the neutral result you first achieved.

Note: In general, viewers respond more favorably to images with a warm color balance, so you may want to explore a shift toward warmer values (red, magenta, and yellow).

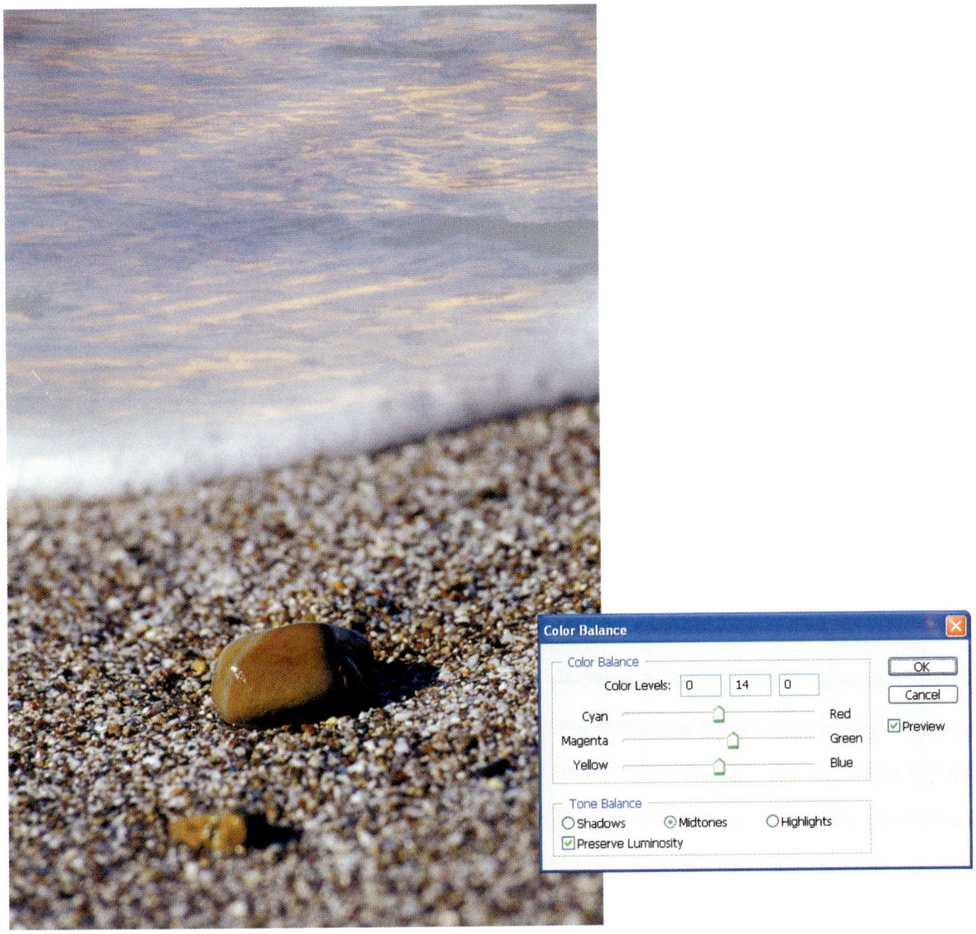

Figure 5.23 A magenta color cast can be corrected by moving the Magenta/Green slider toward Green in the Color Balance dialog box. After you have corrected the color cast in your image, the result is a relatively neutral image with accurate color.

Looking again at our sample image, after producing a neutral result, you might want to explore adding a shift toward warmer values. In this case, I applied a shift toward yellow to warm up the image and enhance the natural earth tones that were already present (Figure 5.24). The result is an image with much greater warmth than the original adjustment produced.

After you've adjusted all three sliders in the Color Balance dialog box, the basic process is complete. Keep going, though. Move all three sliders again, this time making *much* smaller adjustments. Because each slider move affects all of the colors within the image, subsequent adjustments at least slightly alter the image; you might discover an even better result.

For the vast majority of images, all you need to do is adjust the sliders in the Color Balance dialog box after selecting the default Midtones setting in the Tone Balance section at the bottom of the dialog box. However, you can also change the range of tonal values within the image that will be affected by the Color Balance adjustment by selecting Shadows or Highlights and making separate adjustments targeted at those tonal ranges.

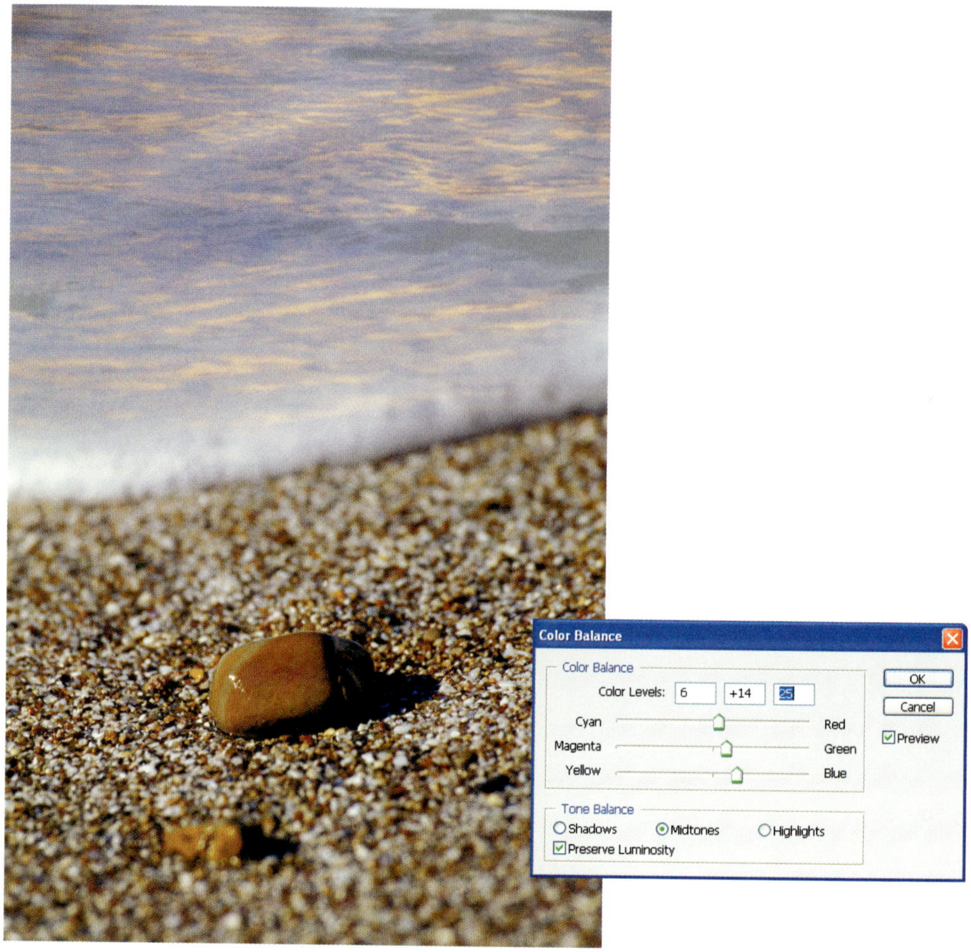

Figure 5.24 After you've made adjustments to produce a neutral result, you can often produce a better final image by making further adjustments. In particular, adjustments that warm up the image slightly are often appealing.

Each of these options for limiting the tonal values to be affected by the adjustment operates independently. When you select Shadows, for example, the adjustments you make will not replace or undo adjustments you made when the Midtones option was selected. The Midtones option will affect most values within the image, whereas Shadows and Highlights will limit the adjustment to the darkest and brightest values within the image, respectively.

Another option in the Color Balance dialog box is the Preserve Luminosity checkbox. With this option selected, when you adjust one slider the color values for the other channels within the image will be modified slightly so that the perceived luminosity of all colors is preserved. I recommend keeping this checkbox selected. The only time I recommend deselecting this option is when you are attempting to produce a perfect neutral value and want to be able to control each channel's color value independently.

Basic Saturation

After you've achieved an appropriate overall tone and an accurate color balance, the next consideration is the saturation of the colors within your image. This calls for a Hue/Saturation adjustment (Figure 5.25). Although this control allows you to perform a wide variety of adjustments, for now I'm going to focus on a basic saturation adjustment (though not as strong an adjustment as I described at the beginning of this chapter when using Hue/Saturation for evaluating the image). In Chapter 8, I'll cover Hue/Saturation in even greater detail, but for now I'll keep it simple.

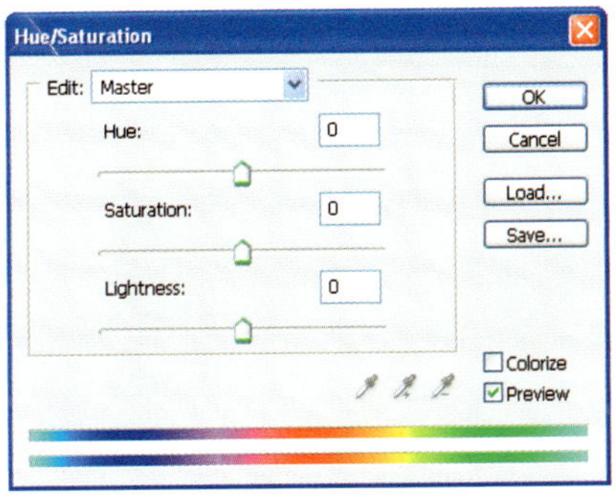

Figure 5.25 Hue/Saturation allows you to perform basic saturation adjustments, along with a variety of other adjustments covered in Chapter 8.

Start by creating a Hue/Saturation adjustment layer, in the same manner that you created the other adjustment layers covered earlier.

In general, photographers want to boost the saturation of the colors in their images, so the most common adjustment is to increase the Saturation value. However, there are certainly plenty of situations where you might want to reduce saturation slightly. For example, if you are producing an image with a watercolor appearance, you'll want to tone down the colors slightly so they don't appear overpowering.

Note: Although it is possible to move the Saturation slider all the way to the left to produce a black-and-white version of an image, this isn't the optimal method. In Chapter 11, "Creative Adjustments," I'll cover a method for producing better black-and-white conversions.

Although reducing saturation can be done to any degree based on your preference for how the image should look, a little more care should be taken when increasing saturation. If you increase the saturation too much, you can create some problems within the image. For one thing, the colors may start to look fake because they are too vibrant. Also, by shifting colors to their most saturated values, you are reducing the total number of possible values and, therefore, increasing the risk of posterization in the highly saturated areas of the image. As a general rule, use caution when increasing the Saturation slider to a value above +20. That doesn't mean you can't increase Saturation further, just that you should carefully review the image to make sure you aren't introducing any problems in doing so.

Other than exercising some care in how much you increase saturation, making an adjustment is really as simple as deciding how strong you want the effect to be. If your image doesn't have very strong saturation (Figure 5.26), you can easily produce a more pleasing image by increasing the Saturation slightly with a Hue/Saturation adjustment.

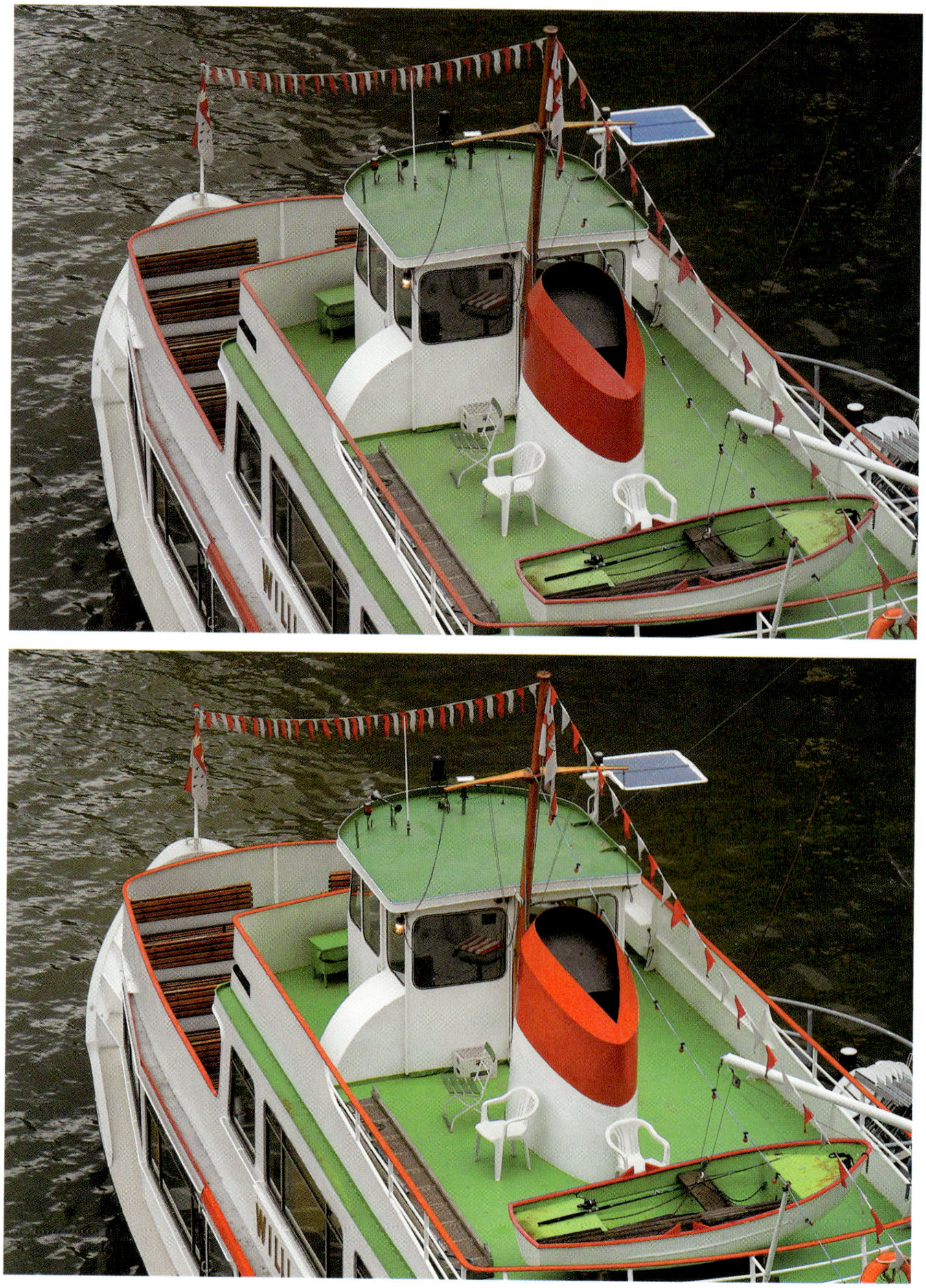

Figure 5.26 When an image has colors lacking in vibrancy, the perception is an image that is flat. (top) Boosting the Saturation adds life to the image. (bottom)

Provided you are cautious not to apply an excessive boost in saturation, a basic increase in Saturation with the Hue/Saturation adjustment is one of the more straightforward adjustments you'll make in a basic workflow for your images.

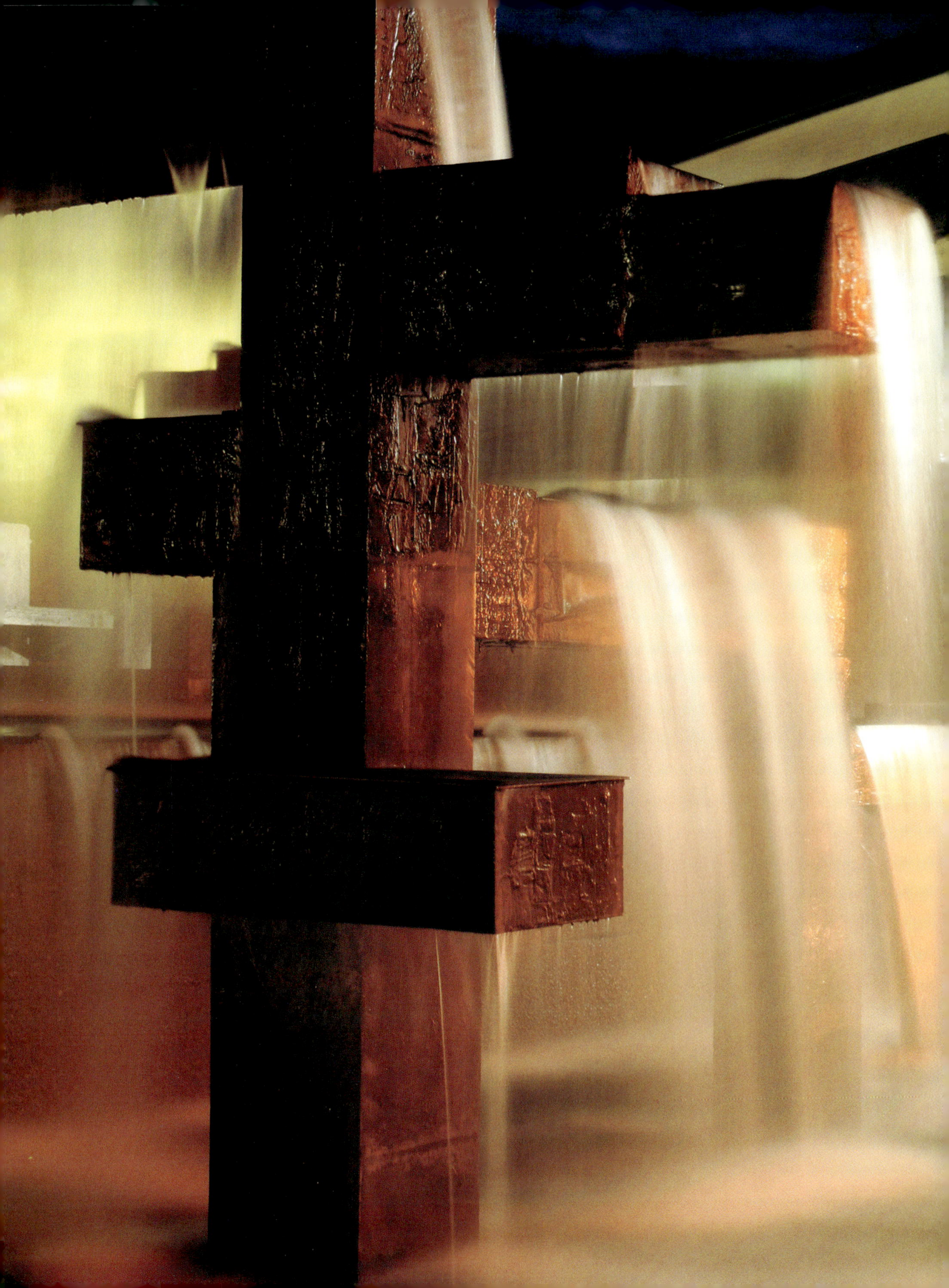

6 Image Cleanup

Chances are you'd like to perform some cleanup on most of your images. Whether it is just a matter of eliminating dust spots, or a more extensive removal of objects you wish hadn't been in the scene to begin with, there are a variety of tools and techniques you can use to remove unwanted elements from your images. In this chapter, you'll take a look at the various tools Photoshop provides to clean up and touch up specific areas of your images.

Chapter Contents

Cleanup Workflow

Virtually every image will require some degree of cleanup work if you're going to get the best results. Cleanup may be required for digital captures because of dust on the sensor, for film scans because of dust or scratches, or for any image in which there's an unwanted element such as a power line across the sky (Figure 6.1).

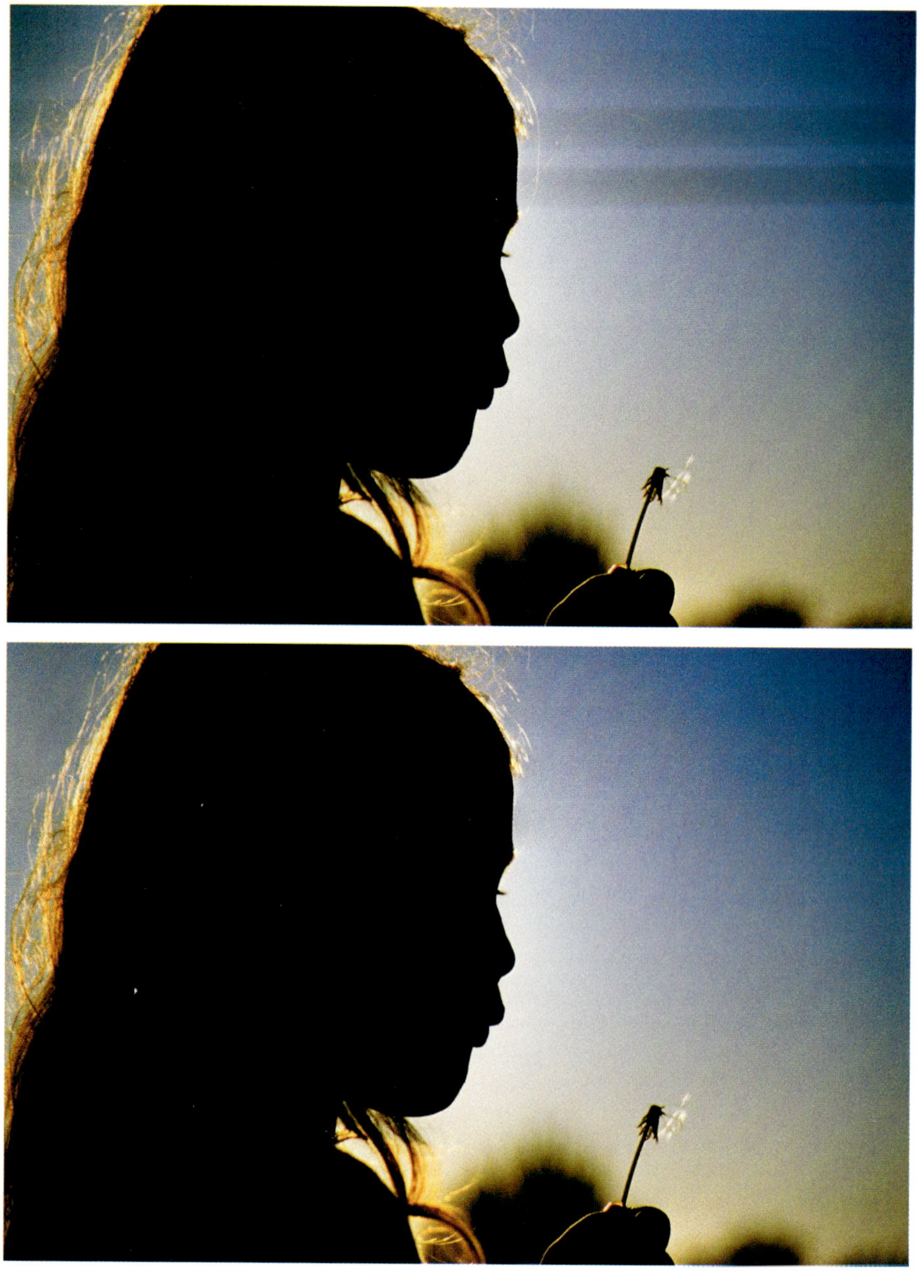

Figure 6.1 There are a variety of situations where you'll need to clean up areas of your image, such as the power lines in the top-right of this photo.

If cleanup is something you'll likely do for most images, the main question is when in your workflow you should perform that cleanup work. When you're using a layer-based approach to your workflow (as I obviously encourage), it isn't critical to perform your cleanup at any particular stage, but I recommend that you don't do it too early in the process of optimizing your images. Cleanup can be a very detail-oriented task and, in many cases, can require considerable time and effort. It doesn't make much sense to invest in the cleanup process until you're sure the image is worth the effort. Therefore, I recommend performing at least a basic optimization on an image before you start with cleanup.

In other words, the basic workflow presented in Chapter 5, "Basic Tone and Color," should be completed, at a minimum, before you begin cleanup work. This will give you an opportunity to determine whether the image really warrants the effort often required for cleanup.

The following are the key tools you'll use for this cleanup process:

Clone Stamp This tool is most effective for cleaning up portions of your image when it is important to preserve the original texture with some precision. It allows you to copy pixels from within your image exactly as they appear to cover up other pixels that represent problem areas. This is useful for most any image, and it is commonly used for cleaning up dust spots or scratches or removing unwanted objects from the scene.

Healing Brush Use this when you need to replace the texture of a problem area in your image but maintain the existing tone and color. The Healing Brush works very similarly to the Clone Stamp tool, except that it blends the copied pixels, preserving texture but blending tone and color to match the destination area. The Healing Brush is most often used for cleaning up blemishes in portraits, but it is also incredibly helpful for cleaning dust or scratches from any area of an image that contains smooth textures.

Spot Healing Brush The Spot Healing Brush is essentially an automated Healing Brush, allowing you to paint away defects without actually selecting a source of pixels to copy. It is helpful for cleaning up dust and scratches in areas of the image with smooth textures, where the area surrounding the defect represents good replacement values. It is an excellent tool for cleaning up dust in the sky, for example.

Patch Tool The Patch tool behaves like the Healing Brush, except that it allows you to fix a selected area in one step. This is a great tool for repairing areas of damage to older photos or for adding texture to areas that lost it due to exposure problems.

Clone Stamp

The most common tool for image cleanup is the Clone Stamp tool. This tool allows you to copy pixels from one area of your image to another, covering unwanted elements within the image with an appropriate replacement. This is much easier than trying to paint replacement pixels yourself, because you can select pixels that are a perfect match for the destination area from directly within the image.

Getting Started

Before you start using the Clone Stamp tool, you should configure the tool and your working environment so you'll be ready to work. As you can probably imagine by now, you should work with the Clone Stamp tool on a new layer, so you aren't actually replacing pixels within the image. Instead, you'll be copying pixels from within your image onto a new layer, so they cover up the pixels in the original that you don't want to have visible.

Start by selecting the Clone Stamp tool from the Tools palette or by pressing the S key. With the tool active, you're ready to start configuring it for the most effective use.

Set Up the Layers Palette

The first step is to create a new image layer to serve as the target for the pixels you'll copy with the Clone Stamp tool. Because the new layer will be placed directly above the currently active layer, first click on the Background image layer to select it. You want the new layer to be above the Background image layer but below all adjustment layers so the adjustments will affect cloned pixels to the same extent as the underlying image layer.

> **Note:** There are a variety of ways you could work with the Clone Stamp tool. I present here what I recommend as the best method, utilizing a separate layer for cloned pixels to maximize flexibility and maintain the ability to fix any mistakes later.

To create a new layer, click the Create A New Layer button on the Layers palette. The new layer will have a name such as *Layer 1*, which won't really tell you a lot about the layer when you open the image later. I recommend renaming the layer, particularly because cloning often requires cleaning up small areas of an image, and the thumbnail for the layer on the Layers palette may make it appear that the layer is empty, leading you to delete it without realizing its importance. You can rename the layer by simply double-clicking the name of the layer. You can then type a new name, such as *Clone Stamp* or *Cleanup*, and press Enter/Return to apply the new name to the layer (Figure 6.2).

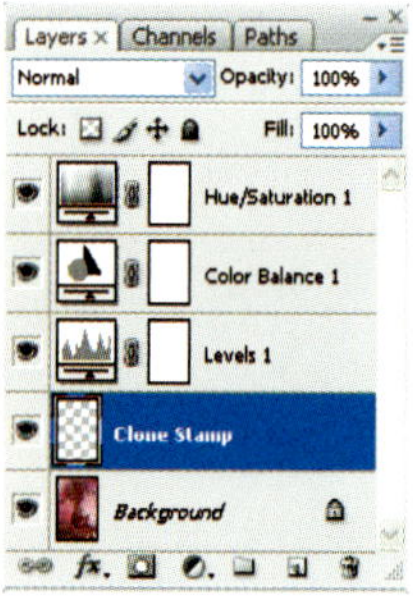

Figure 6.2 Giving the new layer for cloning a new name, such as *Clone Stamp*, helps avoid confusion about the layer's purpose.

Note: You may be tempted to place the Clone Stamp layer above the adjustment layers so they won't affect cloned pixels twice. However, if you ever decide to change the settings in any adjustment layer, the pixels will no longer match properly.

Configure the Options Bar

The Options bar includes several settings you can establish for the Clone Stamp tool. Although these settings offer a variety of ways to configure the tool, the vast majority of the time you'll use the same ones. Therefore, after you've configured the Clone Stamp tool the first time, you'll need to only glance at the Options bar to confirm that the settings are as they should be.

The first setting on the Options bar you should look at is the Brush popup palette, accessed by clicking the brush tip icon. This allows you to define the shape, size, and hardness of the brush (Figure 6.3). In most situations, I recommend using a standard round brush when working with the Clone Stamp tool, although at times you may find a different shape useful. The size setting isn't particularly helpful because you probably don't know how many pixels wide you want the brush to be. Instead, you can set the size later and use the area you want to clean up as a reference. This leaves only the hardness of the brush to be considered at this point.

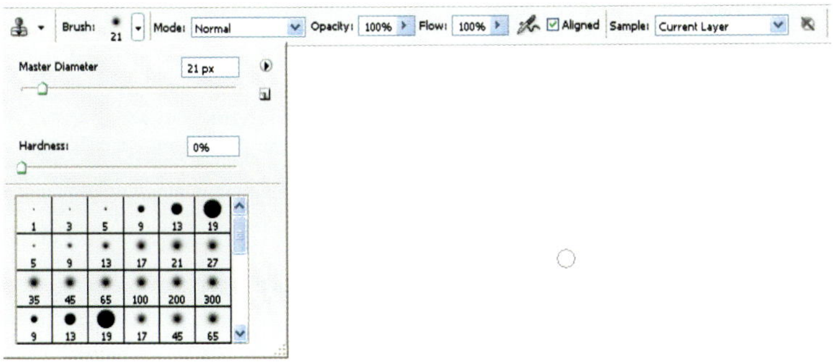

Figure 6.3 The Brush popup palette on the Options bar allows you to adjust the size, hardness, and shape of the brush.

Besides selecting a hard- or soft-edged brush from the Brush popup palette (you can tell the difference by looking at the thumbnail of the brush stroke preview in the Brush popup palette or the brush sample icon on the Options bar), Photoshop includes a Hardness slider. I never recommend using a hard-edged brush with the Clone Stamp tool because it produces a result that is too obvious, with a harsh transition between the pixels you've cloned and the surrounding pixels (Figure 6.4). A soft-edged brush works well when cloning in areas that don't have significant detail, such as when cleaning up dust spots in the sky. However, in areas with crisp texture, a soft-edged brush can also leave obvious indications of your work, in the form of soft areas where the pixels are blended too much, outlining your brush strokes. In most cases, I prefer to use a brush with about a 50% Hardness setting. However, you can certainly experiment with different Hardness settings to find the one that works for you.

Figure 6.4 A hard-edged brush should never be used with the Clone Stamp tool because it leads to obvious transitions between cloned and surrounding pixels, such as the straight lines within the pattern here.

As you're working, you can adjust the Hardness setting with keyboard shortcuts: press Shift+[to reduce hardness or Shift+] to increase it, in 20% increments. You can watch the brush sample icon on the Options bar to see the effect of your change.

The next setting on the Options bar is Mode, which controls the blending mode for the Clone Stamp tool. This changes the appearance of the pixels you're cloning as they are placed on the new layer, in a way that varies based on the mode chosen. As you can imagine, when you're trying to remove elements of an image by copying pixels from elsewhere within the image, you don't want the appearance of those pixels to change. You should, therefore, leave the Mode set to Normal when working with the Clone Stamp tool.

The Opacity control determines whether the pixels you copy with the Clone Stamp tool will be shown at full opacity, or whether they will be partially transparent. Normally, you want to completely replace the underlying pixels, so a 100% Opacity setting would be used. However, in some situations you may want to reduce the impact of an area of your image, without completely replacing the detail. For example, you may want to tone down some blemishes on a person's face without completely removing them. By using the Clone Stamp at a reduced Opacity (perhaps around 50%), you can partially block the underlying pixels to minimize their effect without completely removing them.

Note: Photoshop also includes Flow and Airbrush controls on the Options bar, but they change the behavior of the Clone Stamp tool to make the results somewhat unpredictable, so I don't recommend using them with the Clone Stamp.

The Aligned checkbox controls how the source area is reset with each stroke of the Clone Stamp tool. With the Aligned checkbox selected, each time you release the mouse and then click again, the relationship between source and destination pixels you have defined remains unchanged. For example, if the source of pixels to be cloned is 50 pixels directly to the left of the destination area, each time you release the mouse and click elsewhere in the image, the source will be 50 pixels to the left of the new location. This is generally the preferred behavior, so as a general rule I recommend leaving the Aligned checkbox selected.

If you deselect the Aligned checkbox, after you have set a source of pixels within the image and you release the mouse and click again to start copying more pixels, the source will reset to the original point you established. This is helpful if you want to copy the same pixels repeatedly within the image, but it does increase the chance that the cloning will become obvious in the final image. If you're going to deselect the Aligned checkbox, take particular care to ensure it doesn't become obvious that you have copied the same pixels repeatedly within the image.

The Sample dropdown on the Options bar allows you to select what source for pixels should be used. The default is Current Layer, but since you're working on a new empty layer using this option would result in an ineffective Clone Stamp tool. Instead you'll want to use the Current & Below or All Layers option. In many cases, the Current & Below option will produce the intended result, including pixels that are on the layer you're using to paint on with the Clone Stamp tool along with the Background image layer. However, to allow for situations where you have a composite image with multiple image layers, I recommend using the All Layers option.

The final setting on the Options bar for the Clone Stamp tool is a button that allows you to toggle whether adjustment layers are included in cloning. To ensure pixels you clone onto a new layer actually match, it is critical that they not include the effect of adjustment layers. In other words, you want the pixels you copy onto a new layer with the Clone Stamp tool to match the Background image layer, and then be affected along with that Background image layer by adjustment layers above. Therefore, it is critical that you select this option when working with the Clone Stamp tool on a separate layer. When you click this button, it will appear recessed to indicate the option is selected, and you should always leave it in this state.

Note: In versions of Photoshop prior to CS3, the option to ignore adjustment layers was not available. When you were working with the Clone Stamp tool, you had to turn off the visibility of all adjustment layers manually and utilize the Sample All Layers checkbox on the Options bar.

Cloning Pixels

After you've selected the Clone Stamp tool, configured your Layers palette to work on a separate layer, and established appropriate settings on the Options bar, you're ready to select a source area for the pixels and start cloning them onto a new layer.

Select an Appropriate Source

Selecting an appropriate source of pixels within your image is the most important skill to develop when you are working with the Clone Stamp tool. The pixel source determines how well the pixels you copy match those around the destination area, which in turn determines how seamless the correction you're making will be. It takes some practice to be able to quickly select the best source area, so I encourage you to practice cloning things out of your image.

Note: To improve your skills with the Clone Stamp, give yourself an assignment with a test image. Remove something significant from the scene, trying to produce a result where nobody can tell that anything was removed from the image.

When selecting a source area within the image, you need to choose pixels that will blend in perfectly with the destination area in terms of tone, color, and texture (Figure 6.5). That doesn't mean the pixels you copy have to be an exact match, just that they need to fit in well with the surrounding pixels after you've copied them. As you're learning to use the Clone Stamp tool, take the time to carefully look at the image to find the best source of pixels to place in the area you're trying to clean up.

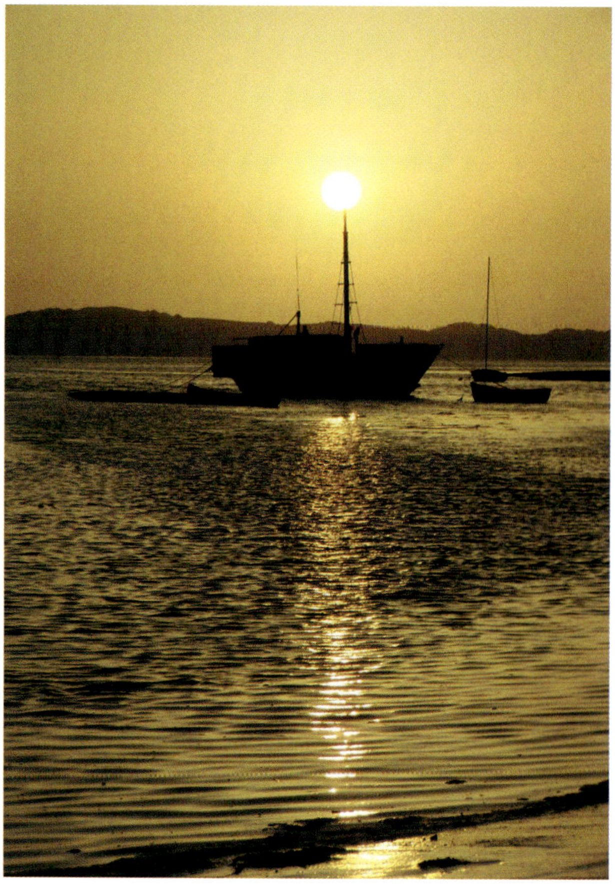

Figure 6.5 Choosing an appropriate source is critical when working with the Clone Stamp tool. Even areas that seem relatively uniform, such as a sky, will have subtle tonal variations as seen in this image. These variations need to be considered when selecting a source for cloning.

After you've chosen an appropriate source of pixels, hold the Alt/Option key and click on that source area. This will establish the point within the image where pixels will be copied from, and the relationship between source and destination will be set when you start painting with the Clone Stamp tool.

Paint with the Clone Stamp

With the source of pixels for the Clone Stamp established, you're almost ready to start painting away the first blemish in your image. However, before you do so, it is important to set the brush to an appropriate size (Figure 6.6).

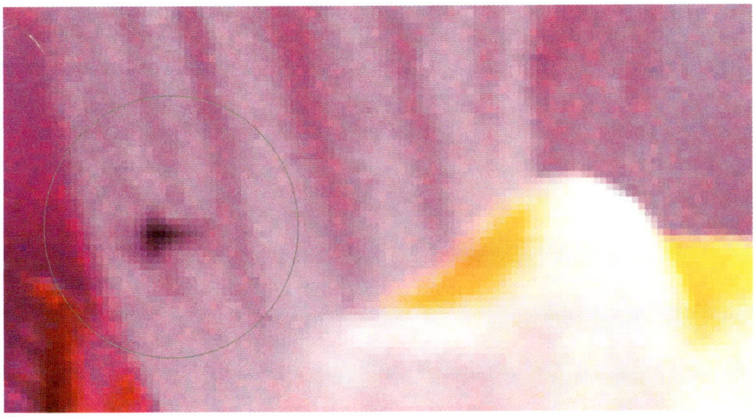

Figure 6.6 If you use a brush size that is larger than the area you are attempting to clean up with the Clone Stamp, you'll affect surrounding areas and increase the risk of having areas that have obviously been altered.

As I mentioned earlier, you can't set the brush size without knowing where you're going to clone—there is no always-correct size. Instead, you care only that the brush is an appropriate size relative to the area you're trying to clean up (Figure 6.7). As a general rule, you want the brush to be no larger than the area you're trying to clean up, and when you're cleaning up a relatively large area you may want a smaller brush, working small sections at a time.

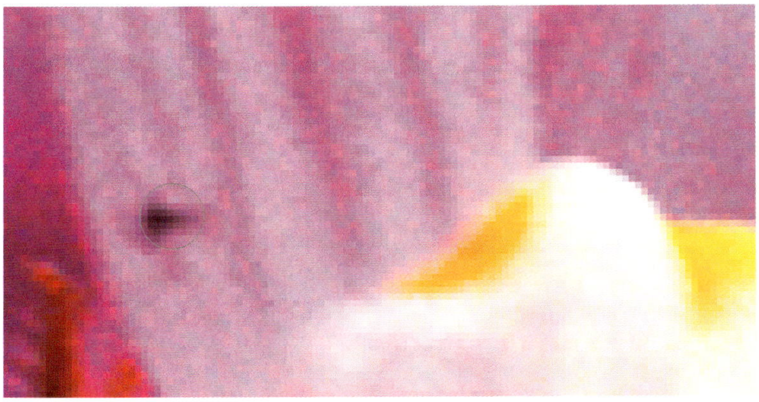

Figure 6.7 The brush size for the Clone Stamp should be no larger than the size of the area you're trying to clean, and often a bit smaller so you can carefully build up your corrections in that area.

Note: If you don't have the Preferences set to show brush size, you can't see the relative size of your brush for the Clone Stamp or other tools. To correct this, choose Preferences > Display & Cursors and set the Painting Cursors option to Brush Size.

To size the brush, place your mouse over the area you want to clean up and then use the left square bracket ([) to reduce the brush size and right square bracket (]) to increase the brush size, until the brush is an appropriate size.

Note: If you have set the proper Preferences setting to display cursors with brush size but still aren't seeing the correct display, make sure Caps Lock is not turned on. The Caps Lock key toggles between Brush Size and Precise options for your mouse pointers.

As you're working with the Clone Stamp tool, there are two basic ways you'll paint with the brush. The first is to simply click on a target area to repair a small blemish. For example, for dust spots in the sky you should click only once on each dust spot. For larger areas, you should click and drag slightly to repair sections at a time. If you click repeatedly, you'll tend to build up an obvious pattern in the cleaned-up portion of your image. At the same time, you don't want to click and drag excessively, or you'll risk having too much repetition of patterns within the repaired area. Instead, use short brush strokes, clicking and dragging over small areas as you build up the correction.

Naturally, if you keep the same relationship between source and destination as you work with the Clone Stamp tool, you'll end up with less than optimal source pixels for certain destination areas. To prevent this problem, and also to avoid the risk of producing duplication within the image that is relatively easy to see, I strongly recommend choosing a new source location frequently. In fact, it is best to select a new source every time you paint with the Clone Stamp tool, selecting a source area that is best suited for the specific area you are cleaning up at a given moment.

Note: Selecting a new source area for the Clone Stamp tool for every blemish you need to fix will help ensure the best match for those pixels as well as reduce the risk of obvious duplication of shapes and textures within the image.

Producing effective cleanup results without any obvious indication that you've changed the image requires a certain amount of practice with the Clone Stamp tool. Start with relatively easy tasks, such as cleaning dust spots out of the sky, before you move on to more advanced efforts. With practice, you'll get to the point that you can select an ideal source area quickly and easily, cleaning up the image seamlessly (Figure 6.8).

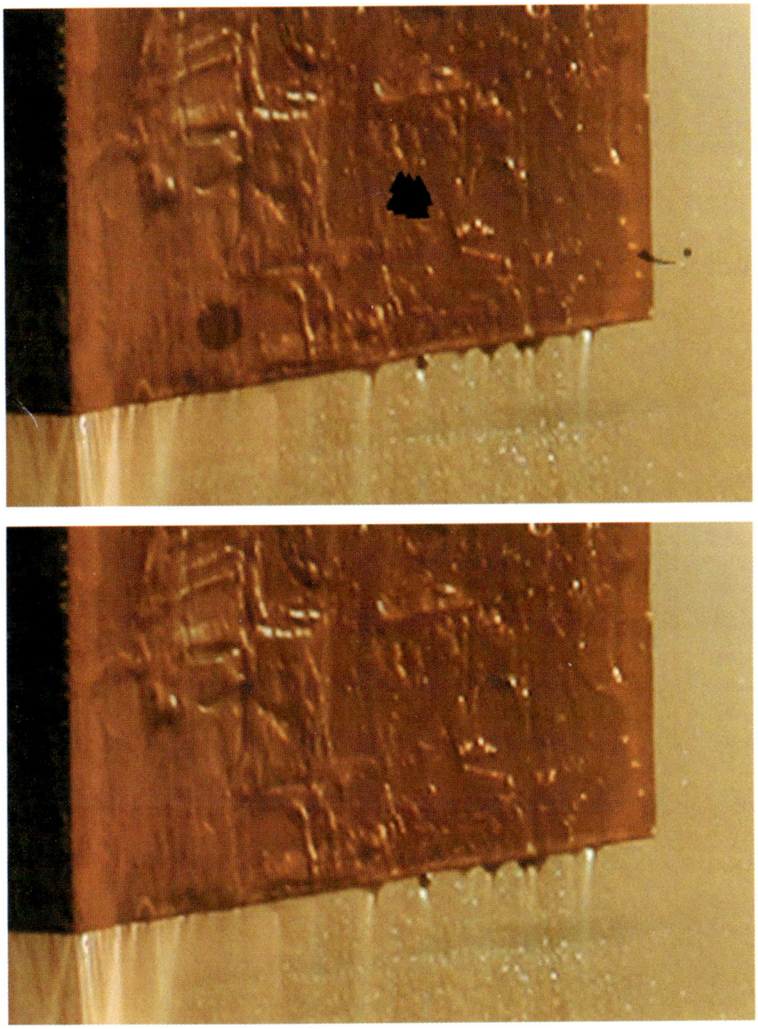

Figure 6.8 With some practice, you'll be able to clean up areas of your image with no evidence that any changes have been made, even in complicated areas.

Fixing Mistakes

In many cases, the Clone Stamp tool is used to fix "mistakes" in the image, although these aren't necessarily mistakes on the part of the photographer. However, even when you're cleaning up problems in your image with the Clone Stamp tool, you may run into situations where the cloning is less than perfect. Fortunately, when you are working with the Clone Stamp tool on a separate layer, fixing mistakes is remarkably simple.

Note: The ability to simply erase pixels from the cloning layer when you make a mistake is one of the best reasons to work on a separate layer with the Clone Stamp tool.

First, be sure the Clone Stamp layer is the currently active layer; if it isn't, click its thumbnail on the Layers palette. Then select the Eraser tool from the Tools palette (the shortcut key is E). On the Options bar, select a brush with the same hardness as you were using with the Clone Stamp tool, and adjust the size of the brush as needed for the area you want to clean up. Then simply "paint" over the image in the area where you want to erase the effects of your cloning. This will remove those pixels from the new layer you created, allowing the original pixels in the Background image layer to show through again (Figure 6.9).

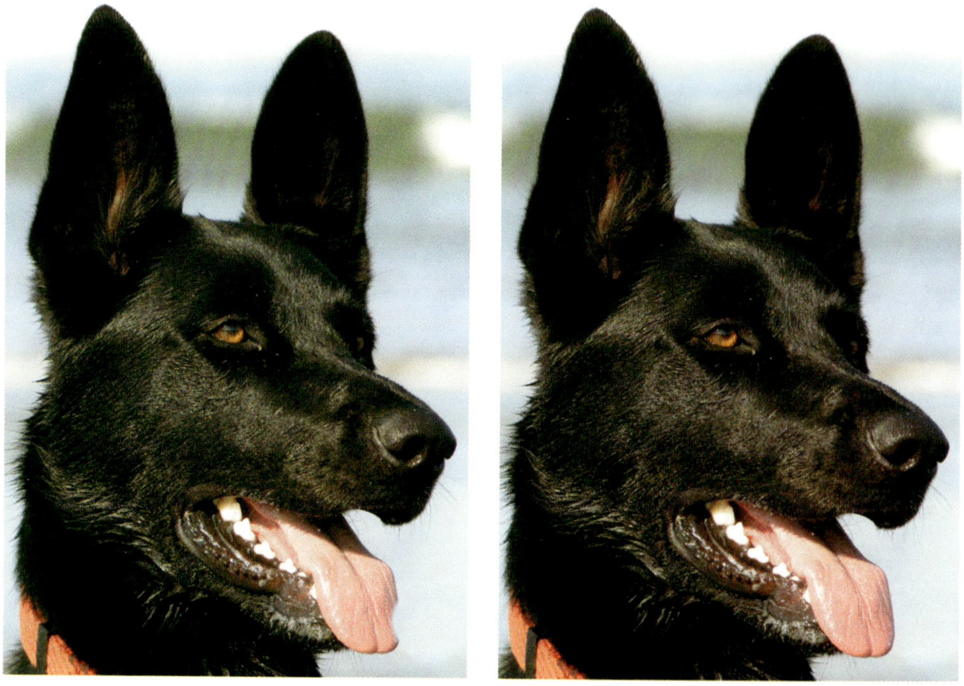

Figure 6.9 When cloning on a separate layer, it is easy to fix mistakes by using the Eraser tool to remove cloned pixels from your Clone Stamp layer. For example, while trying to clean up some clutter in the background, a portion of the dog's tongue was accidentally removed. Erasing pixels on the Clone Stamp layer quickly solves the problem.

Note: It is possible to undo a mistake by clicking a state on the History palette or by pressing Ctrl/Command+Z. However, this doesn't provide a solution when you've closed the image in the meantime, or when you don't realize you've made a mistake until you've already done other cleanup work you want to keep.

Healing Brush

After you know how to use the Clone Stamp tool effectively, you pretty much already know how to use the Healing Brush as well. In fact, the Healing Brush is even easier to use than the Clone Stamp because you don't have to be as careful about the selection of a source area within the image. This is because the Healing Brush copies only texture, automatically adjusting the pixels you copy to a destination area so they match the overall tone and color of that area.

It is an ideal tool for fixing many problems within your image because of the automatic blending it provides. For example, when cleaning dust spots in the sky, you don't have to worry about selecting a source area that matches perfectly in terms of tone and color. Instead, you need to find an area with only an appropriate texture, and the Healing Brush will do the rest.

Note: The Healing Brush is an even better tool than the Clone Stamp for cleaning dust in areas with smooth texture, such as sky. It automatically blends pixels to produce a perfect match with minimal effort.

Getting Started

The first step is to configure the Healing Brush for proper use. The procedure I recommend is identical to that used for the Clone Stamp tool. Create a new layer on the Layers palette; give it a name such as *Healing Brush* so you'll know what that layer is for; then select the Healing Brush tool from the Tools palette (the shortcut key is J). With the tool active, you're ready to adjust the settings on the Options bar.

The brush size, as with the Clone Stamp, should be adjusted with the square bracket keys as you are preparing to paint with the tool. However, the Hardness setting should be set to 100% for a hard-edged brush (Figure 6.10). Because the Healing Brush automatically blends the pixels you copy, using a soft-edged brush will only create more work for it. The Mode should be set to Normal to avoid unexpected results, and the Source should be set to Sampled.

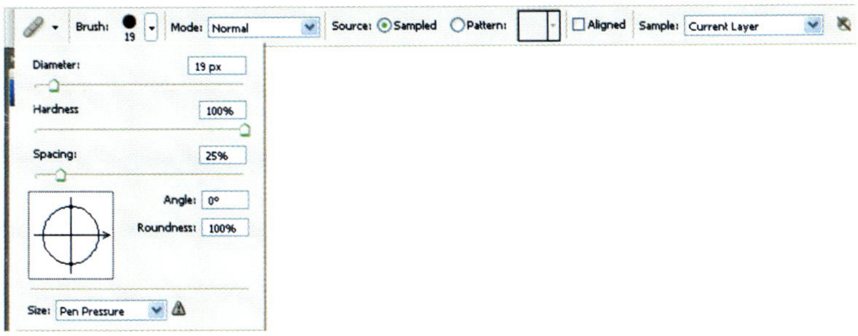

Figure 6.10 A hard-edged brush should be used for best results with the Healing Brush because it automatically blends copied pixels.

Note: If you change the blending mode for the Healing Brush tool to Replace, it will behave exactly like the Clone Stamp tool.

As with the Clone Stamp tool, the Sample dropdown should be set to All Layers and the option should be set to ignore adjustment layers while using the Healing Brush. However, you may not want to select the Aligned checkbox. Because the Healing Brush is used to repair problems by blending the source pixels into the destination, you don't need to be as careful about the source selection or about trying to avoid creating repeating patterns. In fact, it is often helpful to leave the Aligned checkbox unselected so you can select a source with a texture that will work well for a variety of areas within the image you need to clean up. For example, when touching up a portrait, you could select a single area of smooth skin texture as your source, and use that source for a variety of areas on the face.

Note: Although it is possible to use the same new layer for both Clone Stamp and Healing Brush work, I recommend using separate layers for these tasks so you can handle them independently.

Healing Pixels

After you've configured the settings for the Healing Brush, you're ready to start cleaning up your image. Again, this tool functions in exactly the same way as the Clone Stamp tool. Hold the Alt/Option key and click on a source area, selecting that source based on the area of the image that has the best texture for the area you wish to clean up. The pixels will automatically be adjusted to blend with the tone and color of that area. Then click and drag with small strokes (or even a single click) to clean up problem areas within the image (Figure 6.11).

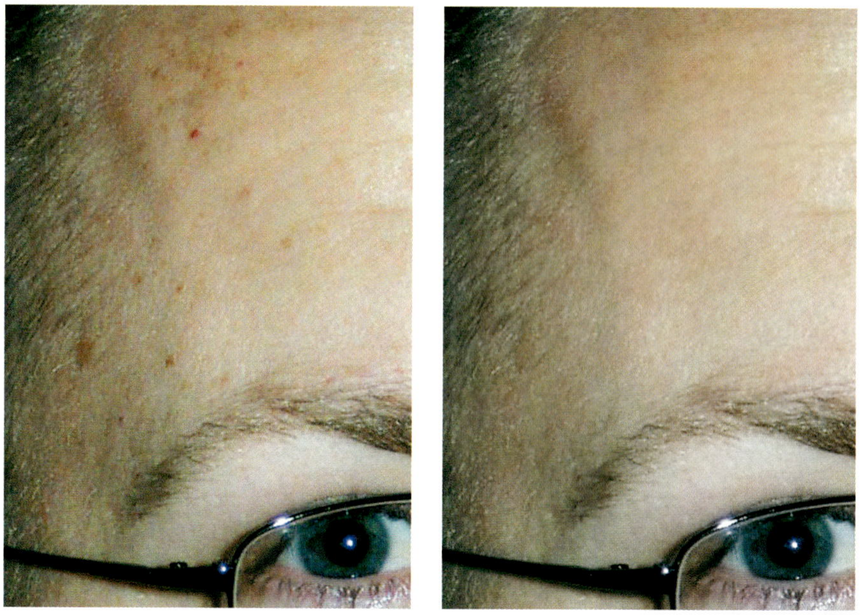

Figure 6.11 When working with the Healing Brush, use small strokes for each area you are trying to correct (left), building up each small correction until you have touched up the complete image (right).

When you first start painting with the Healing Brush tool, you'll notice that as you hold down the mouse button, the pixels you're painting don't match the destination area. However, as soon as you release the mouse, the pixels will be adjusted to blend in, producing an excellent match in most cases, provided you've selected a source with appropriate texture.

Note: I recommend making small brush strokes with the Healing Brush, rather than attempting to clean up large areas at once. This is because the Healing Brush can take time to blend, and a larger area will require considerably more time.

If you are using the Healing Brush near a high-contrast edge, you may get some "blooming," in which the blend near that edge produces a mismatch of tone or color that bleeds into the area you're correcting. In that case, creating a selection around the area you want to clean up will constrain the blending so it won't look beyond the selection for pixel values with which to blend. I'll cover the creation of selections in Chapter 9, "Making Selections."

Note: As with the Clone Stamp, because you're working on a separate layer for the Healing Brush tool, you can easily correct problems even if you don't discover them until much later. Simply use the Eraser tool to erase any cleanup pixels on the Healing Brush layer that you'd like to remove.

Minimizing Healing

The Healing Brush does an excellent job of blending pixels in the area you are cleaning up, but often the effect is too strong. When you're trying to clean up dust spots in the sky, the blending works remarkably well, allowing you to perform the same basic task as you would with the Clone Stamp tool but without being as careful about the source of pixels. With the Healing Brush, you really need to worry about only the texture of the source area.

One of the most common examples used for the Healing Brush is to remove wrinkles from a person's face. However, if you completely remove those wrinkles, the person won't look the same, and chances are they won't like the difference. Although many people would like to take a few years off their face, the Healing Brush doesn't provide a way to reduce the strength of the effect as you're working. The blending it performs is done at full strength and will, therefore, completely replace the area you use it on.

Because you're working with the Healing Brush on a separate layer, however, you can control the strength of the adjustment. By reducing the Opacity setting for the layer you're putting the Healing Brush pixels onto, you can reduce the impact of the adjustment. At the default Opacity setting of 100%, the Healing Brush pixels will completely cover up the underlying pixels. As you reduce this setting, the underlying pixels will be able to show through to some extent, minimizing the effect of the Healing Brush.

By reducing the Opacity setting for the layer, you can produce a more realistic correction for your image (Figure 6.12). Instead of completely removing a person's wrinkles, you can tone them down so they won't be as obvious. Instead of making the person look like they had extensive plastic surgery, for example, you can make them look like they were photographed under more flattering lighting. Each situation will call for a different Opacity setting for the Healing Brush, but in general I recommend starting at a value of about 50% and fine-tuning from there.

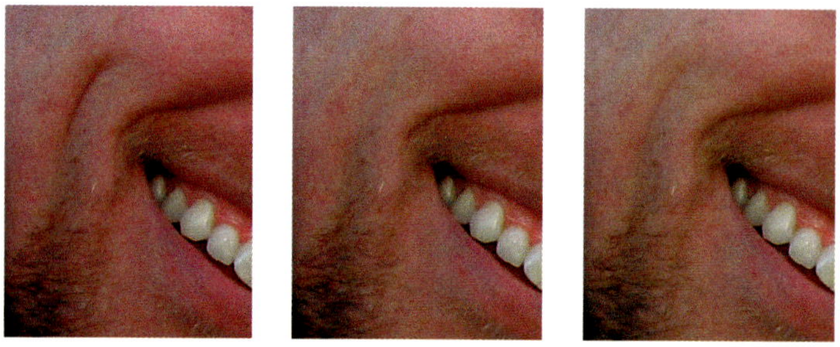

Figure 6.12 When you want to reduce laugh lines or wrinkles in an image (left) but using the Healing Brush causes an unnatural look (center), you can reduce the Opacity of the Healing Brush layer on the Layers palette. This produces a more realistic correction, creating the effect of more flattering light while maintaining the character of the subject (right).

Spot Healing Brush

This tool provides the same blending corrections as the Healing Brush, but without the need to select a source area from within the image. As with the Healing Brush, you should create a new layer to paint on when working with the Spot Healing Brush. Then select the Spot Healing Brush from the Tools palette. If you still have the Healing Brush active, click and hold (or right-click/Control-click) that button and select the Spot Healing Brush from the flyout menu that appears.

Despite not allowing you to choose a source area within your image, the Spot Healing Brush works well when the area you need to clean up is surrounded by pixels that represent an appropriate match. Any time you have a blemish surrounded by an appropriate texture for repair, the Spot Healing Brush is an excellent tool for the correction.

The Options bar for the Spot Healing Brush includes very few controls. The first setting you'll need to consider is the Type option. The Proximity match is the option I recommend, which looks to the pixels surrounding the area you've painted over to find textures that should be blended during the repair. However, in some situations this won't provide a good match, such as when contrasting tones or colors are near the area to be repaired. In that case, try using the Create Texture option. This will cause the Spot

Healing Brush to look within the area you painted over and attempt to produce an appropriate texture based on the pixel values within that area.

The other setting to check on the Options bar is the Sample All Layers checkbox. You must select this checkbox in order to be able to work with the Spot Healing Brush on a separate layer.

Once you've established the settings, using the Spot Healing Brush is remarkably easy. Adjust the brush size based on the area you need to fix, using the left and right square bracket keys ([and]). Then paint over the blemishes you'd like to repair (Figure 6.13). Initially the area you paint over will be covered with a dark overlay, showing you the area that will be affected by the Spot Healing Brush. When you release the mouse, the area you painted over will be automatically adjusted.

Although the Spot Healing Brush isn't a perfect solution for all situations, it does provide a simple way to work when you're just cleaning basic blemishes within your image.

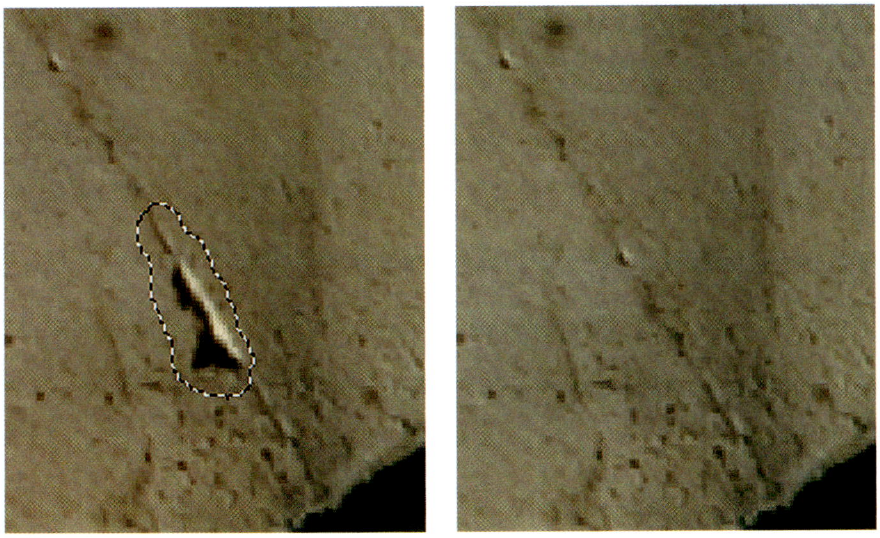

Figure 6.13 With the Spot Healing Brush, all you need to do is paint a selection around the area you want to correct (left), and Photoshop will do the rest (right).

Patch Tool

I think of the Patch tool as being exactly the same as the Healing Brush, except for the way you utilize it. It offers the same blending capability, ensuring that pixels will match the area to which they are copied. Instead of functioning as a brush tool, however, it allows you to create a selection to use as the basis of a patch to correct problem areas of your image (Figure 6.14). This tool is particularly effective when you have large areas you need to repair, or when the area that requires repair has a unique shape that would be difficult to repair with brush strokes.

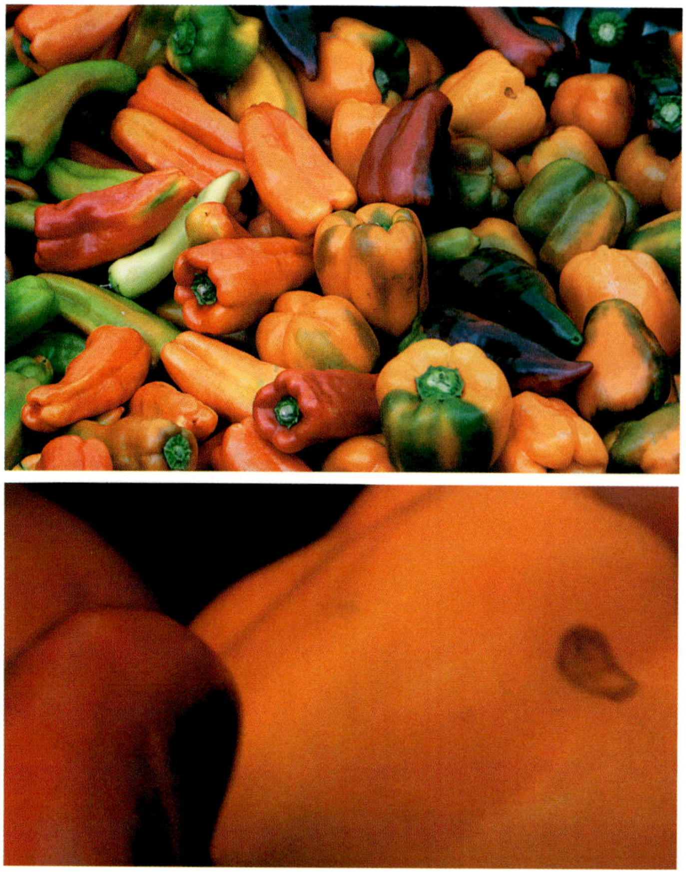

Figure 6.14 The Patch tool allows you to quickly repair sections of your image, such as this blemish on a pepper.

The Patch tool does not allow you to work on a new empty layer, so before you use it you'll need to create a duplicate working copy of your Background image layer. To do so, click and drag the thumbnail for the Background image layer on the Layers palette to the Create a New Layer button at the bottom of the Layers palette. Make sure this duplicate layer is active (highlighted) when you're working with the Patch tool.

The Patch tool is found under the Spot Healing Brush on the Tools palette. To select it, click and hold your mouse on the button for the Spot Healing Brush, and select the Patch tool from the flyout menu that will appear (Figure 6.15). You'll then need to create a selection that defines either the area you want to repair or the area from which you want to copy pixels. I recommend always selecting the area that needs repair, so you are defining the shape of the patch required to apply the appropriate repair.

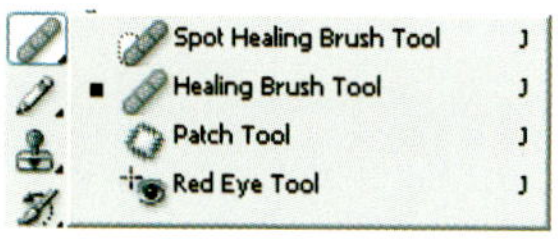

Figure 6.15 The Patch tool is found under the Healing Brush on the Tools palette.

To create that selection, click and drag to draw the shape directly on the image. Hold the mouse button down until you close the shape back where you started. When you release the mouse, the shape will automatically be closed. If you have created a selection that defines the area to be repaired, be sure that the Patch option on the Options bar is set to Source. Then place your mouse pointer inside the selection and click and drag it toward an area that appears to be a good candidate for replacing the selected area. As you drag the mouse, the original selection will be filled with the pixel values from the floating selection, providing a helpful preview of the results before blending is applied (Figure 6.16). Find an area of the image that contains an appropriate texture to repair the selected area, and then release the mouse. The pixels will be copied into the source area and blended for the best match (Figure 6.17).

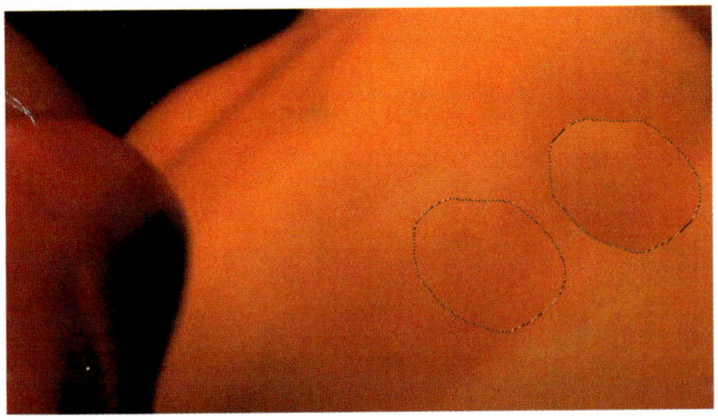

Figure 6.16 When the Source option is set on the Options bar and you drag a selection, a preview shows you the pixels that will replace the target area when you release the mouse.

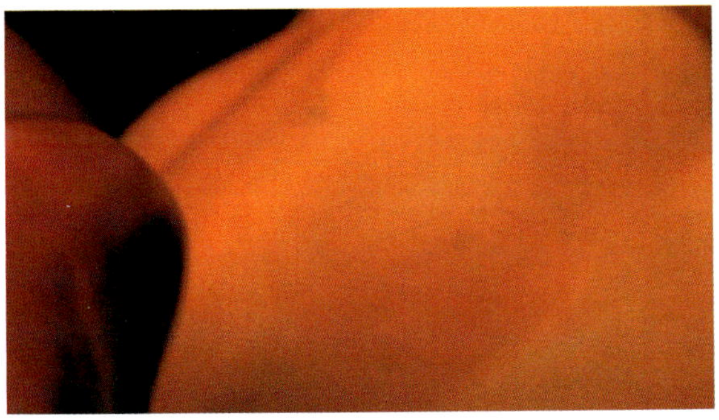

Figure 6.17 When you release the mouse button after dragging the Patch tool selection, the patch will be used to automatically repair the blemish and blend the copied pixels into the surrounding area.

Note: Besides using the Patch tool to create a selection, you can use any of the other selection methods discussed in Chapter 9 to create more precise selections to use in conjunction with the Patch tool.

If you prefer to create a selection that defines the source of pixels and then copy those pixels to the destination area that requires repair, choose the Destination for Patch on the Options bar. Then create your selection of the pixels you want to copy and drag that selection onto the area you want to repair, and the pixels will be blended.

Note: The Patch tool also includes a Transparent checkbox that causes pixels to be combined in the destination area rather than blended. I don't recommend using this option to repair photographic images.

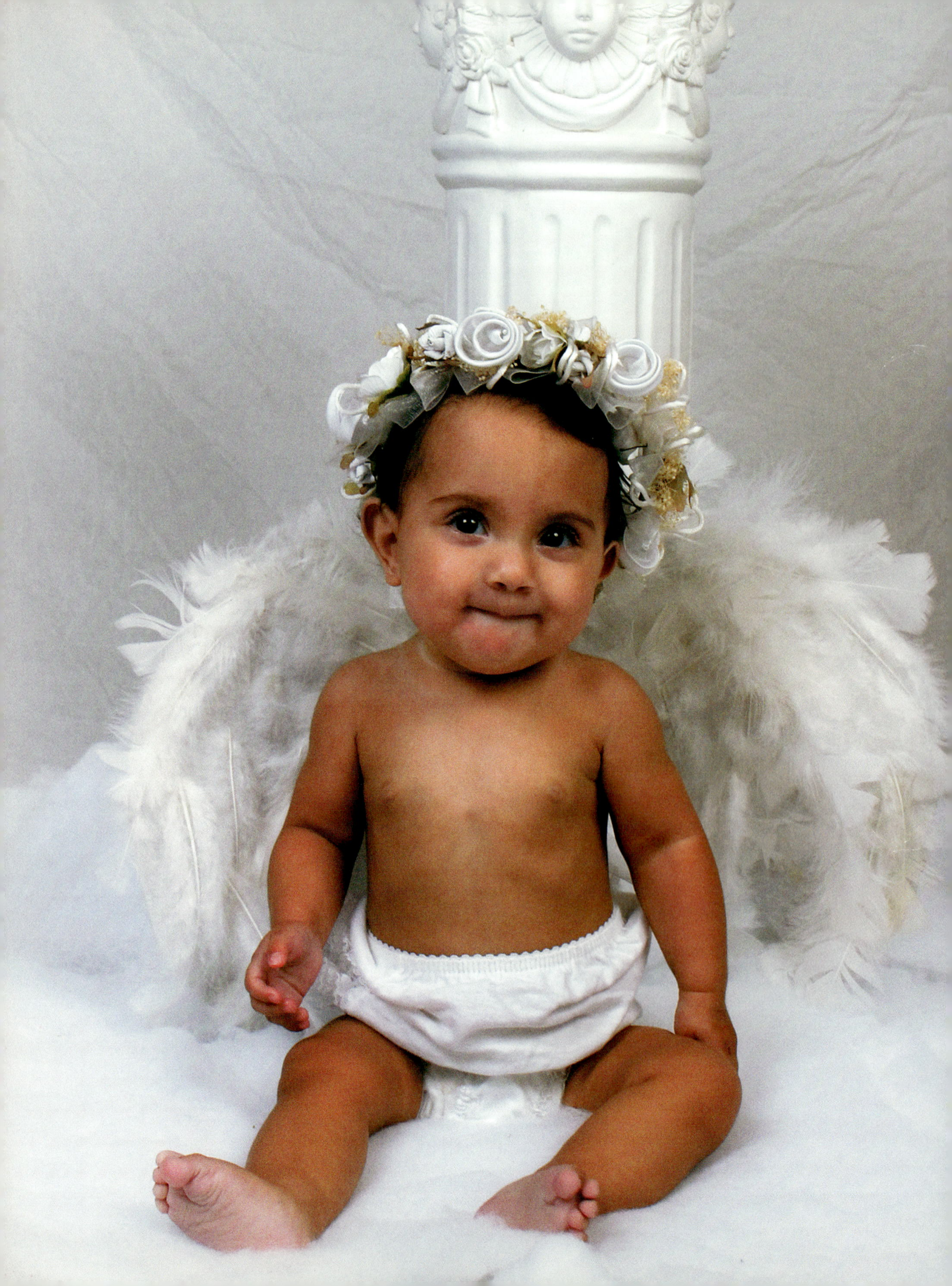

Advanced Adjustments

III

Producing the very best image in a digital workflow requires considerable control in the adjustment process. Previous sections have helped you organize and perform basic optimization on your images. Now it is time to roll up your sleeves and focus on getting exactly the results you envision. This includes making more advanced adjustments than were covered in previous sections, as well as targeting adjustments to specific areas of your images.

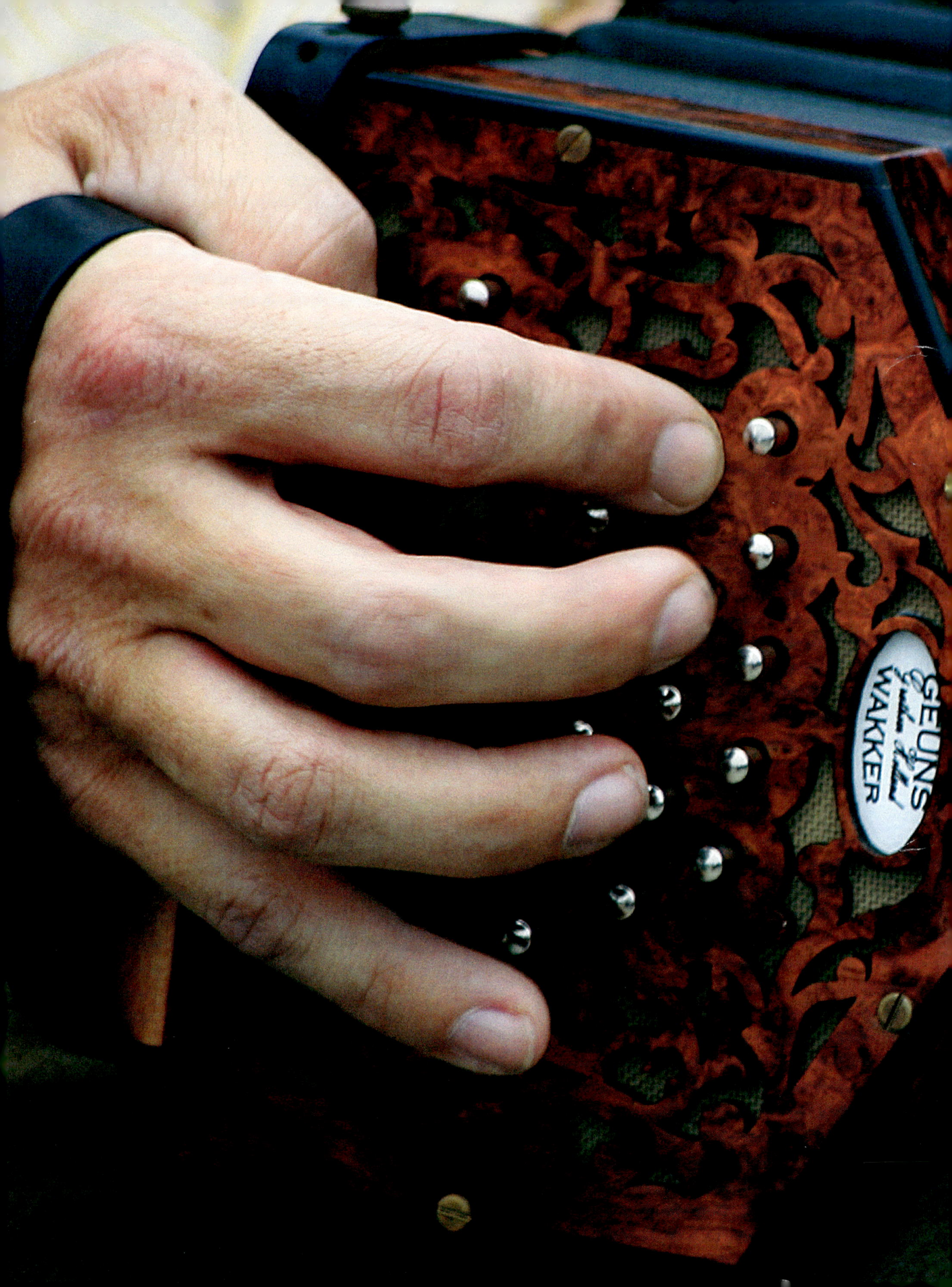
GEUNS
WAKKER

7 Advanced Tonal Adjustments

Performing tonal adjustments seems like a relatively simple task because you are focused on perfecting only two straightforward qualities of your image: the brightness and contrast. However, there are a variety of advanced techniques you can use to produce sophisticated tonal adjustments within your images. This chapter will focus on helping you exercise greater control over those adjustments.

Chapter Contents

Shadow/Highlight

An improper exposure can result in an image with shadow or highlight detail that has been permanently lost. The Shadow/Highlight control allows you to recover detail that has been lost in shadow or highlight areas because of excessive contrast (Figure 7.1). In many respects, this tool simply offers an easier method than that offered by other tonal adjustment tools such as Curves to make complicated adjustments to various areas of your image based on their tonal value. More specifically, it represents a good way to perform at least an initial recovery of image detail that you might have thought was lost for good.

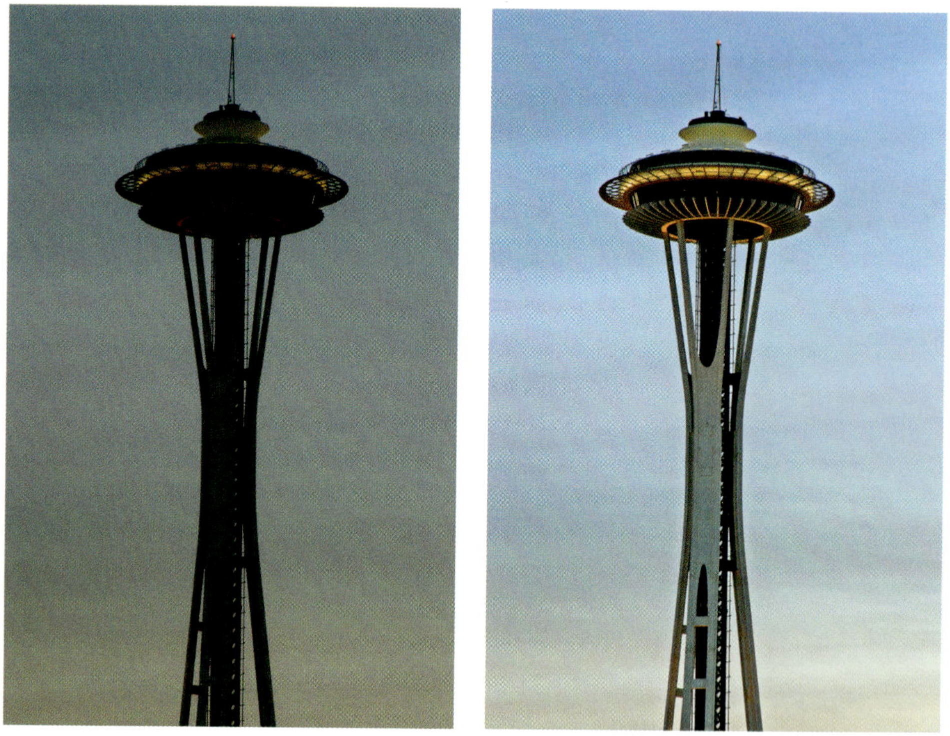

Figure 7.1 The Shadow/Highlight control provides a way to salvage images that have lost detail in excessively dark shadows or bright highlights.

I tend to prefer Curves for most of these tonal adjustments. However, I put Shadow/Highlight to use when I don't want to spend too much time or effort, especially when I just want a quick and easy way to extract shadow detail from the image. This is a relatively low percentage of the time, but Shadow/Highlight is still a valuable tool for pulling out shadow detail or toning down excessive contrast. This adjustment typically fits at this point in the workflow because you would have likely already tried other tonal adjustment methods and found they didn't help extract adequate shadow detail.

Because the Shadow/Highlight adjustment can't be applied as an adjustment layer, I recommend duplicating your Background layer as the first step. To do so, click the thumbnail for the Background layer and drag it to the New Layer at the bottom of the Layers palette (Figure 7.2). With the duplicate image layer active, choose Image > Adjustments > Shadow/Highlight from the menu.

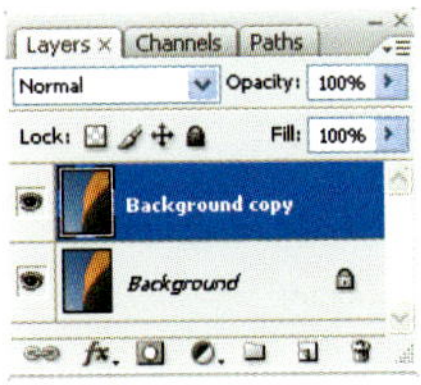

Figure 7.2 Because Shadow/Highlight can't be used on an adjustment layer, create a duplicate of the Background layer to work on.

The default dialog box for Shadow/Highlight in Photoshop includes only the Amount sliders for Shadows and Highlights (Figure 7.3). In effect, you can think of the Amount slider for Shadows as allowing you to decide how much to lighten the darkest areas of your image. The Amount slider for Highlights provides a similar ability to darken the brightest areas. Your first reaction may be that doing so will simply reduce contrast and produce a muddy image. However, keep in mind that this adjustment is designed for situations where contrast is too high or when you want to extract more detail from the darkest and brightest areas of your image. When used with modest settings, the result is an effective increase in detail without a problematic loss of contrast.

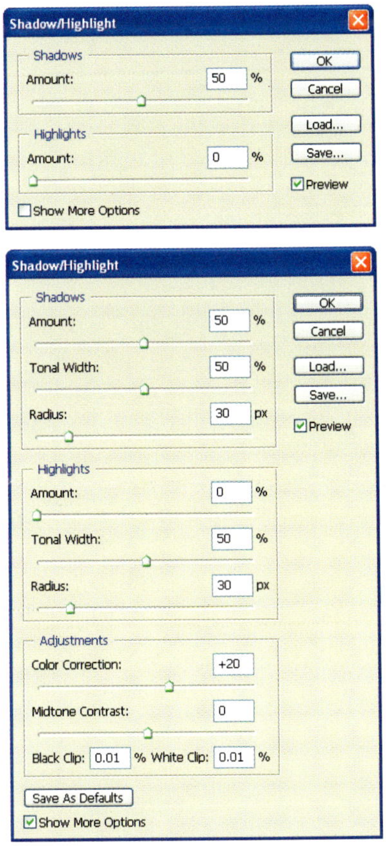

Figure 7.3 The default settings for the Shadow/Highlight dialog box enable you to adjust only two sliders. Selecting the Show More Options checkbox provides considerably more options.

Using the basic Shadow/Highlight control is a simple matter of adjusting the sliders to extract the desired level of detail in the image. As you make these adjustments, use care not to overcorrect, which can create an image that is excessively flat or that has an artificial appearance (Figure 7.4).

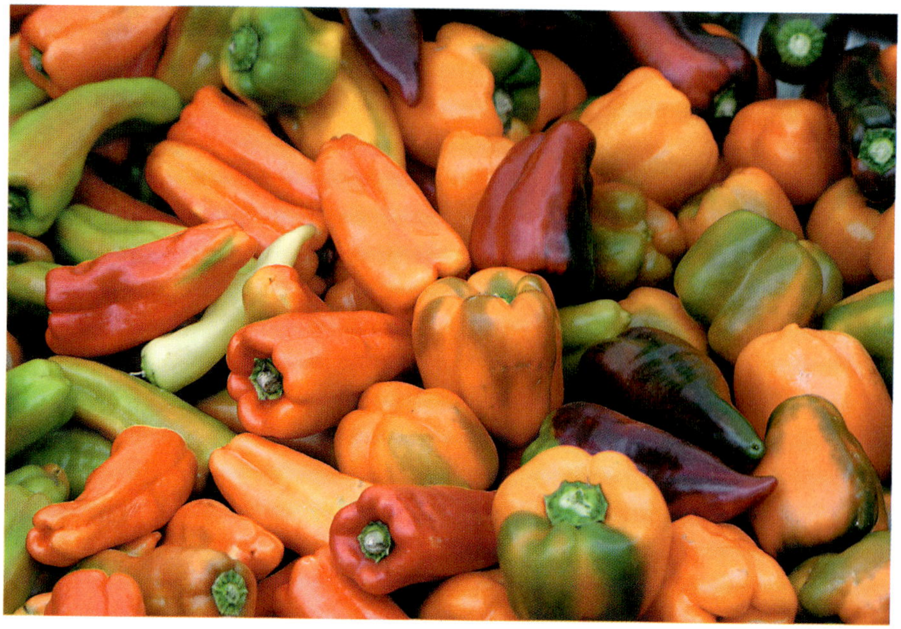

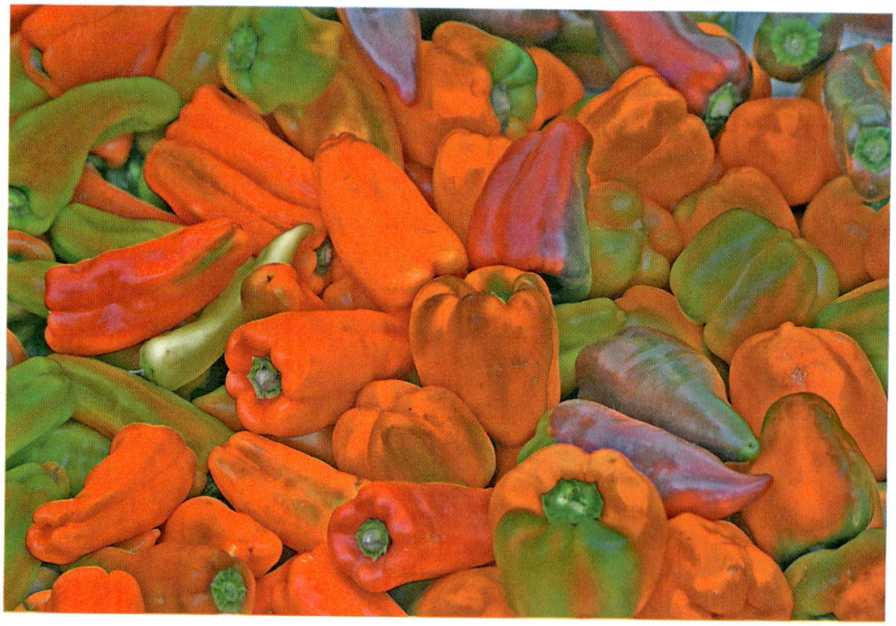

Figure 7.4 Extreme adjustments with Shadow/Highlight will result in images with an artificial appearance, although this could be used to create a new artistic interpretation of your image.

The real power of the Shadow/Highlight control is enabled when you select the Show More Options checkbox. This enlarges the dialog box to include many additional controls for fine-tuning the adjustment. The controls are divided into three sections. The Shadows and Highlights sections provide similar controls for adjusting areas of your image based on tonal value; the Adjustments section provides additional controls for improving specific aspects of the image.

The controls in both the Shadows and Highlights sections are the same, although they obviously target different areas of the image based on tonal value:

- The Amount slider affects the strength of the adjustment you're making to the area (Figure 7.5).

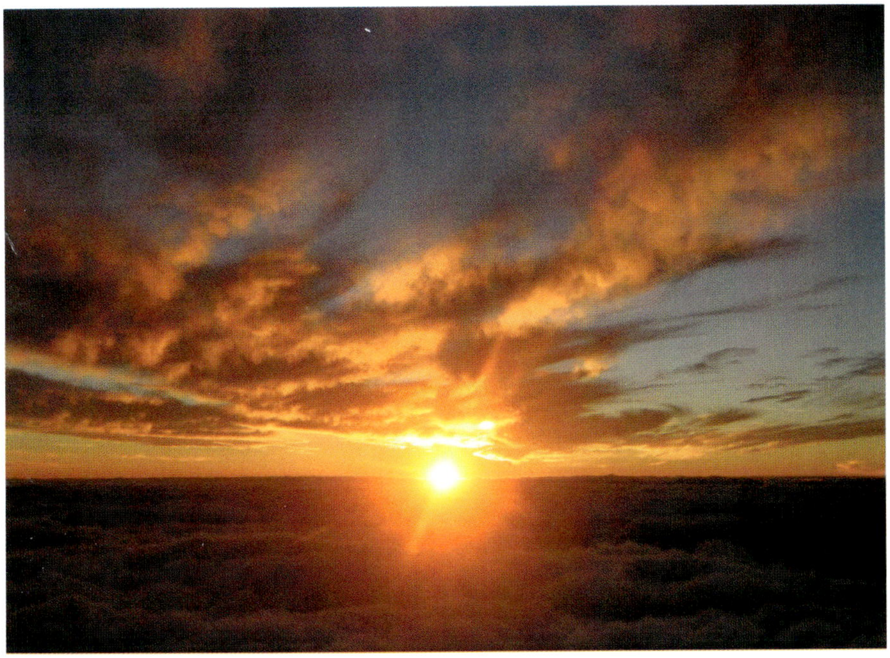

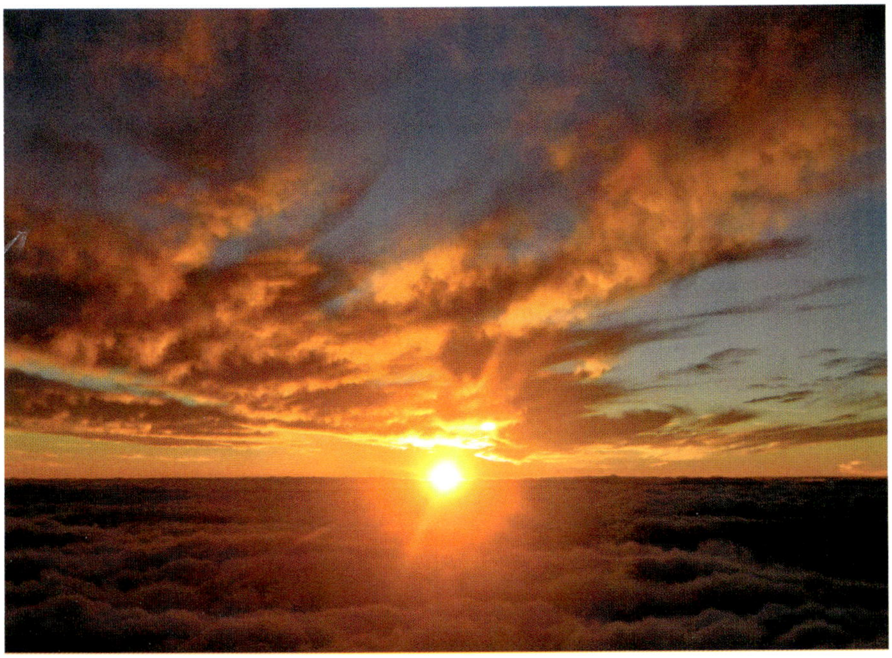

Figure 7.5 The Amount slider adjusts the strength of your adjustments for Shadow and Highlights. In this image, detail has been enhanced in the clouds by adjusting the Amount for Shadows.

- To adjust the range of tonal values that will be affected by this adjustment, use the Tonal Width slider (Figure 7.6). A low value will cause only a limited range of tonal values within the image to be affected, whereas a high value will allow the adjustment to apply to a wider range. In other words, you expand or contract the area to be adjusted by defining a tonal range.

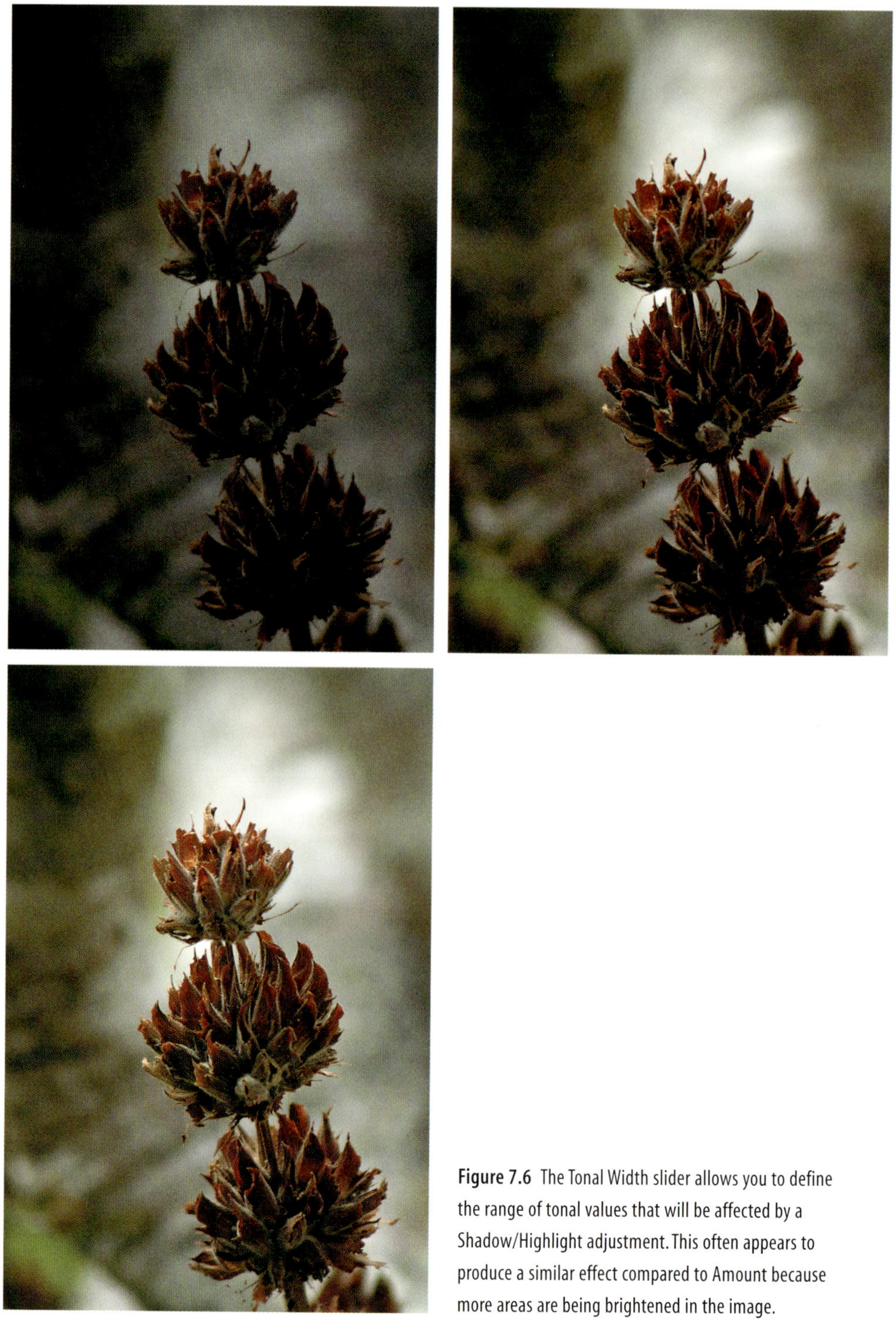

Figure 7.6 The Tonal Width slider allows you to define the range of tonal values that will be affected by a Shadow/Highlight adjustment. This often appears to produce a similar effect compared to Amount because more areas are being brightened in the image.

- Finally, the Radius slider determines how far outward from pixels that fit within the defined tonal range the adjustment will spread (Figure 7.7). This provides the ability to blend the adjustment to produce a more realistic effect.

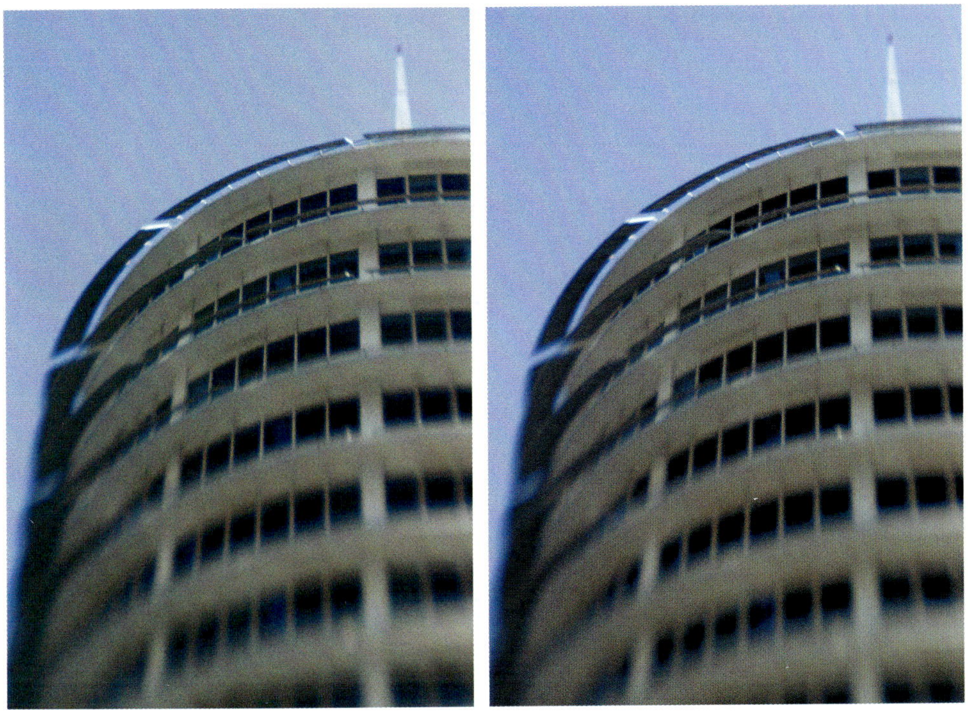

Figure 7.7 The Radius slider provides control over the blending of adjusted areas.

Note: Although the best settings will be found through experimentation with your image, I recommend setting Tonal Width values between about 40% and 60% and Radius settings between about 30 and 100 pixels.

After you've adjusted the controls in the Shadows and Highlights sections, use the Adjustments section to fine-tune the final result. The Color Correction slider is really a saturation adjustment that affects the darkest areas of your image. This control allows you to compensate for shadow areas that often have reduced saturation compared to other areas of the image because there isn't adequate light to enhance the colors. After you've brightened up shadow areas, you'll likely want to increase the saturation slightly so those areas will match the rest of the image (Figure 7.8).

Similarly, brightening shadows and darkening highlights helps to extract more detail but results in an overall reduction in contrast. The Midtone Contrast slider allows you to apply compensation by adjusting contrast for just the middle-tone values within the image, leaving the shadow and highlight areas you've already adjusted relatively unchanged (Figure 7.9).

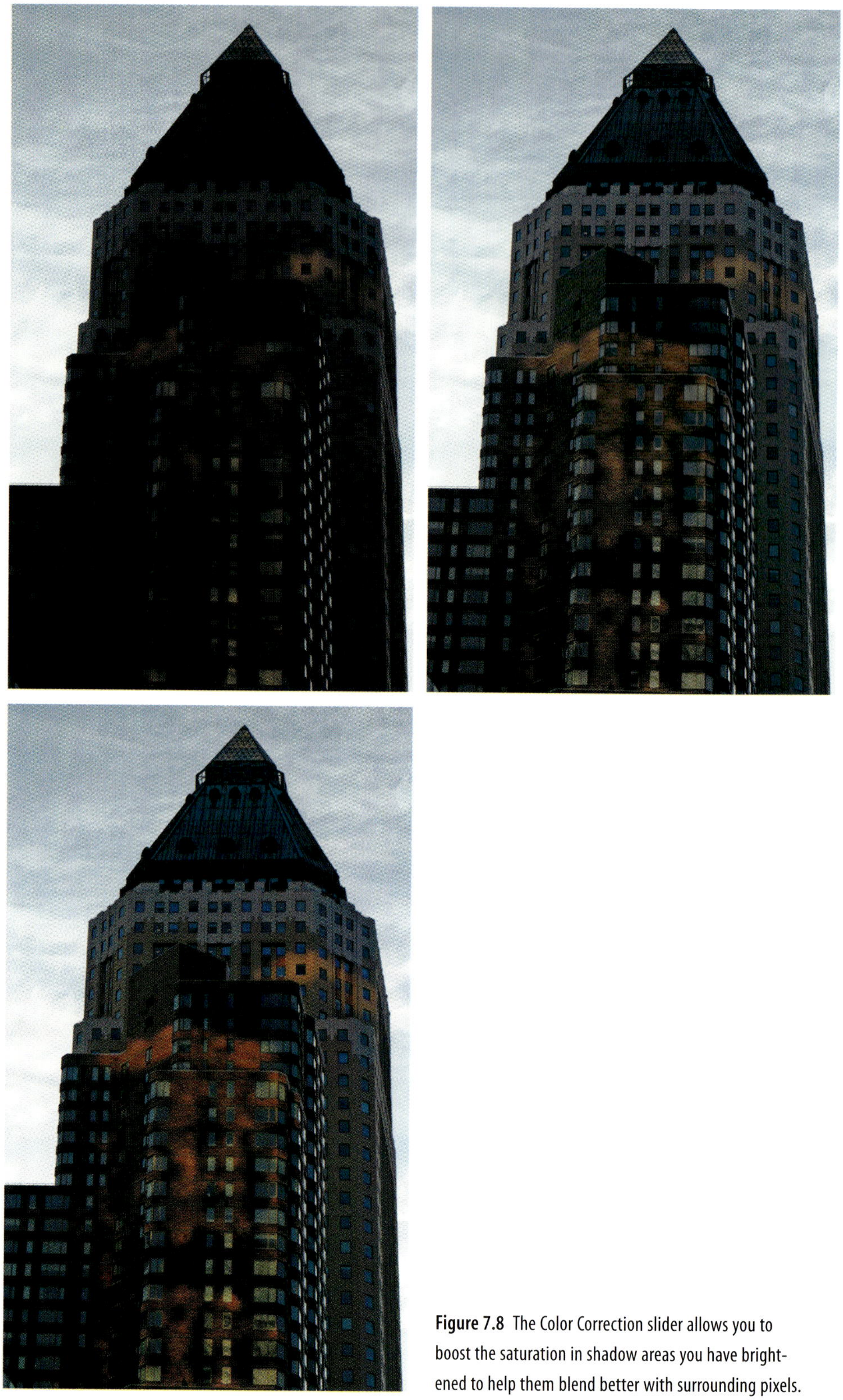

Figure 7.8 The Color Correction slider allows you to boost the saturation in shadow areas you have brightened to help them blend better with surrounding pixels.

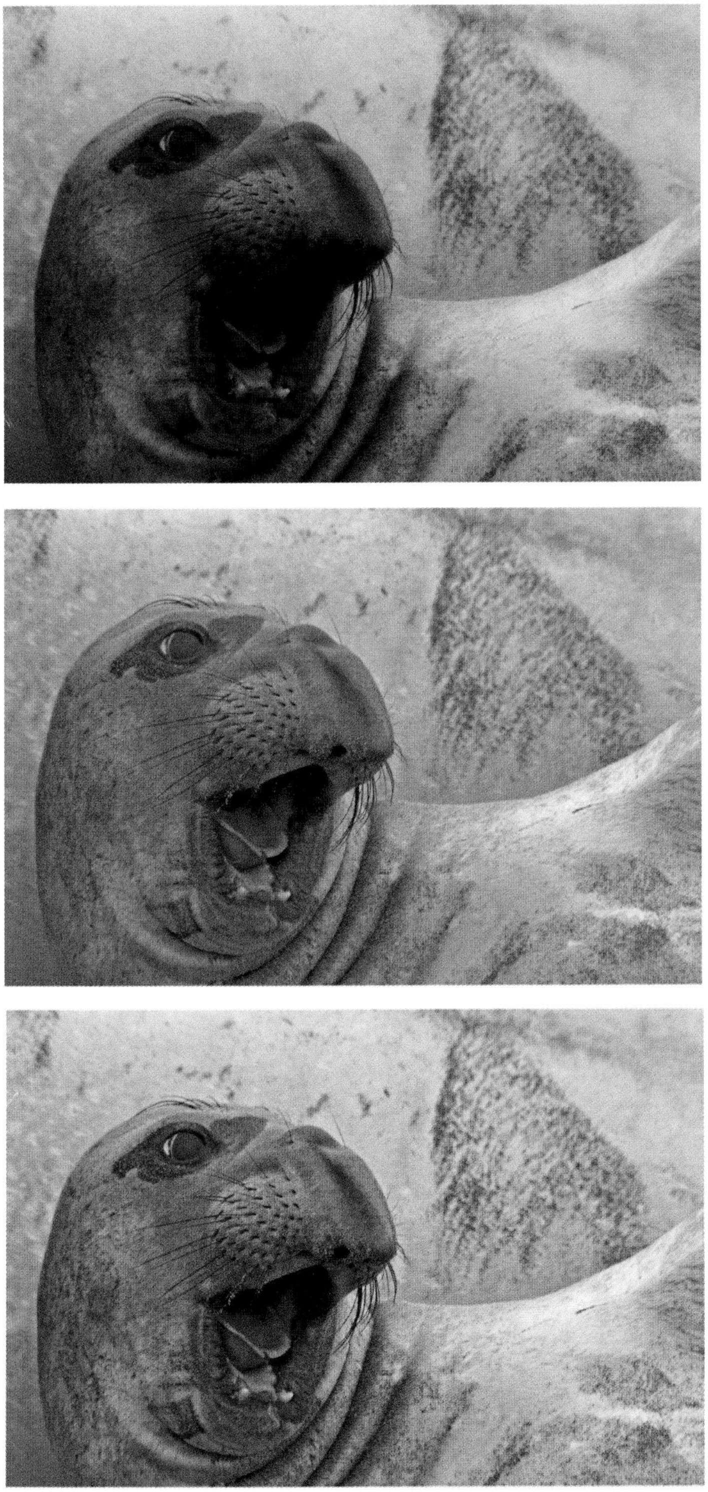

Figure 7.9 The Midtone Contrast slider allows you to compensate for the general loss of contrast that typically occurs with a Shadow/Highlight adjustment.

The Black Clip and White Clip settings allow you to specify how much detail can be sacrificed in the image when making adjustments by using Shadow/Highlight. I recommend leaving these values at their default of 0.01% to minimize the loss of detail.

Note: Don't let the Save As Defaults button lull you into thinking you can establish one set of adjustments for Shadow/Highlight that will be appropriate for all images. Each image deserves its own custom settings.

Curves

The Curves adjustment in Photoshop has the reputation of being one of the most difficult controls to master. Although becoming comfortable with it can certainly be a challenge, it provides an incredible level of control over your images. In fact, I tend not to use Shadow/Highlight simply because I can achieve the same results with even greater control (although with greater effort) by using the Curves adjustment.

As with all controls that are available as an adjustment layer, the first step in utilizing Curves is to create a new adjustment layer.

The key to understanding the Curves adjustment is the concept of before and after values. All adjustments in Curves are based on shifting the value of all pixels at (or near) a particular tonal value. Therefore, you should think in terms of brightening the midtones or darkening the highlights, for example, when working with Curves.

The Curves dialog box shows a "curve" overlaid on a grid. Of course, at first the curve isn't a curve at all, but a straight line at a 45-degree angle (Figure 7.10). As you learn to "read" the curve, you'll see that this 45-degree line represents no change in the image. The gradient along the bottom of the grid represents the "before" tonal values, and the gradient at the left shows the "after" values. If you follow a vertical line up from a specific tonal value on the gradient below the grid to the point that intersects the curve line, and then follow in a straight line to the left until reaching the after gradient, you'll see that (at this point) the before and after values are exactly the same (Figure 7.11). Changing the shape of the curve will alter the relationship between before and after values, resulting in a change in appearance in your image.

At the bottom of the Curves dialog box is a double-chevron button that provides the option to show Curve Display Options. The first time you use Curves you should expand this section so you can establish your preferred settings, and then you can hide the options again.

The first option allows you to choose whether you want the gradients at the bottom and left of the curve display to reflect the amount of Light (so "up" on the curve represents lightening the image) or Pigment/Ink (so "up" on the curve represents darkening the image). Because photographers tend to think of their images as being created from light (even if the image will ultimately be printed on paper with ink), it generally makes more sense to use the Light option, and that's what I recommend. Changing the gradient configuration won't have any impact on the image, and any adjustments you've made with Curves will automatically be mapped accordingly (Figure 7.12).

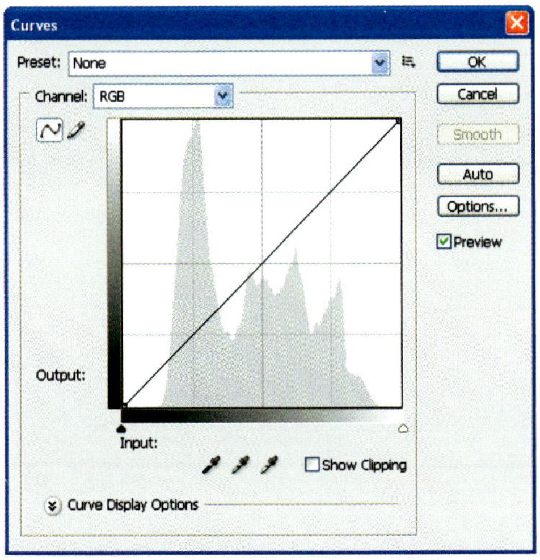

Figure 7.10 The initial "curve" in the Curves dialog box is actually a straight line.

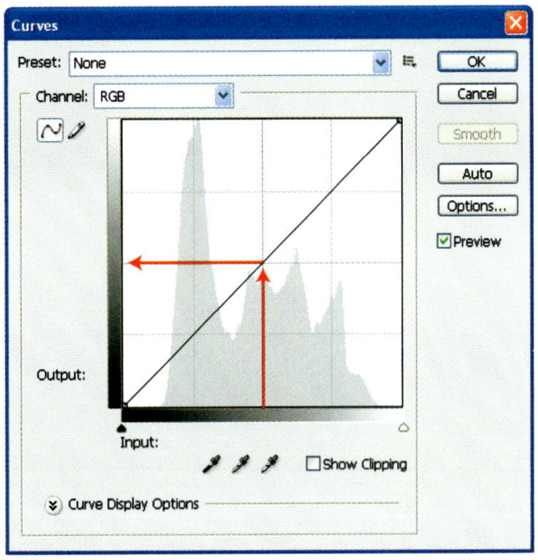

Figure 7.11 The basic concept of Curves is that you are able to "read" and adjust the relationships between before and after values in your image as you reference the gradients.

To the right of the Show Amount control are two buttons that allow you to choose the setting for the grid behind the curve line. The default is for the grid to divide the curve into quarters (25% increments). In general, I find that the 25% increments are preferred by those working in prepress, because they tend to think about quarter tones, midtones, and three-quarter tones. However, most photographers seem to prefer the 10% increments, and that is the setting I recommend. To change the setting, click the appropriate button. You can also toggle the setting by holding the Alt/Option key and clicking the mouse within the actual grid. Keep in mind that changing the increments has absolutely no effect on the actual adjustment being applied.

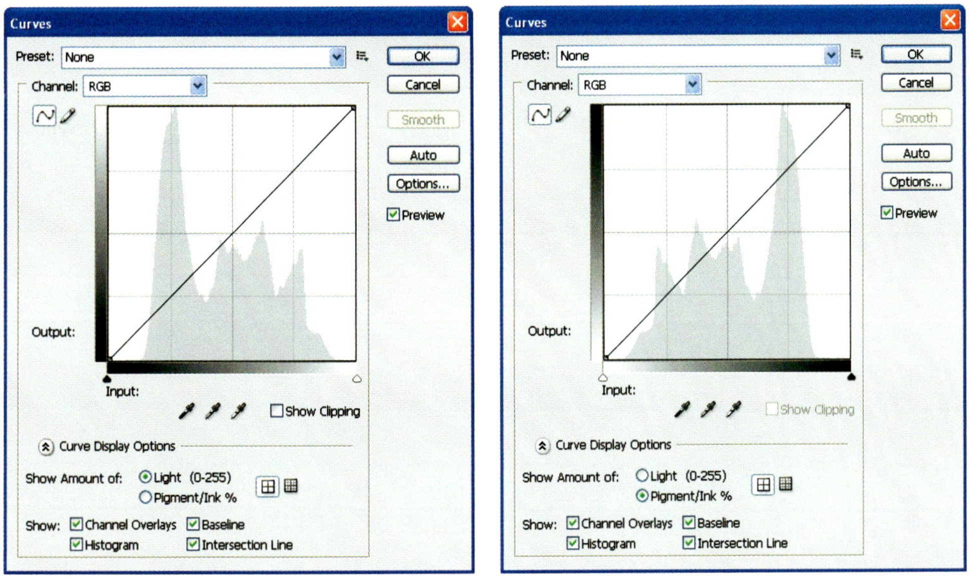

Figure 7.12 The Show Amount option allows you to toggle between having black at the bottom and left, or top and right, of the gradients in Curves.

Note: The adjustments discussed in this section assume you have the gradients set with white at the top and right (using the Show Amount of Light option). If you're using them with black at the top and right, you'll need to reverse the direction of anchor point movement discussed here.

The next set of options has checkboxes that allow you to toggle the display of specific elements within the Curves dialog box. The options are as follows:

Channel Overlays determines whether the individual curve lines for each color channel will be displayed. If you adjust only the RGB curve, you won't see any overlay because the individual channels aren't adjusted. This setting can be helpful to give you a sense of what other adjustments have been applied. The channel overlays are displayed only when you are working with the RGB channel.

Histogram determines whether a histogram display is shown in the grid area behind the curve. Having the histogram visible can be helpful as you're making adjustments, so I recommend leaving it turned on.

Baseline causes a light gray line to appear showing you the starting position of the curve line (a straight line at a 45-degree angle going from bottom-left to top-right). Keeping this setting turned on makes for a very "fast read" of the adjustment you've made, so I recommend keeping it turned on unless you find it distracting.

Intersection Line will cause a vertical and horizontal line to create a "crosshair" showing you where the anchor point is as you move it, and where that anchor point intersects the "before" (bottom) and "after" (left) gradients. This makes it much easier to quickly visualize the change being created as you move the anchor point around. When this option is turned on, you will see only the intersection lines when you are actually dragging an anchor point with the mouse.

Once you've established all the desired settings, I recommend clicking the double-chevron button again to hide the Curve Display Options simply to de-clutter the display.

Black and White Points

The Curves adjustment has always included "ends" to the curve that you could move to adjust the black and white points in the image, much as you can adjust those values with Levels. In Photoshop CS3, the Curves interface has been updated to provide sliders similar to those found in Levels for the black and white points. The "handles" to control these settings are found below the gradient under the curve display. To make an adjustment, simply click and drag the black or white point as you would in Levels. In fact, as of Photoshop CS3, I no longer feel the need to use Levels at all for tonal adjustments. Instead, I can use the new capabilities in Curves to accomplish the same thing.

The key to being able to make the best adjustment of black and white points with Curves is to use the clipping preview display. As you learned in Chapter 5, "Basic Tone and Color," the clipping preview allows you to see what areas are losing detail in highlights or shadows based on your adjustments so you can make an informed decision about the adjustment. Curves now offers the same clipping preview available in Levels, enabled via a checkbox below the curve display called Show Clipping.

The process I recommend for adjusting the black and white points is to first turn on the Show Clipping checkbox. Then adjust the white point and black point based on the clipping preview display. The display will change between highlight clipping (black background with color or white showing areas where highlight detail has been clipped) and shadow clipping (white background with color or black showing areas where shadow detail has been clipped) automatically based on which slider you are adjusting. Once you've established the black and white points, you can clear the Show Clipping checkbox and continue working with Curves to fine-tune your image.

Anchor Points

You will generally want to use anchor points for changing relationships between before and after values in your image, which in turn will create the actual tonal adjustment. Anchor points allow you to place a handle on a particular point on the curve and adjust its position (Figure 7.13). When you do so, Photoshop will automatically smooth out the curve to connect all the anchor points, providing a smooth transition in your adjustments.

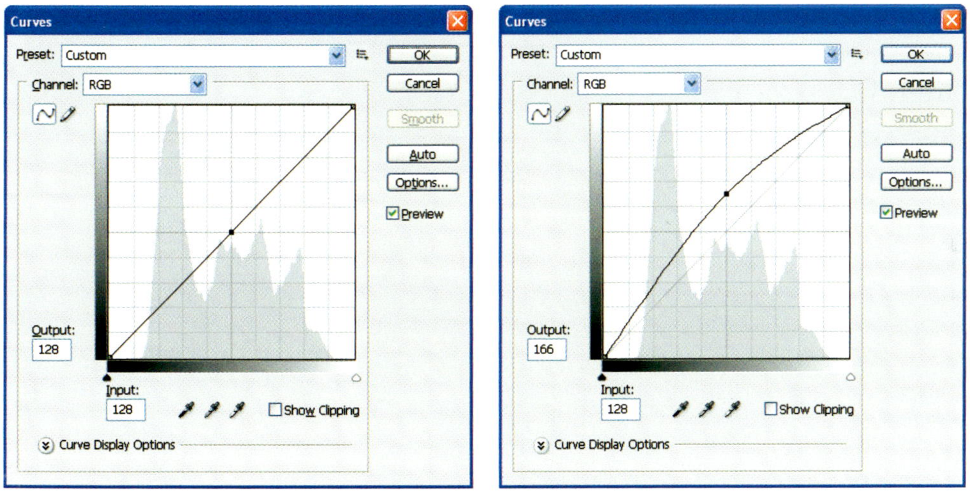

Figure 7.13 Anchor points behave as handles that allow you to change the shape of the curve. Adjusting an anchor point up or down at the center of the curve is very similar to adjusting the Midtone slider in Levels.

To see the basic functionality of anchor points, position your mouse pointer at about the middle of the curve and click. This will place an anchor point, which you can move around to change the shape of the curve, at that position. Move the anchor point upward to lighten the image and downward to darken the image. The result is very similar to adjusting the Midtone slider in Levels.

Of course, this hints at the incredible power of Curves. You can place up to 14 anchor points (in addition to the black and white points included by default) on the curve to perform adjustments on pixels at various tonal values within the image. By carefully positioning and adjusting these anchor points, you can exercise tremendous control over the tonal adjustments applied to the image.

To get a better sense of which area of the curve should be adjusted to affect specific areas (based on tonality) within the image, you can click and drag the mouse pointer on the image. A small circle will appear on the curve showing you where the tonal value for the pixel under the mouse pointer falls (Figure 7.14). If you drag the mouse pointer around on the image, the circle will bounce around as it updates its position based on the tonal value under the mouse pointer. This display allows you to see exactly where particular areas of your image fall on the curve.

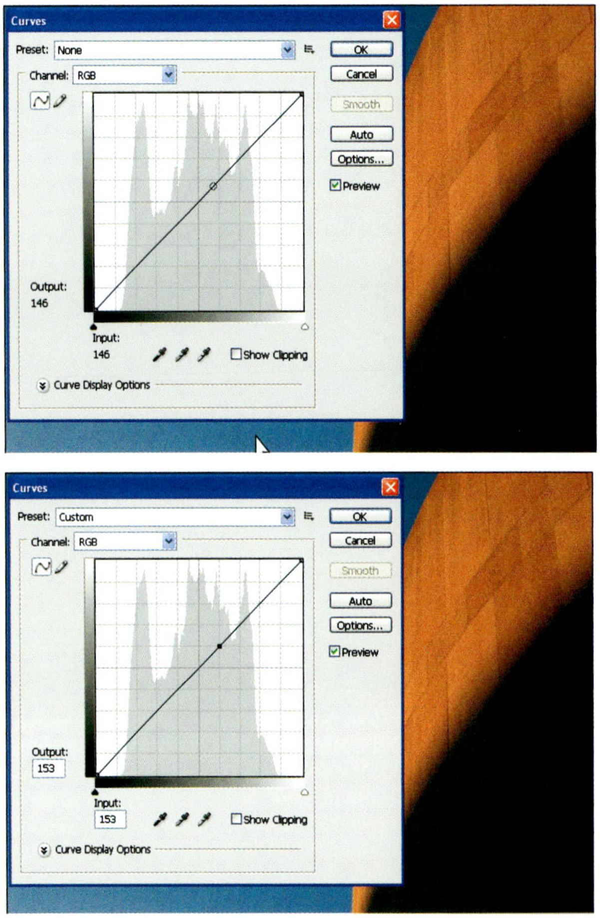

Figure 7.14 Clicking the image will show you a circle on the grid that corresponds to the tonal value of the pixel under the mouse pointer. If you Ctrl/Command+click the image, an anchor point will automatically be placed on the curve in the appropriate position.

Even better, if you hold the Ctrl/Command key when you click the image, an anchor point will be created on the curve for the tonal value of the pixel under your mouse pointer. You can even drag around the image to review the range on the curve before releasing the mouse to place the anchor point. This allows you to place anchor points very precisely based on the area of the image upon which you'd like to focus your adjustments.

Note: The Curves dialog box includes eyedroppers with which you can select black, midtone, and white points in the image. However, I don't like using them because they don't offer the precision you can achieve by directly adjusting the curve.

Adjusting Anchor Points

After you've created one or more anchor points, you can adjust them to change the relationship between before and after values on the curve. You lighten or darken specific values by raising or lowering an anchor point, respectively.

The anchor points can be moved by dragging them with the mouse, but you can apply a more precise adjustment by clicking an anchor point to select it and then using the arrow keys to adjust its position. You are typically thinking in terms of lightening or darkening, and therefore would adjust the anchor points up or down to change the after value, but you can also move the anchor point left or right. Although this is actually changing which "before" value you are adjusting, I prefer to think of this as simply fine-tuning the relationship between before and after by taking greater control over the specific shape of the curve (Figure 7.15).

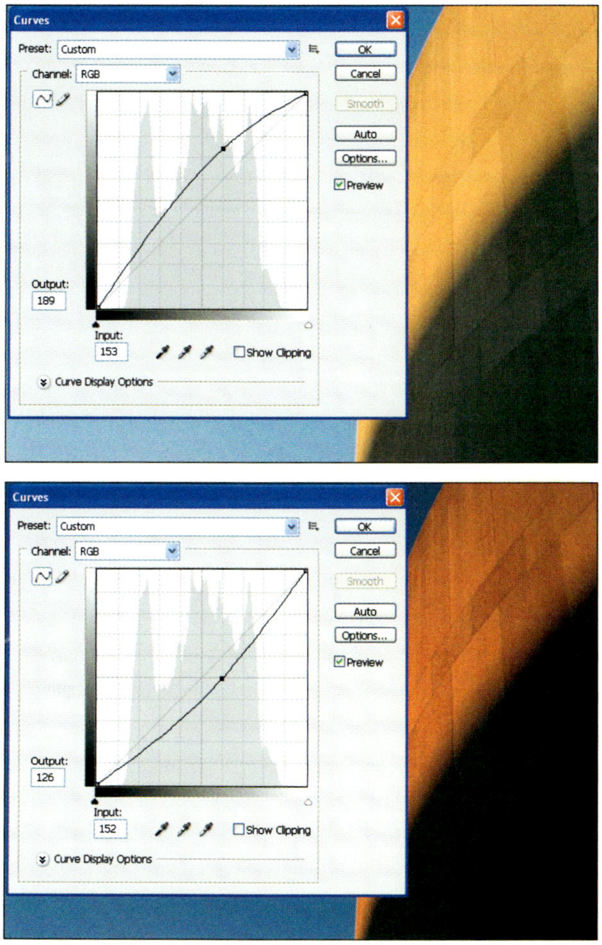

Figure 7.15 Changing the position of an anchor point changes the shape of the curve and, therefore, changes the relationship between before and after values in the image.

Note: At this point, you're performing only tonal adjustments with Curves. In the next chapter, you'll look at adjusting the curves for individual color channels to apply color adjustments to your images.

As you're adjusting the anchor points, you'll begin to see the relationship between the shape of the curve and the effect on the image. Raising or lowering the curve in a particular area affects the brightness of pixels within the tonal range represented by that portion of the curve. Making a portion of the curve steeper than the original 45-degree line represents an increase in contrast; areas that are shallower represent reduced contrast. As you understand these relationships, you'll be better able to read the curve as well as apply the desired adjustments with minimal effort.

Note: If you're still feeling a bit uncomfortable working with Curves, I strongly recommend that you practice using it on grayscale images. This will help you gain confidence with the adjustment as you target specific tonal ranges within the image, without having to concern yourself with the effect on overall color.

Creating the *S* Curve

One of the most common adjustments recommended for Curves is the *S curve* (Figure 7.16). This curve shape applies an increase in contrast to the midtones of your image, while preserving detail in highlight and shadow areas. Because we tend to respond better to photographs with higher contrast, this adjustment can be applied with good results to almost any photographic image.

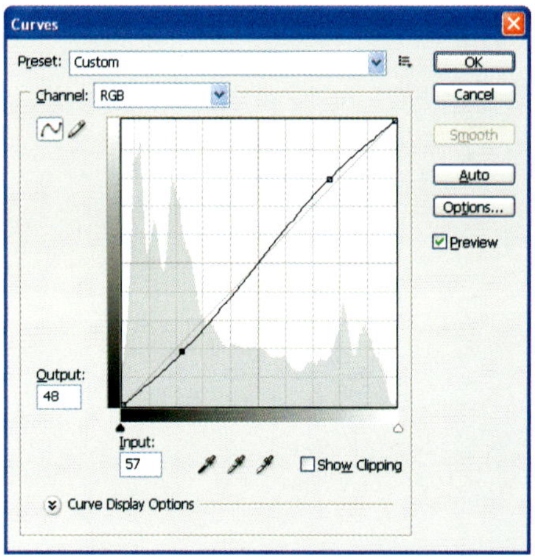

Figure 7.16 The S curve lets you limit your changes to one region of tonal values, improving midtone contrast without losing shadow or highlight detail.

To create an S curve, I recommend placing anchor points about 20% in from the black and white end points on the curve. Then move the upper of these anchor points to the left slightly, and the lower to the right. You won't need to move them much to produce a nice boost of contrast in your image.

Another great thing about using Curves for such an adjustment is that you're able to focus your S curve on either the highlights or shadows within your image. If you want to boost the brighter tones more than the darker ones, move the anchor point that's closer to the white end point farther inward than the anchor point you added near the black point.

If you'll also be applying more sophisticated adjustments with Curves, you may want to make one Curves adjustment layer specifically for the S curve, and another for adjustments that apply to various tonal values within the image. Renaming each of these adjustment layers will help you stay organized as you move through your workflow and when you return to the image later.

Locking Down the Curve to Limit Changes

When you move anchor points on the curve, Photoshop will automatically adjust the shape of the curve to provide a smooth transition between all anchor points. Although this is a good thing, sometimes it causes adjustments in areas where you don't want any applied. When this happens, you must prevent changes—"normalize" the shape of the curve—in the areas you don't want altered.

For example, if you're trying to focus some adjustments to the brighter areas of your image, you'll find that adjusting the anchor points causes a bend in the curve that also affects the darker areas (Figure 7.17). To lock the curve, place a new anchor point near the existing anchor point on the side representing the tonal values you want to limit changes to (Figure 7.18). Drag this new anchor point to find a position that will result in the rest of the curve being as close as possible to the original 45-degree angle (Figure 7.19).

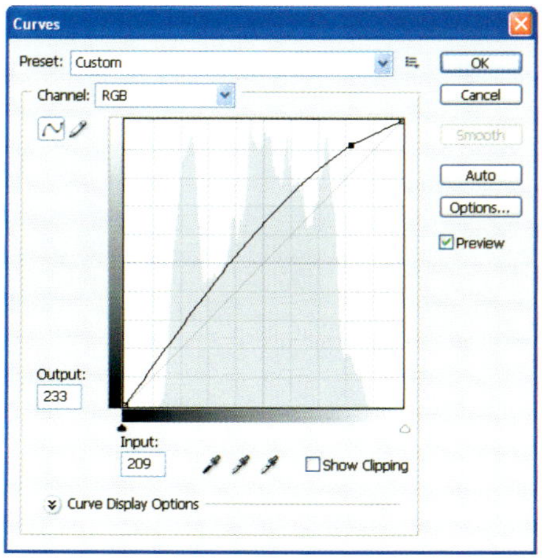

Figure 7.17 When you adjust the curve in one area, the entire curve changes because Photoshop creates a smooth transition.

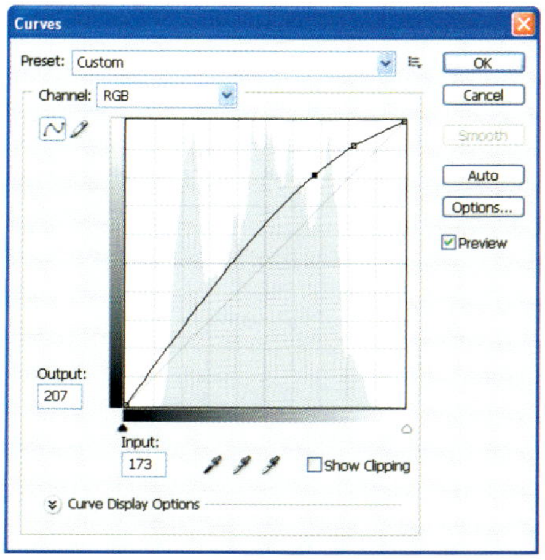

Figure 7.18 To "lock down" part of the curve, place an anchor point between the area you want to adjust and the area you want to leave uncorrected.

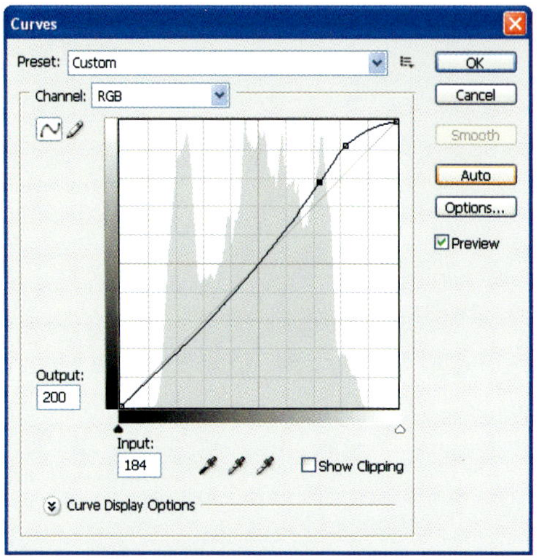

Figure 7.19 By adjusting the "lock-down" anchor point, you can normalize one side of the curve and limit the adjustment to the other side to only those areas you want to adjust.

You can also place anchor points outside those you placed for adjustment, producing something of a barrier outside the range you're adjusting. This won't always prevent adjustments from applying to the rest of the curve, but it will help when the adjustments you're making are relatively minor.

The bottom line is that you are able to use anchor points not just for producing desired changes within the image, but also to adjust the shape of the curve to compensate for unintended consequences of your adjustments. Think of these anchor points as handles that allow you to control the shape of the curve, and use them to produce exactly the result you have in mind.

Note: The best advice I can offer for working with Curves is to use very small adjustments. It doesn't take much to cause a significant change in the image, and frustration with Curves is most often caused by adjustments that are simply too strong.

Curves Pencil Tool

At times you'll find it is challenging to get the curve to do exactly what you want it to by using only anchor points to apply your adjustments. As you adjust one anchor point, the curve moves on both sides, producing an effect that might not be exactly what you intended. In those situations, you'll want to take full control over the precise path of the curve. The Pencil tool within the Curves dialog box provides exactly this control.

Click the Pencil button near the top-left corner of the curve grid, and the anchor points will disappear, leaving only the curve (Figure 7.20). You can then drag with the Pencil tool directly on the curve grid, defining a new curve shape. It is possible to redraw the entire curve if you know exactly what it should look like; however, I recommend using this tool to apply spot corrections to specific, small areas of the curve.

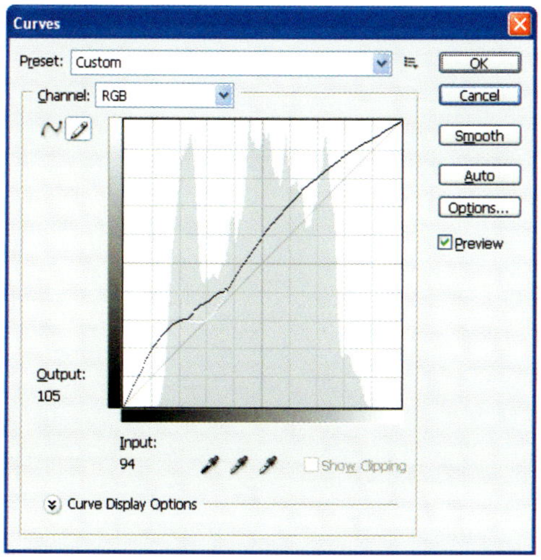

Figure 7.20 When you use the Pencil tool in Curves, the anchor points are hidden. You can draw directly on the curve to define a new shape, fine-tuning areas you weren't able to control as well with anchor points.

I like to use the Pencil tool to manually smooth out small portions of the curve, where the position of anchor points has caused small but radical "bumps." By drawing a smoother curve in that area, you can avoid the problem of abrupt changes within the image and bring the adjustment under control.

When you're finished drawing with the Pencil tool, if your hand wasn't as steady as you'd have liked, you can click the Smooth button to further smooth out the bumps in the curve (Figure 7.21). After refining the shape of the curve, you can click the Anchor Points button to the left of the Pencil button to return to a curve with defined anchor points. The position and quantity of the anchor points will be updated based on the new shape of the curve (Figure 7.22).

Note: Avoid repeatedly clicking the Smooth button; doing so will reduce the effect of the adjustments you've made using Curves.

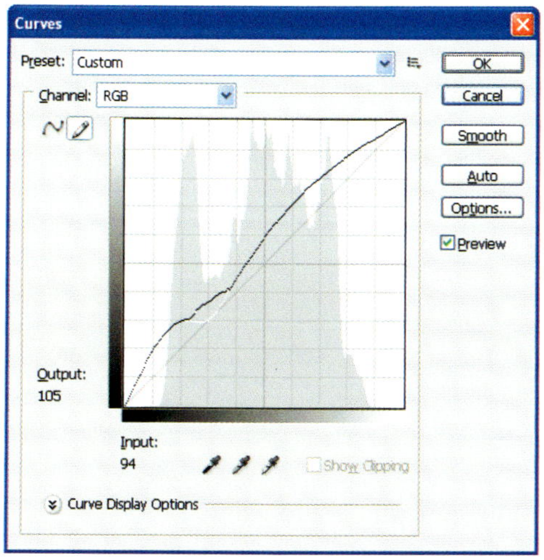

Figure 7.21 Clicking the Smooth button when using the Pencil tool will smooth out the bumps in your curve.

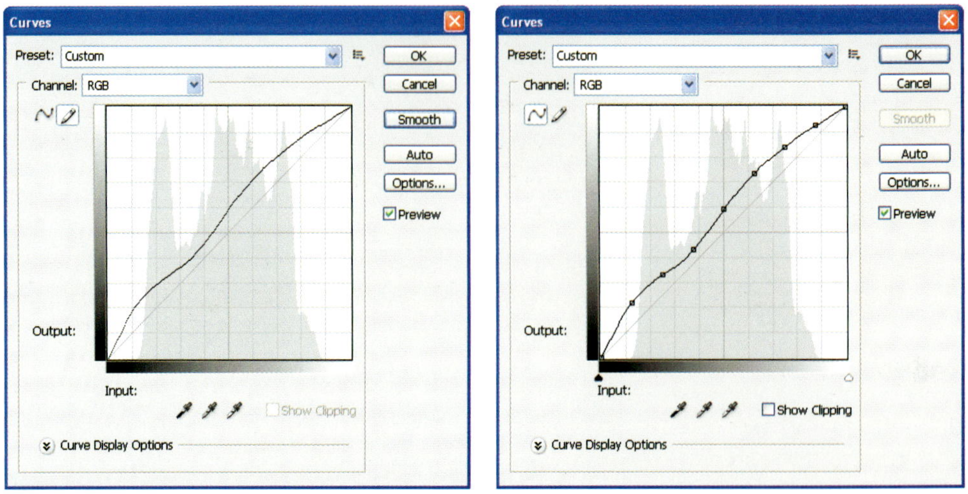

Figure 7.22 After you've used the Pencil tool and switched back to anchor points, the number and position of points will automatically change to maintain the curve you adjusted with the Pencil tool.

Note: If your Curves adjustment is causing undesirable color shifts in your image, change the blending mode for the Curves adjustment layer to Luminosity (using the dropdown at the top of the Layers palette). This will ensure that the Curves adjustment layer will affect only tonal values, not color values, within the image.

Note: Photoshop CS3 includes a new Exposure adjustment, which is designed for adjusting images that will be merged together to produce a high dynamic range (HDR) image. I recommend using Curves instead of Exposure for tonal adjustments to individual images.

Exposure

The Exposure adjustment was added in Photoshop CS2 to provide a way to adjust images that will be merged together to produce a high dynamic range (HDR) image. With CS3, the Exposure adjustment is now available as an adjustment layer, making it more appealing for the type of workflow presented in this book. However, because it is really specifically created for this purpose, I don't recommend using it for tonal adjustments for individual images, preferring Curves instead.

However, there are some photographers who find this new feature helpful. The thing that makes the Exposure adjustment unique is that it adjusts the image in a linear color space rather than the current working space, which is how RAW images are adjusted in Adobe Camera Raw.

The following settings can be adjusted with Exposure:

- **Exposure** emphasizes its adjustment on the highlight end of the tonal range in your image, with very little effect on the shadow areas. This is similar to the Exposure adjustment in Adobe Camera Raw discussed in Chapter 3, "RAW

Conversion," but with the Exposure adjustment this setting is much more focused on the highlights in the image.

- **Offset** allows you to adjust the brightness of the darkest areas of the image. It has only minimal effect on highlight areas, though it isn't as constrained in this manner as the Exposure setting. I recommend making only modest adjustments with this setting, as it can quickly lead to an artificial appearance in the image.
- **Gamma Correction** can be thought of as an overall brightness adjustment that focuses its effect on the midtones in the image.

Dodge and Burn

Up to this point, the tools in this chapter have allowed you to target adjustments to a particular area of the image, but that targeting has been based upon tonal values for the pixels, not their "geographic" location within the image. Now you're going to explore an adjustment that allows you to fine-tune tonality for specific areas of the image, regardless of their tonal values.

Dodging and burning is a technique borrowed from the wet darkroom, where you can use your hands or various instruments to block light from specific areas of an image. Blocking light to small areas during exposure is referred to as *dodging*, and results in the blocked areas being lighter in a print than they otherwise would have. *Burning* is the opposite: blocking light from *most* of the image so you can concentrate light for a portion of the exposure on one particular area, darkening that area of the print.

In Photoshop you can produce similar effects. In fact, both include Dodge and Burn tools on the Tools palette, but I don't recommend using them because they must be applied directly to an image layer and they don't offer quite the flexibility of the method I'll present here.

Setting Up

As you know very well by now, any adjustment you apply to an image should be done on a separate layer, so the first step here is to create a new layer to paint on so you can apply selective lightening and darkening to the image. However, you want the layer you create to have special properties. Therefore, Alt/Option+click the New Layer button on the Layers palette. This will bring up the New Layer dialog box so you can adjust the settings for the layer as it is created.

To help stay organized, I recommend giving the layer a name. *Dodge & Burn* seems a good candidate. However, you can enter any name you like that will help you remember why this layer was added.

The most important setting here, and the key to the whole technique, is the Mode setting (Figure 7.23). This will set the blending mode for this layer, which affects how the pixels on this layer will interact with underlying pixels to produce the final effect. I recommend using the Overlay blending mode because it results in a relatively strong effect and slightly increases contrast. However, you could also use Soft Light if you prefer, which produces a more subtle effect.

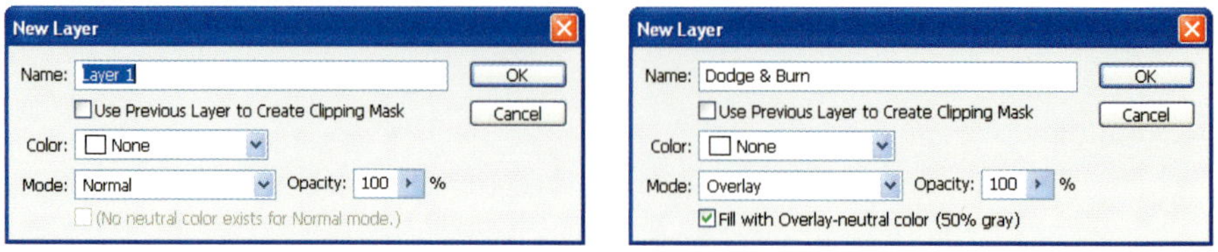

Figure 7.23 Alt/Option+click the New Layer button to open the New Layer dialog box. After the appropriate settings are established for dodging and burning, you can click OK to create the layer.

After you've set the blending mode, the checkbox below will be enabled. I recommend selecting this box so the layer will be filled with 50% gray, which is the neutral color for the Overlay and Soft Light blending modes. Having the layer filled with 50% gray won't cause any change in the image, but it will make it easier to see where you've applied dodging and burning.

Click the OK button on the New Layer dialog box, and the layer will be created based on the settings you've established.

Now you're ready to configure the Brush tool, which will be used to paint with light and apply selective lightening and darkening to the image. Start by selecting the Brush tool from the Tools palette or by pressing the B on your keyboard. Then press D to set the colors on the color boxes in the Tools palette to their default values of black foreground and white background (Figure 7.24). You can also click the small icon below the bottom-left corner of the color boxes to set these defaults. Note that you can switch the foreground and background colors by pressing X as you're working, allowing you to easily switch between black and white.

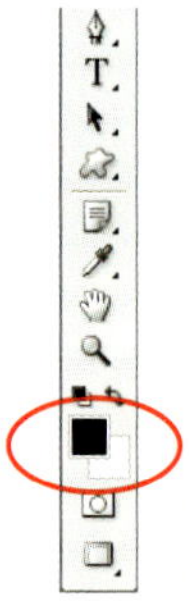

Figure 7.24 Pressing D resets the colors to their defaults of black and white.

On the Options bar, select a soft-edged brush with 0% Hardness. The Mode on the Options bar should be set to Normal because you want the brush itself to behave normally and changes to be applied only by the layer itself.

Note: It is important that the Brush be set to Normal blending mode, and the layer you're painting on be set to Overlay or Soft Light mode.

The tool's Opacity option should be set between 10% and 20%. You can set this value quickly by using keyboard shortcuts: press 1 for 10%, 2 for 20%, and so on. If you want to set the value to something in between, such as 15%, just press 1 and 5 in relatively rapid succession. You'll likely want to adjust the Opacity setting, which controls the strength of the dodging and burning, as you're working on the image (Figure 7.25).

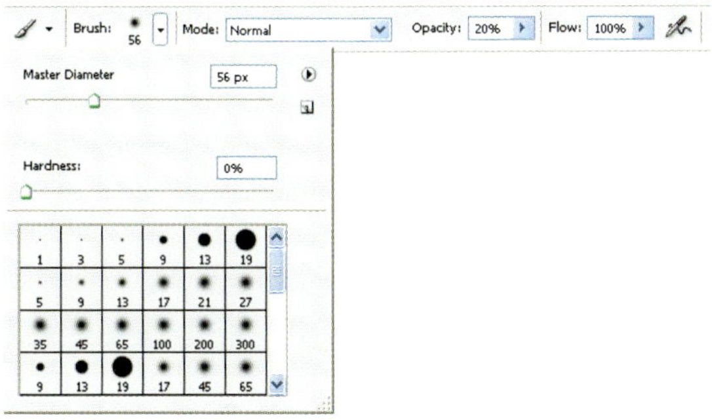

Figure 7.25 On the Options bar, select a soft-edged brush with a reduced Opacity setting for dodging and burning.

Note: If you're using a tablet, you can also use pen pressure of the stylus to determine the Opacity setting when dodging and burning with this method.

Painting with Light

With your new layer and the Brush tool properly configured, you're ready to start painting with light. Paint with black to darken portions of your image, and white to lighten. Because you're painting at a reduced opacity, the result is relatively modest. If necessary, you can paint over areas multiple times to build up an effect. However, the best effect is usually subtle. When someone looks at the final image, they shouldn't get the impression that you were using dodging and burning techniques. However, when you turn off the visibility of the Dodge & Burn layer, you'll see a difference between the images (Figure 7.26).

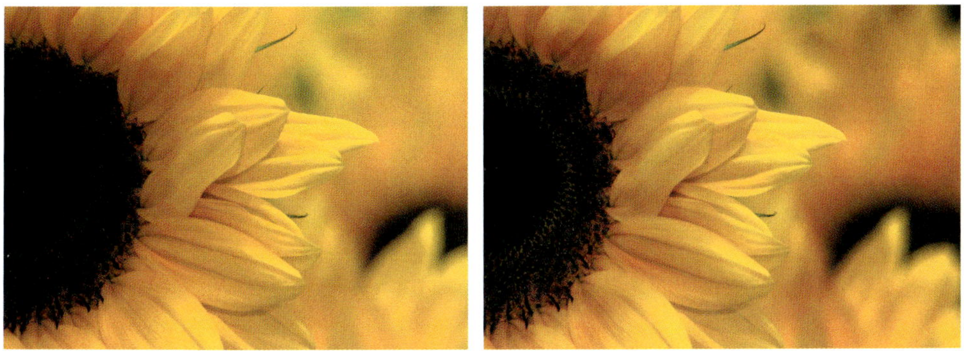

Figure 7.26 The best effect from dodging and burning is one that isn't an obvious modification but that produces a more pleasing final result. Here the center of the sunflower has been lightened to show more detail, and various dodging and burning has been applied to the flower petals to increase contrast.

It is important to understand the behavior of the Brush tool when working at a reduced opacity for this technique. As long as you hold down the mouse button, the effect will not accumulate no matter how many times the mouse pointer passes over a particular area. However, if you release the mouse and start painting again, the effect will be uneven if you partially overlap areas you've previously painted. Therefore, it is important that you click and hold the mouse button while painting until you've covered the entire area you want to adjust. Then release the mouse and start painting again in additional areas you'd like to change.

Dodging and burning is honestly one of my absolutely favorite techniques in Photoshop. I think this has a lot to do with the capability to paint with light, bringing out details in various areas of the image or simply emphasizing particular features. So much of the image optimization process seems very mathematical, adjusting sliders and other controls to apply formulas to an image. The process of dodging and burning is different, allowing you to work directly on the image. As a result, it feels more artistic than other methods and enables you to take great control over tonal adjustments.

Correcting Mistakes

Of course, now and then you may be less than satisfied with an adjustment you've made when using this technique. Fortunately, because it was applied on a separate layer, it is easy to fix mistakes even if it is too late to simply undo a step on the History palette.

There are two basic ways to correct your mistakes. The easiest is to select the Eraser tool and a soft-edged brush, and then erase the areas you don't like (Figure 7.27). Because you're working on a separate layer, all you're erasing are the pixels you painted onto your Dodge & Burn layer.

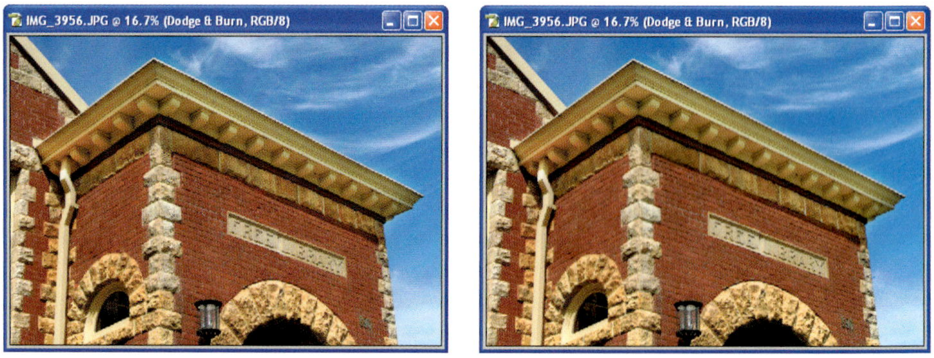

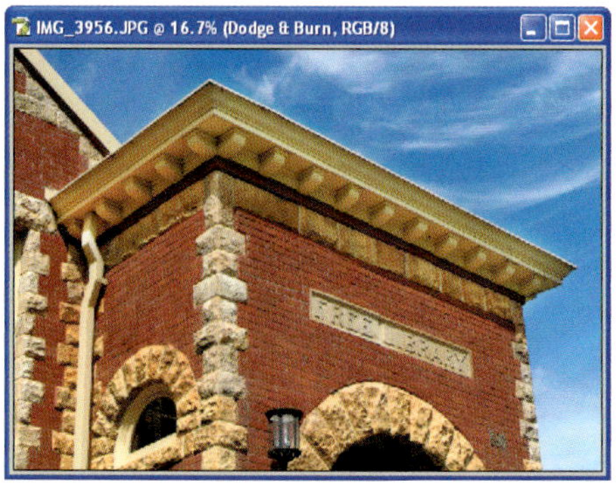

Figure 7.27 You can use the Eraser tool on the Dodge & Burn layer to quickly erase mistakes you made when painting on that layer. For example, here the roof line was over-lightened (top left) and the Eraser tool is being used (top right) to remove that effect from the Dodge & Burn layer (bottom).

Using the Eraser works well, but the disadvantage is that the middle gray pixels that fill the layer will also be erased. This isn't a major problem, but it does make it more difficult to see where you've painted at a reduced opacity if you look at the layer by itself. The checkerboard pattern representing transparent pixels left after erasing doesn't provide good contrast for viewing the partially transparent pixels painted for the dodging and burning effect (Figure 7.28).

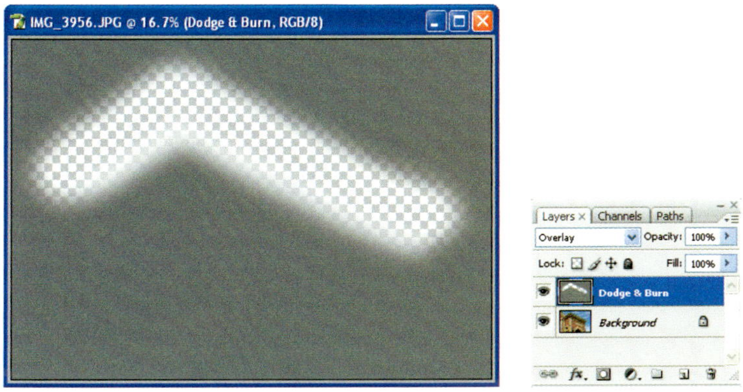

Figure 7.28 When you erase on the Dodge & Burn layer, you'll leave transparent pixels behind (shown as a checkerboard pattern). These transparent pixels, much like 50% gray pixels, won't have any effect on the underlying image.

To avoid this problem, though with a slightly more complicated process, you can instead paint with 50% gray to remove the effect of any dodging and burning in particular areas of your image. To start, click the foreground color from the Tools palette to access the Color Picker. Set the Hue (labeled *H*) and Saturation (labeled *S*) to 0, and set the Brightness to 50. Click OK; then change the Opacity for the Brush tool on the Options bar to 100%, and paint over the image in areas where you want to remove the dodging and burning effect. When you're finished, you can reset the colors to the defaults and adjust the Opacity as desired to continue dodging and burning in other areas of your image.

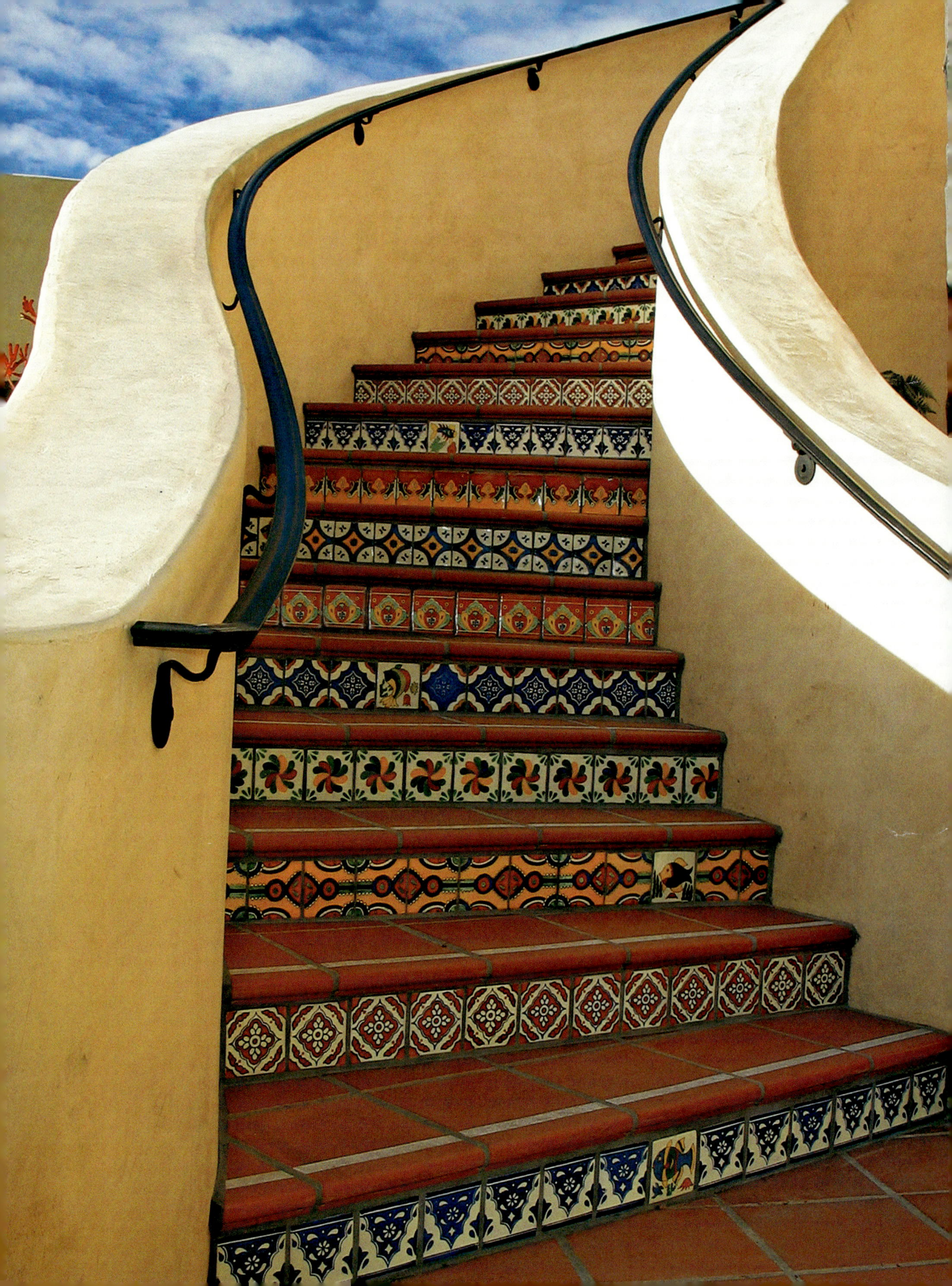

Advanced Color Adjustments

Getting the color just right in a photograph is a major goal for photographers. For many, it borders on being an obsession. When it comes to getting the best results in a photographic image, I think a little obsession is good. Taking the color in your images to the next level requires a collection of techniques that allow you to better control the colors in a relatively targeted way. In this chapter, you'll look at those techniques.

8

Chapter Contents

Hue/Saturation

In Chapter 5, "Basic Tone and Color," we made a basic saturation adjustment by using a Hue/Saturation adjustment layer. However, Hue/Saturation includes considerably more power than that basic adjustment. In fact, it allows you to target specific color ranges within your image to apply fine-tuning to various areas as needed (Figure 8.1). As you become more detailed in your workflow process, you can put Hue/Saturation to greater use to fine-tune various colors.

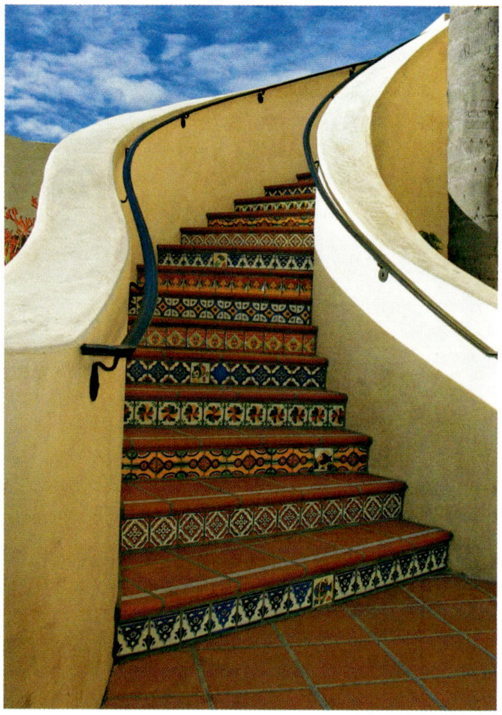

Figure 8.1 When color is critical to the story of a photo, being able to fine-tune the color to perfection is critical. Advanced color adjustments provide this control over the colors in your photos.

Using Preset Color Ranges

The most basic way to target a specific range of colors with the Hue/Saturation adjustment is to select a color option from the Edit dropdown list at the top of the Hue/Saturation dialog box (Figure 8.2). Doing so will limit the adjustments you make with the Hue, Saturation, and Lightness sliders to affect only that color range. You can make individual adjustments for each of the available color ranges or choose the Master option to affect all colors in the image.

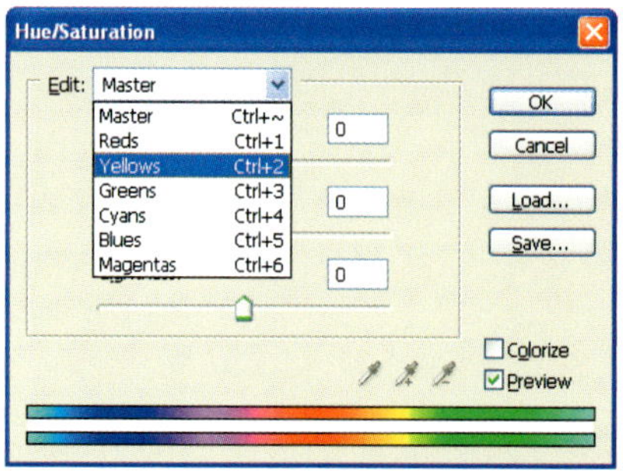

Figure 8.2 You can choose an item from the Edit list in Hue/Saturation to adjust a specific preset range of colors in the image.

For example, if an image has good color balance but a magenta color influence is still causing a problem (Figure 8.3), you can select Magenta from the Edit dropdown and then reduce the saturation. In this case, the saturation adjustment was -44. This will bring the magenta areas of the image toward neutral, eventually to a pure gray if you reduce saturation completely. You aren't limited, however, to just reducing saturation for a given color to remove its influence. You can make any adjustment within Hue/Saturation and have it targeted to a specific range of colors.

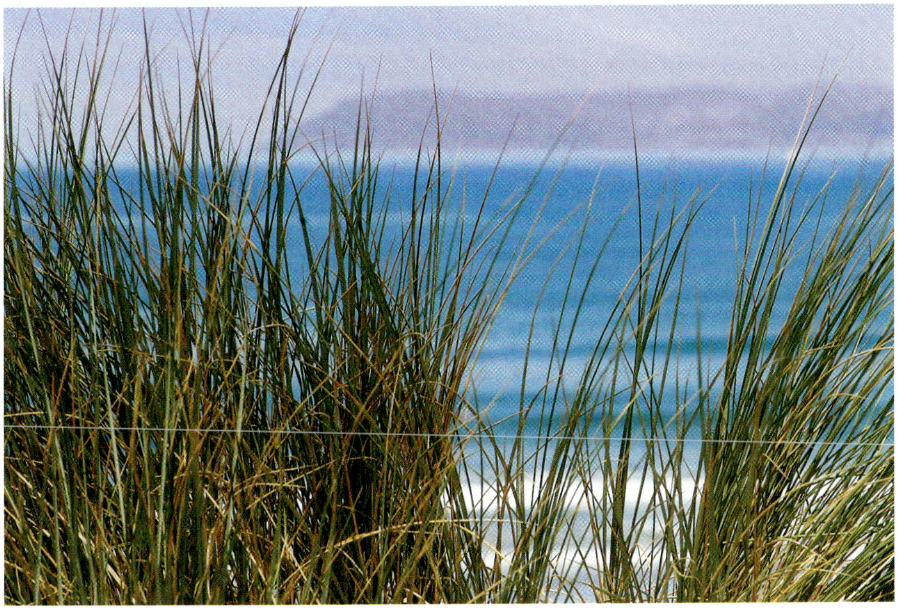

Before

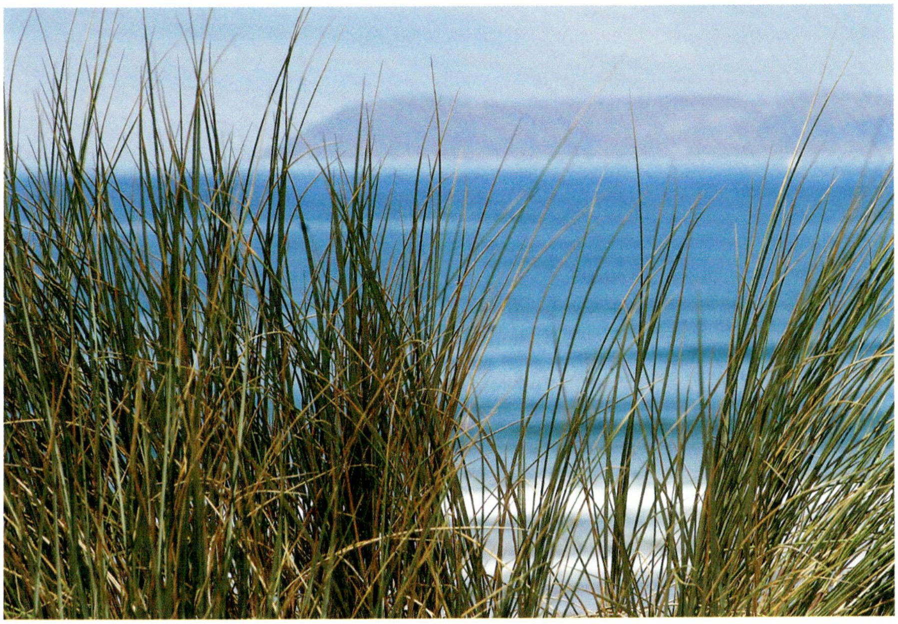

After

Figure 8.3 When an image has an otherwise good color balance but a single problem color, such as magenta in this image, a targeted saturation adjustment provides a solution.

Note: Be sure to check other areas of your image for possible unwanted side effects whenever you are targeting a specific color range for adjustment.

The only problem with this approach is that Photoshop's idea of which colors should be included within a given color range doesn't necessarily match your definition of that range or your goals for the image. Fortunately, you can customize any range of colors to produce exactly the effect you're seeking.

Customizing Ranges

The color gradients at the bottom of the Hue/Saturation dialog box are linear representations of a color wheel. The top gradient represents the range of possible "before" values for the colors in your image, and the bottom one represents the "after" values. When you select a color range from the Edit dropdown, markers appear between the gradients to indicate the colors in the image that will be affected by any adjustment you make (Figure 8.4).

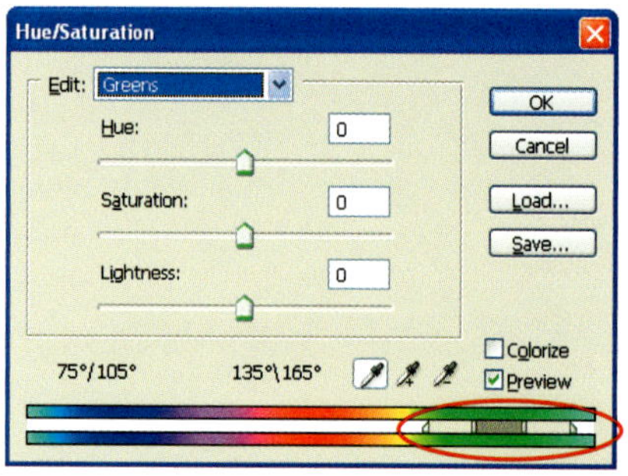

Figure 8.4 When you select a range of colors from the Edit dropdown in Hue/Saturation, that range is indicated by markers between the color gradients at the bottom of the dialog box.

The vertical bars indicate the range of colors to be adjusted. Colors falling between these bars will be completely affected by any adjustments you make. The trapezoid sliders represent the blending of the adjustment. The range of colors between the bar and the trapezoid will have an effect that tapers off, with a stronger adjustment for colors near the bar and a diminishing adjustment near the trapezoid. The distance between the bar and the trapezoid determines how gradual (or abrupt) the transition between affected and unaffected colors will be.

Note: When you change the range of colors for one of the preset ranges, the name may change automatically based on the new range you define.

You can change the color range to be adjusted by simply dragging any of the vertical bars or trapezoids to define a new range. However, identifying an appropriate range of colors just by looking at the color gradient can be a challenge. Instead, I recommend first making an exaggerated adjustment so it will be easier to see the range of colors you've defined within the image. I typically reduce the saturation completely so the range is obvious within the image, but you could also increase saturation completely or shift the hue, depending on what will help that range stand out in your image (Figure 8.5).

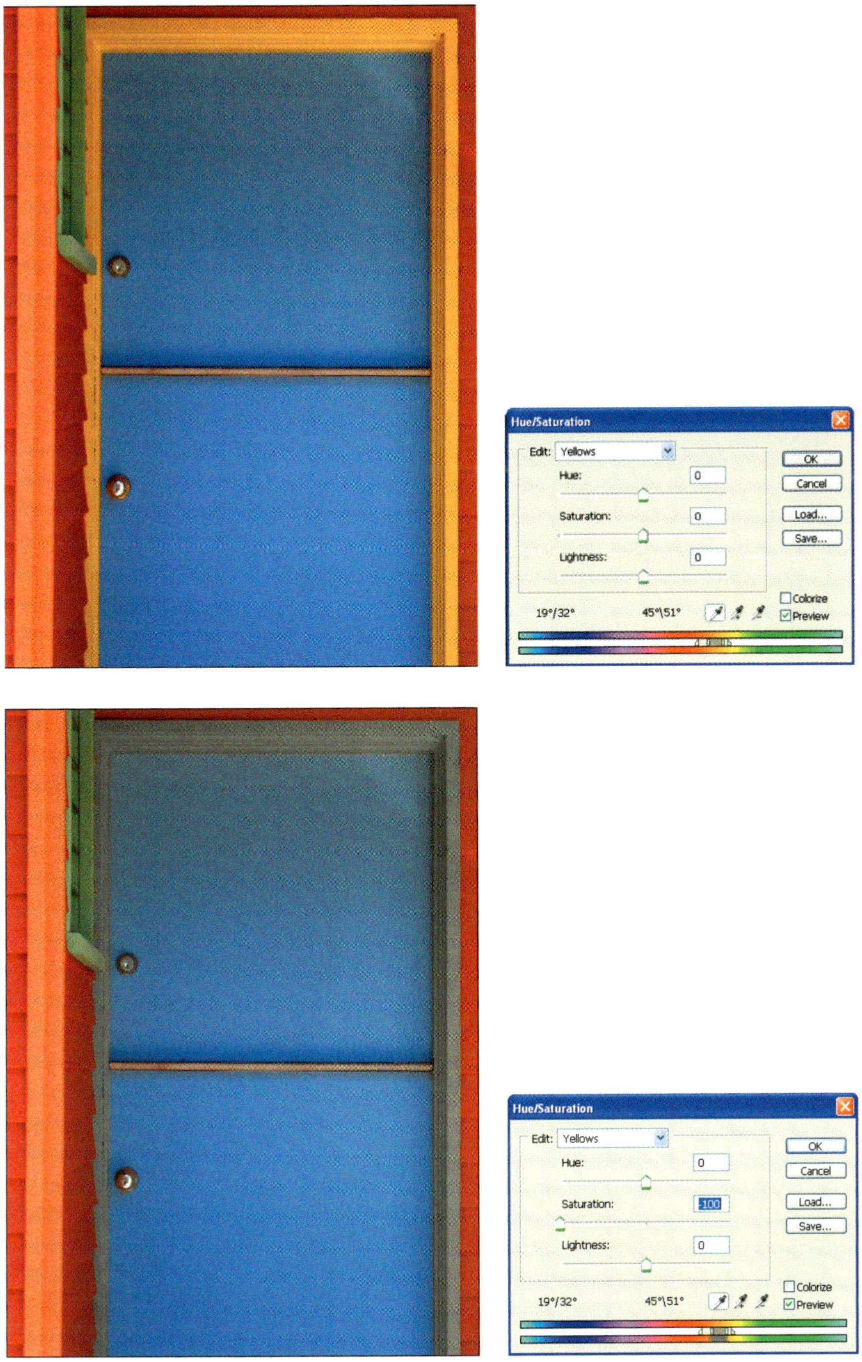

Figure 8.5 It is easier to see the effect of a change in color range by creating a temporary exaggerated adjustment, such as a complete reduction in saturation.

When you start to adjust the range of colors, I recommend keeping the trapezoids pulled in close to the vertical bars in order to see an abrupt difference between included and excluded colors. The vertical bars and trapezoids don't move together, so you may need to shift a trapezoid whenever you move the corresponding bar. After you have positioned both vertical bars so they define the basic color range in the image as accurately as possible, move the trapezoids away from the bars as needed to produce a transition for the adjustment you'll apply. The amount of transition required will depend on how defined the color separation is in your image and on how gradually you want your adjustment to fade away at the edge of the color areas to be affected.

After you've perfectly defined the range of colors, you can undo the exaggerated adjustment (such as a complete desaturation) that you made to help you define the range, and then make the actual adjustment you want to apply to that range. In Chapter 5, I discussed using only Saturation adjustments for an image. However, when you have targeted a specific range of colors within an image, you don't have to restrict yourself in that way to maintain a realistic-looking photo. You can use the Hue slider to adjust the basic color of the specific range you're adjusting, and you may even want to use the Lightness slider (which adds white or black to the color you're adjusting) to adjust the tonality of that range. By using all three sliders, you can fine-tune a specific range of colors to produce the desired results.

Defining Inverse Ranges

At times you may want to adjust the opposite of a given preset range of colors in your image. For example, you may want to boost everything except the shades of blue and cyan found in the sky, so you can improve the vibrancy of colors in a landscape without producing an artificial-looking sky.

To create this range of colors, you essentially need to wrap one vertical bar and trapezoid slider around to the opposite end of the color gradient so you can produce a larger range of colors. To do so, drag the vertical bar off the end of the gradient; it will then show up at the opposite end (Figure 8.6). Drag the vertical bar inward (Figure 8.7), and then adjust the position of both vertical bars so the space between them (where the trapezoids are) defines the range of colors you want to exclude from the adjustment. As in the previous section, it is helpful to have an exaggerated adjustment—such as a complete reduction in saturation (Figure 8.8)—active while you adjust the color range so you can see the effect in the image (Figure 8.9).

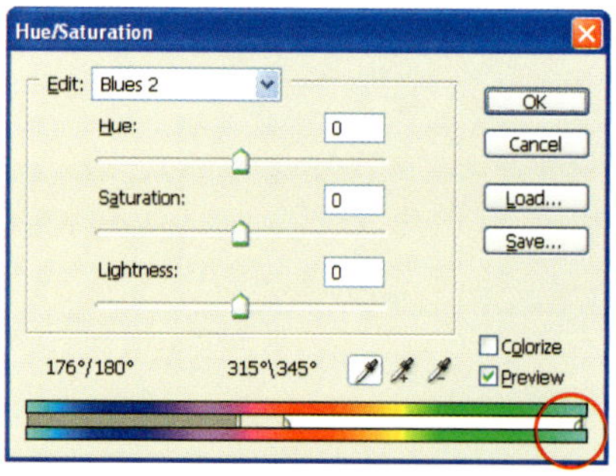

Figure 8.6 When you want to define a range of colors that includes everything except a small range, you'll likely need to drag one vertical bar all the way off the range to place it at the opposite end of the color gradient. For example, here I want to increase saturation of all colors except red, because red is already heavily saturated.

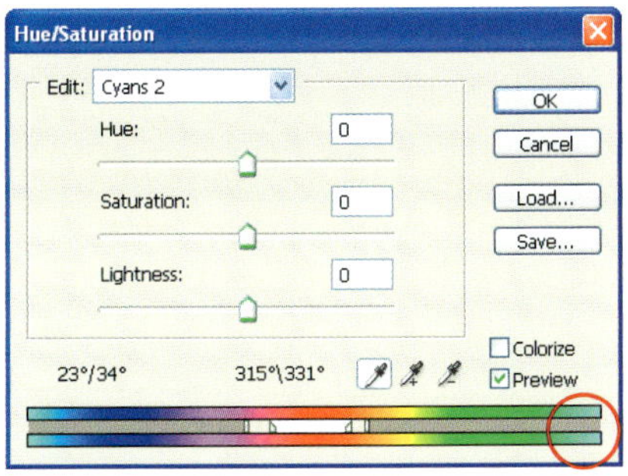

Figure 8.7 After bringing the slider to the opposite end of the color gradient, adjust it to the appropriate position for the color range you want to define.

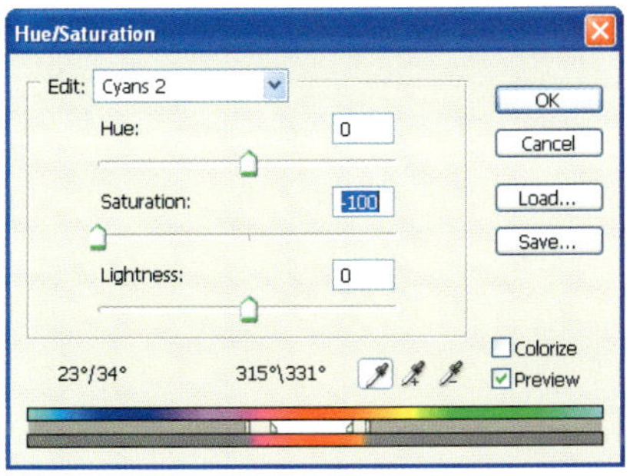

Figure 8.8 A complete reduction in saturation

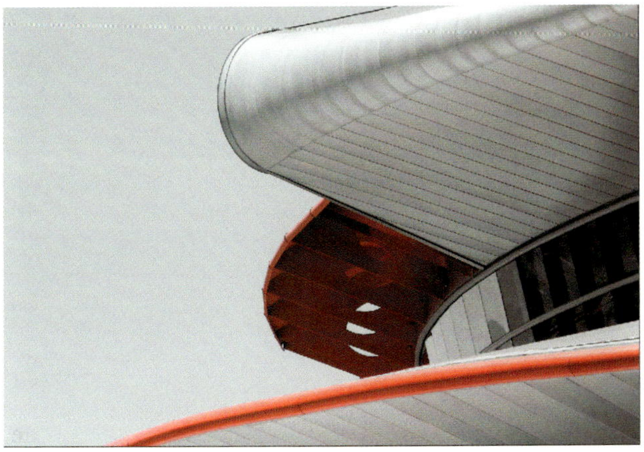

Figure 8.9 An exaggerated adjustment will make it easier to fine-tune the range of colors you want to include in the final adjustment.

With the range of colors defined to include everything except the colors you want to exclude from the adjustment, you can fine-tune the position of the trapezoids to set a blending for the adjustment. Then adjust the sliders as needed to produce the desired effect in the image.

Curves for Color

Chapter 7, "Advanced Tonal Adjustments," provided guidance for using Curves for tonal adjustments. Now that you are comfortable making tonal adjustments with Curves, you're ready to start making color adjustments as well. This is also the point in the workflow where you tend to start making more critical color decisions, requiring tools such as Curves for exercising greater control.

The tonal and color adjustments are performed in exactly the same way, except that the color adjustments are made on an individual channel for the image rather than the composite color image. For an RGB image, that means creating separate curves for the red, green, and blue channels (as needed) instead of (or in addition to) making an adjustment on the RGB composite channel (which affects tonality by default).

The benefit of using Curves for color adjustments is that you can target different color-balance adjustments to different tonal ranges within the image. For example, if your image has too much magenta in the highlights but too much green in the shadows, a color-balance adjustment can be a challenge (Figure 8.10). Even using the Highlights and Shadows options for Tone Balance in the Color Balance adjustment, the overlap is too great to make truly targeted adjustments in those areas. Because green and magenta are opposite colors, fixing the cast in one tonal range will make the cast worse in the other tonal range. Curves allows you to work around this by targeting fine-tuned color adjustments to specific tonal ranges within the image.

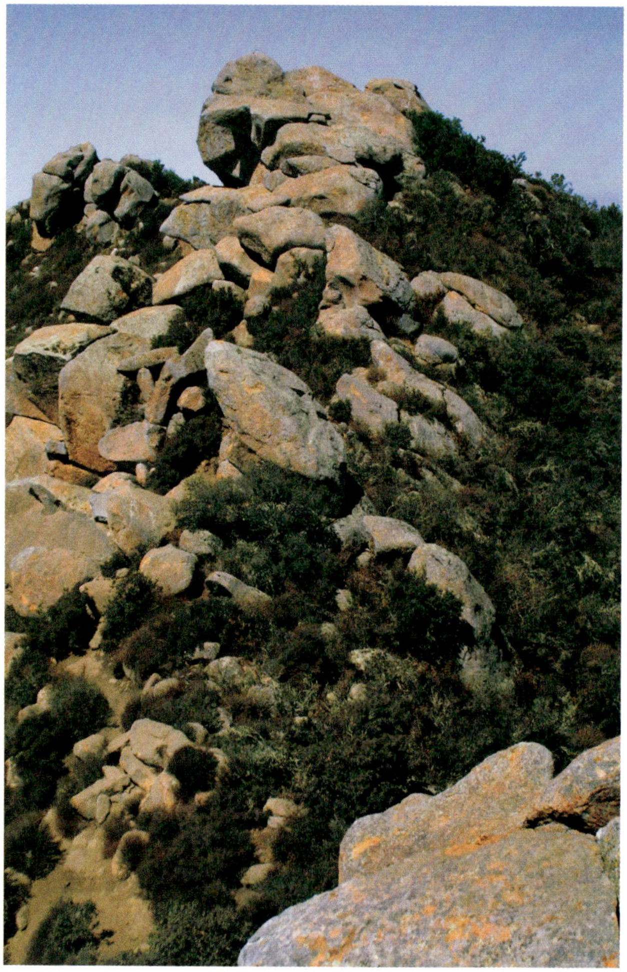

Figure 8.10 In this image, the brighter areas have a bit too much magenta, but the shadows are too green, making a color-balance adjustment a challenge.

Although making color adjustments seems to be very different from making tonal adjustments with Curves, these actions are very similar. Just as a general adjustment to the entire image adjusts overall tonality when you change the shape of the curve, a color adjustment is doing the same thing. The difference is that when you make an adjustment on a particular color channel in Curves, you are adjusting the grayscale image that is the individual channel.

For example, brightening a color channel results in a color shift toward the color represented by that particular channel. So, a brighter red channel would result in an image that is more red and less cyan (the opposite of red). Placing an anchor point at about the middle point on the curve line for an individual channel produces much the same effect as adjusting the slider in Color Balance that represents the same colors (Figure 8.11).

Of course, because you are able to place a large number of anchor points on a curve, you can fine-tune the tonality of the grayscale image for each channel, in turn performing sophisticated color-balance adjustments that target colors of specific tonal ranges within the image.

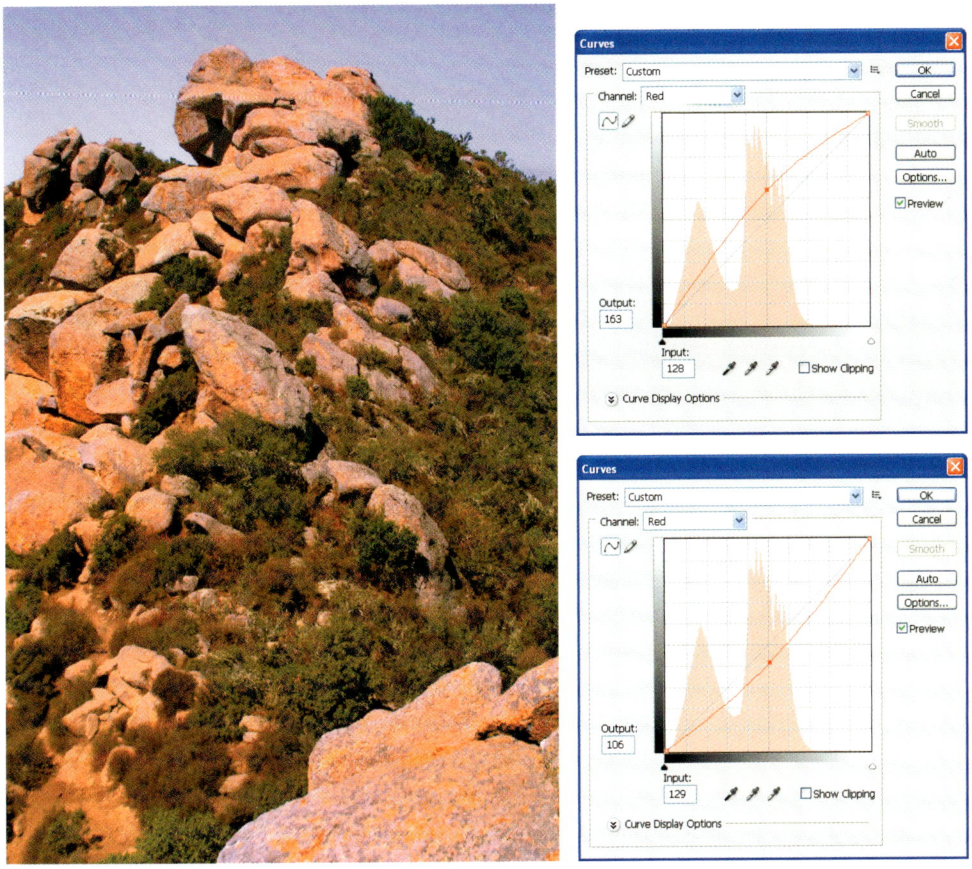

Figure 8.11 Placing an anchor point in the middle of the curve for a single channel and moving it up or down is similar to performing a basic color-balance adjustment for that channel.

Adjusting Channels

The process for making these color adjustments is virtually identical to the way you would perform tonal adjustments in Curves. Start by creating a new adjustment layer for Curves that you'll use for your color adjustments.

Note: You could use a single Curves adjustment layer for both tonal and color adjustments, but I recommend creating two separate adjustment layers to keep these adjustments isolated. You may also want to rename the adjustment layers for clarity.

To make an adjustment, select the color channel you want to adjust from the Channel dropdown list at the top of the Curves dialog box. Then, as you do with tonal adjustments using Curves, click and drag on the area of the image you want to adjust to see the circle that highlights the corresponding portion of the curve. You can hold Ctrl/Command while dragging the mouse so an anchor point will be placed automatically when you release the mouse in the area with the tonality on which you want to focus your adjustment.

With the anchor point created, drag it up or down to adjust the color balance within that range of the image. Dragging the anchor point up or down in the direction of white on the gradient to the left of the grid will shift the image toward the color represented by the channel you are currently adjusting, and dragging toward black will shift the color toward the opposite color (Figure 8.12).

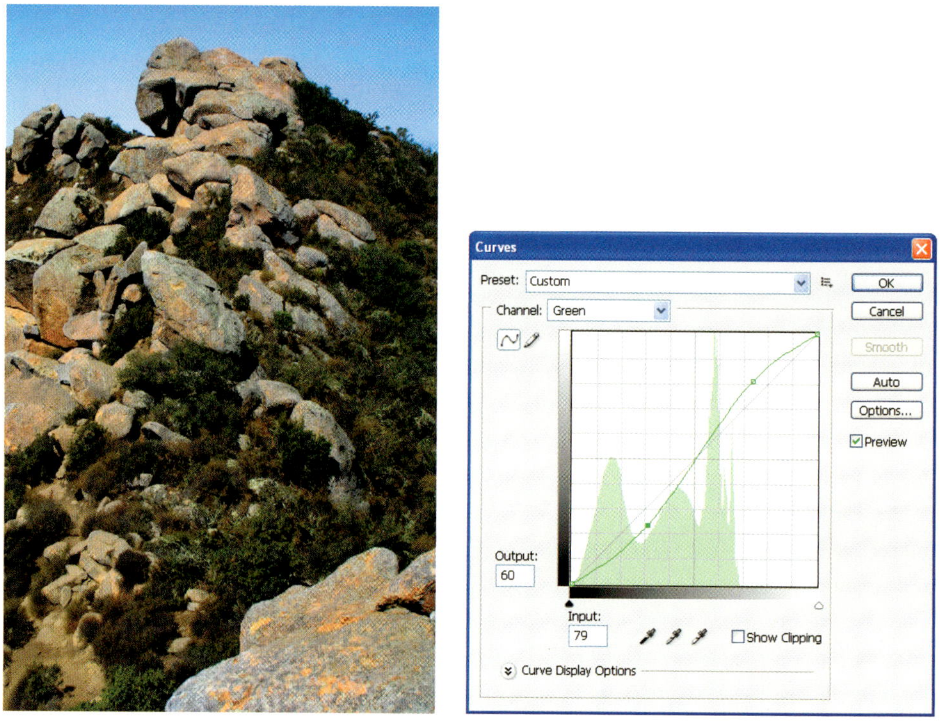

Figure 8.12 To correct complicated color-balance problems in your image, produce a curve for individual color channels that targets the adjustments as needed, based on tonal values within the image.

When making color adjustments with Curves, it is particularly important that you use additional anchor points to lock the shape of the curve (as described in Chapter 7) so you don't introduce color shifts in tonal ranges that shouldn't be adjusted. In other words, the specific shape of the curve is considerably more important when making color adjustments than when making tonal adjustments, so additional care should be taken.

Selective Color

The Selective Color adjustment in Photoshop is designed for prepress work, providing a way to adjust the purity of various ink colors used within an image. It is, therefore, often considered a tool only for CMYK images. However, even for RGB images, it provides an excellent way to fine-tune adjustments for individual colors.

I think of the Selective Color adjustment as a color-balance adjustment that allows you to adjust color balance individually for specific colors. To use this adjustment, first create a Selective Color adjustment layer. In the Selective Color Options dialog box that appears, start by selecting the color you want to work on from the Colors dropdown list (Figure 8.13). Note that besides the basic colors you can also adjust the Whites, Neutrals, and Blacks in the image.

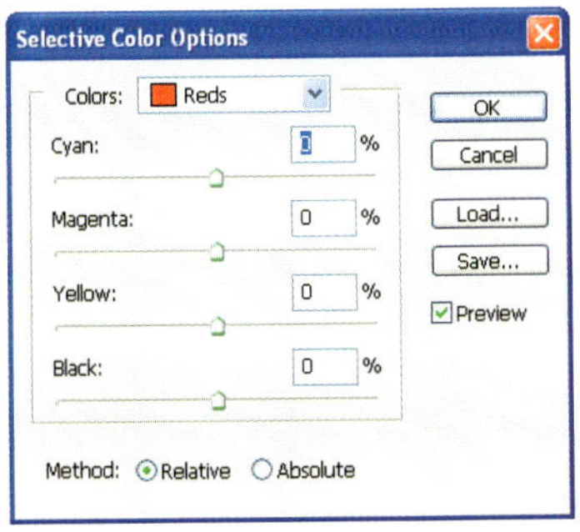

Figure 8.13 The first step to using Selective Color is to choose the color range you want to affect with your adjustment.

Note: The only significant limitation of the Color Range adjustment is that you can't define a custom range of colors, but rather can make adjustments to only the predefined color ranges.

After you've selected a color range to adjust from the dropdown, you're ready to start making adjustments (Figure 8.14). For the most part, making adjustments with Selective Color is the same as using Color Balance, except that the controls aren't quite as user-friendly. Instead of providing sliders that show you the axis between opposite colors, the Selective Color Options dialog box provides sliders only for each of the ink colors used for offset printing (cyan, magenta, yellow, and black). By increasing or decreasing the value for each slider, you are effectively shifting toward the color indicated by the slider (with a positive value) or toward the opposite color (with a negative value). You just need to remember which colors are opposites (red is the opposite of cyan, green is the opposite of magenta, and yellow is the opposite of blue).

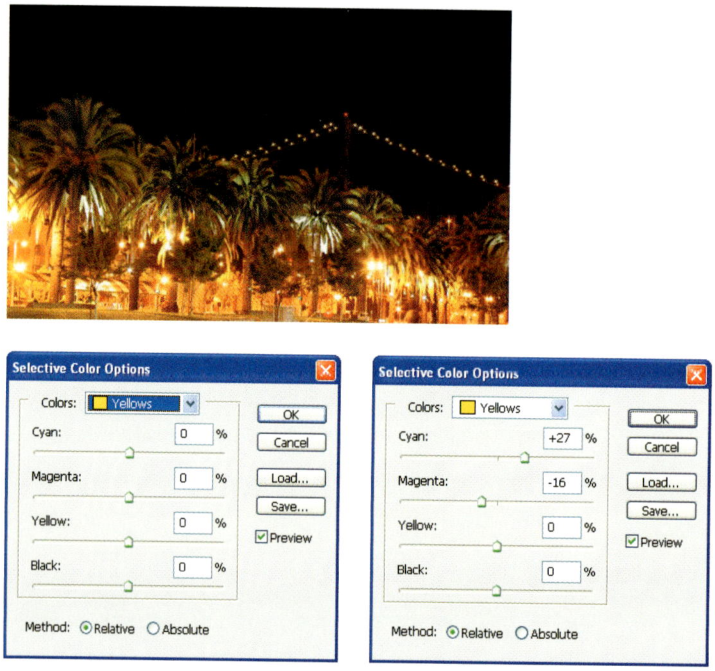

Figure 8.14 Adjustments with Selective Color are essentially the same as Color Balance adjustments applied to a specific color range within the image. Here, adding more green to the yellows improves the color of the palm trees.

The Black slider is, of course, an option you don't have with Color Balance. It allows you to add or remove black from the color you've selected from the dropdown, which in a general sense is like adjusting the brightness of that color. It is more a matter of adding or removing density to those areas, but the perceived result is similar to a basic brightness adjustment.

Note: The Relative versus Absolute option in the Selective Color Options dialog box determines whether the value you adjust represents a percentage of actual color values (Relative) or an absolute percentage increase of the color value (Absolute). I recommend using the Relative option.

I find the Selective Color adjustment to be particularly helpful when the image looks good overall, but one color is just a bit off. For example, if the sky looks a little pink, I can select the Blues or Cyans option from the dropdown (depending on the specific color of the sky in the image being adjusted) and then reduce the value for the Magenta slider. By targeting specific colors and effectively making color-balance adjustments to just the selected color range, you can take greater control over the color in your images than you could have with a general Color Balance adjustment. In later chapters, I'll also show you how to target adjustments to areas of an image based on location within the image rather than color value.

Note: The Selective Color adjustment should be thought of as a fine-tuning adjustment and shouldn't be used until after you've applied a basic Color Balance adjustment to the overall image.

Color Casts

Color casts fall into two basic categories. There are those you want to get rid of, and those you want to add because they are desirable. In either case, there are a couple of methods you can use to apply such a change. A Solid Color adjustment layer can be used to either add or compensate for a color cast, and the average color removal method can be used to remove a color cast. Both solutions can be more effective than a simple color-balance adjustment.

Solid Color

At first glance the Solid Color adjustment layer probably doesn't seem all that useful because the color you add with it completely hides your image. However, it can be used very effectively to add a desirable color cast to an image or to compensate for an undesirable cast.

When you look at your image, you should have a pretty good idea of what color cast you want it to have (Figure 8.15). If you're adding a color cast, this is simply a matter of knowing the color of the cast you'd like to apply. For removing a color cast, the selected color will need to be the opposite of the cast influencing the image. Fortunately, by setting up the adjustment layer properly, you can select a color while observing the change in the image, making it easier to find just the right color.

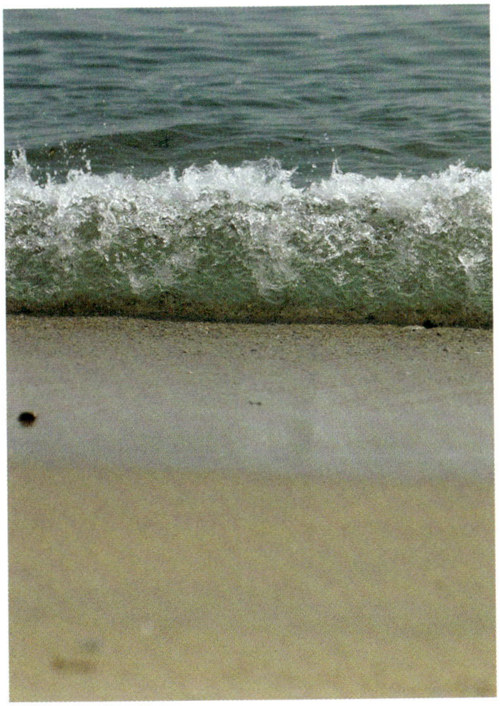

Figure 8.15 When you're going to use a Solid Color adjustment layer, you should have a pretty good idea of the color you'd like to add to the image. For example, with this image I'd like to add a warm cast.

To start, add a Solid Color adjustment layer but then immediately click OK on the Color Picker dialog box that appears. Don't worry about what the color is, as you just want to configure the adjustment layer so you can preview the effect in the image. First, change the blending mode to Color, which causes a layer to be able to alter only the color of the underlying layer without changing tonality or texture. Then reduce the Opacity to about 20% to reduce the effect of the color shift being applied. You'll be able to fine-tune the specific percentage that produces the desired effect, but for now you just want a moderate effect while selecting the color (Figure 8.16).

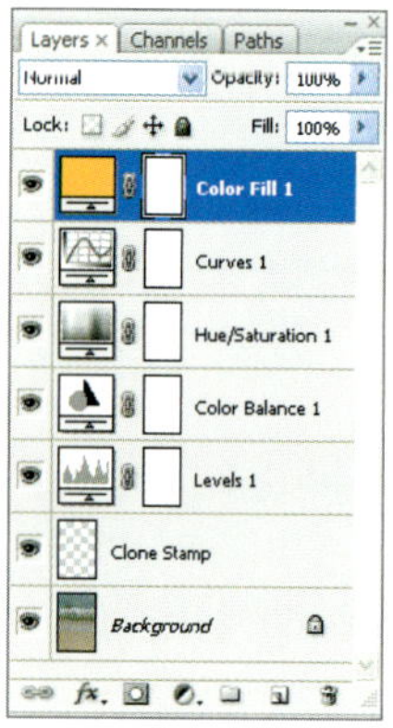

Figure 8.16 When you are using a Solid Color adjustment layer to apply or compensate for a color cast, first create the adjustment layer and click OK; then change the blending mode to Color and the Opacity to about 20%.

With the adjustment layer properly configured, double-click the thumbnail for the Solid Color adjustment layer on the Layers palette. This brings the Color Picker back up, allowing you to select the color you'd like to add (Figure 8.17). Because of the way you configured the adjustment layer, when you select a color the image will update to show you a preview of the effect. With the Hue (H) option selected in the Color Picker, click along the vertical color bar to select a basic color. Then click in the larger color box to define the specific saturation and brightness. Based on the preview in the image, fine-tune your color selection until the desired result is achieved, keeping in mind you'll be able to adjust the strength of the adjustment afterward with the Opacity of the adjustment layer. After you've found the right color, click OK.

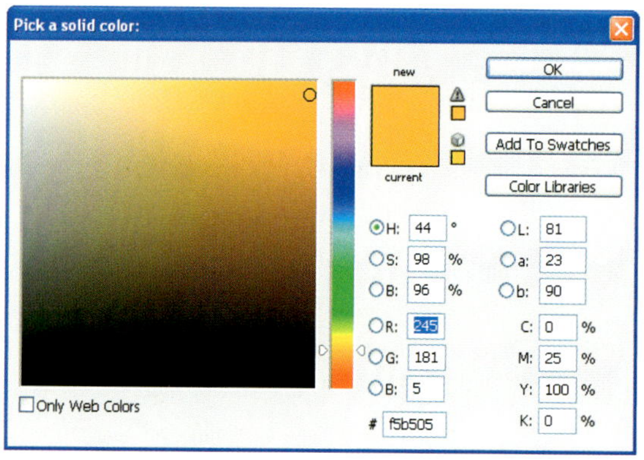

Figure 8.17 The Color Picker is used to select the specific color you'd like to use with the Solid Color adjustment layer.

Finally, adjust the Opacity setting for the adjustment layer to dial in the desired strength (Figure 8.18). Keep in mind that you'll often want to reduce the Opacity lower than you think is necessary to avoid an artificial appearance in the image. I also recommend reviewing the before and after versions of the image by toggling the visibility of the adjustment layer on and off (by using the eye icon to the left of the adjustment layer thumbnail on the Layers palette).

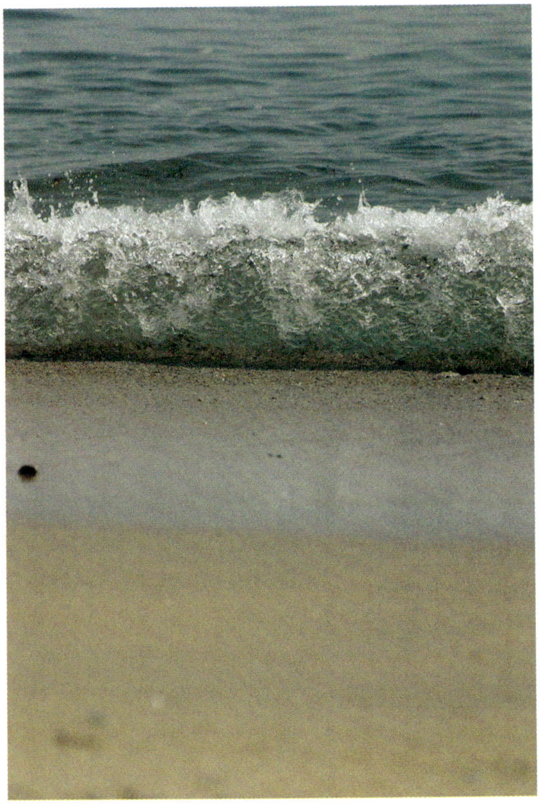

Figure 8.18 With the color selected, adjust the Opacity of the Solid Color adjustment layer to produce the desired effect.

Average Color Removal

When you're trying to *remove* a color cast from an image, trying to find just the right color for the Solid Color adjustment layer can be a challenge. Often, simply compensating for the average color in the image will provide a simple way to remove an undesirable color cast (Figure 8.19).

The first step to using this method is to create a duplicate copy of the Background layer. (Remember, there are several methods for creating or duplicating layers. Here, you can drag the thumbnail for the Background image layer on the Layers palette to the Create A New Layer button; *or* highlight the Background and choose Layer > New > Layer From Background; *or* highlight the Background and choose Duplicate Layer from the palette menu.) You then want to figure out what the average color is for this duplicate layer, which will in turn provide information about the color cast influencing the image. To find the average color, simply highlight the layer and choose Filter > Blur > Average from the menu. The result will be a solid color on this layer representing the average color value for all pixels within the image (Figure 8.20).

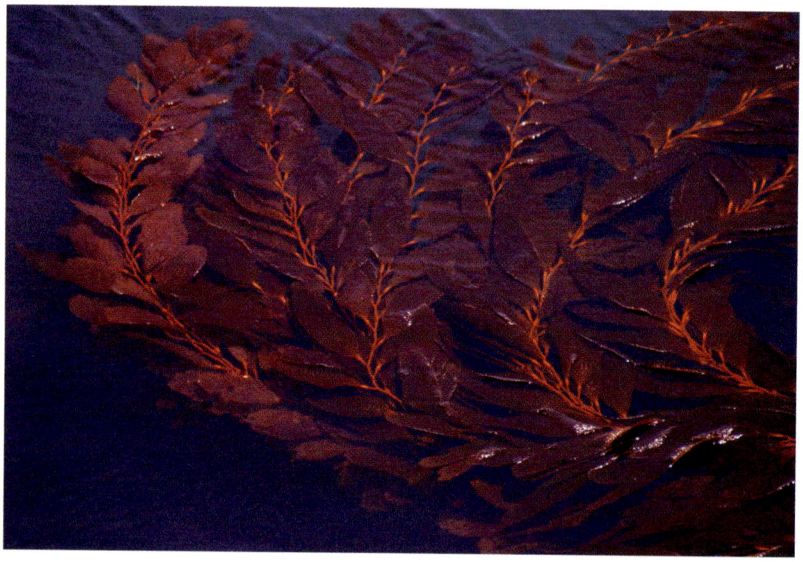

Figure 8.19 The average color removal technique is an excellent way to correct strong color casts in an image.

Figure 8.20 Applying the Average Blur filter to the Background Copy layer results in a layer where all pixels have the same color value.

Because this color is the average of all pixels, it approximately represents the color cast for the image. To compensate for this color cast, you first need to invert it by choosing Image > Adjustments > Invert from the menu. This will "reverse" the color so it represents the opposite of the color cast identified by the Average blur.

Next, change the blending mode to Color so this duplicate image layer can affect only the color of the underlying image (Figure 8.21). Then adjust the Opacity slider for this image layer to adjust the strength of the effect so that it provides a compensation for the color cast in the image (Figure 8.22).

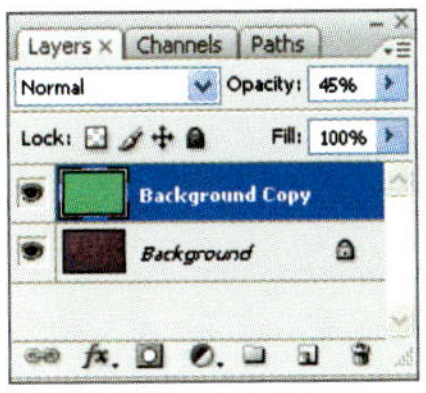

Figure 8.21 After inverting the Background Copy layer, change the blending mode to Color and adjust the Opacity as needed.

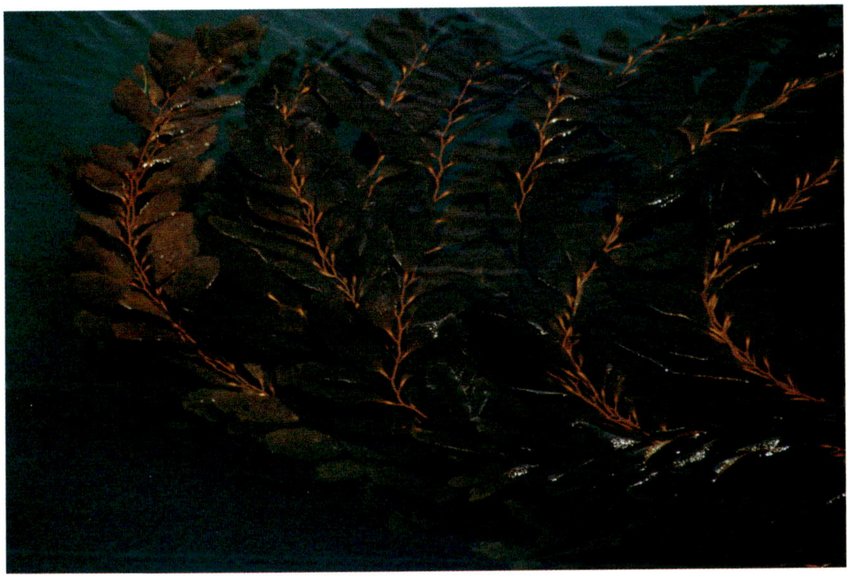

Figure 8.22 With the color cast successfully removed, you may need to boost saturation or contrast to compensate for the "averaging out" of much of the color within the image.

Note: When you're finished applying the average color removal effect, you may need to apply additional adjustments to compensate for the loss of saturation and contrast that can result.

Targeted Color Painting

When you really want to take control over a color fix in your image, sometimes it is best to paint the color right into the image. This provides an opportunity to be precise about the location within the image to be affected, painting color exactly where you need it. Of course, you don't want to simply paint with a solid color over the pixels of your image. Using proper settings, you can paint with color so that the only effect is a change in color in the target areas, without any loss of texture or detail.

I usually use this method to spot-fix color contamination within an image (Figure 8.23). For example, if an object was near the front of the lens when a photo was taken, it will add a translucent color wash to the scene. Photographers often use such an effect intentionally, but when it is accidental it can lead to a color problem. There are many examples of situations that can introduce color contamination without damaging the texture of the underlying areas of the image, and fortunately there's an easy way to fix such problems.

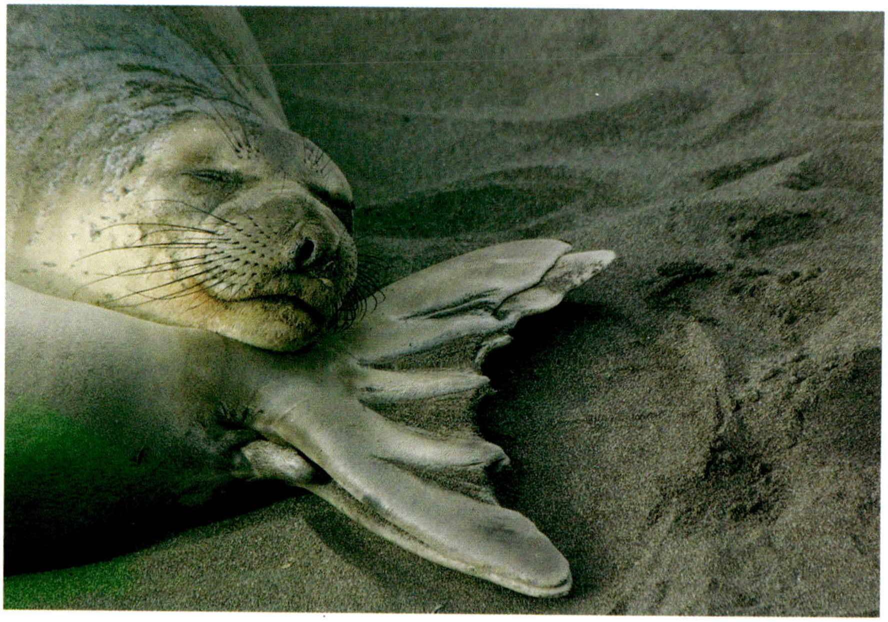

Figure 8.23 Targeted color painting is an excellent technique for fixing isolated color contamination in an image when only the color has been affected but the underlying texture remains, such as the green wash in the bottom-left of this image.

As you can well imagine by now, you shouldn't paint your color adjustment directly onto the Background image layer, so create a new empty layer—not a copy, this time—to apply to the painting. Rename this layer; I usually use *Color Fix* for this type of adjustment, but any name that helps you remember why you added this layer is good.

The key setting for this layer is the blending mode. Because you want to adjust only the color of the underlying image layer, the blending mode should be changed to Color. This will limit the effect of anything painted on this layer so it applies to only the hue and saturation (the overall color) of pixels below, without changing the texture or tonality.

Note: You can also use the Hue blending mode for this technique, which will limit the change to only the basic color value without changing the saturation or brightness of underlying pixels.

With the layer properly configured, the next step is to choose and configure the Brush tool. Click the Brush tool on the Tools palette or press B. On the Options bar, select a soft-edged brush (or set the Hardness to 0% in Photoshop) and set the Opacity to 100%. Now select the color with which you'll be painting. Because you're trying to fix a color in part of the image, it is often best to select a color from directly within the image.

Note: You can also select a color from the Color Picker on the Tools palette if there isn't an appropriate color within the image.

The Eyedropper tool is specifically designed for such a task, but you don't have to switch tools to employ it. Simply hold the Alt/Option key with the Brush tool active, and you'll temporarily get the Eyedropper tool. Before using this shortcut, be sure that you've already set the Eyedropper tool options to use the 3 By 3 Average setting for sampling. While still holding the Alt/Option key, click the image at a point containing the color you'd like to use, and that color will be set as the foreground color (Figure 8.24).

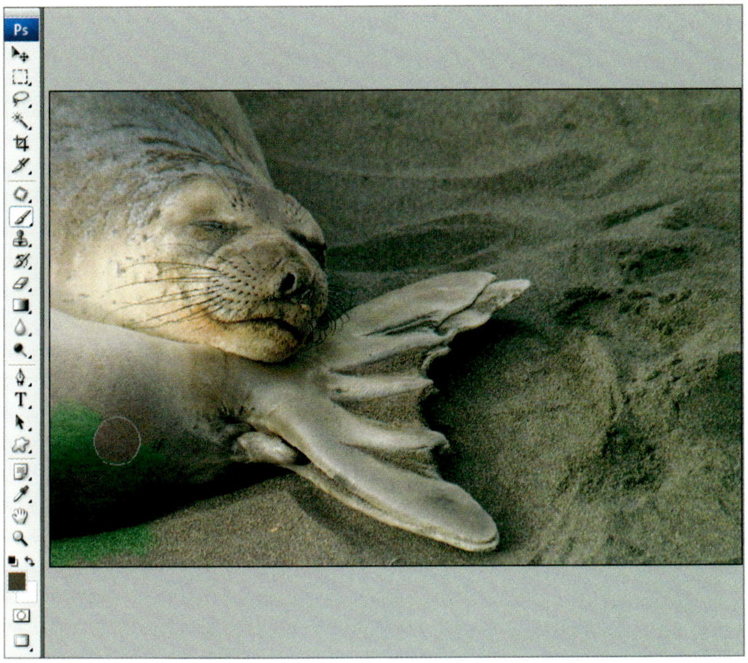

Figure 8.24 By Alt/Option+clicking an appropriate area of the image, the foreground color will be set to the color of the pixel you clicked on so it can be used for painting in the color correction.

Note: Using the Alt/Option key to select a color from within for painting with the Brush tool is similar to the behavior of the Clone Stamp and Healing Brush tools. As a result, it is possible to forget which tool you're using, causing results other than what you expect. Remain aware of which tool you're using, especially if you aren't seeing the behavior you expect.

By painting over the area of the image that exhibits the color problem, you will change the color without affecting the overall tonality or texture of the area (Figure 8.25). You can, therefore, fix minor color contamination quite easily, selecting colors from directly within the image so you'll know they will look appropriate.

Note: If you want to apply a minor compensation for a color problem, rather than completely replacing colors, you can reduce the Opacity for the "Color Fix" layer.

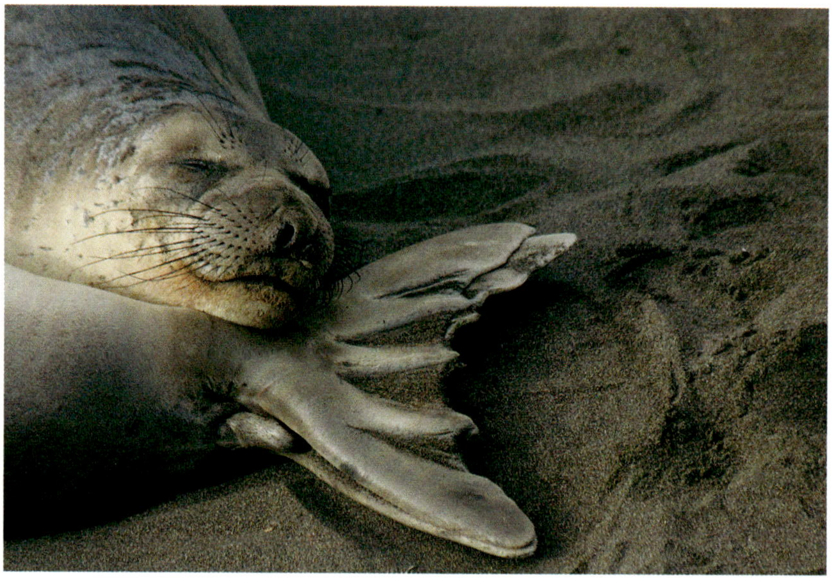

Figure 8.25 Painting the appropriate color with the Color blend mode on the layer will correct the color contamination without altering the tonality of the underlying pixels.

Targeted Saturation Painting

Similar to the technique described in the previous section, it is also possible to paint saturation adjustments to targeted areas of the image. This capability is offered by the Sponge tool in Photoshop, but it requires that you paint directly on an image layer, or on a duplicate layer that doubles the file size unnecessarily. Instead, you can paint targeted saturation adjustments on a new empty layer.

Start by creating a new image layer. Change the blending mode for this layer to Saturation. You may also want to rename the layer to something such as *Saturation Paint* so you'll know why the layer was added (Figure 8.26). Then choose the Brush tool, pick a soft-edged brush, and set the Opacity to 100%.

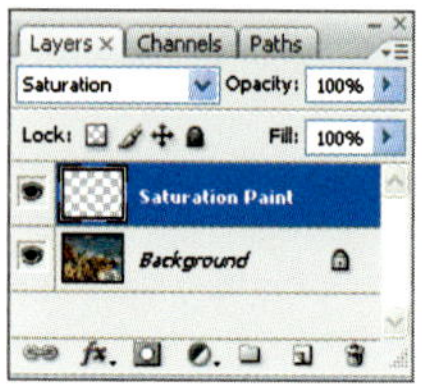

Figure 8.26 To paint saturation adjustments onto your image, create a new layer, give it a name such as *Saturation Paint,* and change the blending mode to Saturation.

The next step is to select a color to paint with by clicking the foreground color of the Color Picker on the Tools palette. However, because the layer you'll be painting on is set to the Saturation blending mode, you need to concern yourself with only the saturation level of the color you select. Therefore, you can click the Saturation (S) option in the Color Picker dialog box, and use the small vertical gradient bar to select the saturation level you want to use (Figure 8.27).

Another alternative to selecting a specific saturation level is to simply choose a fully saturated color if you're working to increase saturation, or choose a completely desaturated color if you're working to decrease saturation. You can then adjust the Opacity setting for the Brush on the Options bar to vary the strength of the adjustment. Just keep in mind that, when painting at a reduced opacity, you should hold the mouse down as you paint over the entire area that you want to adjust before releasing the mouse. Otherwise, you may paint over some areas more than once, causing an uneven adjustment to the image.

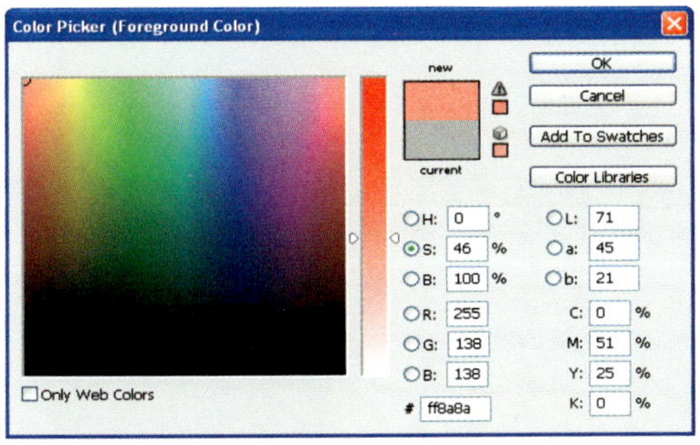

Figure 8.27 Use the Color Picker to select an appropriate saturation level (the actual color doesn't matter) for painting an adjustment on your image.

With the color properly selected, you can simply paint on the image to apply saturation adjustments in a selective way (Figure 8.28). When you need to vary the effect you're applying, simply choose a color with a different saturation level in the Color Picker or adjust the Opacity setting for the Brush on the Options bar.

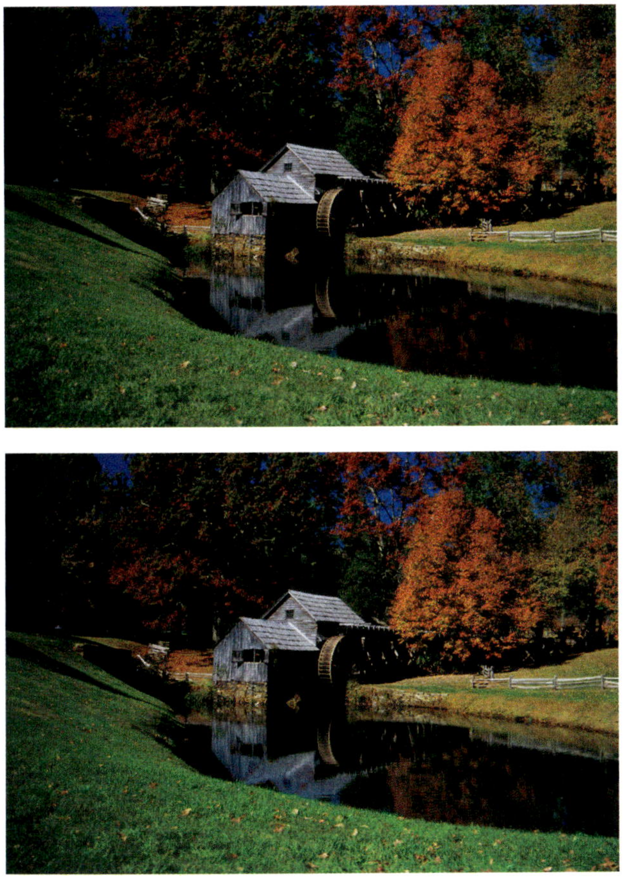

Figure 8.28 Painting with a color at a particular saturation level onto a separate layer set to the Saturation blending mode allows you to perform targeted adjustments to saturation within the image. In this image, the grass in the foreground was made more vibrant without oversaturating the background trees. (Photo by Gabby Salazar)

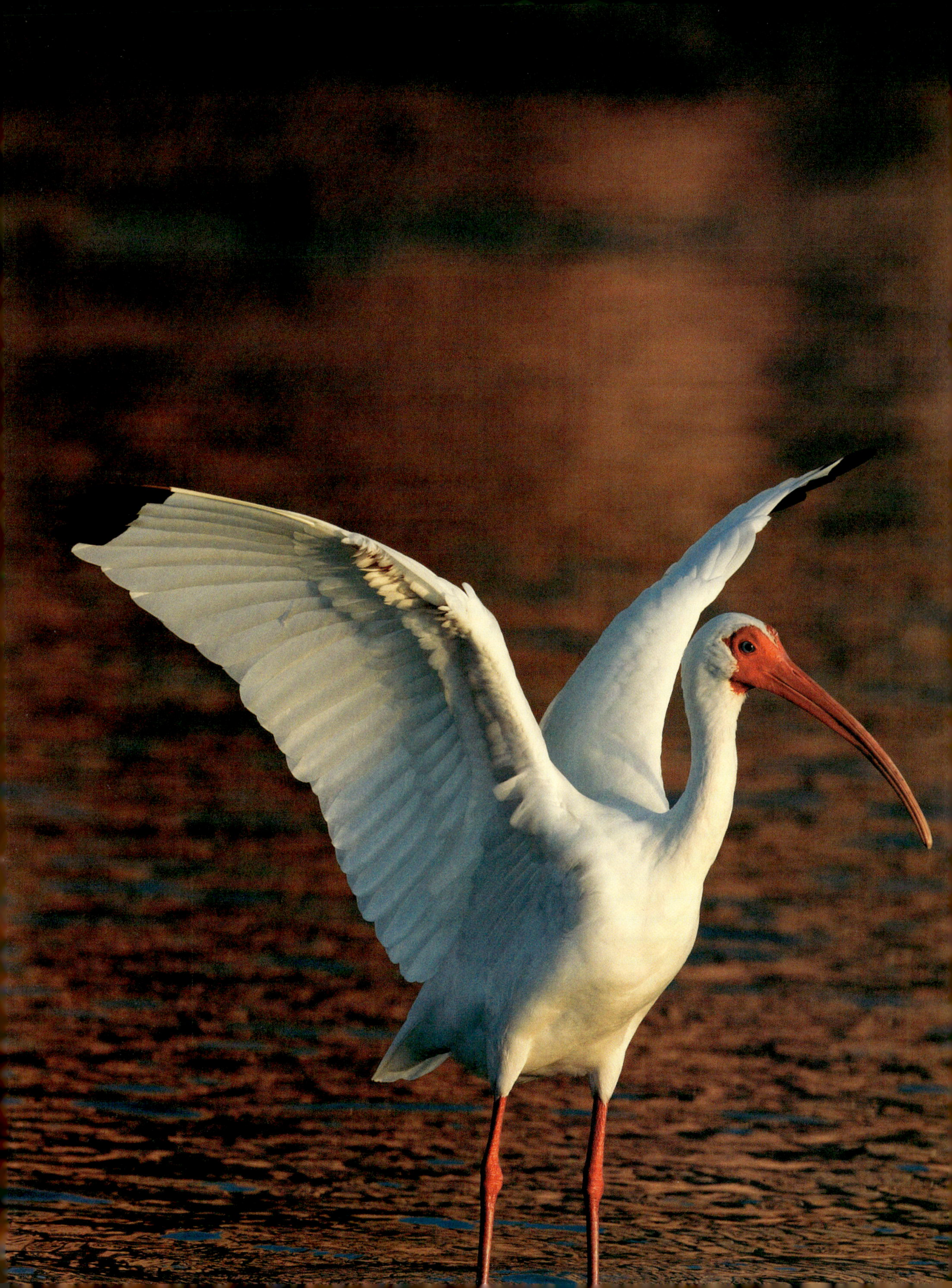

Making Selections

This chapter marks a turning point in the control you will be able to exercise over your images. In previous chapters, the adjustments you made either applied to the entire image or could be targeted in only relatively limited ways. Selections allow you to take full control over your images by enabling you to make adjustments to the specific areas you would like and to produce an image that is exactly what you envision. The first step in exercising this control is to create the selections that define the areas you'd like to adjust within your image.

9

Chapter Contents

Understanding the Selection Tools

Photoshop includes built-in tools for creating selections, most of which can be found directly on the Tools palette. Understanding these selection tools is the key to getting started with targeted adjustments, and it provides a strong foundation for the other selection methods I'll discuss later in this chapter. Creating a selection is the first step toward adjusting specific areas of your images (Figure 9.1).

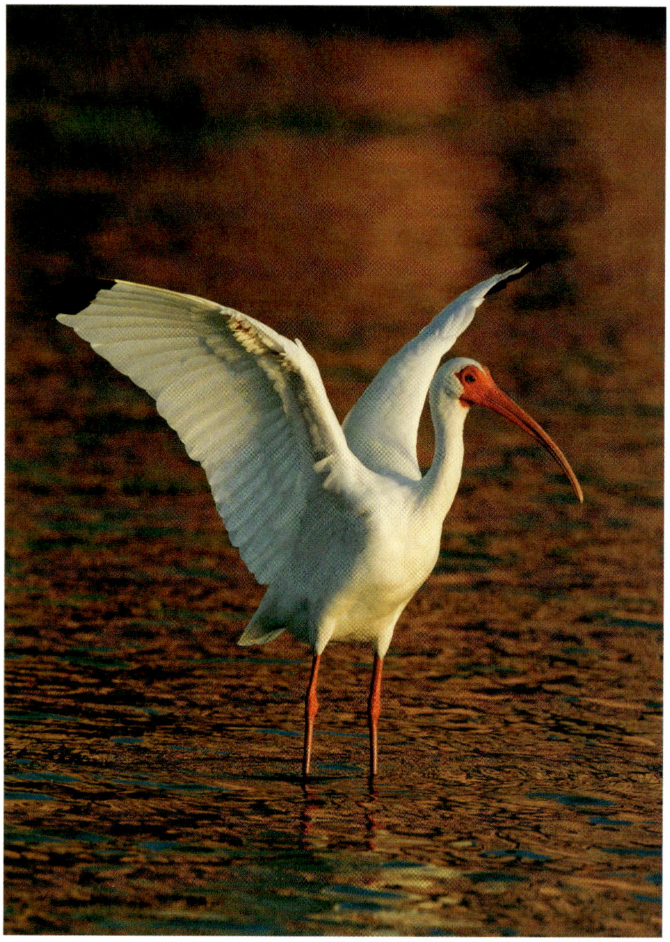

Figure 9.1 When you want to create adjustments targeted to a particular area of the image, a selection is the first step. For example, if you want to increase contrast in the background of this image without creating excessive contrast in the bird, first create a selection that defines the background. (Photo by Art Morris, www.birdsasart.com)

Marquee

The Marquee tools are the most basic selection tools, which is another way of saying they are the least powerful. In fact, when it comes to making targeted adjustments to your images, these tools are frankly not up to the job. However, because the Marquee tools are relatively simple in their operation, starting with them helps to lay the groundwork for selections in general.

There are four Marquee tools: Rectangular, Elliptical, Single Row, and Single Column. However, the Single Row and Single Column Marquee tools simply select one row or column of pixels in line with the pixel you click, which isn't typically useful for photographic images.

The complete set of Marquee tools can be activated by clicking the mouse and holding the mouse pointer on the current Marquee tool on the Tools palette; you can then choose the desired tool from the flyout menu. You can also press M on your keyboard to choose the current Marquee tool, and then press Shift+M to cycle through the various Marquee tools. For our purposes, we'll focus on the Rectangular and Elliptical Marquee tools. They work the same way, with the only difference being the general shape of the selection created.

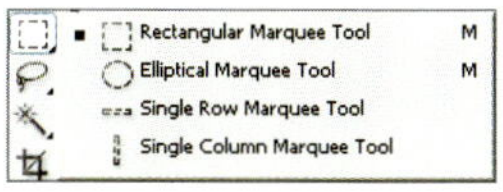

Note: You can remove the requirement to hold the Shift key to switch between tools with the same shortcut key by clearing the Use Shift Key For Tool Switch checkbox in Preferences. However, I don't recommend doing so.

To create a selection with the Rectangular or Elliptical Marquee tool, first imagine a rectangle bounding the area you would like to select in your image. Move the mouse pointer to any one of the corners of that imaginary rectangle, and then click and drag to the imaginary corner diagonally opposite your starting point. As you're dragging, a dashed rectangle or ellipse will be formed. When you release the mouse, that shape becomes the selection, outlined by the "marching ants" display defining the border of the selection (Figure 9.2). All pixels inside the border are selected.

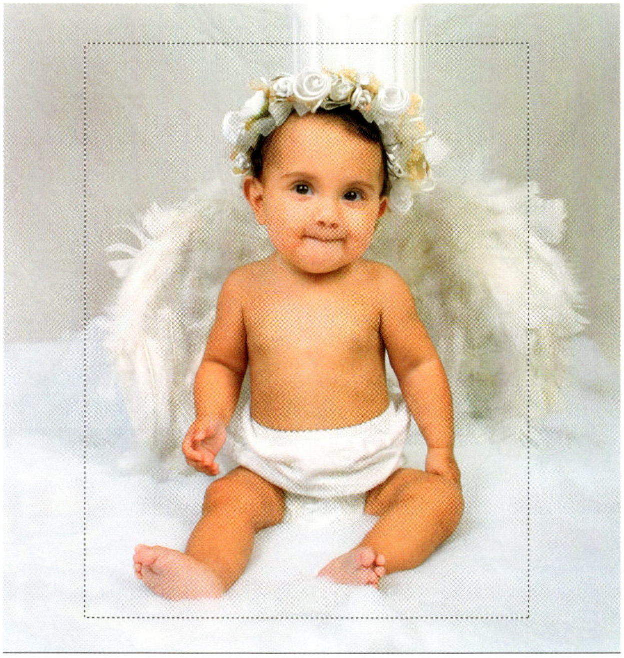

Figure 9.2 When you drag a box with the Rectangular or Elliptical Marquee tool, the selection defined by that bounding box will be created on your image. (Photo by Chris Greene, ImageWest Photography)

While you're dragging to define the selection, there are several modifier keys you can use to change the behavior of the tool. Press and hold the Shift key to constrain the selection to a perfect square or circle. If you press and hold the Alt/Option key after you've started creating the selection, the selection will be centered on your starting point (Figure 9.3). Holding both keys will cause both effects to apply. Keep in mind that these modifier keys must be pressed after you start creating the selection or you won't get the expected behavior because these shortcut keys also enable the Add To Selection and Subtract From Selection options (discussed later in this section).

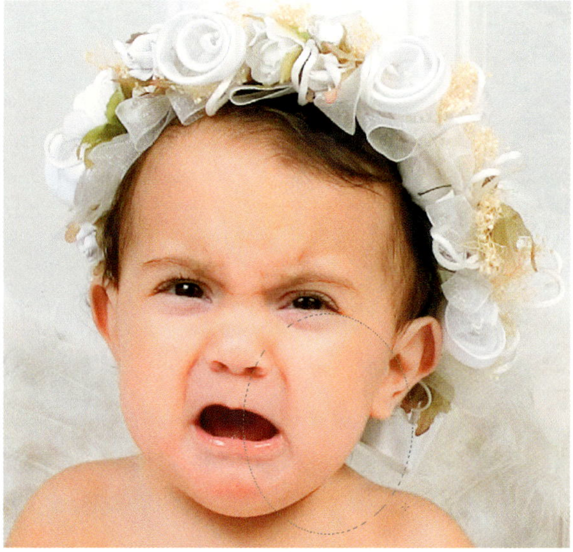

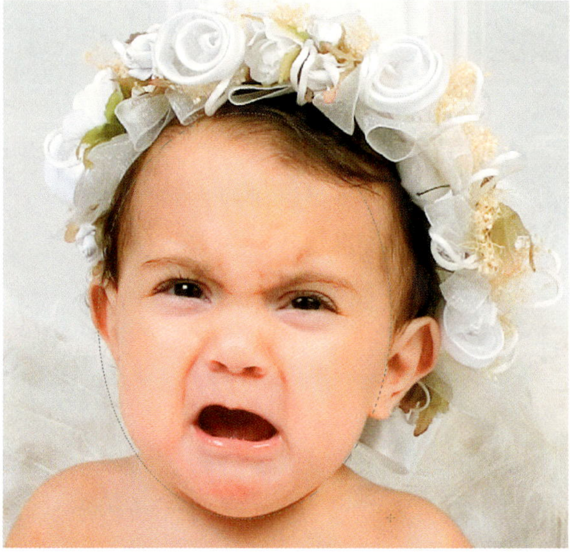

Figure 9.3 Normally, the Marquee tools create a selection that has a corner on your starting point (top), which in this case was near the nose of the baby. Holding the Alt/Option key will cause the selection to be centered on your starting point (bottom). (Photo by Chris Greene, ImageWest Photography)

You can also change the position of the selection as you're drawing it with one of the Marquee tools. After you've started dragging to define the selection, press and hold the spacebar. This will activate the Hand tool temporarily; however, because you're in the middle of creating a selection, it will allow you to move the selection around, rather than the image (Figure 9.4). After the selection is made, the spacebar will go back to allowing you to move the currently active image layer, not the selection.

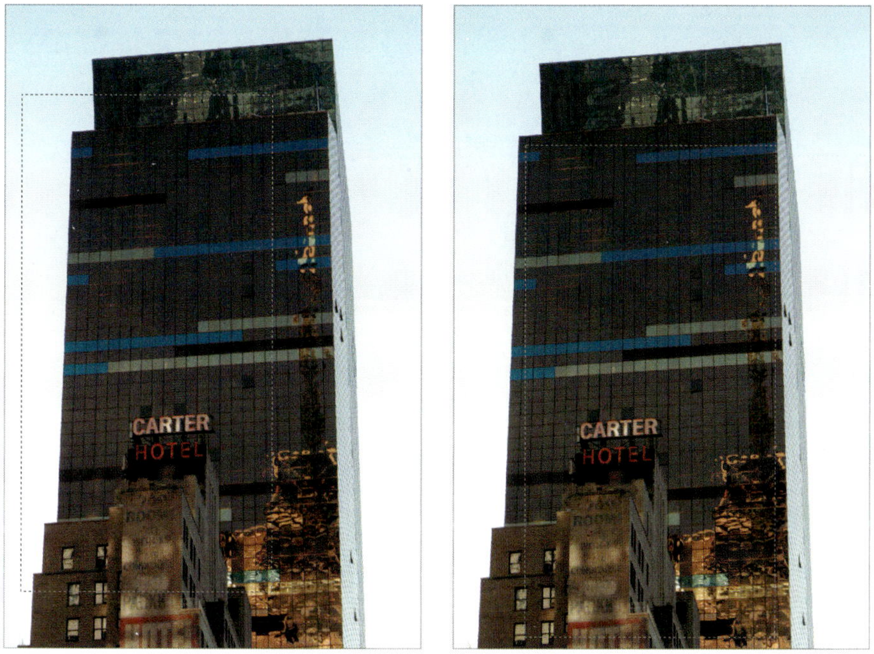

Figure 9.4 Holding the spacebar allows you to drag to move the selection while you're in the process of creating it with one of the Marquee tools.

The Options bar contains settings for the Marquee tools (Figure 9.5). I'll save some of these settings for the next section because they affect all selection tools. For the Feather setting, I recommend using a value of 0 px (zero pixels), so that no feathering is applied. I'll explain how to apply feathering when we get to making targeted adjustments in Chapter 10, "Targeted Adjustments."

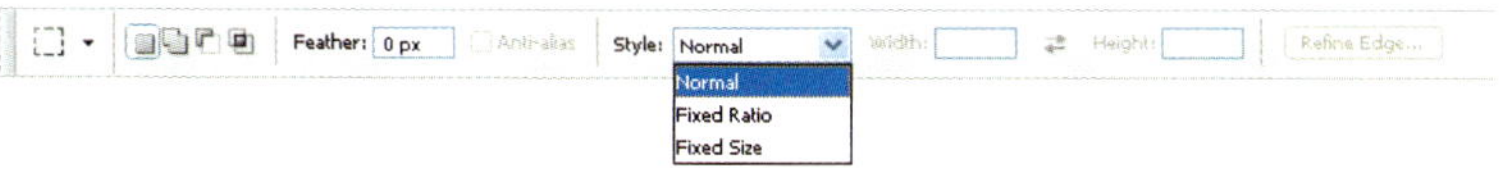

Figure 9.5 The Options bar includes settings for the Marquee tools.

For the Rectangular and Elliptical Marquee tools, a Style dropdown list is available on the Options bar. The Normal option is the one you would usually want to use because it allows total flexibility in the dimensions of your selection. However, at times you may want to constrain your selection to a specific size or aspect ratio. These options are helpful when you want to crop an image to a specific size, vignette an image, or mask out an image with a fixed shape and size.

The Fixed Aspect Ratio option allows you to set a specific relationship between width and height in the selection you'll create. When you choose this option, the Width and Height text boxes become active on the Options bar, and you can enter values for each. This won't limit you to a specific selection size, only a fixed *relationship* between width and height. As you drag the mouse after your initial click, no matter what direction you drag, the general shape of the selection will be fixed, with your mouse movement affecting only the size of the selection.

The Fixed Size option allows you to create a selection of a specific size. When you choose this option, the Width and Height text boxes become available. Enter values for both dimensions, using *px* for pixels, *in* for inches, or *cm* or *mm* for metric measurements. For example, to create a selection that is exactly 8″×10″, set the Width to 8 in and the Height to 10 in. When you click the image, a selection of exactly those dimensions will be created, and the spot you clicked will define the top-left corner of the selection area. If you click and drag, you can't change the shape of the selection, but you can change the starting position of the selection. Note that when measuring in inches, the sizing will be based on the current output resolution for the image, so you should set that first by using the Image Size dialog box (Image > Image Size).

An option that is available for only the Elliptical Marquee tool (not the other Marquee tools) is the Anti-Aliased checkbox. With this selected, the edges of the selection will be smoothed so they don't have a jagged appearance. This is a particular concern for curved edges or diagonal lines, which is why it is an issue for the Elliptical Marquee tool.

Selection Modes

With the Marquee selection tools under control, you can start making more complicated selections by adding pixels to or subtracting pixels from a selection. Start by using one of the Marquee tools to create a basic selection. To the right of the Tool Preset dropdown list on the Options bar is a set of four buttons that allows you to modify the behavior of these (and other) selection tools.

Note: The options discussed in this section can be applied to any of the selection tools in Photoshop.

The first button causes the current selection tool to behave in the "normal" manner, creating a new selection whenever you use the tool. This is the option I typically keep active at all times, using shortcut keys to access the other options.

The second button is the Add To Selection option. With this option chosen, whenever you use a selection tool to surround pixels, the new selection will be added to the existing selection (Figure 9.6). For example, if you use the Rectangular Marquee tool to create a rectangular area, you could then turn that into a more complicated polygon shape by dragging to create additional selection areas. You can also hold the Shift key to access the Add To Selection option regardless of the current state of the tool.

The third button in the set is the Subtract From Selection option, which allows you to subtract pixels from an existing selection. When this button is selected, creating a selection marquee will cause the surrounded pixels to be omitted from the existing selection (Figure 9.7). For example, if you start with a circular selection created with the Elliptical Marquee tool, and then draw another circle inside this selection with the

Subtract From Selection button chosen, the result will be a "doughnut" selection. You can access this option by holding the Alt/Option key when using any selection tool.

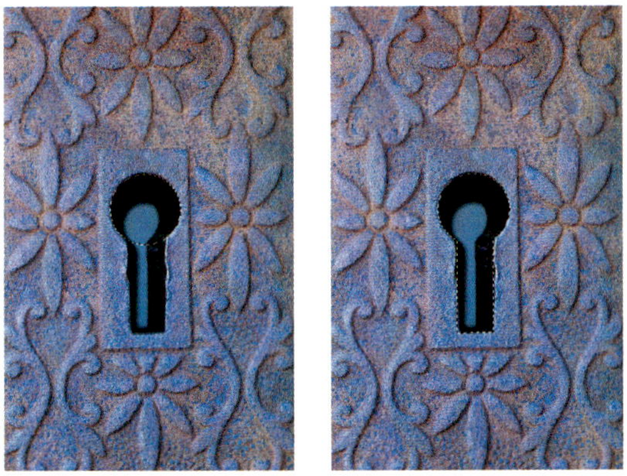

Figure 9.6 The Add To Selection option allows you to build up selections in multiple steps. (Photo by Alice Cahill, www.alicecahill.com)

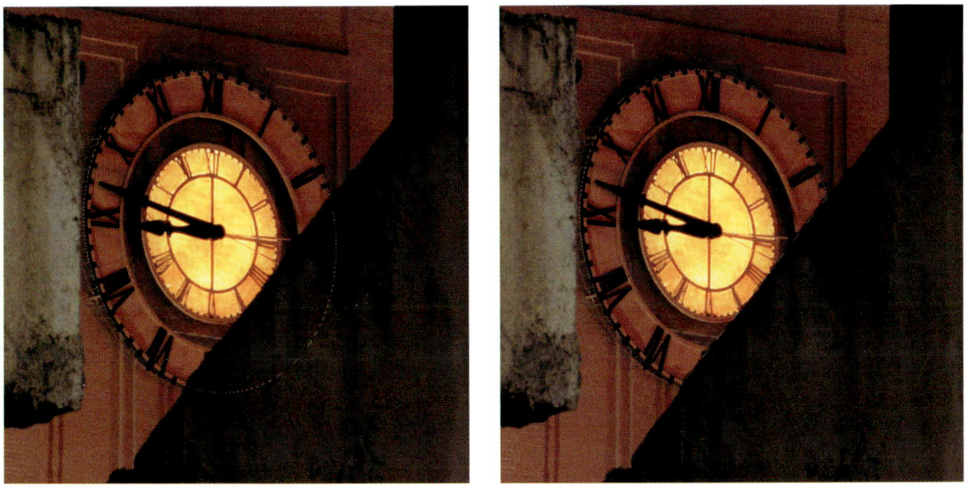

Figure 9.7 The Subtract From Selection option allows you to remove portions of an existing selection.

The add and subtract options are helpful, and you'll use them extensively as you build complicated selections that require a fair amount of fine-tuning, as you'll see later in this chapter.

The last button of the four is one you'll use less frequently but that can be very helpful in certain situations. This is the Intersect With Selection option. When this option is chosen, creating a new marquee when you have an existing marquee will result in a selection of only the pixels in the areas where the two marquees overlap. This option can also be accessed by holding the Shift and Alt/Option keys when using a selection tool.

Lasso

The Lasso tool provides maximum flexibility, because it allows you to literally draw a custom shape around the pixels you want to select. Activate the Lasso by choosing it from the Tools palette or pressing L on your keyboard. Zoom in on the area close enough that you can clearly see the edge of the area you want to select. Carefully position your mouse along that edge; then click and hold the mouse button. Drag the mouse along the edge so you're effectively tracing that edge to define your selection (Figure 9.8). Take the time to be as precise as you can so the selection you create will be as accurate as possible.

Note: For all of the Lasso selection tools, you can use the keyboard shortcuts discussed in Chapter 2, "Download and Sort," to zoom in and out while you are in the process of creating the selection.

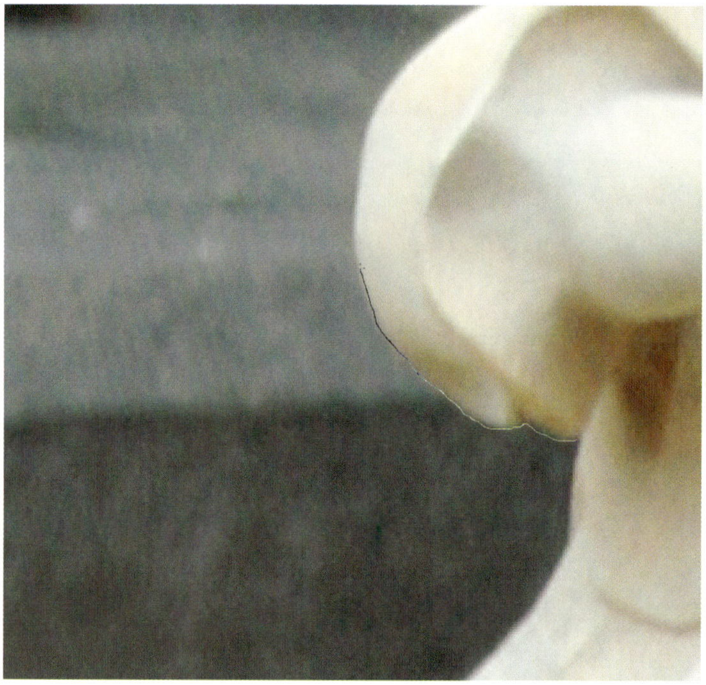

Figure 9.8 The Lasso tool is used to trace along the edge of the object you want to select in your image.

The Options bar for the Lasso tool contains the same four modifier options as the Marquee tools; these options allow you to refine your selection by adding or subtracting pixels from an existing selection, or to create a selection from the intersection of an existing and new selection. Also on the Options bar for the Lasso tool are the Feather and Anti-Aliased controls. As mentioned previously, I recommend leaving Feather set to 0 px and Anti-Aliased selected.

When you are working on a zoomed portion of your image, the area you are trying to select might extend outside the document window. In that case, as you near the edge of the document window, press and hold the spacebar. This will temporarily allow you to use the Hand tool, so you can click and drag the image to change the area at which you are currently looking. When you've finished moving the image, release the spacebar and continue dragging the mouse to extend the selection.

When you've looped around the entire area you want to select, drag the mouse to your original starting point and release the mouse button to finish the selection (Figure 9.9). If you don't finish at the same point you started, Photoshop will automatically complete your selection by extending a straight line from the point where you release the mouse button to your original starting point.

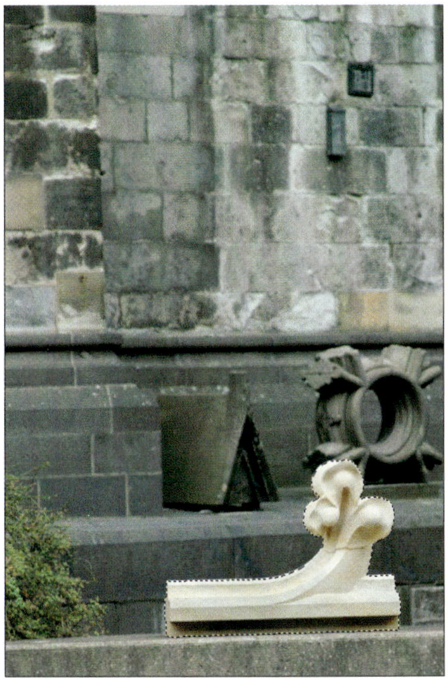

Figure 9.9 The Lasso tool allows you to produce a perfect customized selection with a bit of effort.

Working with the Lasso tool can require a steady hand and a bit of practice. It isn't always the fastest or easiest way to create a selection, but it does offer exceptional flexibility.

Polygonal Lasso

The Polygonal Lasso tool allows you to create selections composed of perfectly straight lines. To choose the Polygonal Lasso tool, click and hold the Lasso Tool button on the Tools palette and then choose Polygonal Lasso Tool from the flyout menu. You can also press L to activate the current Lasso tool, and then Shift+L to cycle through the Lassos until you get to the Polygonal Lasso.

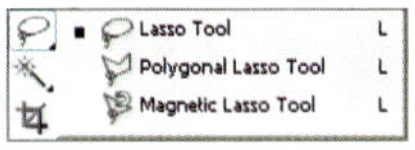

The concept of the Polygonal Lasso tool is that you can create a selection with straight edges by "connecting the dots" with a series of anchor points. Start by clicking along the edge of the object that you want to select in your image. This will create the first anchor point at that position, with a line connecting that anchor point to your cursor (Figure 9.10). Wherever you move the mouse, the line will follow. Position the mouse so the line perfectly aligns with the edge of the object you're selecting and click again to create an additional anchor point. Continue clicking individual points to define the outer edge of the selection.

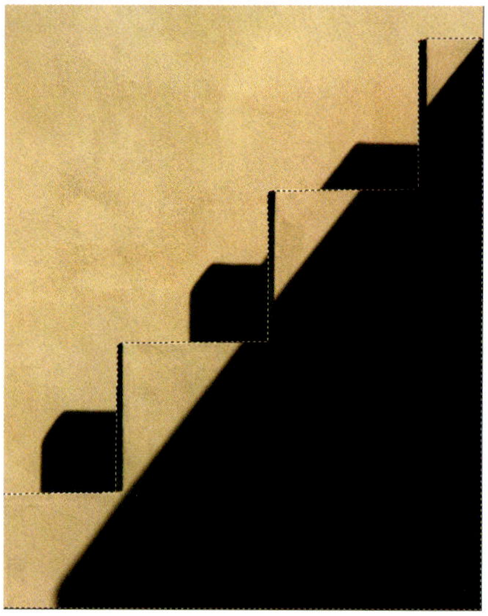

Figure 9.10 The Polygonal Lasso tool allows you to create anchor points that will be connected by straight lines to produce the final selection.

The standard set of four modifier options (new, add, subtract, and intersect) are available on the Options bar for the Polygonal Lasso tool, as are the Feather and Anti-Aliased options. In the case of the Polygonal Lasso, Anti-Aliased will affect both diagonal lines and the junction of two lines at an anchor point.

Although it is possible to create a "curved" line by placing many anchor points very close together, you don't need to go to that extreme. If you reach a place where you can't really use a straight edge effectively (Figure 9.11), press and hold Alt/Option to temporarily switch to the regular Lasso tool, allowing you to click and drag to draw a portion of the selection edge freehand. When you want to return to the straight edges of the Polygonal Lasso tool, simply release the Alt/Option key and you'll be back to placing anchor points to define straight edges within the selection. You can switch back and forth between the tools in this manner as frequently as needed.

As you're defining anchor points with the Polygonal Lasso tool, you may find that you want a particular edge to be perfectly horizontal or vertical. You can constrain the line created from one anchor point to the next by holding the Shift key before you click the new anchor point. Doing so will limit the current line between anchor points to a straight line in 45-degree increments. However, this option works only if you press and hold the Shift key after you've started creating the selection.

If you've placed an anchor point in an incorrect position, you can press Backspace or Delete to remove the previous anchor point. Each time you press the key, you'll delete the prior anchor point, all the way back to the initial anchor. If you decide you just want to cancel the current selection in progress and start over, press the Esc key; the selection will be cancelled and all anchor points will be removed.

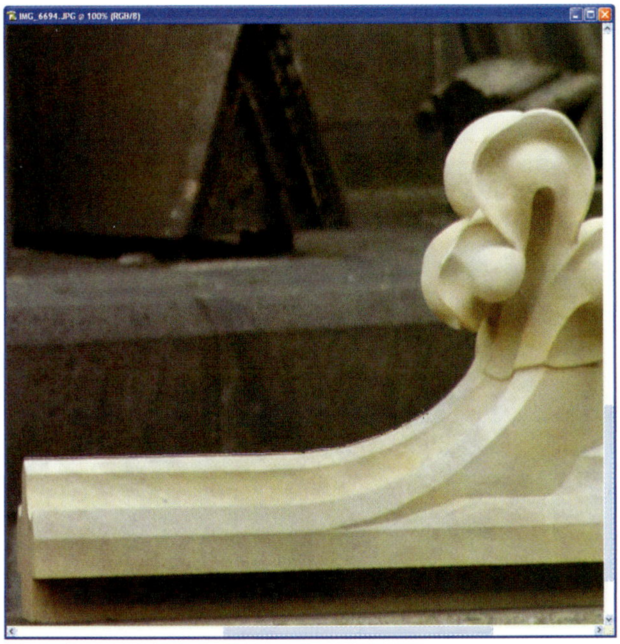

Figure 9.11 In this image, the Polygonal Lasso tool was used on the straight portion of the selection in progress; then the Alt/Option key was used to continue with a free-form selection.

To finalize a selection with the Polygonal Lasso tool, return the mouse pointer to the original anchor point. A small circle will then be added to the cursor, indicating you can click to close the selection shape. If you can't find the original anchor point, double-click in the image and the selection will be closed in a straight line from the point you double-click to the original anchor point.

Magnetic Lasso

The Magnetic Lasso is quite different from the other Lasso tools and in some ways acts like a brush tool. While it bears some resemblance to the other Lasso tools, it has a certain amount of automation built into it that makes it special. Although its name might make it sound like a tool for selecting metallic objects from your images, it instead assists you in selecting objects along their edges based on contrast at those edges. Similar to the Polygonal Lasso tool, the Magnetic Lasso tool defines a selection by placing anchor points. However, whereas you place those points manually with the Polygonal Lasso tool, the Magnetic Lasso places anchor points automatically based on edge contrast.

As with the Polygonal Lasso tool, the Magnetic Lasso is found under the regular Lasso on the Tools palette. Click and hold the mouse on the Lasso tool to bring up the flyout menu, and choose Magnetic Lasso. You can also press L on your keyboard to activate the current Lasso tool, and then press Shift+L to switch tools until activating the Magnetic Lasso.

Besides the standard set of four modifier buttons, the Feather setting, and the Anti-Aliased checkbox, the Options bar contains some special controls for the Magnetic Lasso tool. The first is the Width control; as you "paint" with the Magnetic Lasso, the Width determines the size of the area in which you'd like Photoshop to search for contrast. You could enter a value in pixels to determine the size of the edge width for the Magnetic Lasso, but obviously this is a rather arbitrary decision. Instead, simply place your mouse pointer along the edge where you'll start making the selection, and use the left or right square bracket key ([and]) to reduce or enlarge the size of the edge width, respectively. You want the Width to be small enough that the strongest area of contrast within the sample area will be the edge you're trying to select, but large enough that you don't have to be overly precise in dragging the mouse pointer along that edge.

The Edge Contrast setting determines the amount of contrast for which the Magnetic Lasso should look. For high-contrast edges, you can use a higher setting, and you won't need to be as precise as you move the mouse along that contrast edge. For low-contrast edges, you should use a lower setting, but be more precise in dragging the mouse along the edge you're trying to select. I generally find that a 10% value for Edge Contrast works well in most situations, and the difference in behavior is so slight with different values that I don't recommend changing it.

The Frequency setting determines how often anchor points will be placed as you drag the mouse pointer over the edge. A higher Frequency value will cause anchor points to be placed quickly in close proximity to each other; a lower value will cause them to be placed farther apart. Higher settings are best for well-defined edges, whereas lower settings tend to work well for more nebulous edges. I find that a value of 60 is a good general starting point, and I then revise that number based on whether the anchor points are being placed at an appropriate rate. It is generally better to have a higher frequency with more anchor points rather than a lower frequency, so the shape of the selection will better match the edge of the object you're trying to select.

The final setting on the Options bar is a Pen Pressure checkbox. This setting applies only if you are using a tablet. With the box selected, varying the pressure you apply to the stylus (pen) will affect the edge width. Pressing harder will cause the Width to decrease, as though the pressure is focusing the edge width onto a smaller area. Less pressure will cause the edge width to enlarge, so the Magnetic Lasso will look for contrast across a broader area.

With the Options bar settings established, you're ready to start creating a selection with the Magnetic Lasso tool. Position the cursor over the contrast edge you want to select, and click the mouse button once to place the initial anchor point. Then drag the mouse along the edge of the object you are trying to select. Photoshop will automatically place anchor points at the area of highest contrast within the radius (Width), with spacing based on the Frequency setting (Figure 9.12). If you get to an area of the image where contrast isn't adequate for the Magnetic Lasso to accurately place an anchor point, you can click the mouse to manually place an anchor point.

At times you'll find the Magnetic Lasso doesn't do a very good job of placing anchor points where you want them and will place them in an inappropriate place. When that happens, you'll need to delete anchor points before trying again in the problem area of the image. First, move the cursor back to the last place where you want an anchor point. Then press the Backspace/Delete key once for each anchor you want to remove. The anchor points will be removed starting with the most recently created point. You can then adjust the Width with the square bracket keys, or change other settings on the Options bar, and drag again along the edge. If you can't find settings that work well for a particular area, place the anchor points manually by clicking the mouse.

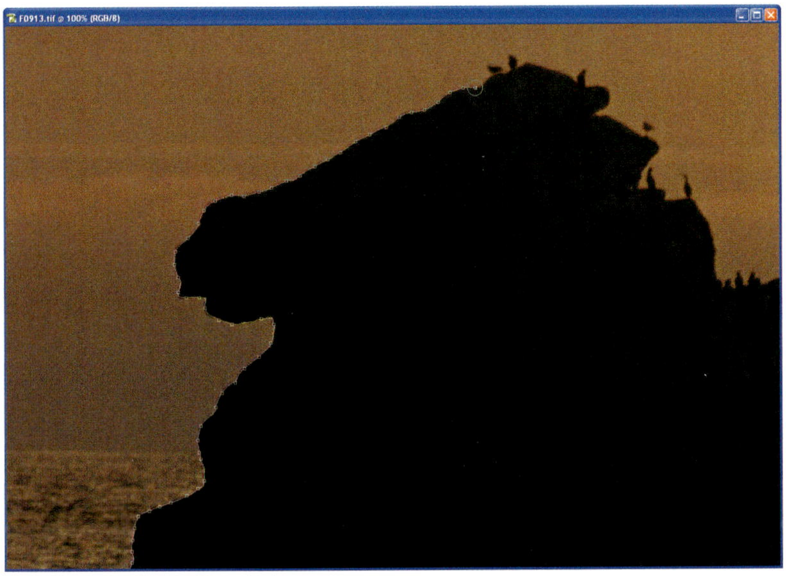

Figure 9.12 As you move the mouse along the edge of the object you're selecting, the Magnetic Lasso tool will automatically place anchor points at the place of highest contrast within the edge width.

If you need to create a straight-line edge along part of the selection, Alt/Option+click at an anchor point. This will add an anchor, but will do so as though you were using the Polygonal Lasso tool, so there will be a line connecting that anchor point to your cursor. Simply move the mouse to the next location where you'd like to place an anchor point and click. The Polygonal Lasso behavior will continue until you Alt/Option+click to place an additional anchor point, at which point you'll return to the Magnetic Lasso tool.

To access the regular Lasso tool while working with the Magnetic Lasso, press and hold the Alt/Option key as you click and drag the mouse along the edge you want to define by drawing freehand. Click the mouse again without the Alt/Option key to return to the Magnetic Lasso.

If you decide you want to cancel the selection in progress, simply press the Esc key; all anchor points will be removed and there will be no active selection (unless there was a selection active before you started using the Magnetic Lasso).

The Magnetic Lasso tool is powerful, but it isn't perfect. Although it does a good job of selecting based on contrast in the area you drag the mouse over, in most cases it won't create a perfect selection. However, it will create a very good basic selection in the vast majority of situations, making it an effective tool that will save you tremendous time in creating selections. I think of it as a tool for creating a rough selection. I know I'll have to modify that selection after creating it, but using the Magnetic Lasso tool will save considerable time in the overall process of creating the perfect selection.

Magic Wand

When the Magic Wand tool can create a selection with a single click of the mouse, it seems truly magical. When too many clicks are required, it can be a bit frustrating. The trick is knowing what type of image is best suited for the Magic Wand tool and how to configure the settings for the best result.

The Magic Wand tool functions by sampling the pixel that you click, and then comparing other pixels to see whether they are a close-enough match. If they are, they are included in the selection.

Before setting the options for the Magic Wand tool, it is important to check a setting on the Options bar for the Eyedropper tool. Although these tools don't seem related, the Magic Wand tool uses the Sample Size setting from the Eyedropper to determine the actual value to use in evaluating pixels for inclusion in the selection. Choose the Eyedropper from the Tools palette, and choose an option from the Sample Size dropdown on the Options bar. There are seven options available, starting with Point Size and continuing with six other options that sample areas of varying size (from a 3×3 pixel grid to a 101×101 pixel grid). Point Sample will cause only a single pixel to be used as the basis for pixel comparison by the Magic Wand tool. This can certainly increase precision, but it also introduces potential errors. For example, you could click a dust spot or a pixel with variation caused by grain or noise, and the resulting selection wouldn't match what you were intending to create. For this reason, I don't recommend using the Point Sample option.

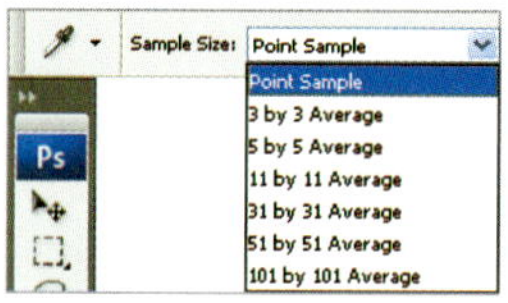

I recommend using either the 3 By 3 Average or 5 By 5 Average. As their names indicate, they sample a grid of pixels (a total of 9 or 25 pixels, respectively) surrounding the one you click and average their values. This average value is then used as the basis of the Magic Wand tool selection. Averaging helps to compensate for any local variation among pixels. In most cases, I'll use the 3 By 3 Average option, but when there is significant variation in the area I want to select I'll sometimes use the 5 By 5 Average setting. The other settings generally sample too large an area to be effective, although there are situations (such as an image with significant noise) when they can be useful.

After you've established an appropriate Sample Size setting on the Options bar for the Eyedropper tool, choose the Magic Wand tool (it is under the Quick Selection tool, so click and hold or right-click the Quick Selection tool button to access the Magic Wand tool) so you can adjust the settings and create your selection.

The key to using the Magic Wand tool effectively is the Tolerance setting. This setting determines how far apart pixel values can be and still be considered a match (Figure 9.13). With a low setting, pixels must be very close to the value of the pixel you clicked to be included in the selection. With a high setting, even pixels with very different values can be included in the selection.

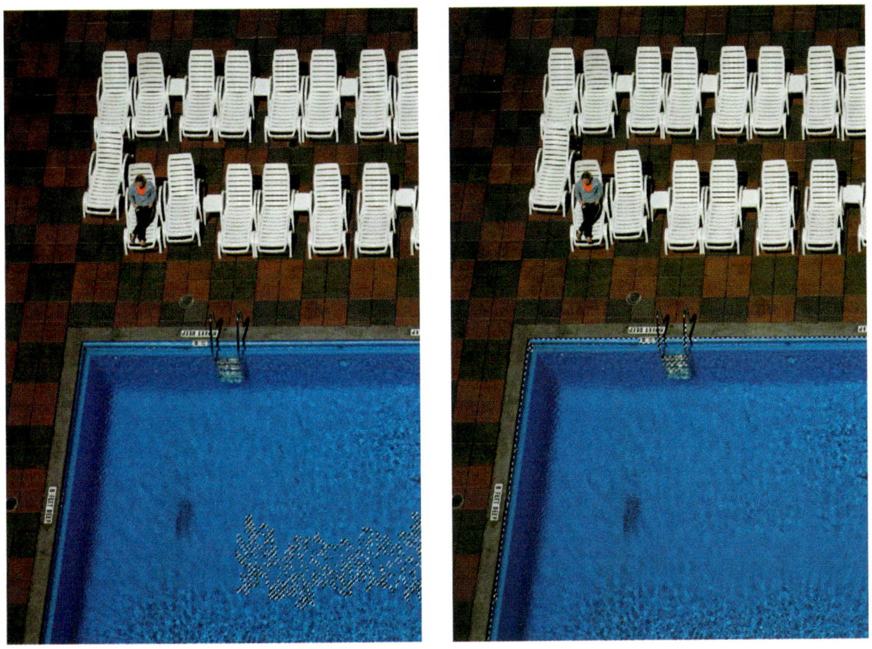

Figure 9.13 The Tolerance setting determines whether a few (left) or many (right) pixels will be included in a selection.

The Magic Wand tool is obviously best suited for images that have broad areas of similar tone and color you want to select. An example is an area of open sky with no clouds. Because the pixels already have similar values, a relatively low Tolerance setting should be appropriate. I typically start with a Tolerance value of 16 and work from there.

Click the area of the image you want to select, and adjust the Tolerance setting based on the result. If too many pixels from areas you didn't want to select were selected, deselect (Select > Deselect from the menu) and reduce the Tolerance setting. If you didn't get the complete area you wanted to select, deselect and increase the Tolerance setting. My approach is to double the Tolerance setting when a higher value is needed, and halve it when a lower value is needed. Then I'll narrow the value down by working between the established "border" values. For example, if 16 is too low, I'll use 32. If 32 is still too low, I'll use 64. If that is too much, I'll go back to 48 (halfway between 32 and 64) and continue "meeting in the middle" until I find an appropriate value.

Note: The method of refining the Tolerance setting here is an example of what is sometimes referred to as a *binary split* method.

Of course, you could spend a lot of time chasing the right Tolerance value. I recommend taking a tempered approach, trying to find a *good* value without spending too much time finding the *perfect* value. If you can't find a good value relatively quickly, opt for a Tolerance setting that is a bit lower than needed. Then use the Add To Selection option to build up the final selection.

Note: It is better to start with a Tolerance value for the Magic Wand that results in a selection that encompasses less than the area you are trying to select and then build up the selection with the Add To Selection option.

It is important to keep in mind that when you add pixels to or subtract pixels from a selection by using the appropriate options with the Magic Wand tool, the selection is modified based on the pixel you click the second time. The natural tendency when adding to a selection with the Magic Wand tool is to Shift+click an area that isn't selected to add it to the selection. However, this will often cause areas you don't want to have selected to be added, based on the new sample point you clicked. You may need to Shift+click inside the existing selection, but at a different location than you originally clicked, to add the appropriate range of pixels to the selection. Also, keep in mind that you can adjust the Tolerance setting between mouse clicks when using the add and subtract options, giving you even greater control. Each time you click with the Magic Wand tool, pixels throughout the image are evaluated based on the Tolerance setting, regardless of whether the pixels are already selected.

Although the Tolerance setting is the pivotal setting for the Magic Wand tool, there are other settings on the Options bar you'll want to consider. The Anti-Aliased checkbox serves the same purpose as it does with the other selection tools discussed previously in this chapter, and I recommend leaving it selected.

The Contiguous option affects which pixels are evaluated. When you click a pixel with the Magic Wand, Photoshop looks outward from that pixel to find matching pixels. If it meets a pixel that doesn't match closely enough based on the Tolerance setting, that pixel creates a border, so that pixels outside the areas defined by that border won't be considered (Figure 9.14). In other words, all pixels in the final selection will be contiguous to each other.

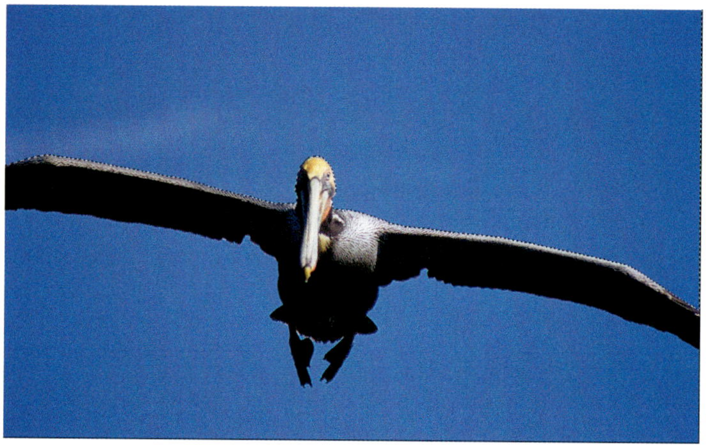

Figure 9.14 With the Contiguous option selected, pixels that are separated from the area of matching pixels won't be included in the selection.

With many images, you'll need to select similar areas that are noncontiguous. For example, you may need to select a sky in an image where the sky shows between the leaves and branches of a tree. Turning off the Contiguous option will cause Photoshop to evaluate every pixel based on the pixel you click with the Magic Wand tool (Figure 9.15).

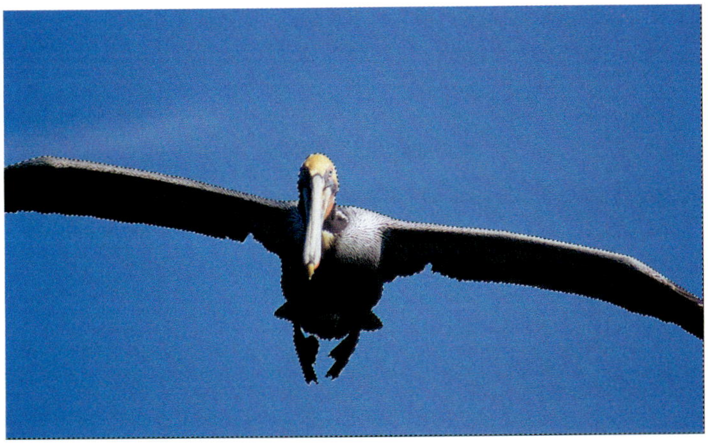

Figure 9.15 With the Contiguous checkbox deselected, all areas that match the pixel you clicked with the Magic Wand will be included in the selection.

The Sample All Layers checkbox allows you to determine whether Photoshop will evaluate pixel values based on all layers in the image or on only the currently active layer. Because you're viewing the image based on all visible layers, it usually makes sense to keep this option turned on. In fact, you can use this setting to make the Magic Wand tool more effective by creating a temporary adjustment layer that accentuates the difference between areas you do want to select and those you don't.

The Magic Wand tool is best for selecting areas of an image that have similar tone and color. If the area you are trying to select contains too much variation, evaluate the image to see if you can easily select the opposite of what you really want. For example, if you want to select the foreground of an image, it might be easier to select the sky and then invert the selection.

Quick Selection Tool

Photoshop CS3 includes a new selection tool that takes the concept of the Magic Wand selection tool to new heights. The tool allows you to paint over areas of the image to define the appearance of the areas you want to select, and automatically creates a selection based on the appearance of surrounding pixels.

To get started, choose the Quick Selection tool from the Tools palette or press W on the keyboard. Then simply "paint" over the image to define the area you want to select. The approach I recommend is to paint "stripes" through the various areas that define the total area you want to select. If the object you're attempting to select is well defined compared to surrounding areas, you'll find this tool is remarkably good at producing accurate selections. When you release the mouse, an initial selection will be created (Figure 9.16). The Quick Selection tool will automatically switch to Add To Selection mode after the initial selection is created, so you can continue enlarging the selection by clicking and dragging over additional areas that need to be included in the selection.

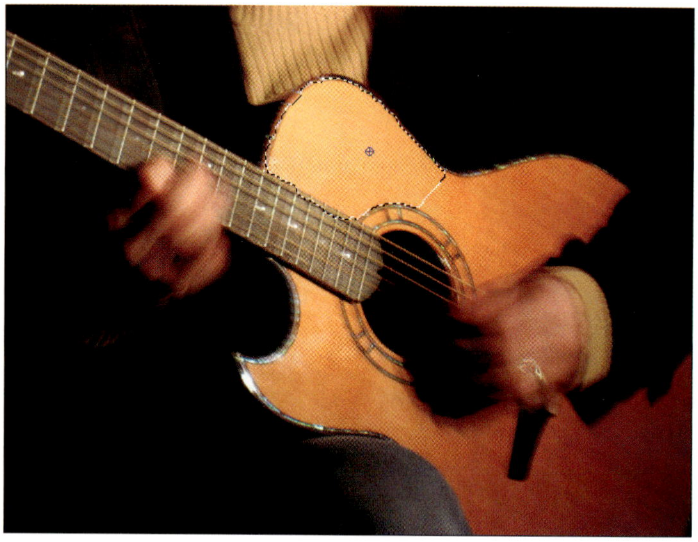

Figure 9.16 The Selection Brush tool allows you to paint the selection onto your image.

You can adjust the size of the brush by pressing the left square bracket key ([ ) to reduce the brush size or the right square bracket key ( ]) to increase the brush size. This is particularly helpful if you need to move the brush through relatively small areas that need to be included in the final selection.

You can reverse the behavior of the tool (removing from the selection in Selection mode or adding to the selection in Mask mode) by holding the Alt/Option key as you paint, or by selecting the Subtract From Selection option on the Options bar.

Using the Quick Selection tool makes it incredibly easy to create selections as long as there is reasonably good definition around the edge of the object you're trying to select. It is the tool I use first whenever attempting to create a selection.

Note: The Refine Edge option found on the Options bar with all selection tools and on the menu at Select > Refine Edge enables you to create artistic selection shapes. I'll talk about using this tool in Chapter 11, "Creative Adjustments."

Color Range

When you need to target a specific range of colors in an image, the Color Range selection feature can be helpful. It is similar in capability to the Magic Wand tool but offers an interactive approach to creating selections. To get started with the Color Range selection function, choose Select > Color Range from the menu. This will bring up the Color Range dialog box, which provides controls for creating a selection based on color values (Figure 9.17).

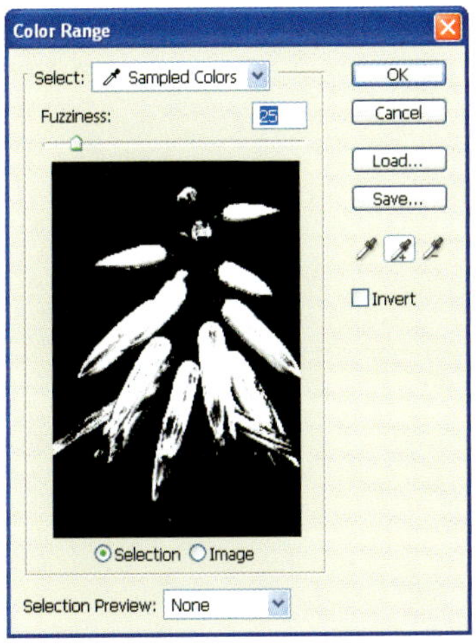

Figure 9.17 The Color Range dialog box allows you to create a selection based on color values within your image.

The Select dropdown allows you to select a range of colors within the image automatically, but I don't consider this feature very useful because you can't adjust the range of colors to be included. It will simply select a range based on Photoshop's definition of a given range. Instead, I recommend leaving this setting on Sampled Colors.

Click the eyedropper button on the right side of the dialog box, and click a pixel that is the color you want to select (note that as with the Magic Wand selection tool, the Sample Size setting for the Eyedropper tool affects the behavior of this eyedropper). Then click the "plus" eyedropper button and click additional areas you would like to add to the selection. The preview in the Color Range dialog box will update with each click, showing the area to be selected in white and nonselected areas in black.

The Fuzziness setting is similar to the Tolerance setting with the Magic Wand tool, with an important difference. The Tolerance setting for the Magic Wand determines what range of colors (based on a sampled color) will be included in the selection, and all of those pixels will be completely selected. The Fuzziness setting, in contrast, allows you to effectively feather the edge of the selection, partially selecting pixels that are close to the sampled value. For most selections, it is best to keep the Fuzziness setting as low as possible. However, with images that have gradual transitions in color values, this setting can help blend the adjustment you make by feathering the selection based on color similarity.

The Selection Preview dropdown specifies how the selection-in-progress should be reflected in your image—that is, in the document window. (Selection Preview has no effect on the preview pane within the Color Range dialog box; that preview is always in gray.) Choosing None will cause the document window to be displayed with no preview of the final selection. Grayscale creates a grayscale preview in which white pixels are selected, black pixels are not selected, and values in between are partially selected. The Black Matte and White Matte options will leave the selected area with a normal display, but with either a black or white matte over the areas that are not selected.

All of these preview options provide a less-than-ideal way to preview what the actual selection will be, and they make it a challenge to modify the selection in the Color Range dialog box. I recommend using the Quick Mask preview option, which creates a preview that is exactly the same display as you would get with the Quick Mask mode discussed later in this chapter. Basically, a defined color mask is overlaid over nonselected areas but is partially transparent so you can still see through to those areas, making it easier to determine when you have a completed selection (Figure 9.18). When you have the selection defined as accurately as possible in the Color Range dialog box, click OK to create the selection.

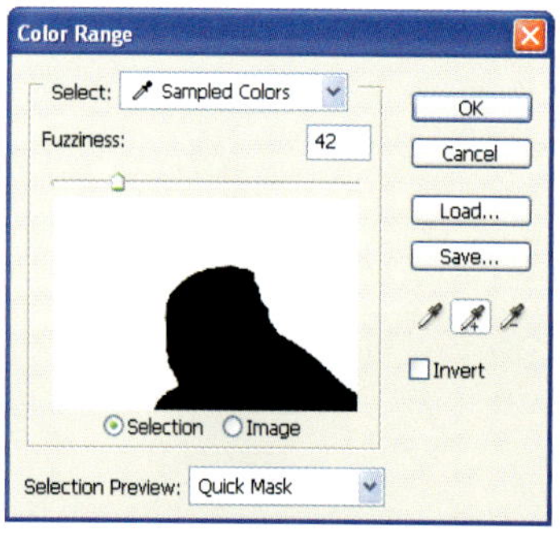

Figure 9.18 The Quick Mask preview option in the Color Range dialog box provides one of the best options for evaluating the selection as you are creating it. Here it shows a Quick Mask preview with a red overlay.

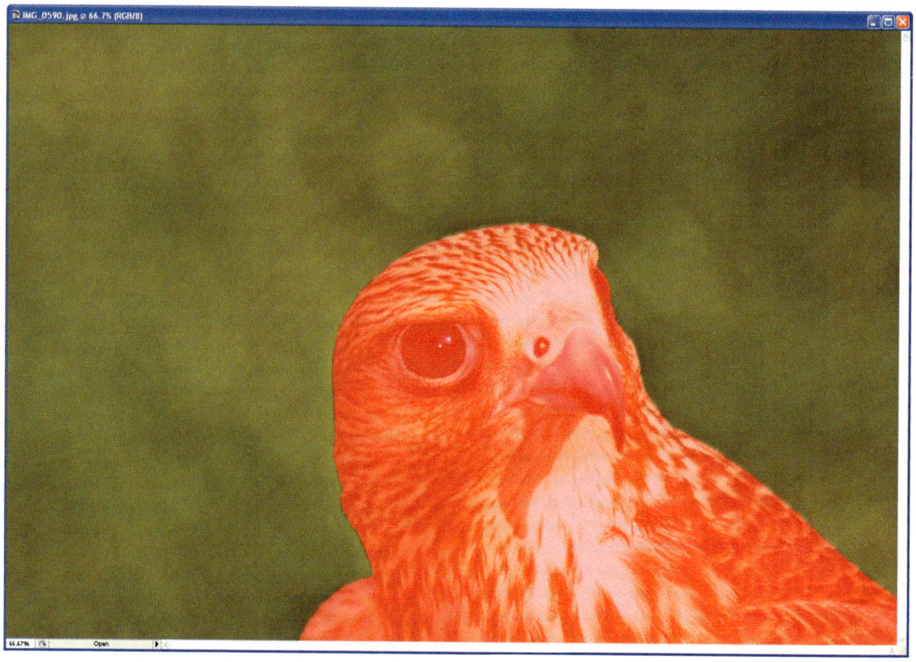

Note: For more information on using the Quick Mask display available in Color Range to modify your selections, see the "Quick Mask Mode" section later in this chapter.

Making Advanced Selections

The selection methods covered so far in this chapter all use Photoshop features that are intended specifically for creating selections. There are some other methods you can use to create a selection—various tricks and techniques made possible with other features of Photoshop.

Threshold Technique

In many situations, you'll want to select all of the pixels in your image based on tonal value. Perhaps you'll want to select all the highlights to tone them down a bit, or select the shadows to extract a bit more detail. Either way, if you want to select all pixels above or below a given tonal value, a handy trick will make your work easier. It involves duplicating the image and using the Threshold command to alter the layer based on tonal values.

Start by duplicating the image layer from which you want to create a selection. I recommend reducing the Opacity of this new layer to about 50%, to make the next step easier to accomplish accurately (Figure 9.19).

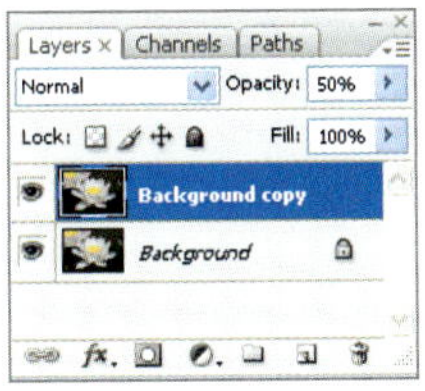

Figure 9.19 The first step in the threshold selection technique is to create a duplicate of your layer and reduce Opacity to about 50%.

Then run Threshold by choosing Image > Adjustments > Threshold from the menu. The Threshold dialog box has only one value to adjust, which you can manipulate by using the slider. The value you set will determine the tonal value at which the pixels will be split. Any pixels at or above that value will be made white, and any pixels below that value will be made black. Adjust the setting so the split between black and white occurs over the border of the area you want to select (Figure 9.20). Because you reduced the Opacity setting for this layer, you can see through it to help you determine the best value. When you have the value set, click OK.

Note: Moving the Threshold Level slider significantly left and right can help you get a better sense of how the image is being split between black and white and, therefore, what the final selection will look like.

Return the Opacity for this layer to 100% so it will be fully opaque. If there are areas you know shouldn't be included in the range to be selected, you can paint on those areas to clean up this template for the selection. For example, if there are black pixels scattered around an otherwise white sky, you can paint with white to clean those up. Next, use the Magic Wand tool with the Contiguous option turned off and click the area of the image you want to select. This will create a selection based on the specific tonal range you defined using Threshold (Figure 9.21). Chances are this won't produce an absolutely perfect selection, but it will quickly get you started with a good basic selection you can modify to perfection.

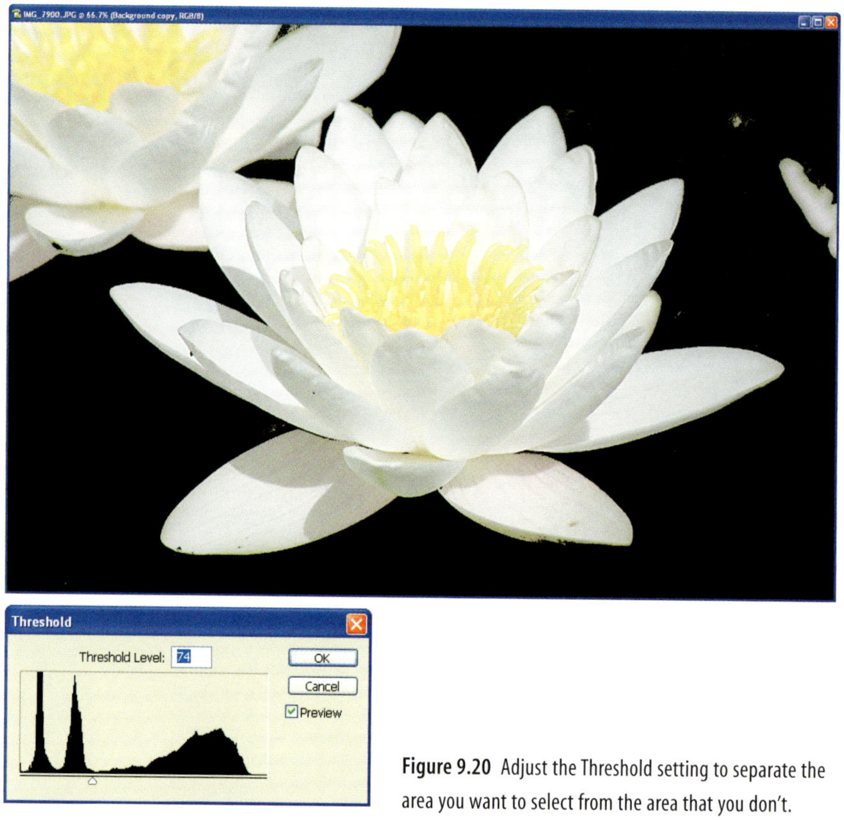

Figure 9.20 Adjust the Threshold setting to separate the area you want to select from the area that you don't.

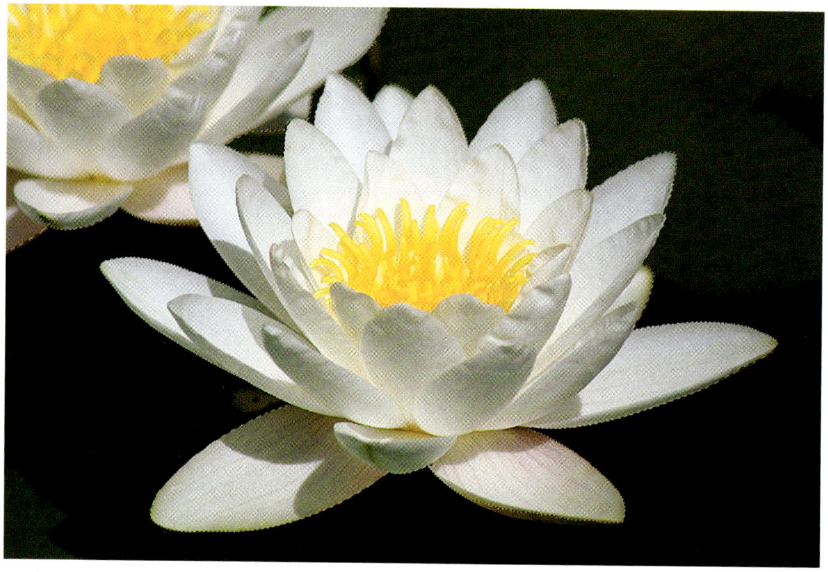

Figure 9.21 The result of the threshold selection technique is a selection that is easy to create. Threshold produces a good selection when the image demonstrates tonal separation.

Selection from Channel

When color contrast exists within an image, creating a selection based on a channel can be an excellent way to quickly create a selection. This process produces similar results to the Threshold method but with a bit more control over the selection.

Start by viewing the individual channels on the Channels palette (Window > Channels). Click each of the channels in turn and decide which channel represents the best contrast for the area you want to select (Figure 9.22). Then duplicate the channel: choose Duplicate Channel from the palette menu, or drag this channel to the Create New Channel button (the blank sheet of paper icon) at the bottom of the palette.

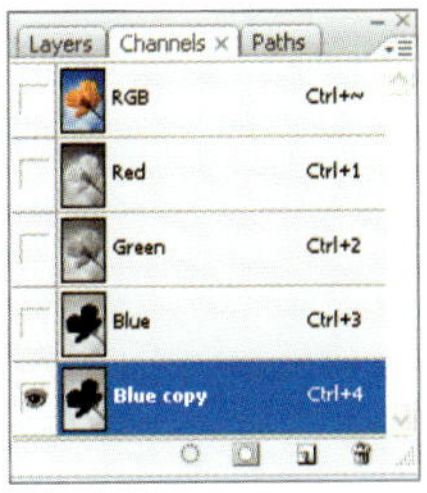

Figure 9.22 To create a selection from a channel, start by reviewing the channels to see which offers the best contrast for the area you want to select and then duplicate that channel.

To create a selection, you'll first need to exaggerate the contrast to define the edge of the area you want to select. To do so, run Levels directly on this new channel (Image > Adjustments > Levels). Bring the Black Point and White Point sliders inward to increase contrast by an extreme amount, placing them so the edge of the area you want to select becomes the focus of maximum contrast (Figure 9.23). You can fine-tune the Midtone slider to adjust the transition between the two values. When you have the adjustment perfected, click OK.

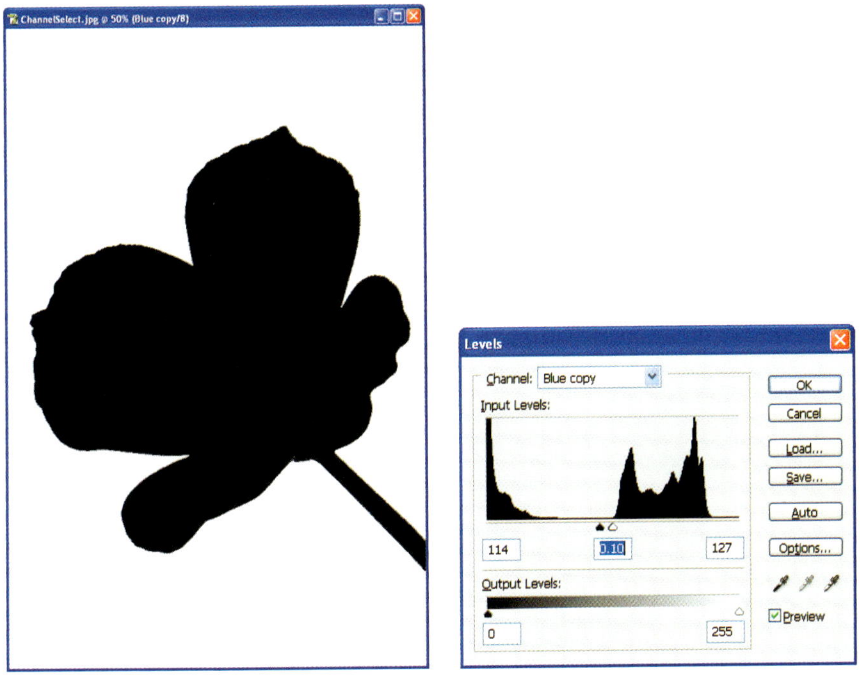

Figure 9.23 Use Levels to exaggerate the contrast of the duplicate channel and create a mask that defines the final selection.

At this point, you can paint on the duplicate channel to further refine the area to be selected. If small areas within the high-contrast channel don't match their surroundings but should, you can paint over those areas and adjust the template to be used for the selection. When you are happy with the result, Ctrl/Command+click the channel. This will load the channel as a selection, with white areas selected and black areas not selected. You may need to invert the selection (Select > Inverse). Click the RGB channel at the top of the Channels palette, and you'll see the selection over the actual image. Again, you can use the other selection tools as needed to change the selection, but this method helps you achieve a good basic selection very quickly when color contrast exists in an image.

Extract a Selection

The Extract filter in Photoshop is designed to extract areas of your image from a background. It doesn't do a perfect job with every image, but it is great for cutting out complicated subjects such as a person with windswept hair or a bird with fuzzy feathers. However, the Extract filter operates by permanently removing pixels from an image, which I prefer to avoid at all costs. Fortunately, you can use the Extract filter to create an excellent selection for difficult subjects.

Start by creating a duplicate of your image layer (highlight the layer, and then choose Duplicate Layer from the Layers palette menu or drag it to the Create A New Layer button at the bottom of the palette). This allows you to destroy pixels on the new layer but preserve the original image on the layer below. Choose Filter > Extract from the menu to bring up the Extract dialog box (Figure 9.24).

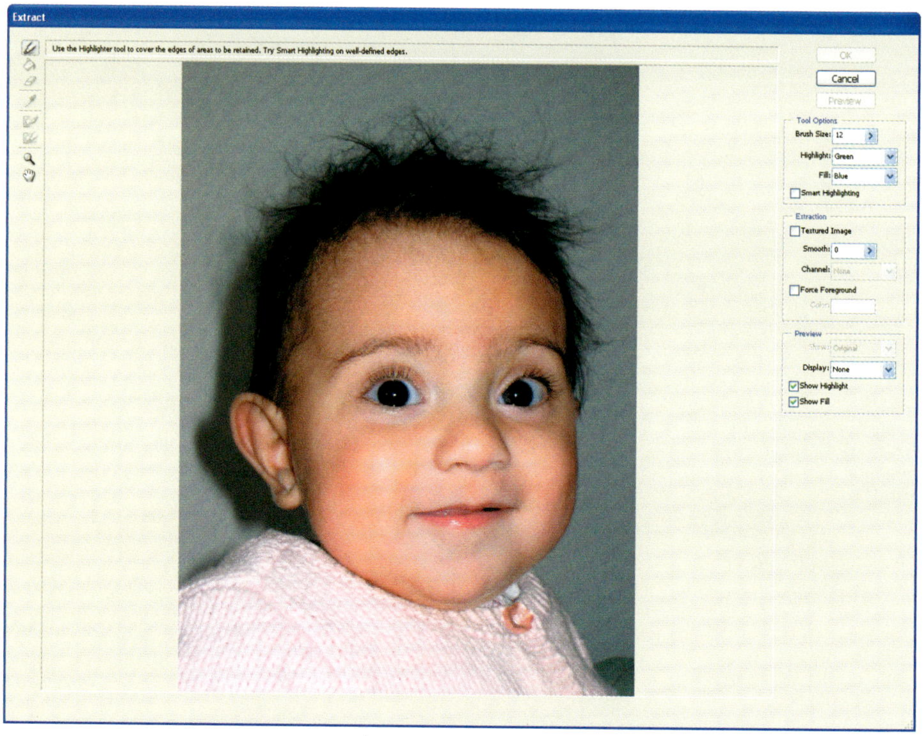

Figure 9.24 The Extract filter is designed to remove backgrounds from an image, but it can be used to create a selection as well.

The basic concept with Extract is that you need to paint along the border of the image to define the area you want to cut out, and fill that border to mark those pixels as protected. The more accurate you are in this process, the more accurate the final selection will be.

When the Extract dialog box opens, the Highlighter tool will be active by default. Zoom in closely on the edge of the subject you want to select, and use the smallest brush size possible for the Highlighter tool (use the left and right square bracket keys to adjust brush size). Paint along the edge of the subject, being sure that any border area is covered in highlighter (Figure 9.25). For example, if you're trying to select a person in an image, be sure to cover up any areas of the background that show through the hair. Paint around the complete border of the subject until you have a closed shape.

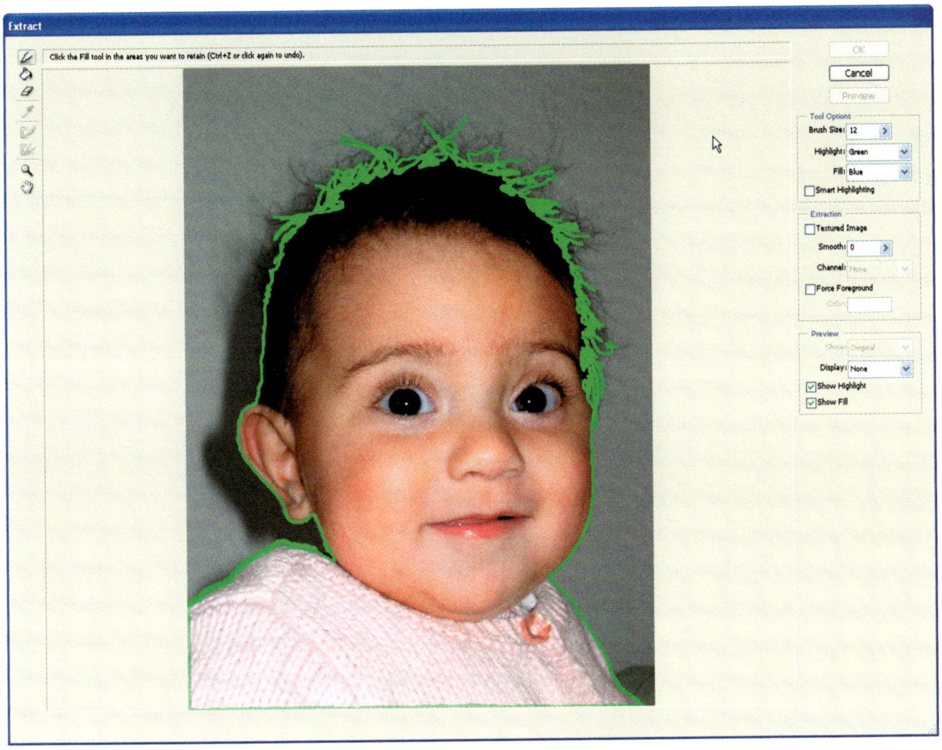

Figure 9.25 Use the Highlighter tool in the Extract dialog box to carefully outline the subject you want to select.

With this outline of your subject painted with the Highlighter tool, choose the Fill tool in the Extract dialog box and click inside the area you have highlighted. This will fill the inside of the highlighted area with a fill color (Figure 9.26). All pixels covered by this fill color will be *retained* in the final extraction. If the fill color spills out beyond the highlighted area, it indicates you didn't close the highlight border completely. If this is the case, press Ctrl+Z/Command+Z to undo the fill and closely examine the highlight border to find (and cover up) the gap.

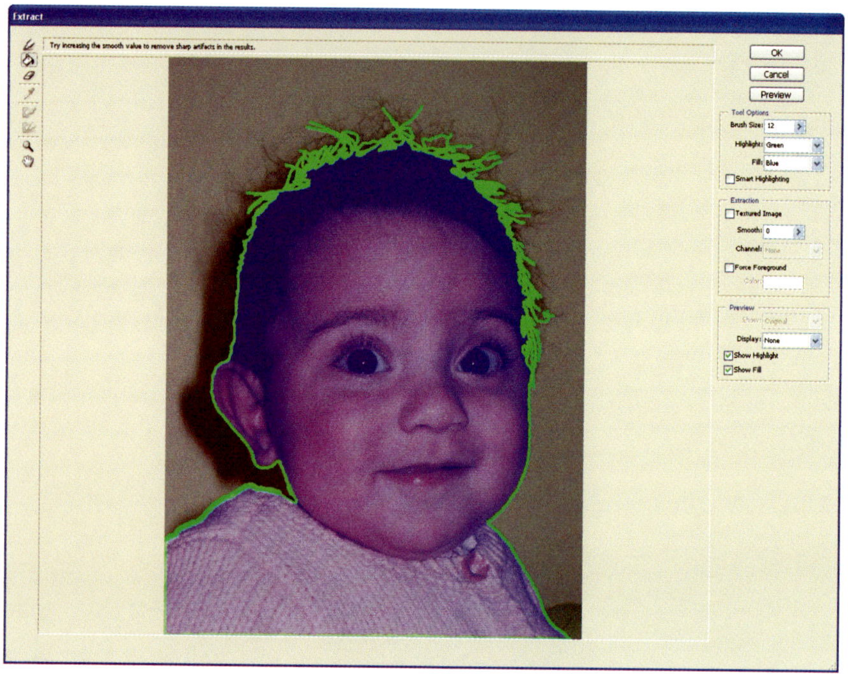

Figure 9.26 After creating the highlighted edge, use the Fill tool to fill in the area you want to have selected in the final result.

If you make any mistakes, choose the Eraser tool in the Extract dialog box and erase portions of the highlight. This will automatically clear the fill, so you'll need to adjust the highlight and perform the fill again.

When you're finished marking the subject to be extracted, you can click OK to apply the extraction. All pixels outside your highlight mark will be discarded, and all pixels covered by the fill color will be retained. The pixels under the highlight will be evaluated and compared to the pixels inside and outside of the highlight, and extracted or retained based on their appearance. The result is an image layer with many pixels removed, as shown by the checkerboard pattern indicating transparency. To see the effect of the extraction on the duplicate image layer, turn off the visibility of the underlying layer by clicking its eye on the Layers palette.

You have the basic shape of your subject defined, thanks to the Extract filter. Now it's time to turn that extraction into a selection. To do so, simply Ctrl/Command+click the thumbnail for this layer on the Layers palette. This will create a selection of pixels in the layer based on their transparency (Figure 9.27). Fully opaque pixels will be completely selected, partially transparent pixels along the edge of the subject will be partially selected, and fully transparent pixels around your subject won't be selected at all. If you turn off the duplicate layer you applied Extract to and turn on the underlying layer, you'll see the selection overlaid on the image. You can then modify this selection to correct any mistakes Extract made.

Note: Extract doesn't recognize the edge of your image for what it is, so if the subject you're trying to select extends beyond the image, the selection in those areas won't be very good. After making the initial selection, you can easily fix this with the Lasso tool.

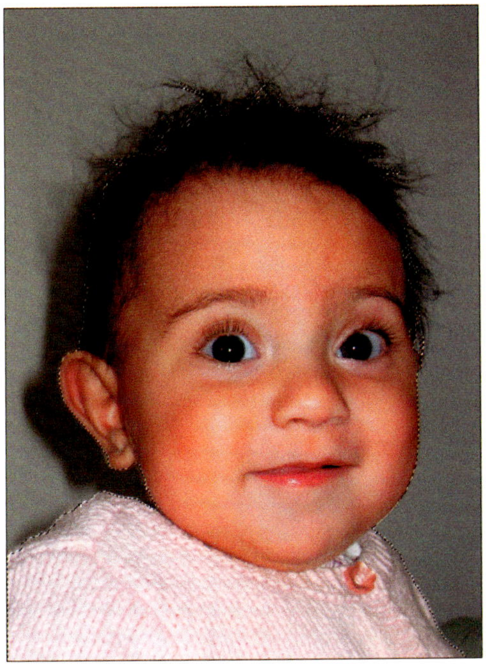

Figure 9.27 When you Ctrl/Command+click the layer you applied Extract to, a selection will be created based on the extracted area of the image.

Note: The selection won't look as good as it really is because this method creates partially selected areas where there is blending, and selections show the boundary between pixels that are at least 50% selected and those with a smaller percentage.

Modifying Selections

Using the selection tools to create a selection is an important start, but often you'll need to modify a selection slightly after creating it. A variety of options enable you to fine-tune your selections after they've been created.

Quick Mask Mode

If you find painting easier than tracing, Quick Mask mode is a great way to modify your selections. It allows you to define which areas of the image should be included or excluded in a selection by painting in white or black over your image.

The first step is to configure the Quick Mask settings. To do so, double-click the Quick Mask button on the Tools palette . The first option in the Quick Mask Options dialog box allows you to decide whether you want color to be placed over Masked Areas (those you don't want to select) or over Selected Areas (Figure 9.28). I recommend using the Masked Areas option because you are then "blocking out" areas you don't want. This is simply a matter of preference, though, and you can work with either setting. I'll assume you're using the Masked Areas option here. Otherwise, you'll need to reverse the instructions about whether to paint with black versus white.

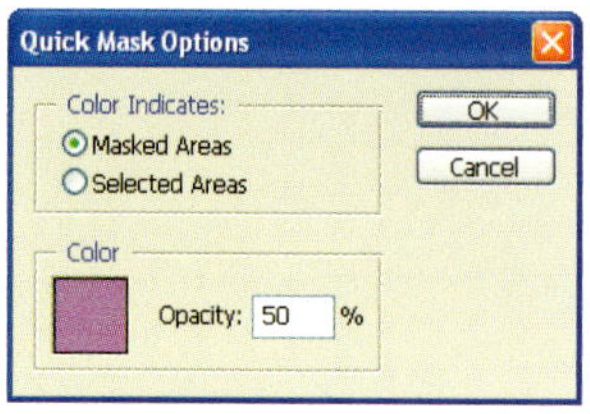

Figure 9.28 The Quick Mask options let you establish settings for the use of Quick Mask mode.

In the Color section, choose the color that will be displayed over the image as you adjust the selection, as well as the opacity of that color. I recommend using a highly saturated color that doesn't appear anywhere in the image. For example, an intense green or magenta usually works well. The Opacity setting allows you to "see through" the mask, so you can get a better sense of where you need to make modifications. A setting of 50% or slightly lower works well for most images. Click OK to apply these options.

Because you double-clicked the Quick Mask button on the Tools palette, the image will be in Quick Mask mode. You can now paint on the image to define the selection. Paint in black over areas that you don't want included in the selection, and white over areas you do want to include in the selection (Figure 9.29). I recommend starting with a basic selection and then modifying it by using Quick Mask. You can switch back and forth between Standard and Quick Mask modes by using the buttons below the Color Picker on the Tools palette or by pressing Q on the keyboard.

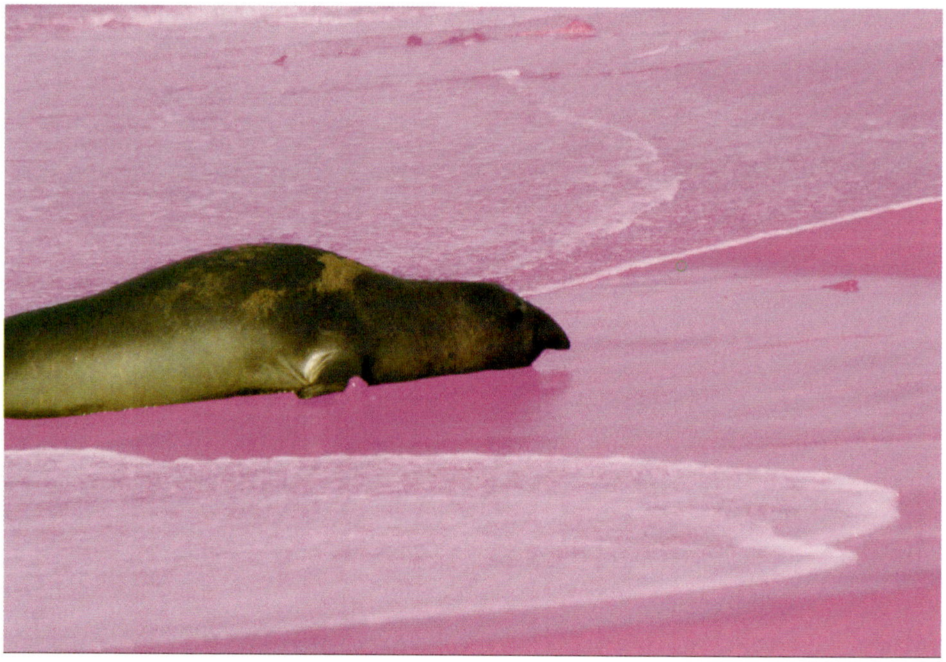

Figure 9.29 When you are working in Quick Mask mode, painting in black will block out areas that won't be included in the selection. This will cause a color overlay to be displayed based on the settings you established in the Quick Mask Options dialog box.

Besides painting with black and white, you can also paint with shades of gray to define relative percentages of selection. The closer to white the color is, the "more selected" that area will be. In effect, you can create complicated feathered edges for your selection by using this process. Any tool that allows you to place pixels on an image can be used in Quick Mask mode; however, only the luminosity of pixels placed will affect the mask.

Modify Options

Some commands allow you to modify the size and shape of a selection after it has been created. These offer even greater flexibility in the creation of complicated selections.

Under the Modify section of the Select menu are four options for altering the selection. The Border option (Select > Modify > Border) allows you to change the selection, so it includes only an area along the border of what had been selected. You can define how many pixels wide you want this final selection to be, and they will be split on either side of the existing selection (Figure 9.30). This can be helpful if you need to apply a blur around just the edge of a subject in a photo, for example.

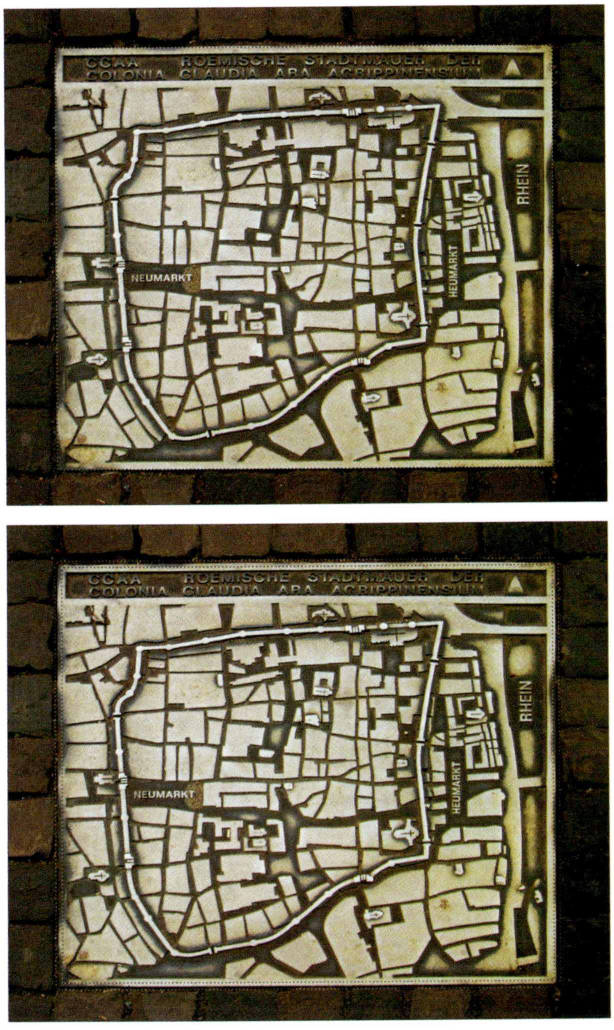

Figure 9.30 The Modify > Border option produces a selection that defines the border of the original marquee.

The Smooth option (Select > Modify > Smooth) smooths out rough edges or tiny flaws of a selection. You define a radius size in pixels, and Photoshop will examine the selection and smooth it out accordingly. If you have jagged lines in a selection, this will solve the problem. This option is also helpful when random small specks aren't included in a selection. For example, dust or grain in the sky can cause scattered individual pixels to be excluded from the selection. Using the Smooth option adds these areas to the existing selection (Figure 9.31). Be careful when using this on selections of fine detail; it can cause the selection to smooth out to the point that the details are no longer selected accurately.

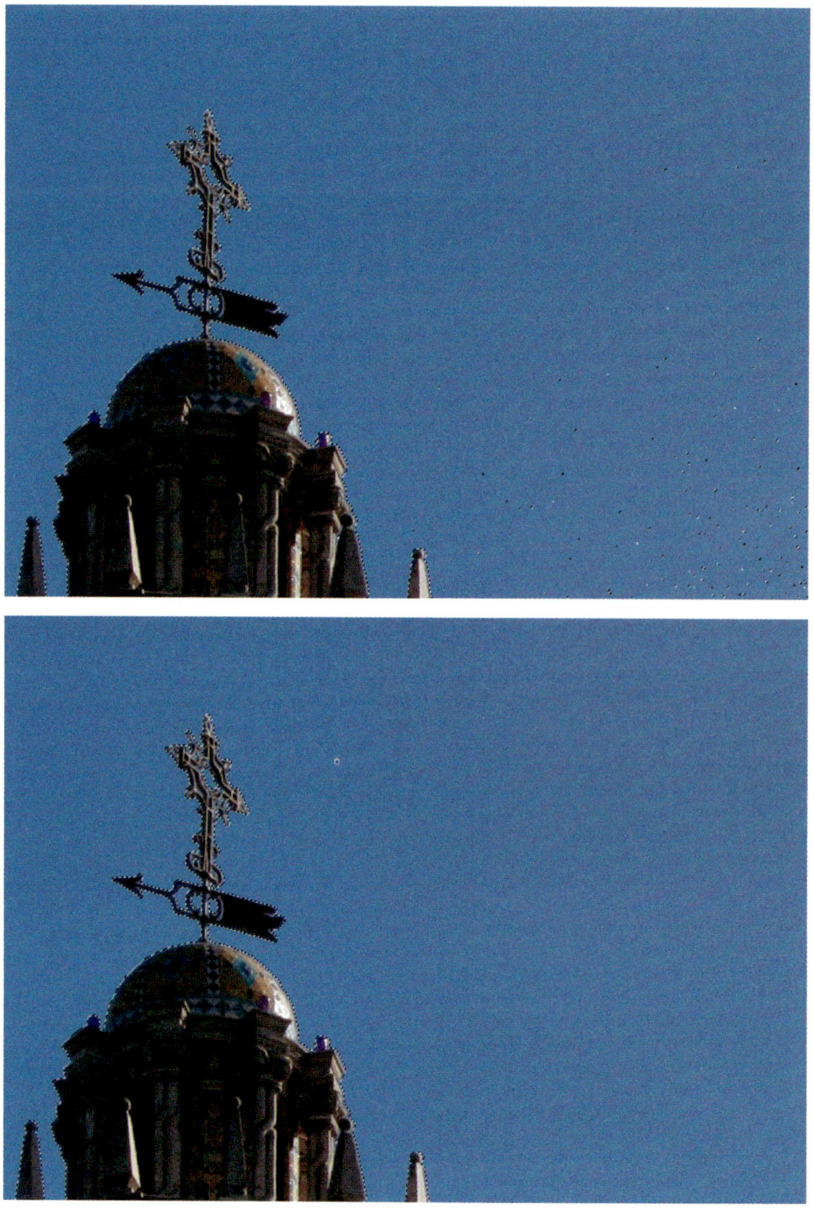

Figure 9.31 The Modify > Smooth option is a great way to clean up a selection that left tiny areas excluded.

The Expand (Select > Modify > Expand) and Contract (Select > Modify > Contract) options do exactly the opposite of each other. Expand allows you to enlarge the selection by a set number of pixels, and Contract allows you to reduce the size of the selection by a set number of pixels. Both respect the outer edge of your images; if a portion of the selection is along the outer border of the document, the selection won't be adjusted in that area.

The Grow and Similar options found on the Select menu also have similar behavior. The Grow option uses the Tolerance setting of the Magic Wand tool to expand the selection based on similar color values, but only contiguous pixels will be selected. The Similar option does the same thing, except that it selects noncontiguous pixels.

In some cases, you may have a selection that is close to selecting the desired object, but not perfect. Particularly if the desired selection has a geometric shape, the Transform option can be helpful. To stretch or skew a selection, choose Select > Transform Selection from the menu (or right-click/Ctrl+click the image with an active selection). A bounding box will be placed around the outside of the selected area. You can move the selection by clicking inside the box and dragging, resize the image by moving the boxes along the bounding box (hold Shift while dragging a corner box to constrain the proportions of the selection), and rotate the selection by moving your cursor outside the bounding box and clicking and dragging. When you're finished transforming the selection, double-click inside the bounding box or press Enter/Return on the keyboard.

So far I've talked primarily about creating selections without a feathered edge. A feathered selection has a gradual transition between pixels that are and are not selected, so any adjustments made will also taper off. You can feather the edge of a selection by choosing Select > Modify > Feather from the menu. However, I prefer not to use this option because it requires an arbitrary decision about the number of pixels by which the selection should be feathered. Instead, I'll apply a Gaussian blur to the final result of the selection, which is typically a mask on an image or adjustment layer, as you'll see in Chapter 10.

Saving and Loading Selections

After you've created a selection, you'll probably want to save it for future use, just in case. My feeling is that any selection requiring more than 10 seconds to create should be saved, even if you don't think you'll use it more than once. The selection is then saved as part of the image file, so you can always reload the selection in the future if needed.

Note: Not all image file formats allow you to save selections because they don't all allow you to save alpha channels. If you're going to save a selection, it should be part of your master image file saved as a Photoshop PSD or TIFF image file.

To save a selection, choose Select > Save Selection from the menu. Although you can save selections in different documents with the same dimensions, I recommend saving them within the current document. Therefore, leave the Document setting to the default value, which will be the name of the current document. The Channel dropdown should be set to New so the selection will be saved as it is. If an existing selection has been saved, you can also choose that selection from the Channel dropdown, and merge the current selection with the previously saved selection. I don't recommend this option because it merges two separate selections together, so they can't be used separately in the future.

The Name is the key setting (and generally the only one you'll need to change) in the Save Selection dialog box (Figure 9.32). Be sure to save the selection with a descriptive name that will make sense to you in the future when you need to load a selection.

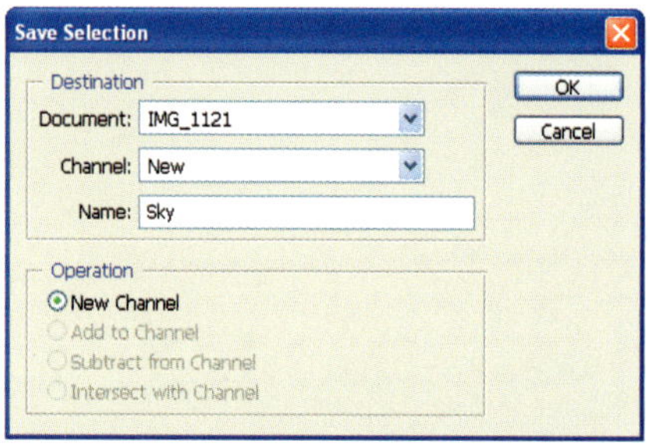

Figure 9.32 When saving a selection, give it a name that identifies it clearly so you'll be able to select it from a list later.

If you are using the New option from the Channel dropdown, the Operation section of the dialog will have only a single option to create a new channel. Otherwise, you'll have the same options as you have for each selection tool to create a new saved selection (Replace): Add To Channel, Subtract From Channel, or Intersect With Channel. When you click OK, the selection will be saved as an alpha channel, which you can view on the Channels palette.

Note: Saved selections aren't truly saved until you save the image in which you stored them. If you save a selection but then close the image without saving it, the selection won't be saved.

In the future, you can load the selection by choosing Select > Load Selection from the menu and choosing the name from the Channel dropdown (Figure 9.33).

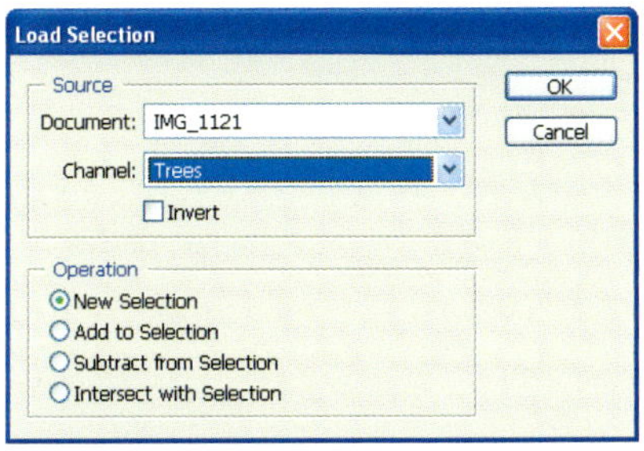

Figure 9.33 You can recall any saved selection by choosing it from the Load Selection dialog box.

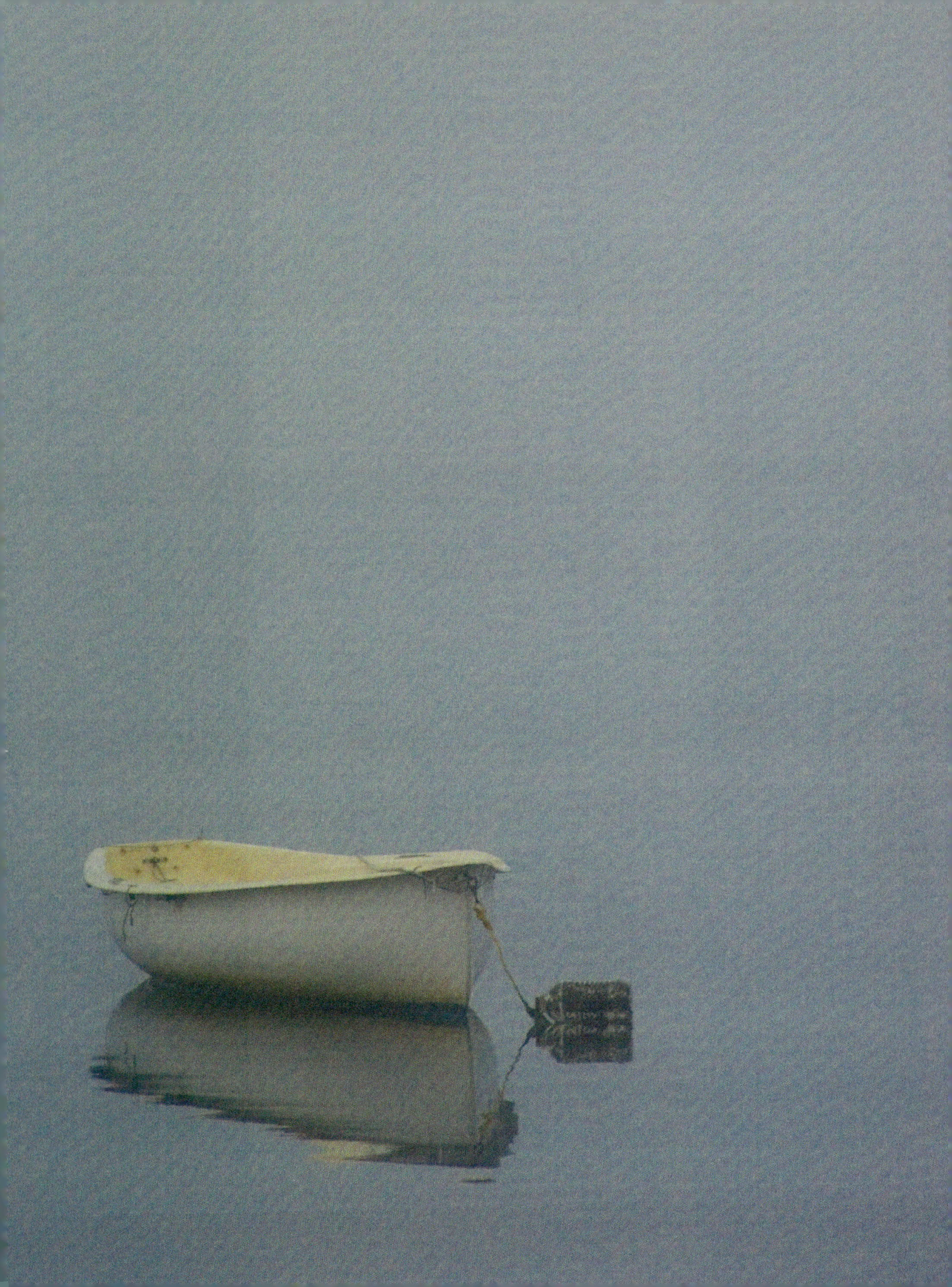

Targeted Adjustments

Up to this point, each task in the image-optimization workflow has been leading up to the topics covered in this chapter. When I'm working on an image, I tend to see the initial steps of the workflow as laying the foundation for the final adjustments that are most important. Being able to exercise control over specific areas of an image—making adjustments to those areas specifically—frees you; it means you are limited only by your own imagination when it comes to producing the image you are trying to achieve. In this chapter, I'll cover the concepts and techniques that will allow you to produce an image that matches your vision.

10

Chapter Contents

Introduction to Masking

Targeted adjustments for your images utilize a method called *masking*, which enables you to define the areas of an image that should be affected by the adjustment. To help you understand the concepts of masking, I'll start with some basic principles.

To understand the concept, think about how you might go about creating an animated cartoon the "old fashioned" way, by painting onto clear acetate sheets. In traditional cartooning, the artist paints a background and then paints a character by itself on a second sheet. Additional characters and props are also painted onto separate acetate sheets. When these sheets are stacked up, the result is a composite scene in which the individual elements can be moved independently. Changes to one element won't affect the other elements.

When creating a composite image in Photoshop—taking an element from one image and placing it on the background of another image, for example—new complications arise. In theory, you could simply place one image on top of the other, and then erase the areas of the top layer you don't want to have visible so that the top layer would blend into the background produced by the underlying layer. The problem with this approach is that you shouldn't simply erase unwanted pixels, even if you know for sure you don't want them included in the final composite image. Doing so would remove all flexibility to return later and revise the areas you've erased.

Masking provides a way to perform such tasks without having to erase pixels from the top image. Instead, you can hide the pixels so they aren't visible, but retain the option to "un-hide" them later if you discover you made a mistake. For example, if you create a composite image by placing a dog into a new environment, but discover you accidentally erased part of the dog's tail, you'll want a way to fix the problem even if it is too late to undo a step by using the History palette (Figure 10.1). With masking, you aren't erasing and "un-erasing" pixels, but rather blocking and revealing them.

Note: Some people use the terms *hide* and *reveal* for masking. I use *block* instead of *hide* to provide an association with *black*; I teach in my workshops, over and over, that "black blocks, white reveals."

Creating Composite Images

Creating a composite image in which, for example, a single element from one image is placed onto the background created by a separate image is an excellent way to gain confidence with masking techniques. Ultimately, these methods can then be applied to mask adjustment layers to target their effects to specific areas of an image.

There are two ways to create a mask to block portions of an image. You can either start from a selection or you can paint on a mask to define the areas to block or reveal.

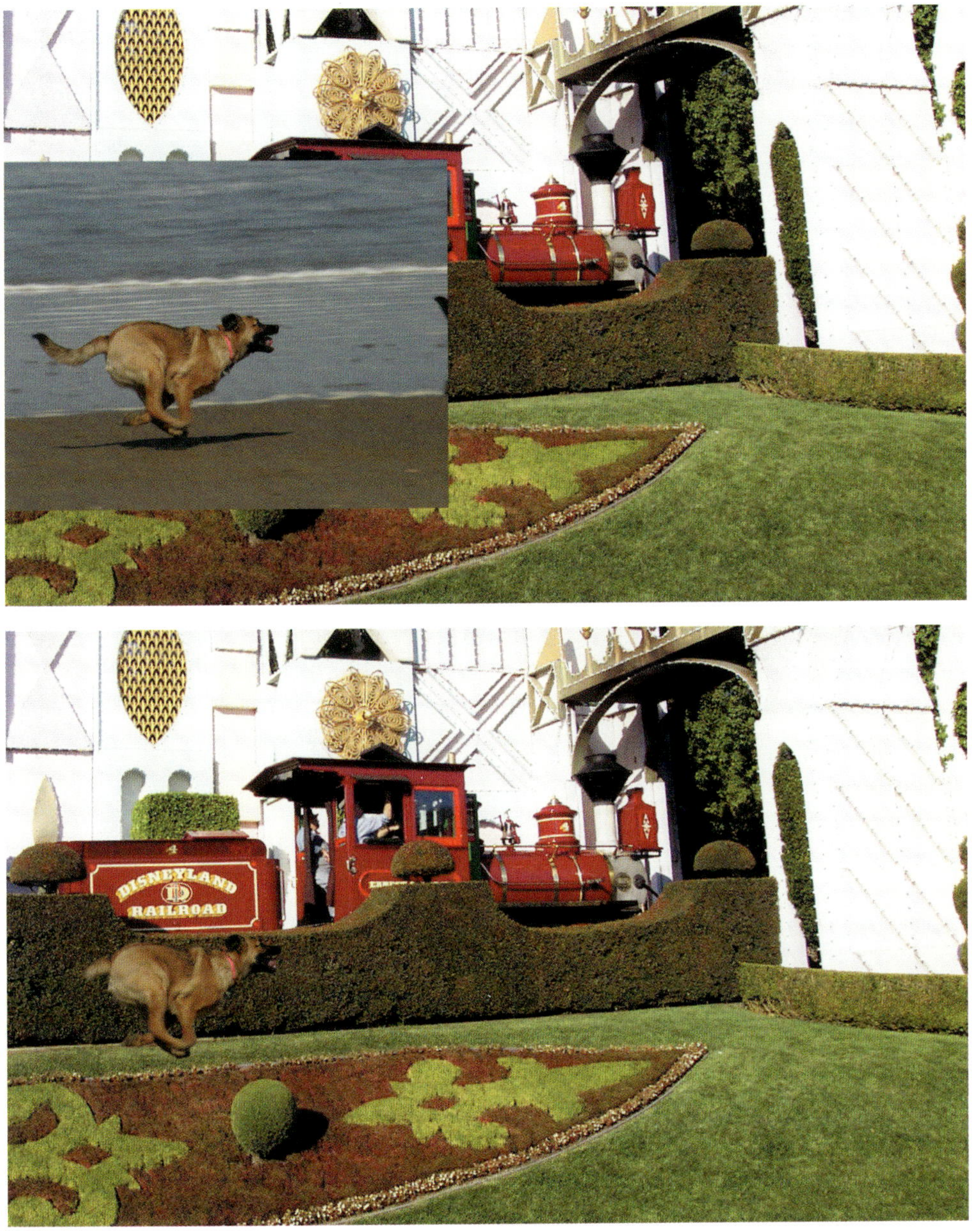

Figure 10.1 If you create a composite image that contains an error, masking provides a solution even if you've since saved and closed the image file.

Mask from Selection

In Chapter 9, "Making Selections," you learned how to create selections with a variety of tools and techniques. Using a selection as the basis of a mask is remarkably easy. The most challenging part is creating a good selection in the first place.

To start, open two images from which you'd like to create a composite image. One will represent the background, and the other will contain the subject you want to place on that background. Using the Move tool, drag the image with the subject you're adding to the background image. Be sure that you drag the layer all the way into the background image before releasing the mouse button. This will place the image onto the background image as a separate layer, as you can see on the Layers palette (Figure 10.2).

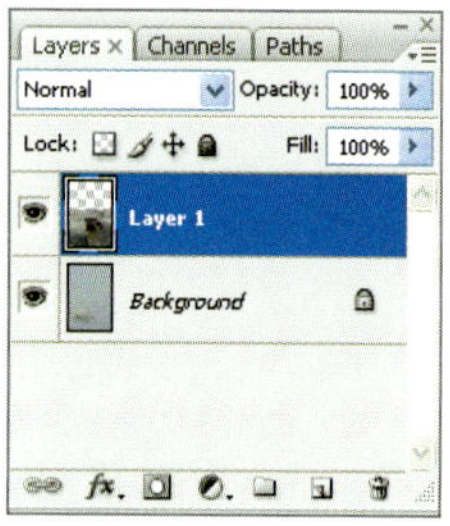

Figure 10.2 When you drag one image onto another, a layer is added to the Layers palette.

Note: If the image you're dragging into the new background contains layers, you must flatten the image first so the effect of all layers is preserved. Just be sure not to save the image after flattening it.

With the two layers brought together into a single document, create a selection that perfectly defines the subject of the top image layer that you want to maintain (Figure 10.3). Anything that *isn't* selected in this image will be blocked after a mask is created, leaving only the selected pixels visible.

Note: If you need to resize the image layer you brought into the new background, choose Edit > Transform > Scale from the menu, hold the Shift key, and drag one of the corners to resize. Press Enter/Return to apply the resize using the default interpolation setting you have established in Preferences.

After the selection is perfected, you're ready to use it as the basis of a layer mask that will reveal only the area you've selected. Make sure the top image layer is active on the Layers palette, and then click the Add Layer Mask button (the one with the circle inside a square icon) at the bottom of the Layers palette. Because a selection is active, Photoshop assumes you want to mask the image based on the current selection and creates the mask accordingly. Areas that were not selected are blocked on the active layer, while selected pixels are revealed (Figure 10.4).

Note: Don't use any feathering in the selection you create. Instead, apply the same effect as feathering after the mask is created by blurring the mask, as discussed in this section. This method provides an opportunity to change the effect based on a preview of the result.

Pixels are hidden from view because of the layer mask that was added to the active image layer. Notice that a layer mask thumbnail is added to the right of the image layer thumbnail on the Layers palette. Areas that had been selected before you created the mask are white on the mask, indicating those areas are visible in the image (revealed). Black areas on the mask correspond to areas that were not selected and are, therefore, blocked from view.

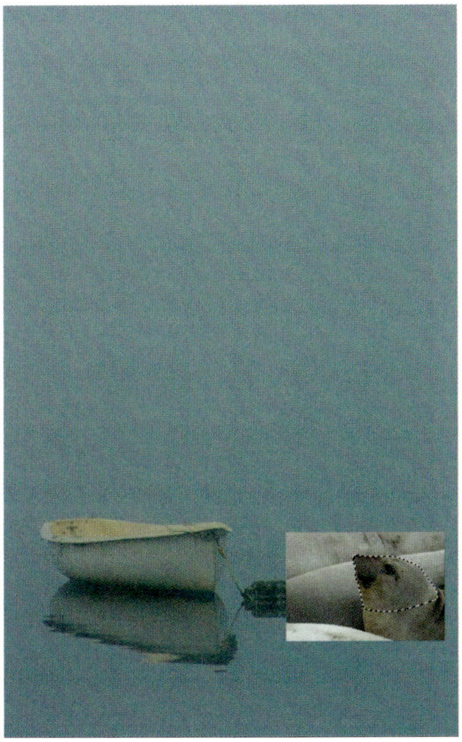

Figure 10.3 Create a selection that perfectly defines the area you want to keep in the image layer added to the background.

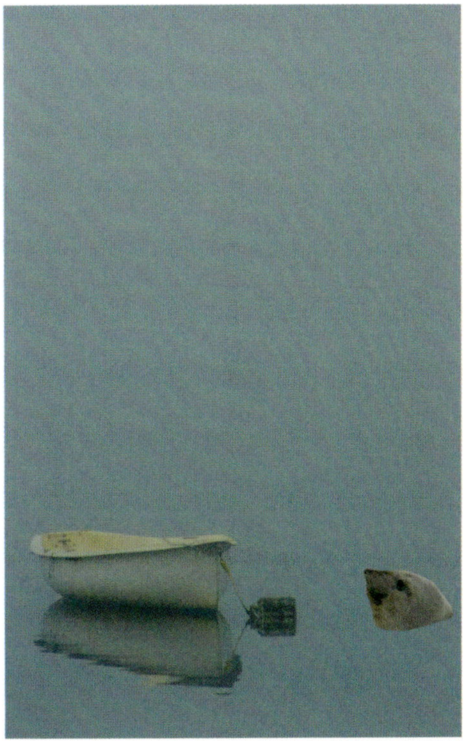

Figure 10.4 When you create a new layer mask with an active selection, the active layer will be masked based on the selection.

Note: When viewing a layer mask, remember that black blocks and white reveals.

If you'd like to see what the layer mask looks like and to have the ability to take a closer look, hold the Alt/Option key as you click the layer mask thumbnail. This will cause the mask to be displayed as a black-and-white image in place of your actual image so you can see the exact shape of the mask (Figure 10.5). This is a great way to determine whether there are areas you missed in the mask and to fix them by painting on the mask if necessary (painting on masks is covered later in this section).

When you're creating a composite image, seeing what the image looked like before and after you created the mask can be helpful. To toggle the mask on and off, hold the Shift key and click the mask thumbnail. A red X will appear on the mask thumbnail when the mask is disabled.

At this point you have a basic composite image. However, because the selection wasn't feathered, a harsh transition occurs between the subject in the top image and the background image layer, resulting in a very "cut-out" appearance. To produce a more realistic effect, you need a more gradual transition between the foreground subject and the background image. You could have done this by feathering the selection, but then you would have had to decide in advance how many pixels by which to feather. Instead, I recommend producing the same effect after creating the mask and while observing a preview.

Figure 10.5 When you Alt/Option+click a layer mask thumbnail, you can see the black-and-white representation of that mask.

To apply a more natural edge to the mask, blur it slightly. This will smooth the transition between areas that are blocked and areas that are revealed, producing a more gradual and realistic transition. First, make sure the layer mask, not the image layer, is selected. You can click the layer mask thumbnail to make it active if it isn't already. When the layer mask is selected, the mask to the right of the image layer thumbnail on the Layers palette will have an extra white box around it.

With the layer mask active, choose Filter > Blur > Gaussian Blur from the menu. While observing the effect on the composite image, select an appropriate blur setting (Figure 10.6). For objects with a relatively crisp edge, a value of 1 or 2 pixels is probably best. For subjects with a "fuzzier" edge, you may need to blur by a higher value. By applying a blur after creating the mask, you're able to determine the best setting for that specific situation, rather than trying to guess how many pixels to feather a selection by before you can even see any effect of the masking. You can then continue applying additional special effects as needed to produce the most realistic result possible (Figure 10.7).

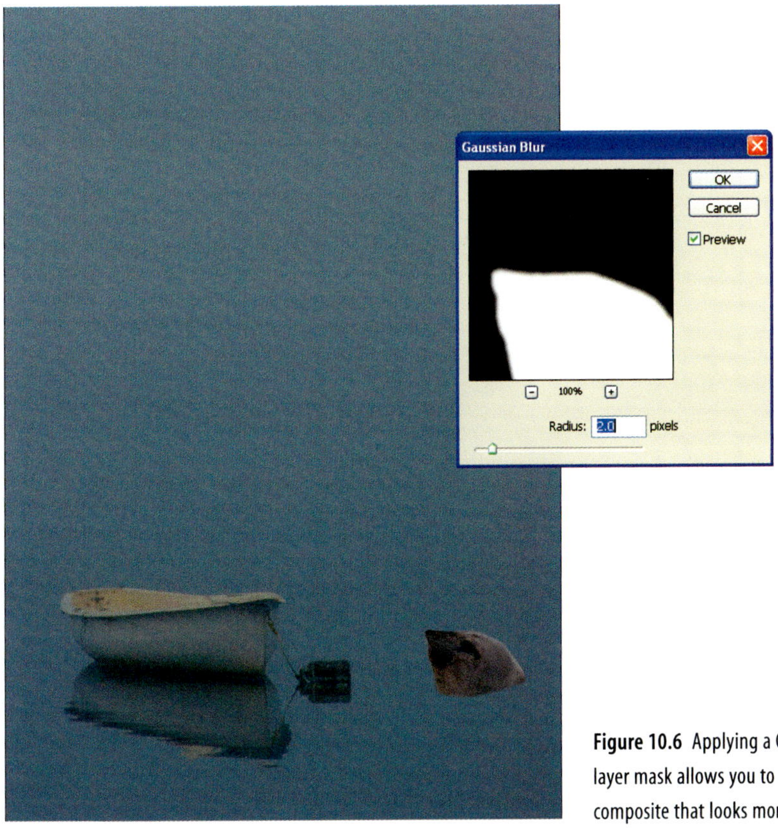

Figure 10.6 Applying a Gaussian Blur to the layer mask allows you to create a blended composite that looks more realistic.

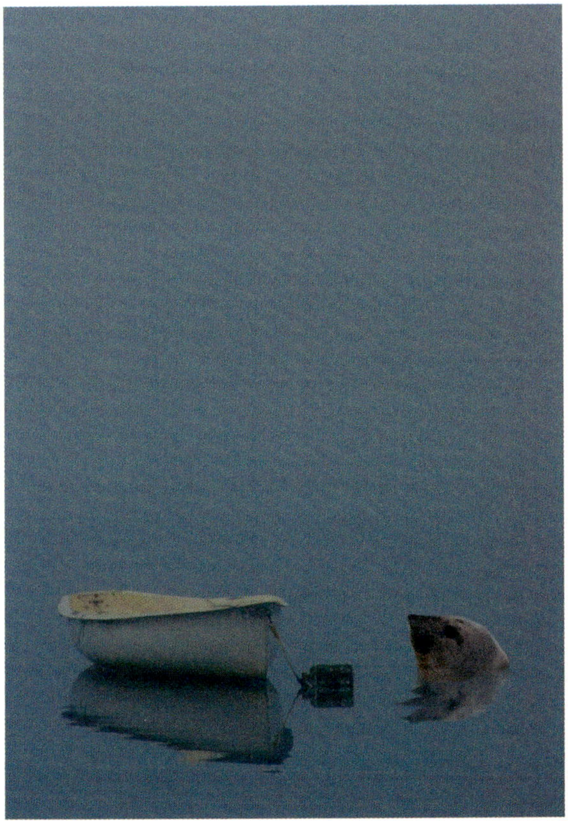

Figure 10.7 Using a variety of techniques, you can work to produce a more realistic composite image.

Painting on Mask

Creating a mask from a selection is simple, but at times it is best to *paint* the mask to block or reveal pixels as needed. As you've already seen, the mask blocks pixels where there is black on the mask and reveals pixels where there is white on the mask. Therefore, you can simply paint on the mask with black or white to block or reveal pixels as needed, respectively.

To create a mask with painting, make sure that you don't have an active selection and that the correct image layer is active, and then click the Add Layer Mask button on the Layers palette. This will create a new layer mask associated with the active image layer. The mask will be filled completely with white, meaning that all pixels are revealed.

Make sure the mask is active by clicking directly on the mask thumbnail on the Layers palette, and then select the Brush tool. On the Options bar, select a brush with a hard edge, and press D to set the foreground and background colors in the toolbar to the defaults of black and white. You can reverse the foreground and background colors by pressing X. Now paint with black in areas where you want to block pixels, and with white in areas where you want to reveal, or "un-hide," pixels that have been blocked (by default all pixels are visible). You can think of this as erasing that can easily be undone (Figure 10.8). Paint in black to effectively erase pixels, but then paint in white to reveal those pixels again.

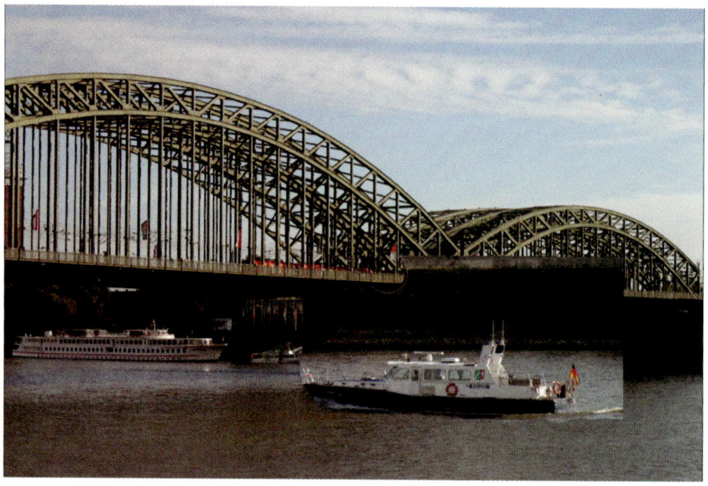

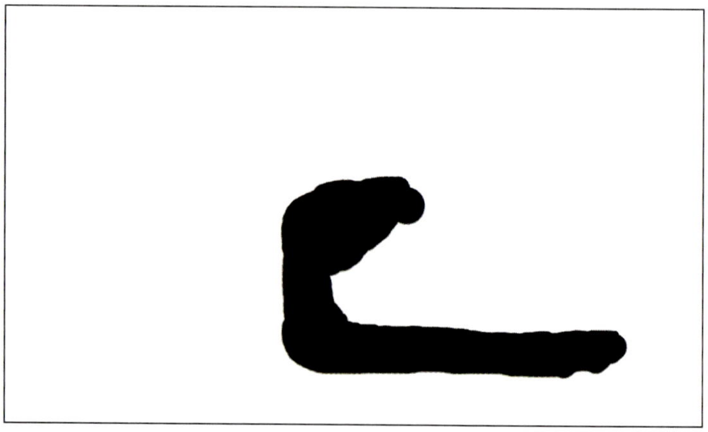

Figure 10.8 When painting on a mask, you can think of black as erasing and white as "un-erasing."

Note: You can always start with a selection to produce a basic layer mask, and then paint on that mask to adjust it.

Clipping Groups

When creating composite images, you'll often need to make adjustments to one of the layers to make it better match the other layers. Naturally, you should produce such a change with adjustment layers. However, if you create an adjustment layer above the top layer, it will affect all image layers below. This makes it impossible to adjust one layer to match another because the layers all change in synch with one another.

One solution is to produce a clipping group composed of the adjustment layers and the image layer you want them to affect exclusively. Click the image layer you want to adjust on the Layers palette to make it the active layer, so that when you add an adjustment layer it will be placed directly above that active layer. Then create a new adjustment layer of the desired type. As soon as the dialog box appears for the adjustment, click OK to close the dialog and allow the adjustment layer to be created. The next step is to group this new adjustment layer to the image layer. Hold the Alt/Option key and point your mouse at the line between the new adjustment layer and the image layer below it on the Layers palette. The cursor will change into a pointer with a left-pointing arrow and two overlapping circles (Figure 10.9). Click to group the adjustment layer with the image layer in a clipping group. You'll know the adjustment layer is in a clipping group because it will be indented and there will be an arrow pointing from the adjustment layer thumbnail down to the image layer thumbnail.

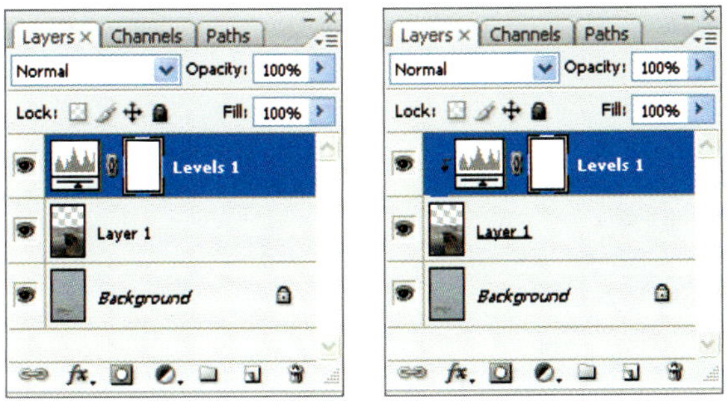

Figure 10.9 Holding the Alt/Option key while pointing the mouse at the line between the adjustment layer and image layer on the Layers palette changes the cursor. When you Alt/Option+click the line, the adjustment layer is grouped with the image layer in a clipping group.

With the adjustment layer grouped with the image layer, double-click the thumbnail for the adjustment layer to bring up the adjustment dialog box. When you make an adjustment, it will apply only to the image layer in the clipping group (Figure 10.10). If you have the same image layer selected when you create additional adjustment layers, those new adjustment layers will be added to the clipping group automatically, so they will also affect only the single adjustment layer.

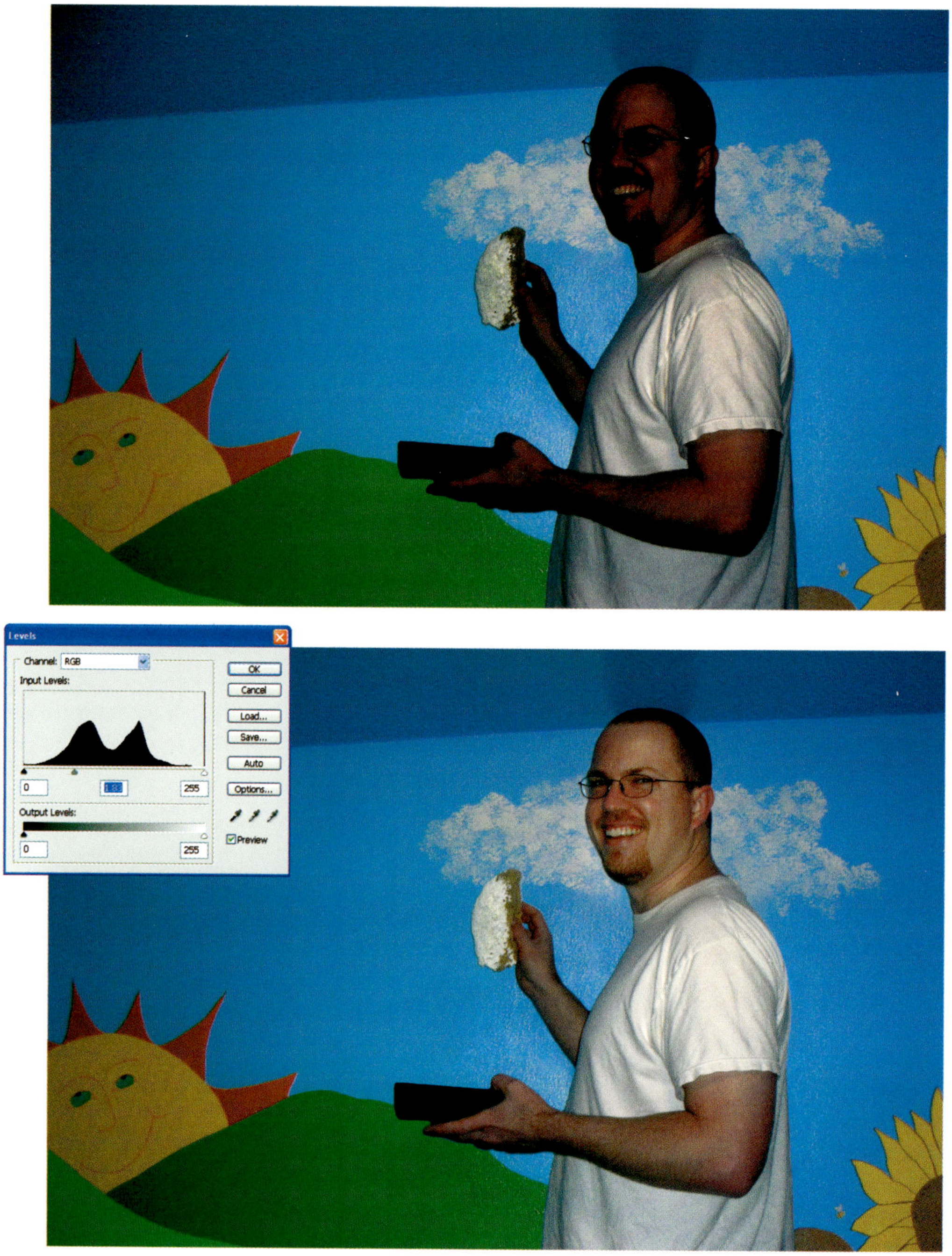

Figure 10.10 Here, an adjustment layer is grouped with an image layer in a clipping group. Changes to that adjustment layer will affect only the layer it is grouped with.

Note: If necessary, you can toggle adjustment layers in and out of the clipping group by Alt/Option+clicking between them and the image layer they are grouped with.

Adjustment Layer Masking

After you understand the principles of masking, it is easy to apply those principles to layer masks for adjustment layers. This allows you to target an adjustment to a specific "geographic" area of your image, which is the key to exercising maximum control. Unlike the adjustments covered in Chapters 5 through 8, which either apply to the entire image or apply selectively to specific tonal or color ranges, when you mask an adjustment layer you can choose which areas of the image you would like to be affected by the adjustment.

For adjustment layers, the principles of masking are exactly the same as for masking image layers. The only difference is that instead of blocking or revealing pixels, you are blocking or revealing the effect of an adjustment layer by altering its attached layer mask.

Mask from Selection

Creating an adjustment layer that is masked based on a selection is easy, especially since you've already seen how such a mask can be used on an image layer when creating a composite image. To mask an adjustment layer, first create a selection that defines the area within the image you'd like to adjust (Figure 10.11). Then create a new adjustment layer of the desired type. Because a selection is active when the new adjustment layer is created, the adjustment layer will apply only to the areas that were selected by automatically creating a layer mask that reflects the selection (Figure 10.12).

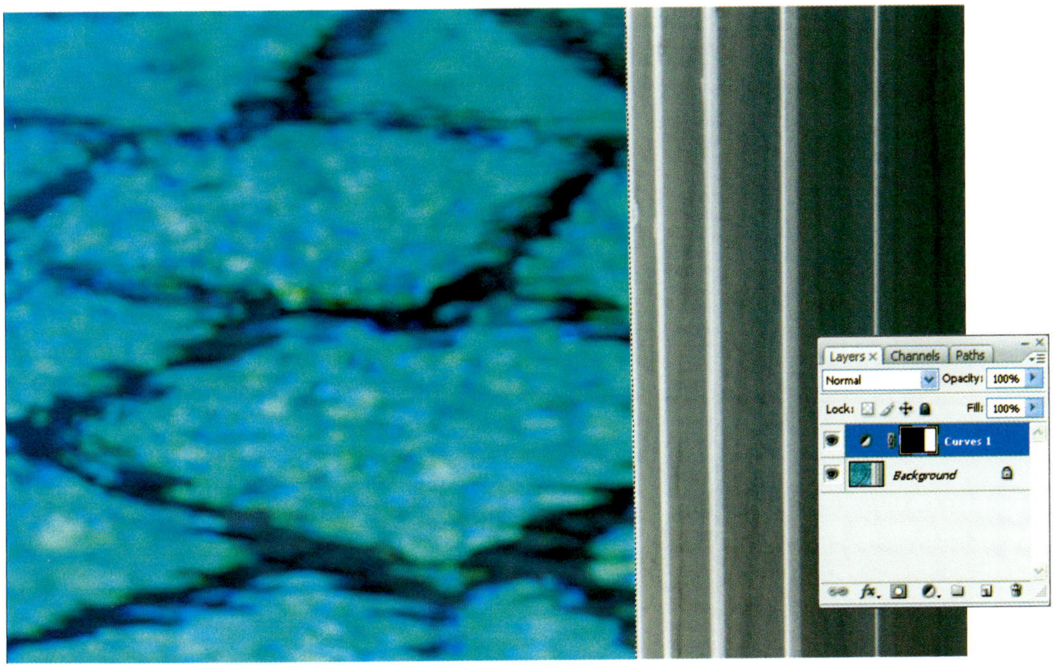

Figure 10.11 To create an adjustment layer that is targeted to a specific area of the image, start by creating a selection of the area you want to adjust. The adjustment layer will automatically be masked based on the selection.

Note: For details on creating selections to use as the basis for masking, refer to Chapter 9.

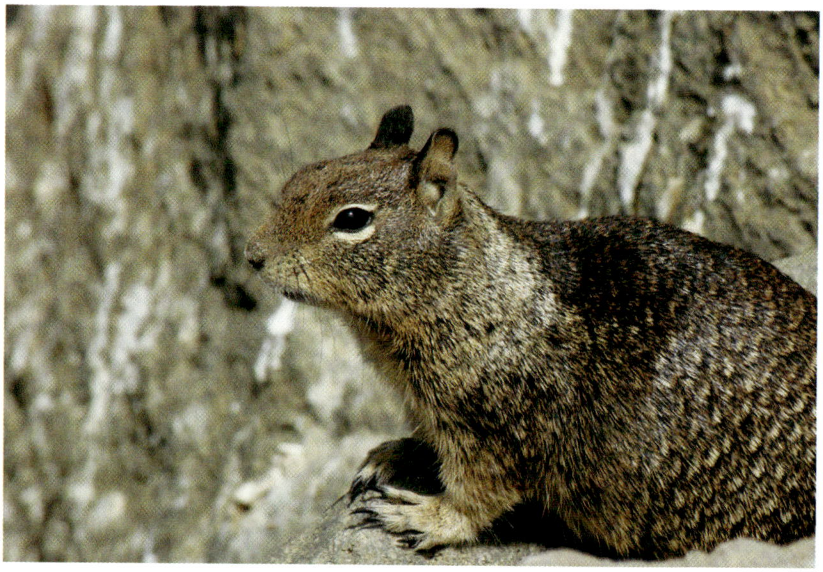

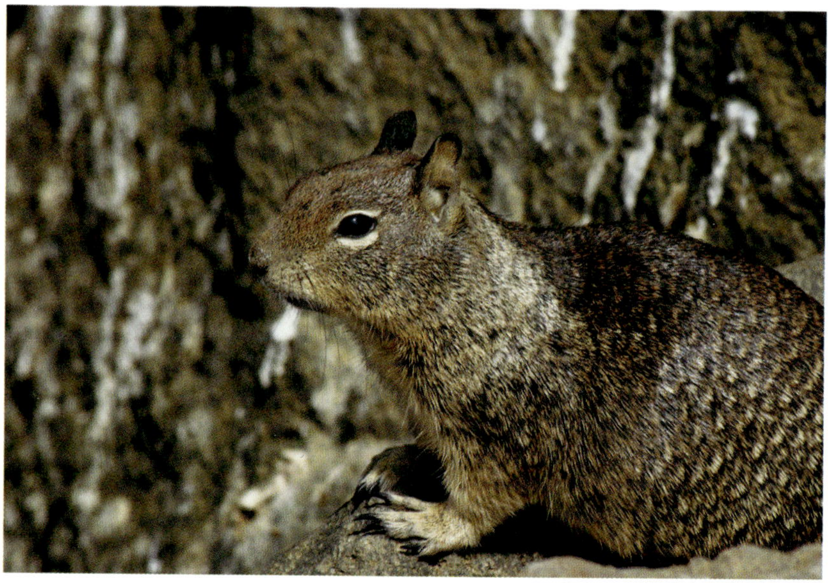

Figure 10.12 The background of this image was a bit too bright, so a selection was created and used as the basis of a mask for a Curves adjustment layer to darken the background.

After you've created a masked adjustment layer, keep in mind that if the selection wasn't feathered (and as discussed earlier in this chapter, I don't recommend feathering the selection for this purpose), the transition between the areas that are affected by the adjustment and those that aren't will be abrupt. To smooth the transition, simply make sure the adjustment layer is active on the Layers palette and apply a Gaussian Blur (Filter > Blur > Gaussian Blur) as discussed earlier in this chapter. Find the blur setting that produces the desired smooth transition.

Painting on a Mask

In some situations you won't want to create the adjustment layer mask based on a selection. For example, when you're going to adjust an image area that is defined by relatively nebulous edges, creating a selection to start from can be a challenge. In those situations, painting to define the mask provides a solution. In fact, adjustment layers are always created with a layer mask attached, so you don't even need to create a layer mask if you have created an adjustment layer when there wasn't an active selection. In that case, the mask will simply be filled with white.

Start by creating an adjustment layer; make an adjustment so you can see an effect in the image. I recommend making an exaggerated adjustment so it is easier to see exactly where in the image the adjustment layer will apply. When you've made the adjustment, click OK in the dialog box. To modify the mask for an adjustment layer, select the Brush tool, press D to set the foreground and background colors to their defaults of black and white, and then press X as needed to switch foreground and background colors, making the desired color the foreground color. Paint with black to block the effect of the adjustment in specific areas of the image, or paint with white to reveal the adjustment (Figure 10.13). When you're finished fine-tuning the mask, you can apply a Gaussian Blur to produce a smooth transition between areas that are and are not affected by the adjustment. Then double-click the thumbnail for the adjustment layer and revise the adjustment to produce the desired final effect.

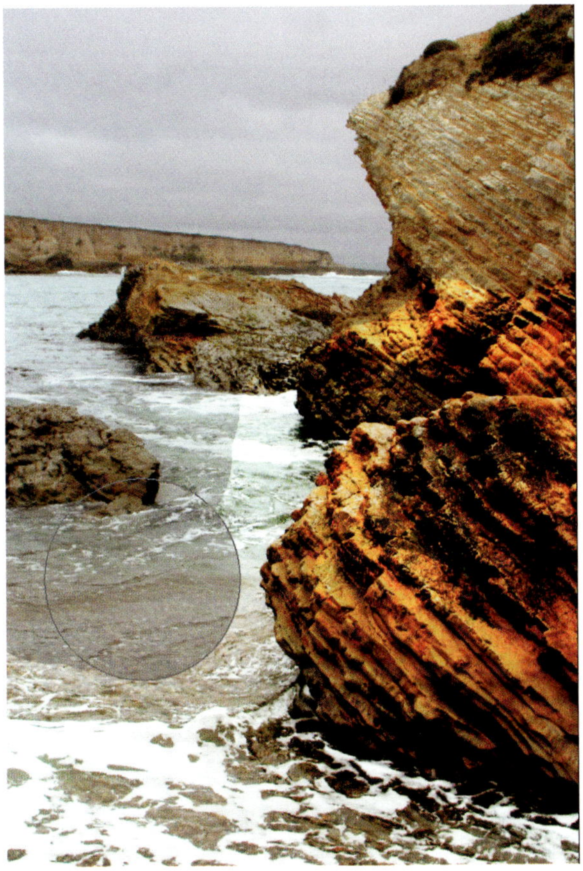

Figure 10.13 After creating an exaggerated adjustment, paint with black on the adjustment layer to mask out the areas you don't want to be affected by the adjustment.

Note: Remember, you can Alt/Option+click the layer mask to view only the mask and clean up small areas that may have been missed in painting.

If you later decide to further revise the adjustment layer mask, simply click the adjustment layer to make it active and paint as needed to change the areas where the adjustment is blocked or revealed. If you've already applied the Gaussian Blur to the layer mask for the adjustment layer, reduce the brush's Hardness setting so you'll continue to produce a soft edge with a smooth transition between areas that are and are not affected by the adjustment layer.

At times you'll want the adjustment layer to apply to a very small area of your image, but that area won't be conducive to making a selection. In such situations, it may seem that the only solution is to paint with black throughout most of the image. However, you can also fill the initially white adjustment layer mask with black so it doesn't apply to any of the image, and then paint with white in the areas where you want the adjustment to be revealed. After creating the new adjustment layer, choose Edit > Fill from the menu, select Black from the Use dropdown list, and click OK. This will fill the layer mask with black, blocking the effect of the adjustment from the entire image. You can then use the Brush tool with the foreground color set to white to paint the adjustment in the areas where you'd like it to be applied.

Note: You can also use Alt/Option+Delete to fill a layer mask with the foreground color and Ctrl/Command+Delete to fill a layer mask with the background color.

So far you've seen how you can paint with black or white on an adjustment layer mask to target specific areas where the adjustment should be blocked or revealed. However, it is helpful to keep in mind that you can use any method at all to place pixels onto a layer mask.

For example, if you'd like to only partially block or reveal the effects of an adjustment layer, you can paint on the layer mask with a shade of gray. This will cause the effect of the adjustment to be blocked or revealed to the extent that the shade of gray you use is nearly black or white, respectively. You could also paint at a reduced opacity to produce a similar effect. As I mentioned previously, you can paint with a soft-edged brush if necessary to produce a gradual transition between the areas that are and are not affected by the adjustment layer.

Note: Any method or tool that allows you to place pixels on a layer can be used to place pixels onto a layer mask, so be creative when you're trying to solve a particular problem with a mask.

Applying a Gradient to a Mask

One particularly helpful example of a tool that can be used to place pixels onto an adjustment layer mask is the Gradient tool. This allows you to place a gradient on a layer mask, resulting in an adjustment that affects one side of the image completely but gradually tapers off in a given direction until it has no effect at the other side of the image. The most common example of using such a gradient is in a composition where you would otherwise use a graduated split neutral-density filter, such as when you need to darken the sky without darkening the foreground of an image (Figure 10.14).

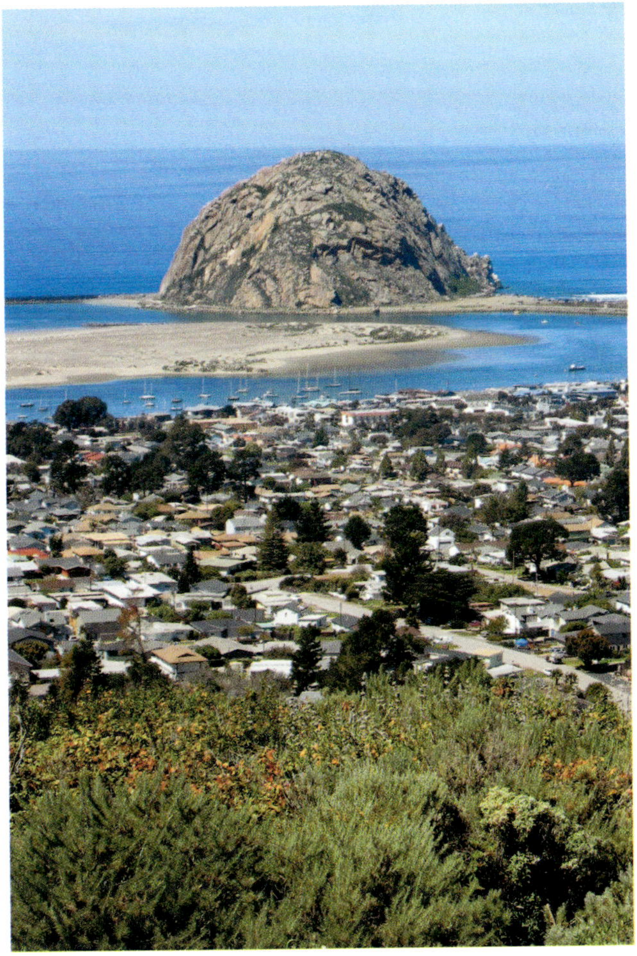

Figure 10.14 To darken this sky without darkening the foreground, a gradient on a mask for an adjustment layer will provide a perfect solution.

To create an adjustment layer with a gradient mask, start by creating a new adjustment layer that produces the desired effect in the area of the image to which you want it to apply. For example, you might create a Levels adjustment layer that darkens the sky in an image. After you've made the adjustment, click OK in the dialog box for the adjustment to apply the settings on the layer.

Then select the Gradient tool from the Tools palette (the shortcut key is G). On the Options bar, click the dropdown for the gradient editor and choose the first gradient thumbnail on the list, which is the Foreground To Background gradient. Next, select the Linear Gradient option from the set of five buttons allowing you to choose a style for your gradient (Figure 10.15). Finally, press D to set the foreground and background colors to the defaults of black and white, and set white to the foreground color (pressing X to switch foreground and background colors if necessary). You're now ready to create a gradient that transitions from white to black.

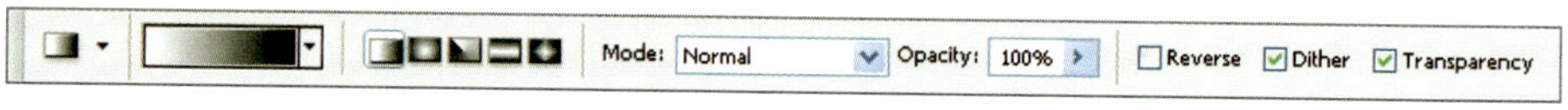

Figure 10.15 The Options bar for the Gradient tool provides the options needed to produce the desired effect when masking an adjustment layer with a gradation.

You want to create the gradient on the layer mask for the adjustment layer you just created, so make sure that is the active layer on the Layers palette. Then click and drag on the image to create a gradient: the foreground color will start where you first click, with a smooth gradation to the background color where you release the mouse. The length of the line you drag determines the distance over which the gradient will transition, and the direction determines the angle of that gradient. To lock the gradient to 45-degree increments, simply hold the Shift key as you drag.

In our example of darkening the sky, click in the area of sky that represents the lowest area you still want the adjustment to affect completely, and drag downward to the point where you don't want any effect at all. If you're not happy with the initial gradient you created, simply click and drag again to replace the gradient with a new one. The result is an adjustment that blends smoothly, from applying completely in one area of the image to having no effect on another area (Figure 10.16).

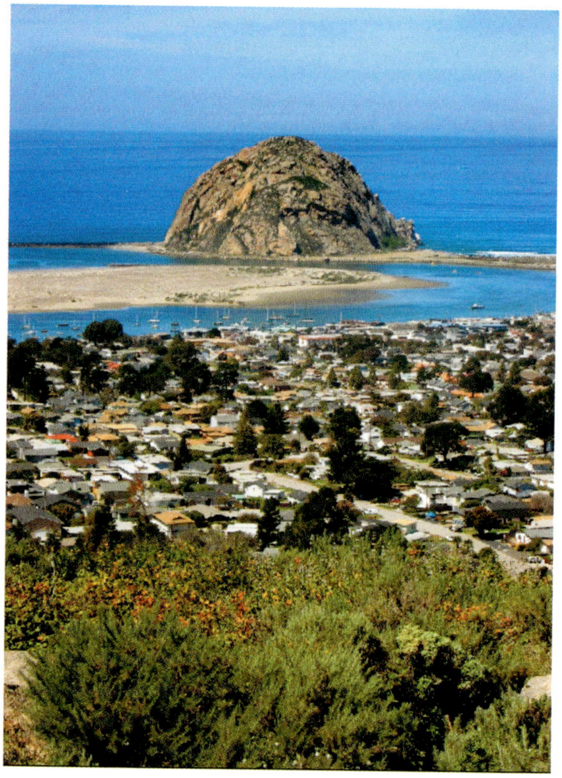

Figure 10.16 Applying a gradient to the layer mask for an adjustment layer produces an effect similar to the use of a graduated split neutral-density filter when capturing an image.

Layer Groups

Layer groups provide a way to organize the layers on your Layers palette when they become so numerous as to be out of hand. On a basic level, they provide a simple organizational tool, allowing you to group layers into a folder (the layer group) that can then be collapsed to hide the layers contained within the layer group and help to de-clutter your Layers palette. However, beyond this simple organizational benefit, layer groups also provide a way to exercise greater control over your images.

Creating Adjustment Versions

The most basic way to extend the simple capability of layer groups is to use them to produce multiple versions of your images in a single master image file. For example, to have a color and grayscale version of your image, you can create layer groups to contain the separate adjustments for each. When you turn off the visibility of a layer group, all layers within that group are also hidden. This allows you to determine which version of the image will be viewed or printed by turning on the visibility of only one layer group at a time.

To create a layer group, click the Create A New Group button at the bottom of the Layers palette. You can then create adjustment layers and drag them into the layer group by clicking the adjustment layer thumbnail and dragging it to the folder icon for the layer group you have created (Figure 10.17). If you create an adjustment layer (or new image layer for that matter) while a layer group is active, the new layer will automatically be added to the group.

Note: You can rename a layer group by double-clicking its name on the Layers palette, typing a new name, and pressing Enter/Return.

When you are finished adding adjustment layers to a layer group, you can click the arrow button to the left of the folder icon to collapse (or later expand) the folder. When you collapse the folder, the layers inside that layer group remain visible in the image but are hidden on the Layers palette, providing a more organized palette.

By creating multiple layer groups, you can produce multiple versions of the same image. Start by turning off the visibility of the layer group by clicking the eye icon to the left of it on the Layers palette. This will hide the contents of the layer group so the adjustment layers contained in the group don't have an effect on the image. Then create a new layer group and add adjustment layers to it. By turning off the visibility of all but one layer group at a time, you can keep multiple versions in a single image file but have only one version active at a time (Figure 10.18).

Note: When you have multiple layer groups containing adjustment layers to produce different versions of your image, be sure that you turn on the visibility of only one layer group at a time.

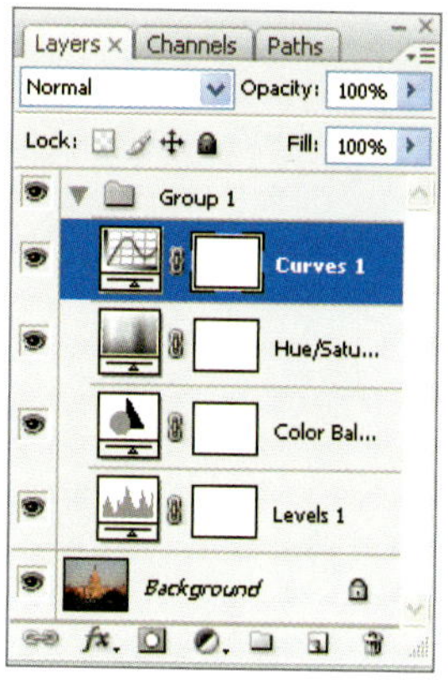

Figure 10.17 Placing adjustment layers inside a layer group keeps them organized and provides the opportunity to produce multiple interpretations of an image within the same document.

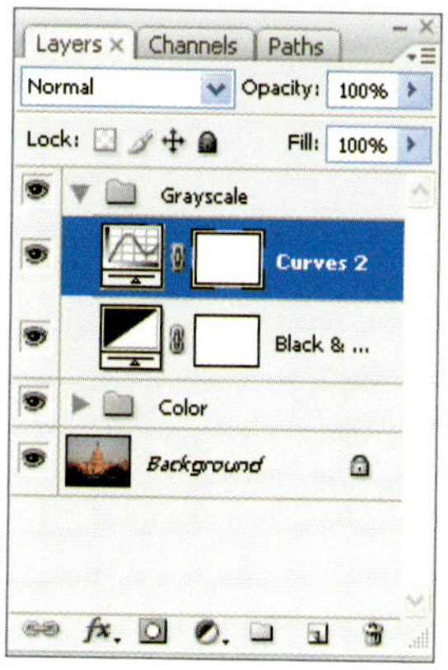

Figure 10.18 When you create layer groups for different versions of an image, keep only one layer group visible at a time.

Masking Multiple Adjustments

Another benefit of layer groups is the ability to mask multiple adjustment layers at once with a single layer mask. When you want to create a targeted adjustment for a particular area of your image, often multiple adjustment layers will be needed to get exactly the desired result. However, if you were to use the same selection as the basis of the masks for these adjustment layers, you'd end up with a duplicate mask for several adjustment layers. This isn't a problem unless you later discover that the selection wasn't perfect. You must then modify all the individual layer masks to correct the problem for all adjustment layers targeted to that area of the image. A layer group allows you to avoid this problem.

When you know you'll be making multiple adjustments to a targeted area, start by creating a layer group. Add an adjustment layer (or several) to this group, and make an adjustment that is obvious so you can see the effect in the image. With the layer group active on the Layers palette, add a layer mask directly to it either by creating a selection and then clicking the Add Layer Mask button, or (without an active selection) by clicking the Add Layer Mask button and then using any of the methods discussed earlier in this chapter to modify the mask. You can then modify the adjustments you placed in the layer group with a single layer mask to perfect the result. The adjustment layers will affect only the area defined by the layer mask for the layer group, because those adjustment layers are contained within the group (Figure 10.19). If you later discover the mask wasn't perfect, you can adjust it in a single place (for the layer group), and it will change the area that all adjustment layers within that layer group affect.

Note: When using this method, leave the blending mode for the layer group to the default value of Pass Through.

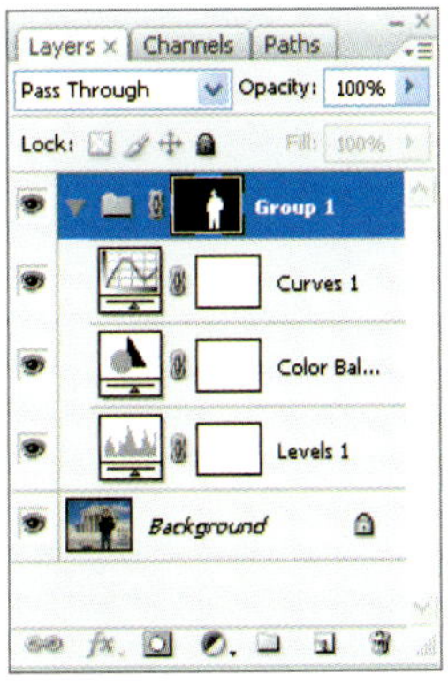

Figure 10.19 Creating a layer mask for a group with multiple adjustment layers allows you to modify only a single mask when needed while affecting the area adjusted by the whole group of adjustment layers.

Applying Multiple Masks

Because you can add a layer mask to layer groups, this opens up the ability to create multiple layer masks for a single layer by having a layer mask associated both with the layer and the layer group. Even better, because layer groups can be nested within each other, you can create multiple masks to apply to a group of adjustment layers by creating multiple nested layer groups. This is helpful when you need to make relatively complicated masks for adjustments.

For example, I often want to target several adjustments to just the sky in an image. This situation benefits from placing those multiple adjustments into a layer group, and then masking the layer group so it affects only the sky in the image. However, if I also want the adjustments to be stronger at the top of the sky than at the bottom, I can't easily solve the problem with a single mask. Instead I'll nest an additional layer group folder, so I have adjustment layers inside a layer group inside another layer group. One layer group will be masked for the sky, and the other layer group will be masked with a gradient (Figure 10.20). The two combine to mask the adjustment layers so they affect only the sky but with a graduated effect.

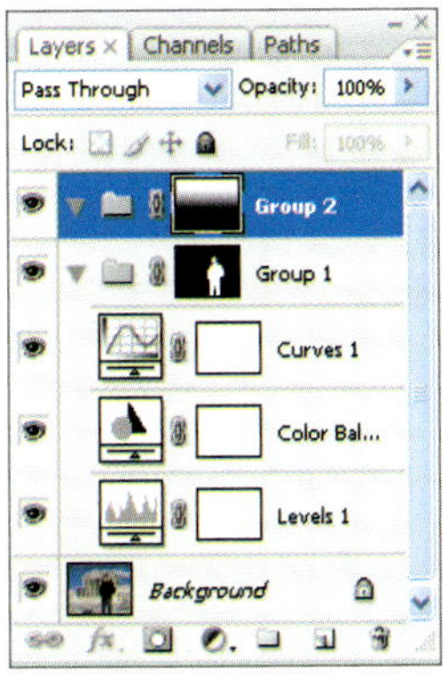

Figure 10.20 By nesting layer groups, you can create multiple layer masks that affect a single group of adjustment layers.

To nest layer groups, create two layer groups and then drag one layer set onto the folder icon of the other layer set. You can then add adjustment layers to the "inside" layer group, and add layer masks to both of the layer groups as needed. You can nest layer groups up to five folders deep, providing enough flexibility to satisfy even the most complicated masking requirements.

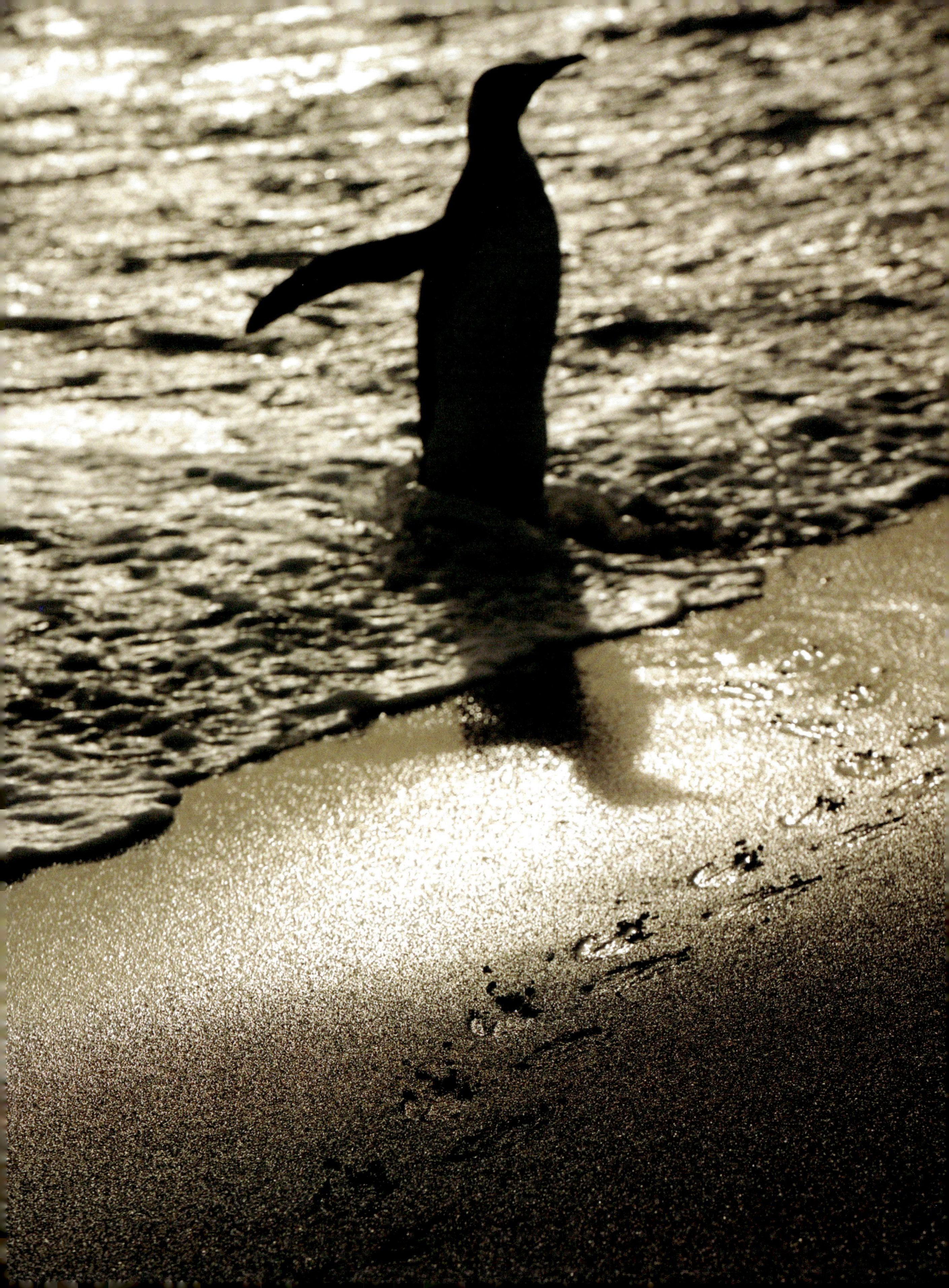

Creative Adjustments

Up to this point, I've presented components of an overall digital workflow that allow you to optimize your images to achieve the very best results that match your vision. However, all of the methods presented have been aimed at producing a "normal" photographic image. Although this is the goal of most photographers with most images, at times you'll want to take some creative license and present a unique interpretation of an image.

11

Chapter Contents

Getting Creative

After you've gone through the full workflow for optimizing your images, you're ready to think about any creative adjustments you'd like to make. I recommend waiting until you reach this stage of the workflow before you start thinking about creativity because that will help you focus on getting the best quality possible from your master image before you move on to other interpretations of it. Even if you think you'll be presenting a black-and-white version of the image exclusively, I still recommend starting with an optimization of the color image. This will help ensure the original master is of the best quality and will provide a better frame of reference as you apply creative adjustments.

In this chapter, I present only a handful of creative adjustments you may want to consider for your images. As you reach the end of your workflow, you'll likely find yourself wanting more and more to explore additional interpretations of your images. Think of this chapter as an introduction to creative adjustments, providing some insight into what is possible. Then, each time you reach the end of your optimization workflow, you'll be better prepared to think of new ways you could present some of your favorite images.

Colorize

In Chapter 5, "Basic Tone and Color," and Chapter 8, "Advanced Color Adjustments," I discussed many aspects of the Hue/Saturation adjustment but didn't discuss one of the available creative options. The Colorize checkbox provides a way to apply a color in such a way as to produce a *monochromatic* image, in which a single color is used at various tonal values. You can think of this as a black-and-white image that uses a colored ink instead of black.

Note: You can also use the new Black And White adjustment layer discussed later in this chapter to apply the same effect as Colorize during the process of creating a black-and-white version of your image, utilizing the Tint settings. This provides more control over the final result you'll achieve because you can adjust the overall tonality as well as the color effect at one time.

Although it is possible to include both a basic saturation adjustment and the Colorize feature in a single Hue/Saturation adjustment layer, I recommend creating a new adjustment layer for the Colorize adjustment. This also makes it easier to switch between different versions of your image, choosing between the full-color and Colorize options by toggling the visibility of a single Hue/Saturation adjustment layer. Therefore, the first step is to create a new Hue/Saturation adjustment layer for your image.

In the Hue/Saturation dialog box, select the Colorize box, which will cause some aspects of the controls to change (Figure 11.1). The Hue slider will change to a representation that includes zero at the far left rather than in the center, and it will have a scale from 0 to 360 rather than from –180 to +180 (these numbers represent position on the color wheel as an indicator of actual color value). The Saturation slider's original range of–100 to +100 will change to a range of 0 to 100. Adjusting these sliders will change the color (Hue) of the image as well as the intensity (Saturation) of that color. You'll also notice that at the bottom of the Hue/Saturation dialog box, the color bar representing the "after" value for colors will change to reflect only the single color that will now exist within the image. The Edit dropdown list will become disabled because you won't be able to adjust individual color channels when working with Colorize.

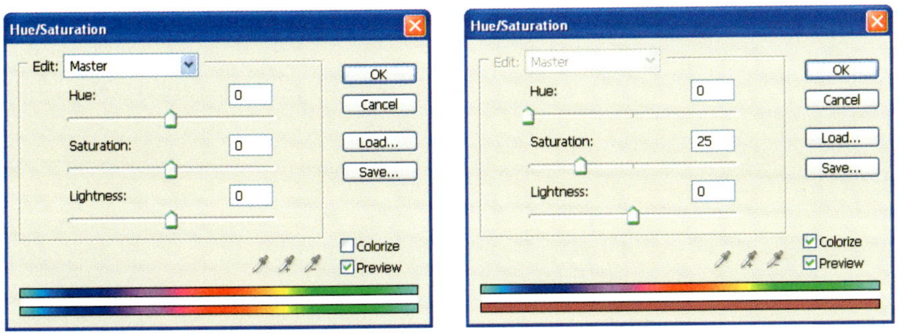

Figure 11.1 When you select the Colorize checkbox in the Hue/Saturation dialog box, the controls change.

Start with the Hue slider to find the particular color you'd like to use for the Colorize effect. Think about the psychology of the colors you're considering and the context of the image. For example, scenes with snow and water tend to look good with cooler colors such as cyan or blue, and images with metal or "rugged" subjects tend to look better with warmer tones such as red or magenta. You have tremendous flexibility and can literally choose any color of the rainbow (Figure 11.2), but it is generally best to find a color that suits the subject of the photo.

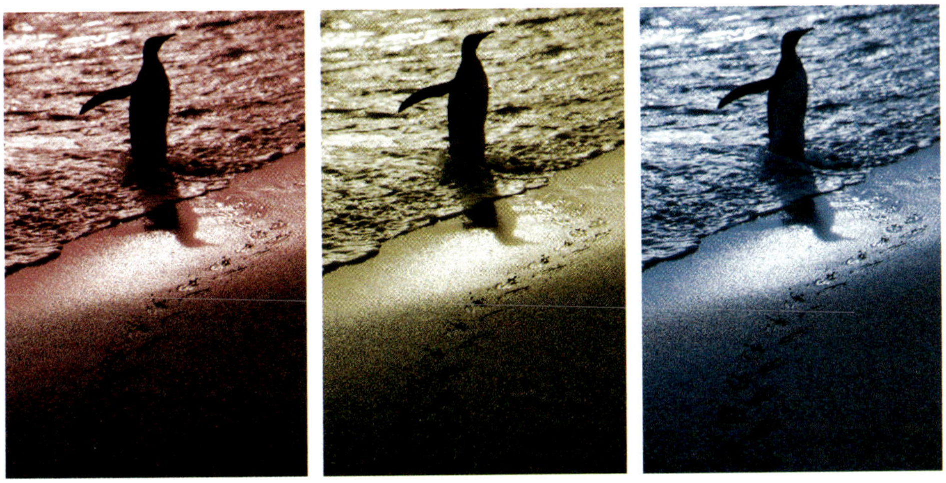

Figure 11.2 You can use any combination of settings for Hue and Saturation for the desired effect with the Colorize option. These images show Hue/Saturation settings of 0/20 (left), 50/25 (center), and 195/27 (right).

After you select the basic color for the image, use the Saturation slider to adjust the intensity of the color. I generally prefer to use relatively low settings, in the range of about 15 to 25. Sometimes I prefer to have an image that looks like a black-and-white at first glance, but gives you an emotional response because of the perception of a color element that you almost don't see. Other times I want to make a more dramatic statement with an image. I usually won't use a setting above about 35 or 40 because the image will then seem to have excessive color. The key is to find settings that you like for the image (Figure 11.3).

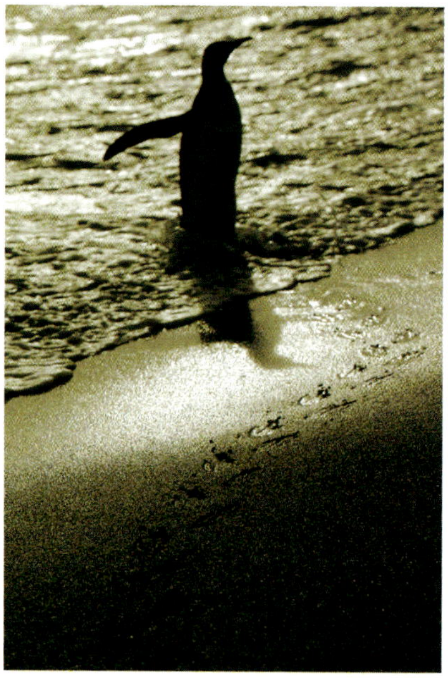

Figure 11.3 To find the values that work best for the image based on your preferences, use the Hue and Saturation sliders with the Colorize checkbox selected.

Note: Many photographers like to produce a "sepia tone" effect, which is a popular way of processing black-and-white images in a traditional wet darkroom. To achieve such an effect, use the Colorize option with a Hue setting of about 50 and a Saturation setting of about 20, fine-tuning these values to your liking.

Because you're using this Hue/Saturation adjustment layer for the sole purpose of adding an artistic effect to your image, it is a good idea to rename the adjustment layer so you'll know in the future why it is there. To do so, double-click the name of the new Hue/Saturation adjustment layer you created, type a new name (such as *Colorize*), and press Enter/Return (Figure 11.4).

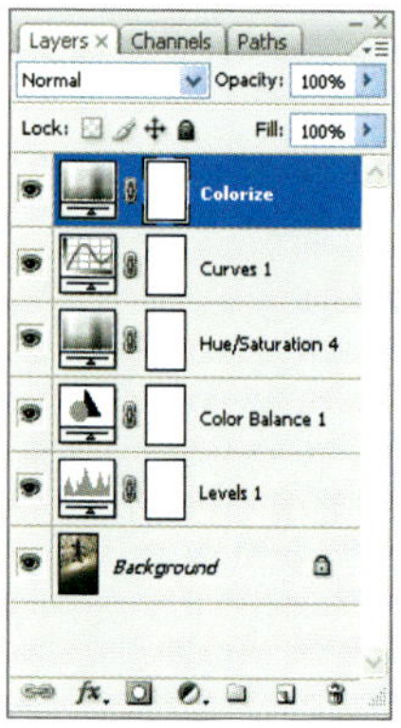

Figure 11.4 Renaming the Hue/Saturation adjustment layer you created to apply the Colorize effect will help you stay organized when reviewing or revising your images later.

Grayscale Conversion

Although digital cameras default to capturing images in full color, and most photography is captured in color, many photographers still enjoy producing black-and-white versions of their images. There are a variety of ways you can convert a color image to black-and-white. I recommend using only methods that preserve the original color data in the image, providing maximum detail in the final result and greater flexibility. There are two primary methods I use for producing these conversions.

Grayscale Hue Shift

One of the easiest methods for producing a grayscale conversion is to use a special technique involving a Hue/Saturation adjustment layer. This solution provides the simplicity of adjusting a single slider to produce variations in the grayscale interpretation of the image.

To use this method, start by creating an empty image layer at the top of your stack of layers on the Layers palette (you can do this by first clicking the topmost layer on the palette and then clicking the Create A New Layer button). Fill this layer with black (or any neutral value) either by using the Edit > Fill command or by pressing D to set the colors to their default values, holding Alt/Option, and then pressing Delete. Change the blending mode for this image layer to Color, so that it affects only the color of the underlying image. The result will be a grayscale image, but you will still need to apply an adjustment to change the result based on your preferences (Figure 11.5).

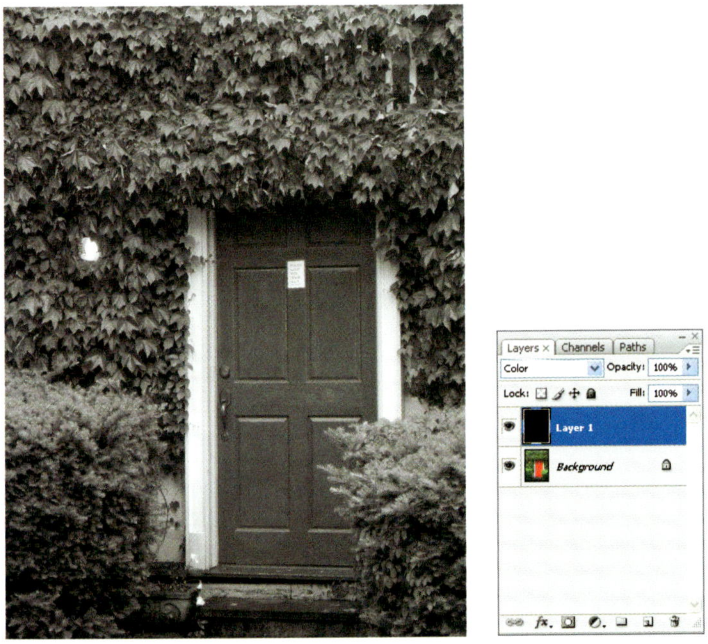

Figure 11.5 The first steps in the process of producing a grayscale image with control provided by a Hue/Saturation adjustment are to create a new empty layer, fill it with black (or another neutral value), and change the blending mode to Color. This will cause the image to appear as a black-and-white version.

The next step is to create a Hue/Saturation adjustment layer that will allow you to fine-tune the effect of your grayscale conversion. This adjustment layer should be placed directly below the new layer you just added, so first click the layer below the new layer and then create a new Hue/Saturation adjustment layer. In the Hue/Saturation dialog box, slide the Hue slider to create a range of different interpretations for the image (Figure 11.6). What's happening is that you're changing the color values in the underlying image, which in turn changes the tonality of those colors. However, you're not seeing the underlying color shift because the topmost new layer you created is causing the image to be seen in only a black-and-white form. You can also use the Saturation slider as a rudimentary brightness/contrast adjustment. However, it doesn't offer much control, so I recommend adding a Levels or Curves adjustment to the top of the Layers palette after you've produced your black-and-white interpretation of the image to further fine-tune the tonality.

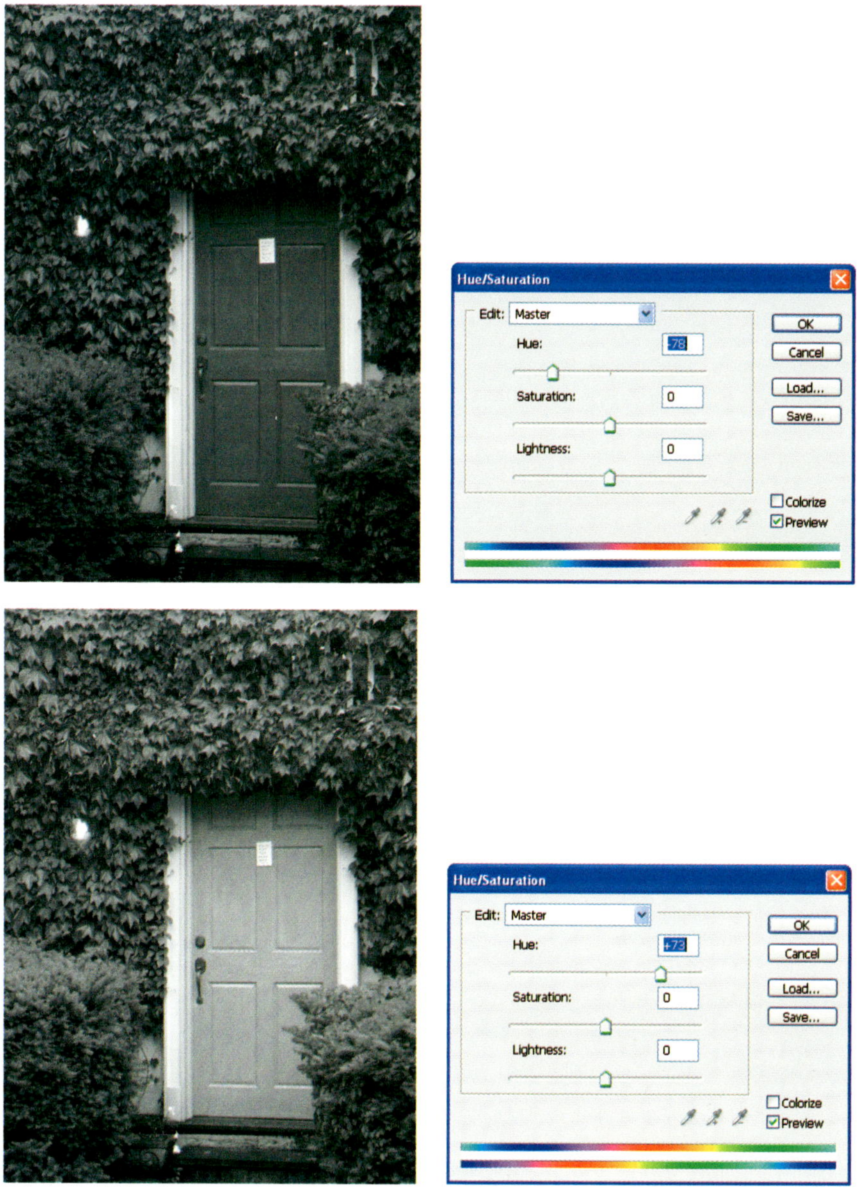

Figure 11.6 Adjusting the Hue slider in the Hue/Saturation dialog box when using this method will allow you to produce various interpretations of the black-and-white image.

Black and White Adjustment

Photoshop CS3 has added a new Black And White adjustment layer option that gives you tremendous control over the process of creating a grayscale version of your image, while still being easy to use. The basic concept is that you are able to adjust the relative brightness for individual color ranges within the image, fine-tuning the final grayscale result. By changing the relationships between colors in the image, you can change the final appearance in terms of brightness levels of various objects within the image, enabling you to create a variety of different interpretations of the image quickly and easily (Figure 11.7).

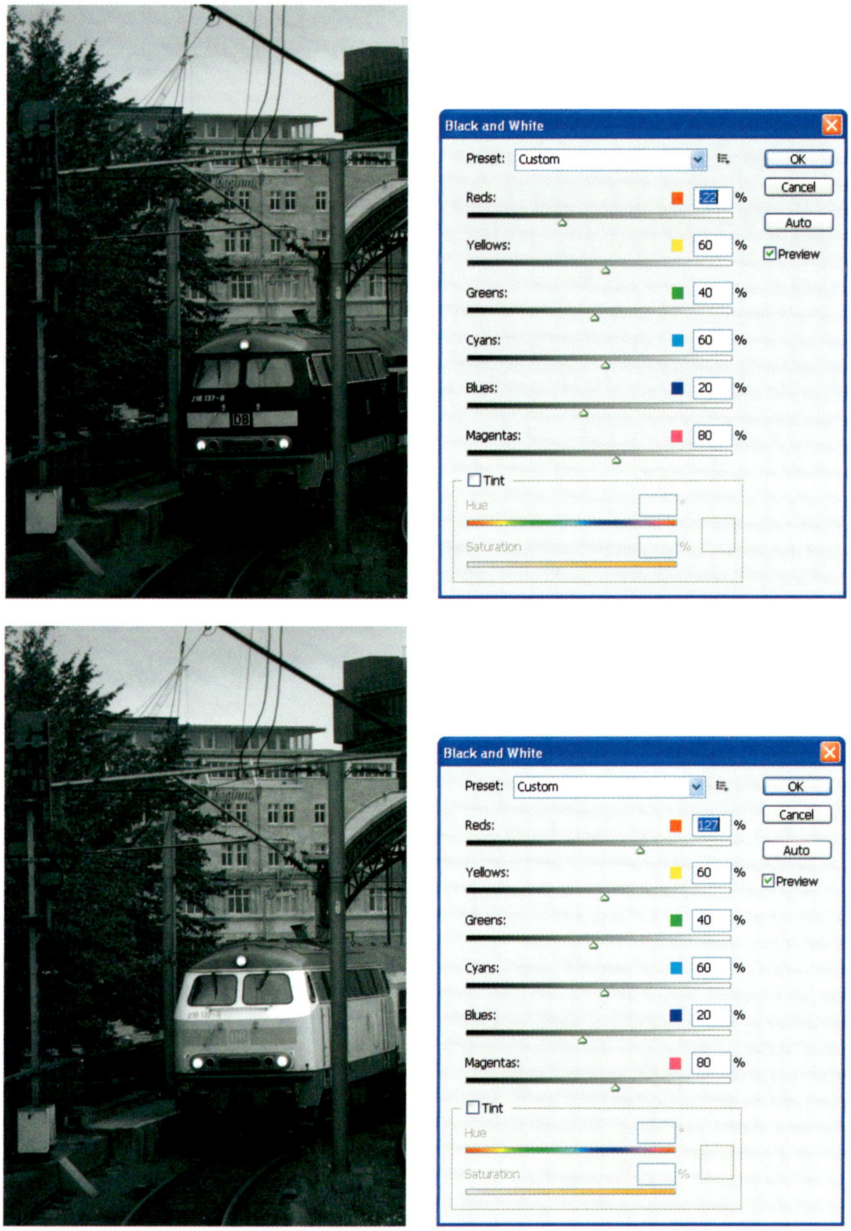

Figure 11.7 By changing the relative brightness for individual color values in an image, you can create a variety of different interpretations for a single image.

To get started, add a new Black And White adjustment layer in the normal manner to bring up the Black And White dialog box. At the top of the dialog box is a drop-down that allows you to select a preset to use as the initial settings for your image. If you're familiar with filters for use in black and white photography, you will recognize many of these. Selecting one of these options can be helpful in providing a starting point closer to your final intend, so you may want to go through these choices to see if one appeals to you. In general you'll probably find the Green Filter option to provide the most pleasing "basic" black-and-white appearance. You might also consider Red Filter when you want to produce a result with particularly high contrast.

The next step is to adjust the individual color sliders. Each of them adjusts the brightness values for the specified color. For example, moving the Reds slider to the right will lighten the pixels that started out red, and moving it to the left will darken those pixels. You can simply go through the list and move the sliders back and forth to get a sense of how you want to fine-tune the controls, but it is much more effective to have a particular goal in mind. For example, if you had a photograph of an orange flower against a blue sky, you might move the Reds and Yellows sliders to the right to brighten the flower and the Cyans and Blues sliders to the left to darken the sky.

Note: As you're working with the Black And White adjustment, you can clear the Preview checkbox at any time to see the original image so you can remind yourself of where particular color values appear within the image.

It can be very helpful to work through all of the sliders at least twice to help you find the optimal settings. The first time you're making larger adjustments and also learning how each will affect the image. The second time you're able to refine the adjustments to work toward the best result possible, having developed a better understanding of how each slider will affect the image.

At the bottom of the Black And White dialog box is a section that allows you to apply a color tint to the image, with results that are very similar to using the Colorize option in the Hue/Saturation adjustment discussed earlier in this chapter. If you'd like to add a color tint to the newly created black-and-white version of your image, select the Tint checkbox. This will enable the Hue and Saturation sliders in this section. Use the Hue slider to select the color you'd like to use for the tint, and then use the Saturation slider to adjust the intensity of the color (Figure 11.8). In most cases, a subtle color tint is best, so you're not likely to want to use a value above about 15% for Tint.

Note: After making a black-and-white version of your image, you may want to add a Levels or Curves adjustment to fine-tune the overall tonality to produce the best result.

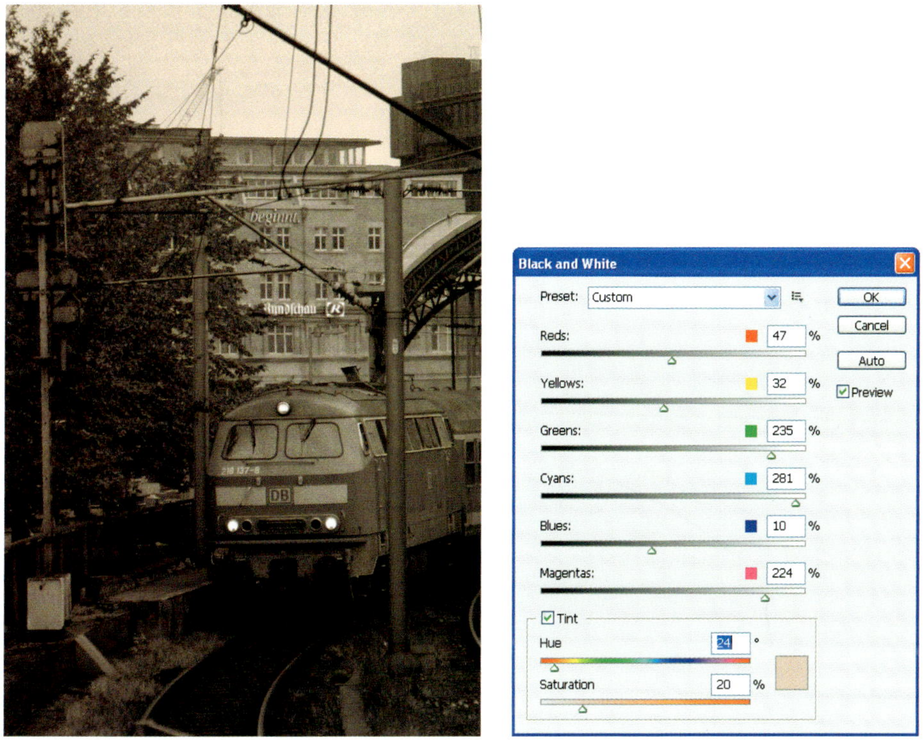

Figure 11.8 The Hue and Saturation sliders allow you to apply a color tint to the image after applying a grayscale conversion with the Black And White adjustment.

High Pass Sharpening

The method of applying a sharpening effect by using the High Pass filter is something I think of as providing a way to sharpen smooth textures (Figure 11.9). This sounds a bit odd, but when you see the technique, you'll see what I'm talking about. The method enhances edge contrast, making it similar to sharpening. However, it doesn't enhance noise, grain, or small artifacts, and it works great as a creative application of a sharpening effect.

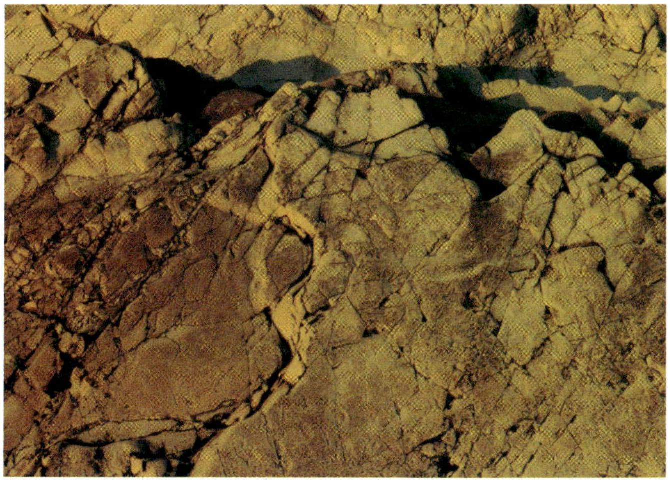

Figure 11.9 An image such as this one, which includes smooth textures, is an ideal candidate for the High Pass sharpening technique.

The first step is to create a copy of your Background image layer (for example, by choosing Layers > Duplicate Layer from the menu). Then change the blending mode for this new layer to Overlay (Figure 11.10). The effect will be strong contrast within the image, but you'll change the effect by applying a filter.

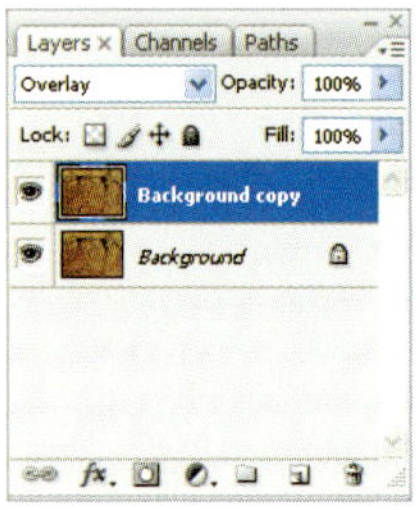

Figure 11.10 To use the High Pass sharpening technique, first create a copy of the Background image layer and change the blending mode for this copy to Overlay.

Choose Filter > Other > High Pass from the menu, which will bring up the High Pass filter dialog box (Figure 11.11). This filter produces something of an embossing effect within the image, producing many middle gray pixels, and brighter and darker values along contrast edges within the image. Because you're using the Overlay blending mode, this is similar to dodging and burning along contrast edges within the image. Adjust the Radius setting to achieve the desired effect and click OK (Figure 11.12).

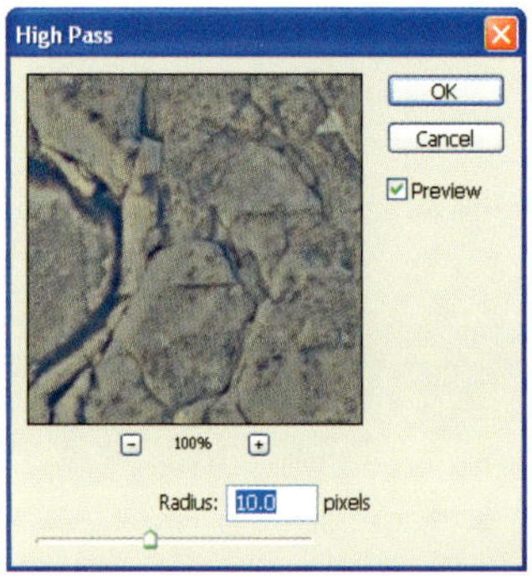

Figure 11.11 The High Pass filter applies an embossing effect to the image, and you can control the strength of the effect by adjusting the Radius slider.

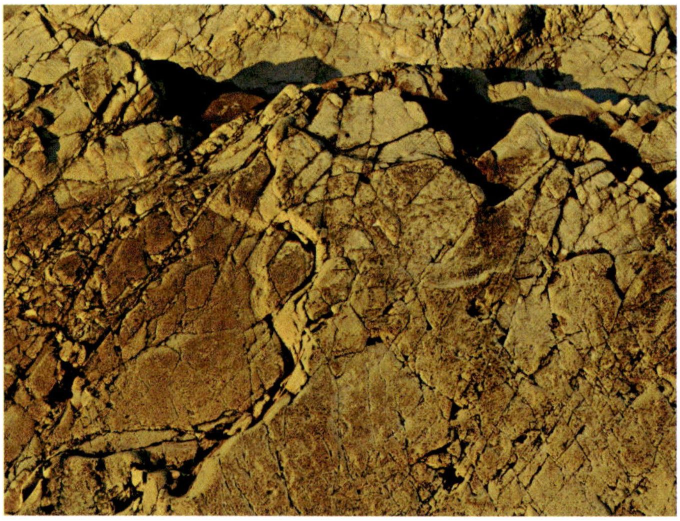

Figure 11.12 When you've found the desired Radius setting for High Pass, click OK to apply the final result.

Note: In most cases, I find a value of 10 pixels for the Radius in the High Pass filter produces the best effect for this technique, but any value that produces a result you're happy with is a good setting.

Filters

When you really want to produce creative interpretations of your images, using some of the many filters available within Photoshop (or as third-party plug-ins) is a great way to extend the possibilities. There are a wide variety of filters, all of which produce some distortion in the image. In some cases, the effect is minor, whereas in others it is dramatic. Even better, you can mix various filters to produce a completely new interpretation of an image.

Smart Filters

Photoshop CS3 allows you to apply filters as *Smart Filters*, applying them as instructions for the image instead of actually altering pixel values. This provides greater flexibility, allowing you to go back and modify the settings you used for the filter to change the effect without any penalty in image quality. From a conceptual standpoint, this can be thought of as applying filters as an adjustment layer. This is a powerful new capability and I recommend taking advantage of it.

Note: The only reason I might choose not to use Smart Filters is that they are a bit more resource-intensive, resulting in slow performance if you don't have a fast computer.

In order to apply filters as Smart Filters, you first need to prepare your image layer for this process, which means converting the Background Copy image layer into a Smart Object. To do so, click on the Background Copy image layer to make sure it is the active layer on the Layers palette and then choose Filter > Convert for Smart Filters from the menu.

Once you have converted the Background image layer into a Smart Object, you're ready to apply filters in the normal manner, but they will then appear as a Smart Filter attached to the image layer. If you want to change the filter settings, simply double-click on the applicable item on the Layers palette and refine the settings you used for that filter.

Note: If you decide not to use Smart Filters, then instead of using the process outlined in this section, create a copy of your Background image layer (by dragging it to the Create New Layer button at the bottom of the Layers palette) and continue using filters as discussed in the next sections.

Filter Gallery

The best way to apply filters with maximum flexibility is to use the Filter Gallery. It is certainly possible to apply individual filters one at a time by selecting them by name from the Filter menu. However, the Filter Gallery allows you to apply multiple filters at one time to an image, similar to the use of adjustment layers on the Layers palette. You can then mix and match various filters, adjusting the settings for each as desired (Figure 11.13). You can launch the Filter Gallery by choosing Filter > Filter Gallery from the menu.

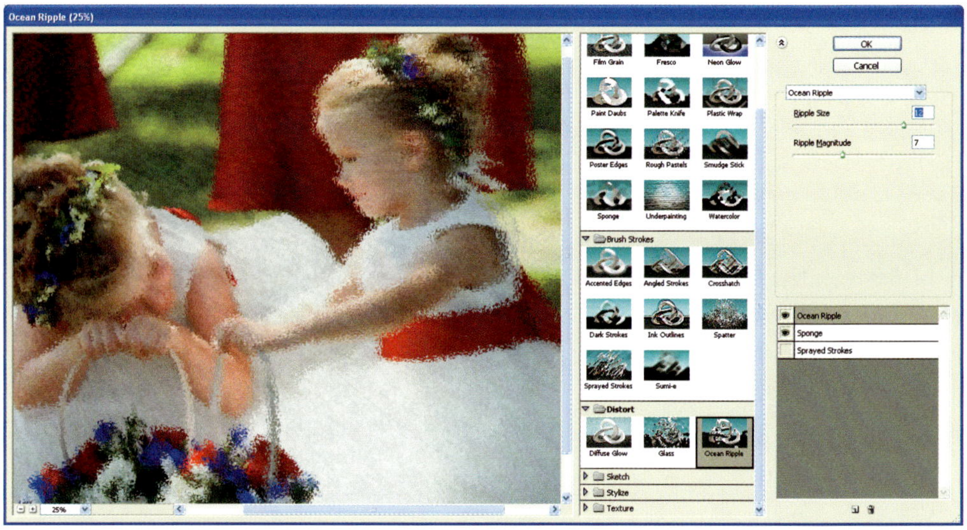

Figure 11.13 The Filter Gallery allows you to apply multiple filters at once to an image, adjusting the settings for each filter until you achieve the desired result.

Note: Not all filters found under the Filter menu are available in the Filter Gallery, but most of the "artistic" ones are included.

When you first launch the Filter Gallery, a single filter will be listed in the bottom-right of the dialog box. You can then expand the various categories of filters by clicking the right-pointing arrow to the left of each category name. Thumbnail previews of the filters will be shown, and you can click any thumbnail to apply that filter to the current filter layer within the Filter Gallery.

After you've selected a particular filter, the settings specific to that filter will be displayed on the right side of the dialog box. Adjust the settings as desired, using the preview image on the left to evaluate the settings. If you'd like to apply multiple filters, simply click the New Effect Layer button at the bottom of the Filter Gallery. This will initially create a duplicate of the same filter you're using, but you can then click a new filter from the thumbnails to change that filter layer and then change the settings for the filter being applied.

You can also change the order of filters, which can change the appearance of the final result, by dragging them on the list. As you're working, you can also toggle the visibility of individual filter layers by clicking the eye icon to the left of the layer.

After you've found the combination of filters and settings that produces the effect you like, click OK to apply the filters all at once to your image (Figure 11.14).

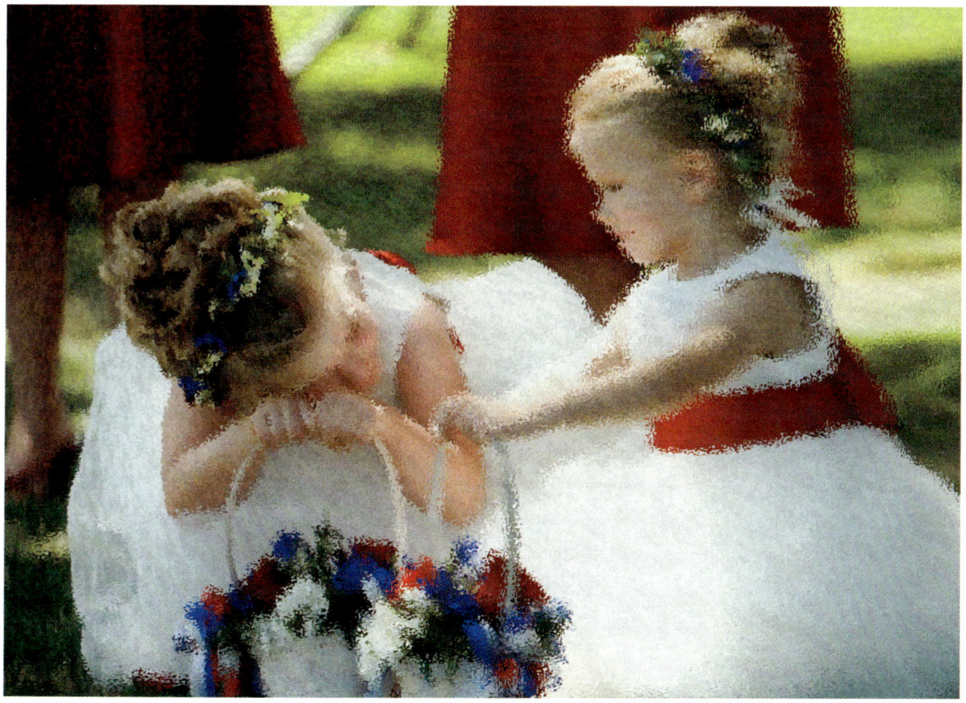

Figure 11.14 After you've established the desired filter settings, you can click OK in the Filter Gallery to produce the final result in your image.

Masking Filters

When you're trying to produce a completely abstract version of an image, you'll often want to apply filters to the entire image. However, in some cases you may want to apply a filter to selective areas, in which case a layer mask provides a perfect solution.

> **Note:** If you want to mask individual filters in different ways, you'll need to first duplicate the image layer and apply the filters separately so you can mask them separately.

When working with filters as Smart Filters, masking specific areas to reveal the original unfiltered image is incredibly easy. You already know how to use masking after reading Chapter 10, "Targeted Adjustments." Because you are applying filters as Smart Filters, a layer mask called Smart Filters is added automatically to the Layers palette, with the individual filters applied shown below that layer mask. The unique thing about this layer mask is that it will appear below the image layer rather than to the right of the image layer. However, it still behaves exactly the same as a normal layer mask. Simply click on the layer mask thumbnail called Smart Filters on the Layers palette, then use any of the painting tools (I generally use the Brush tool) to paint with black to block the filter effect and reveal the original image, or white to reveal the filter effect again in areas that have been blocked. The result is the ability to target where you want the filter effect to appear in your image (Figure 11.15). You can also create selections and then fill the selection with black or white as appropriate using the Edit > Fill command.

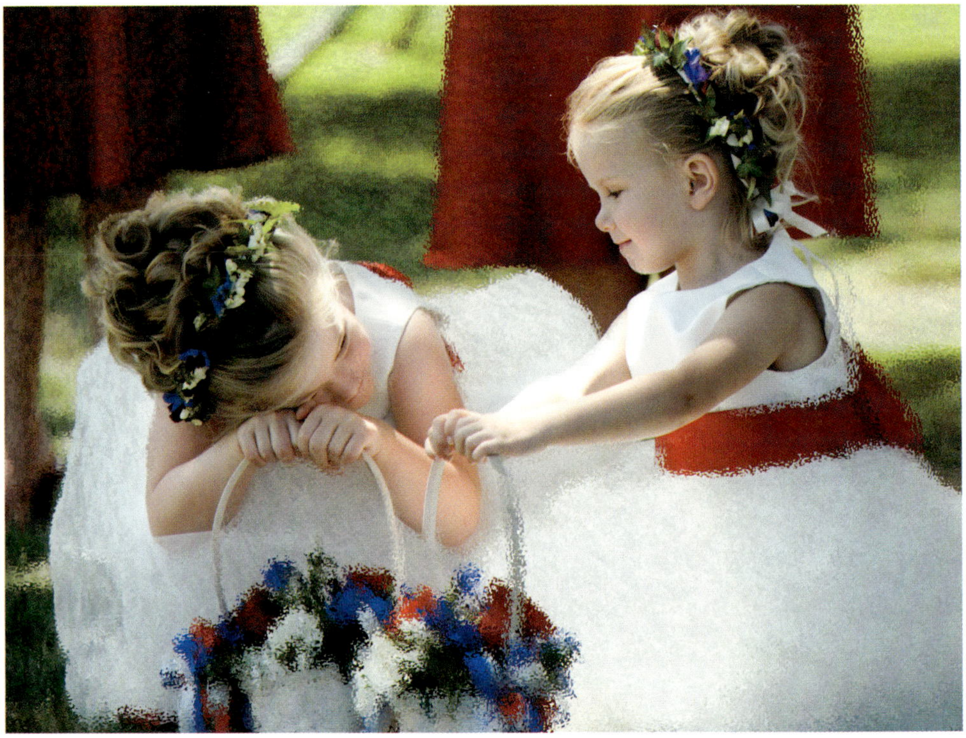

Figure 11.15 By masking out a portion of the Smart Filters layer, you can create an image with some parts that look like a normal photograph and other parts that have the filter effect.

Creative Edges

You can add impact to your images by applying a creative edge around the outside, effectively applying an artistic shape around the image instead of presenting it as a rectangle with crisp edges.

Refine Edge

Photoshop CS3 adds the ability to refine the shape of any selection you create, which provides a starting point for applying a creative edge to the image. Start by creating a selection that defines the area where you want the creative edge to apply. This would generally be very near the outside edge of the image so you are still retaining as much of the image as possible after applying the creative edge. I typically use the Rectangular Marquee tool for creating this selection, but you can use any of the methods for creating selections to do this (for more details on creating selections, see Chapter 9, "Making Selections").

With the selection created, click the Refine Edge button on the Options bar (you must have one of the selection tools active to see this option) or choose Select > Refine Edge from the menu. This will bring up the Refine Edge dialog box (Figure 11.16), where you can adjust the settings affecting the shape of the selection, and thus the edge you'll ultimately apply to the image.

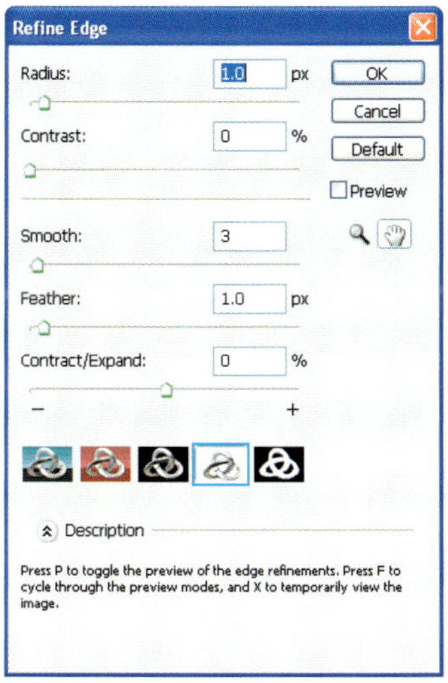

Figure 11.16 The Refine Edge dialog box provides settings that allow you to alter the shape of a selection.

The preview on the image is crucial to producing a good result with the Refine Edge command, so the first thing I recommend doing is setting an appropriate preview option. This naturally requires that you have the Preview checkbox selected (it is selected by default). Below the sliders, you'll find a set of five "picture" buttons that allow you to choose between the available preview modes. I recommend using the On White option (the fourth button) because it shows you what the image will look like when it is printed. In some situations (such as when the final image will be displayed online), you might want to use On Black instead. If you like the Quick Mask display (which I discussed in Chapter 9), you can use the third option to use that preview. I don't find the first and last options very helpful. The first shows you only the selection shape as an animated dashed line (often referred to as the "marching ants" display), which doesn't take into account the feathering along the edge of this selection. The last shows you only the final shape of the selection as a black-and-white mask, which doesn't provide the context of the image itself.

Next, adjust the five sliders to produce the desired edge shape. The sliders have the following effect:

Note: When your mouse is over any of these sliders, a description is provided at the bottom of the dialog box. You can hide the description by clicking the double-chevron to the left of the Description label.

Radius allows you to move the edge inward in a feathered fashion, but the shape of the edge will follow gradations and detail within the image. Sharp details will be preserved more than smooth areas, producing an edge with an irregular shape well-suited to the content in the image.

Contrast will clean up artifacts created by the Radius setting, effectively making the irregular edge created by an increased Radius setting crisper.

Smooth will help clean up jagged edges in your selection, producing an edge that is smoother. After smoothing, you can recover some detail with an increased Radius value.

Feather applies a softening to the edge. At first glance this appears to produce the same effect as the Radius setting. However, it doesn't vary based on the content of the image, instead applying a uniform feathering of the full selection edge.

Contract/Expand allows you to change the size of the original selection and, therefore, the position of the creative edge you are applying to the image.

Note: The Default button can be used at any time to reset the controls to their default values.

Once you have applied the desired settings, click OK to change the shape of the selection with Refine Edge. The selection is now refined, but you'll notice the image itself doesn't reflect the creative edge you're working to create. You may also notice that the selection edge doesn't quite reflect the shape you saw in the Refine Edge dialog box. That's because the animated dashed line showing the selection edge defines the boundary between pixels that are greater than 50% selected and less than 50% selected. Feathered edges in the selection are not reflected. However, the underlying selection still reflects the shape you saw in the Refine Edge preview.

Producing a creative edge from this selection requires a couple more steps. First, you'll want to convert the Background image layer to a "normal" layer by double-clicking its thumbnail on the Layers palette and clicking OK in the New Layer dialog box that appears. Next, click the Add Layer Mask button at the bottom of the Layers palette. The image will be masked based on the selection, producing a creative edge just as you saw in the preview for the Refine Edge command (Figure 11.17).

Note: You'll see a checkerboard pattern around the outside of your image once you have masked it to produce the creative edge with this method. That represents the lack of pixels in those areas. If you prefer to have something behind the image, you can add a new empty layer behind the image layer and fill it with the color of your choice (use white if you don't want the color to print).

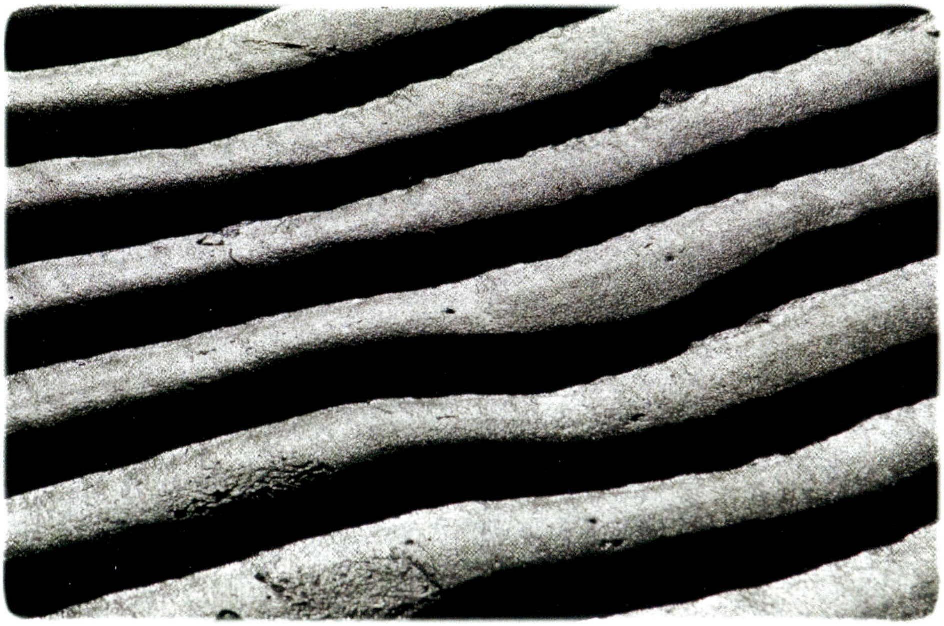

Figure 11.17 Once you've converted the selection to a layer mask, the image will have a creative edge applied to it.

Filtered Edge

You can also use filters to apply a creative edge to your image, providing a bit more flexibility in the type of effect you're able to produce. This is actually a relatively simple technique, but it provides virtually unlimited potential in terms of the creative edge effects you're able to produce.

Start by creating a selection using the Rectangular Marquee tool to define the edge of the border area where you would like the creative edge to appear. Next, enter Quick Mask mode by pressing Q or clicking the button below the color picker on the Tools palette. You'll see the selection represented by a mask, with a color overlay appearing over areas that are not selected and no overlay in the selected area (Figure 11.18).

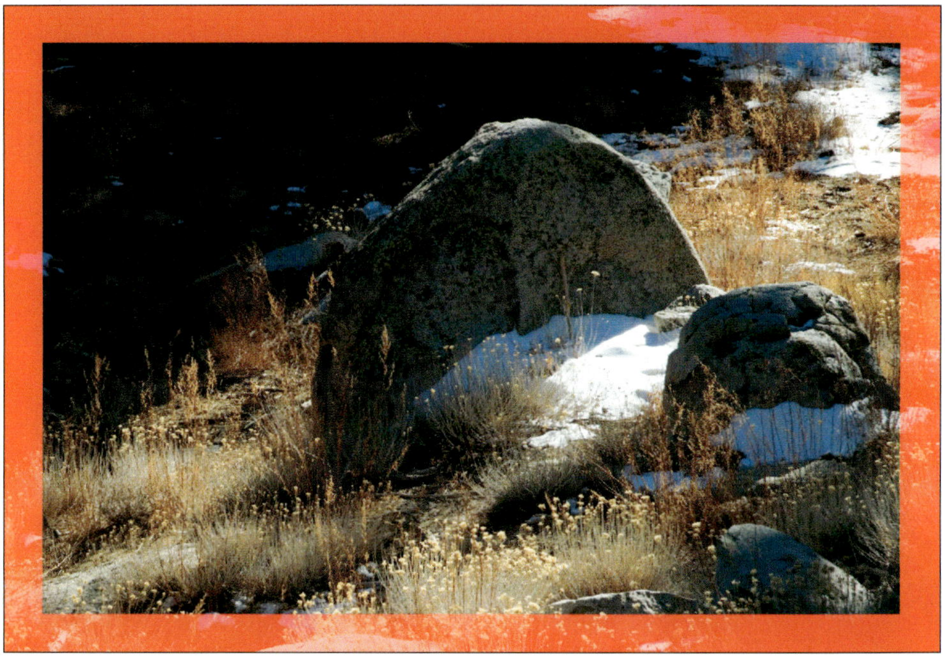

Figure 11.18 When you are viewing the image in Quick Mask mode, the selected areas appear normal and nonselected areas have a color overlay.

Next, select Filter > Filter Gallery from the menu. Using the methods discussed earlier in this chapter, apply one or more filters to alter the shape of the edge for your selection. Make sure the preview is showing you an area along the edge of your selection (it will appear as a transition between black and white because you're working on a mask representation of the selection) so you can make decisions about the settings to use. I recommend using more than one filter to alter the selection edge so you can produce a more unique and random effect. When you're done applying filters, click OK. Press Q or click the Quick Mask button on the Tools palette again to return to the normal selection view.

Note: The Refine Edge command discussed in the previous section can be used once the selection is created at this stage of the process if you'd like to further refine the edge shape you are creating.

To apply this selection to the image as a creative edge, first double-click on the thumbnail for the Background image layer and click OK in the New Layer dialog box in order to convert this layer to a "normal" layer. Then click the Add Layer Mask button to convert the selection into a layer mask, hiding the pixels outside the selection and producing a creative edge for the image based on the filter effects you applied (Figure 11.19).

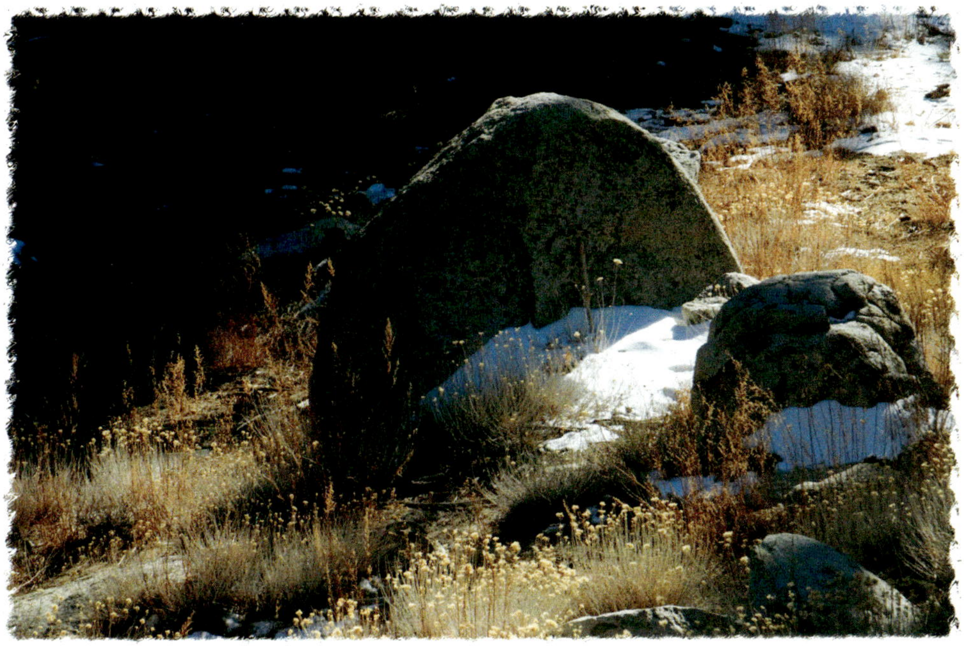

Figure 11.19 Using filters to alter the shape of your selection allows you to produce unique creative edge effects for your images.

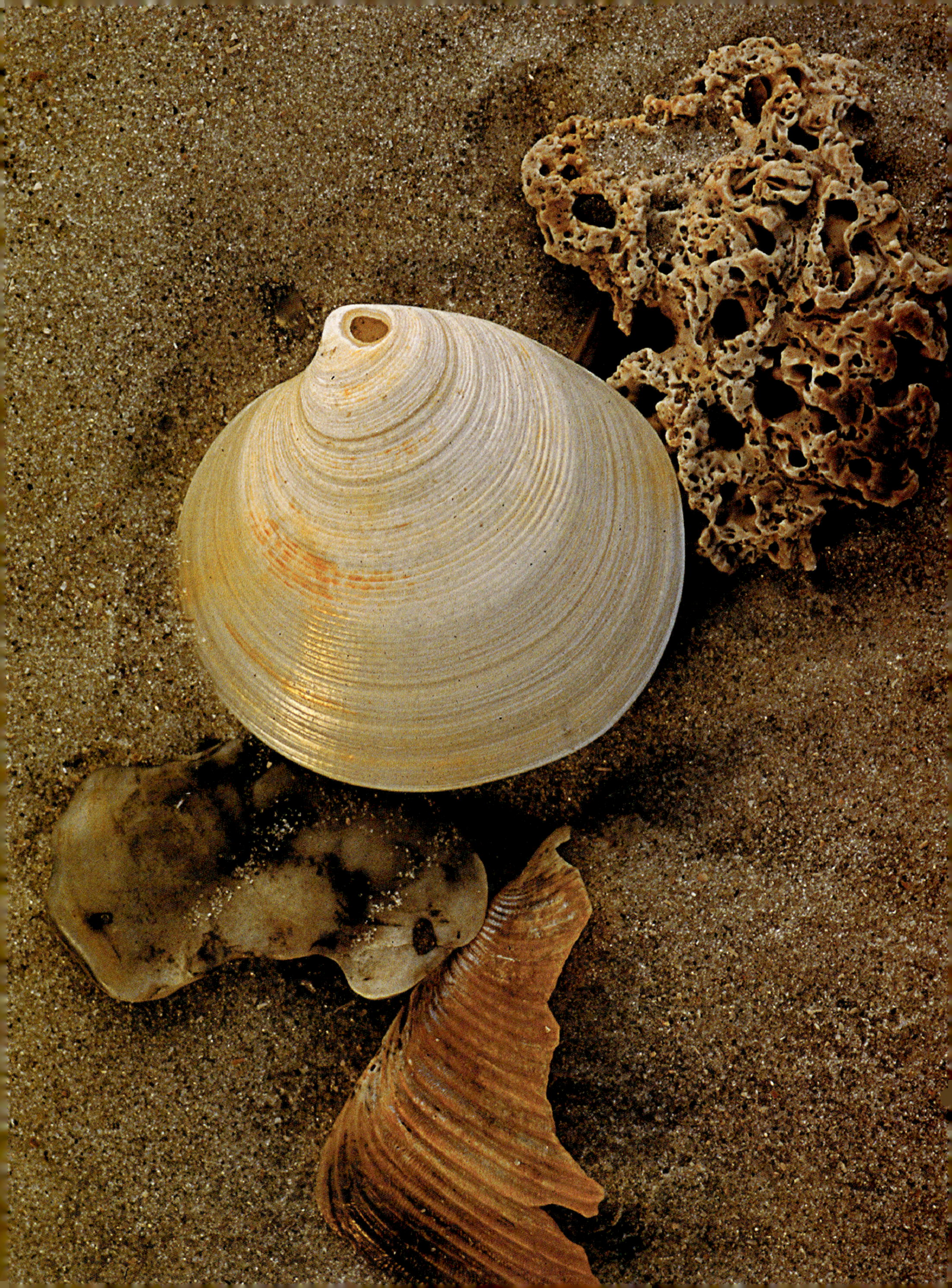

Finishing the Workflow

IV

Many photographers might assume the workflow ends after the image has been optimized to perfection, using adjustment layers and image layers in various ways as outlined in previous chapters. However, a key part of the workflow is "closing out" the process and achieving your ultimate goal. That includes saving your image files after you've optimized them, as well as preparing them for the final output, which is most often the print. Part IV will focus on these topics, as well as provide some tools for automating portions of your workflow.

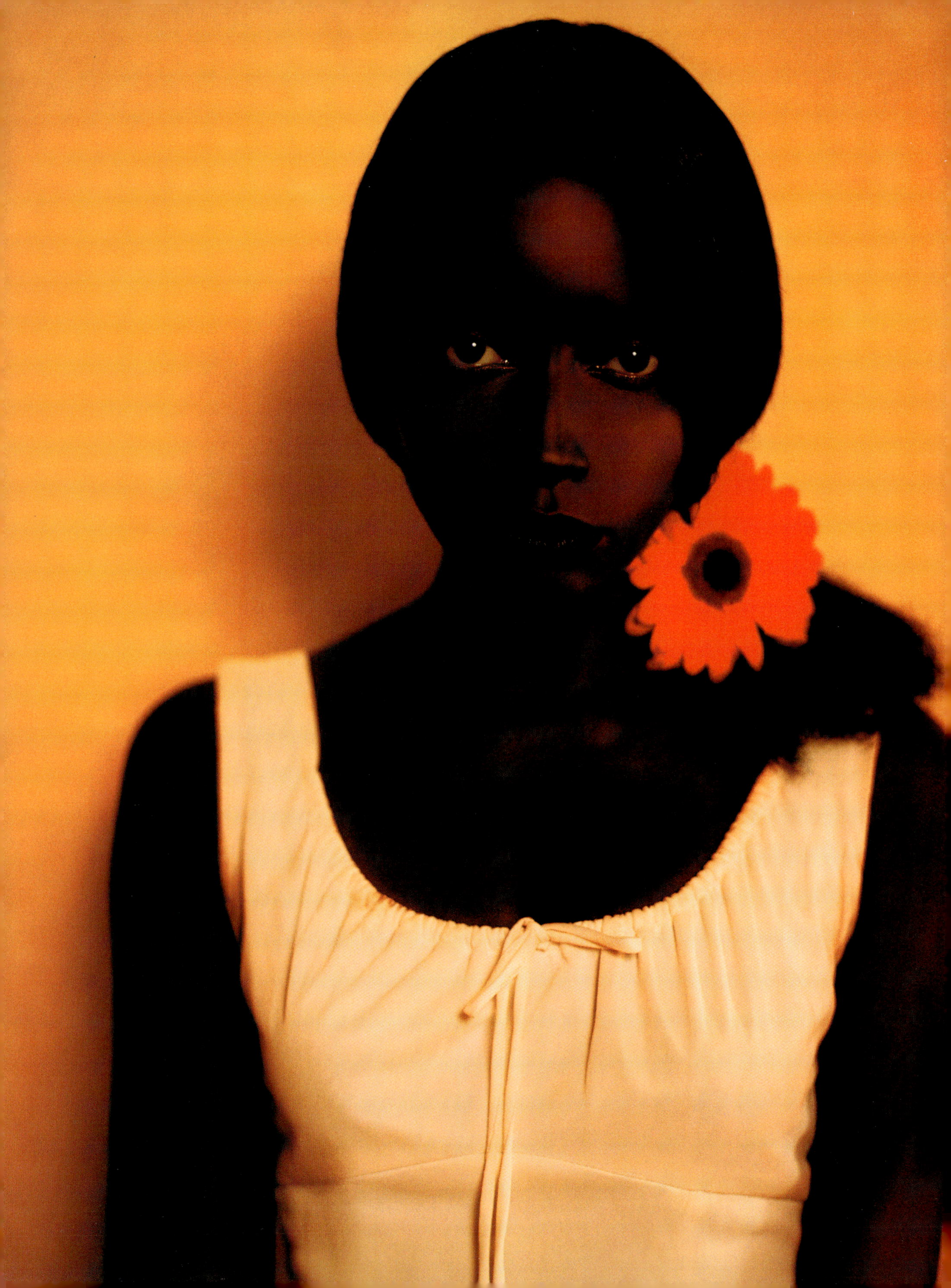

Saving Files

The most efficient workflow and all the optimization in the world aren't going to do you much good—at least not for long—if the efforts you've made are lost as soon as you close the image. Saving your image file is a critical conclusion to your image-optimization workflow, and this chapter will help you understand the issues involved with saving your files properly.

12

Chapter Contents

Master Image Concept

Throughout this book I've focused on techniques for adjusting your images within a workflow process that preserves your original pixel values, utilizing adjustment layers and image layers to change the appearance of the image without altering the original data. This approach provides maximum flexibility, enabling you to return later to modify the adjustments you've made. At the same time, it provides maximum protection of your image by ensuring you aren't permanently discarding image detail you might want to recover later.

After you've optimized the image, investing time and effort in the process, the result is a master image that contains your complete interpretation of the image (Figure 12.1). In fact, you might even include multiple interpretations of the image within a single image file by using different adjustment layers organized into layer sets for each interpretation.

Note: Although saving the image is being discussed at the end of the workflow, it is important to remember that you should save the image early in the workflow, and often throughout the process of optimizing the image.

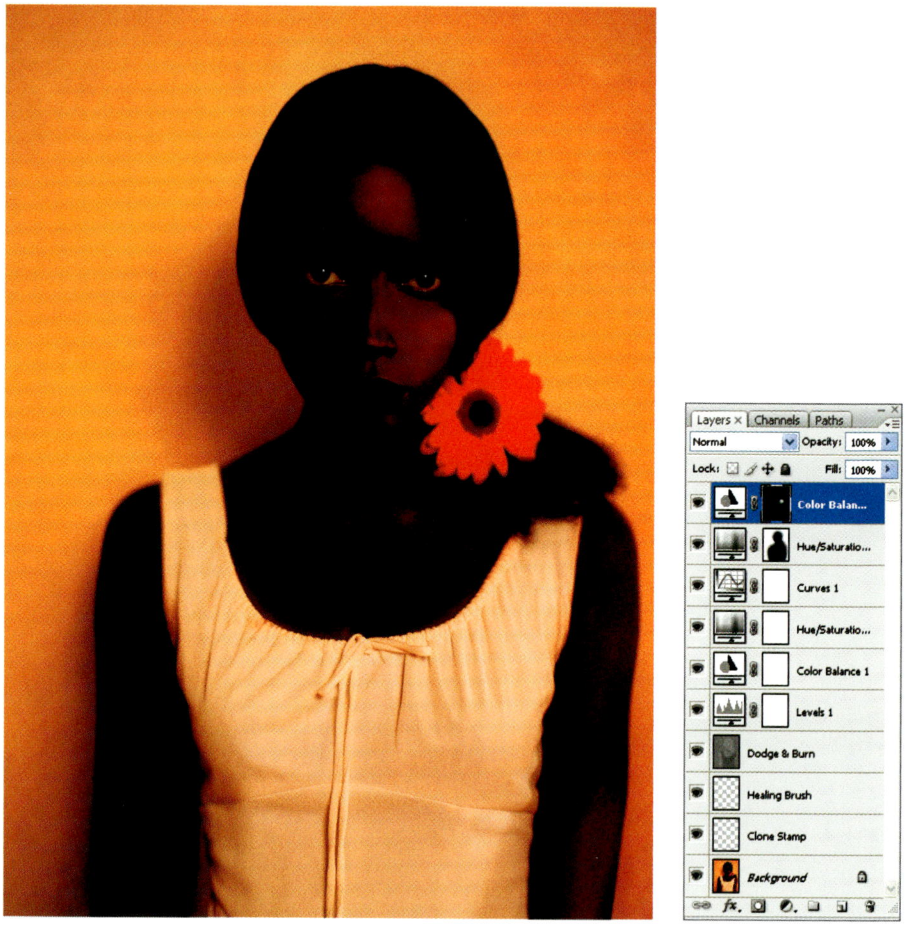

Figure 12.1 After you've perfected your image by using the steps outlined in previous chapters, the result is a master image that should be saved for all future output. (Photo by Matthew Jordan Smith, www.matthewjordansmith.com)

It is important that the final image containing all layers be saved as the master image, which will serve as the starting point for all future output from that image. This master image file should contain the original, unaltered pixel data from the digital capture or film scan, with no resizing and with no changes applied directly to the background image layer. Of course, in the case of a RAW capture, what you're storing is the capture after it has been processed during RAW conversion (unless you're utilizing Smart Objects, as covered earlier in this book), which is why I recommend archiving the original RAW capture in addition to the master image file that results at the end of your workflow. Furthermore, all adjustment layers and image layers used in addition to the background image layer to produce the final result should be saved.

To be sure, saving a master image file in this way can result in very large files. However, to me this is a worthwhile investment in the quality and flexibility of the image. You may be tempted to flatten the image to reduce the file size after you feel confident you've achieved exactly the results you were seeking. However, I still feel it is important to preserve the original image data along with your modifications. For one thing, our tastes tend to change with time. By maintaining the original image data as well as all adjustments within the same file, you can comfortably change your mind later and revise the image as desired. Also, you may learn new techniques at a later date that allow you to produce even better results. Saving a master file enables you to take full advantage of any future preferences or opportunities.

The bottom line is that you've invested considerable time perfecting your image (Figure 12.2). That effort deserves to be preserved in such a way that you won't have to start over if you change your mind about the best interpretation of the image or learn new techniques that allow you to improve your results.

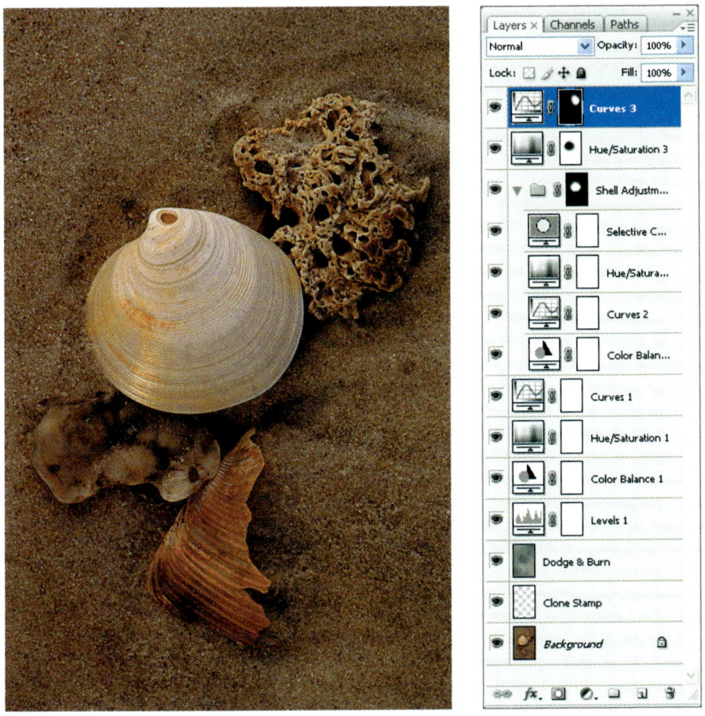

Figure 12.2 After spending considerable time achieving exactly the results you desire, including the creation of many layers to optimize your image, you should save the master image file with maximum information to maintain quality and flexibility. (Photo by Gabby Salazar, www.gabbysalazar.com)

When to Sharpen

There tends to be a lot of discussion about the proper time and method for applying sharpening to digital images. The simple fact is that just about all digital photos need to be sharpened to some degree, whether they are digital captures or film scans. The question is when that sharpening should be applied.

My feeling is that sharpening should not be applied to your master image. Sharpening by its nature is a destructive process, in that it changes pixel values. Furthermore, resizing an image after sharpening can mitigate sharpening or exaggerate artifacts caused by sharpening. Also, your sharpening settings should be tailored to the specific output size of the image. Because the master image contains the original pixel dimensions of the digital capture or film scan, it won't likely match the exact image dimensions of the final output. For all these reasons and more, my preference is to not apply sharpening to the master image. Instead, sharpening should be applied when the image is being prepared for final output, after it has been resized for that output.

Sharpening in the output workflow will be covered in Chapter 14, "Output Processing."

Filenames, Locations, and Formats

Saving your master image file means you need to decide what file type to use to save the image. There are only two file formats you really need to consider for the master file, because you need to be able to save all of your layers and saved selections as part of that file. These are the native Photoshop Document (PSD) and Tagged Image File Format (TIFF) formats.

What about JPEG?

Although the JPEG file format is perfectly acceptable for digital capture, it isn't an ideal format for saving images after you've worked on them. There's no need to convert your JPEG captures to another format if you haven't adjusted the images, so by all means keep those JPEG images saved as they are until you decide to work on each file.

After you have worked on the file, you'll want to preserve the master image. Because JPEG files don't support layers, and because they always apply at least some image compression to your image, this format is not appropriate for saving your master image file.

In addition to being viable for capture, JPEG is an excellent format for saving images for digital slideshows, websites, e-mail, and other purposes for which file size is at least as important as image quality.

The first time you save the image file, you'll need to choose File > Save As from the menu (Figure 12.3). In fact, if you choose File > Save from the menu without previously saving the image (or after adding adjustment layers to an image that was already saved in a file format that doesn't support layers), the Save As dialog box will automatically be invoked. In the Save As dialog box, you'll first need to select the location where you'd like to save the image file. You can do so by selecting a location from the Save In dropdown list. If necessary, you can use the Save In dropdown to navigate to a specific drive, and then double-click the desired folder (or multiple folders in turn) to navigate to the folder in which you'd like to store the image. You can also create new folders at any time by clicking the Create New Folder button in the Save As dialog box and then typing a name for the new folder.

Note: I prefer to keep the master image file in the same folder as the source image that was used to create the master, but other photographers prefer to keep these master images in a special folder within the source folder or somewhere else entirely.

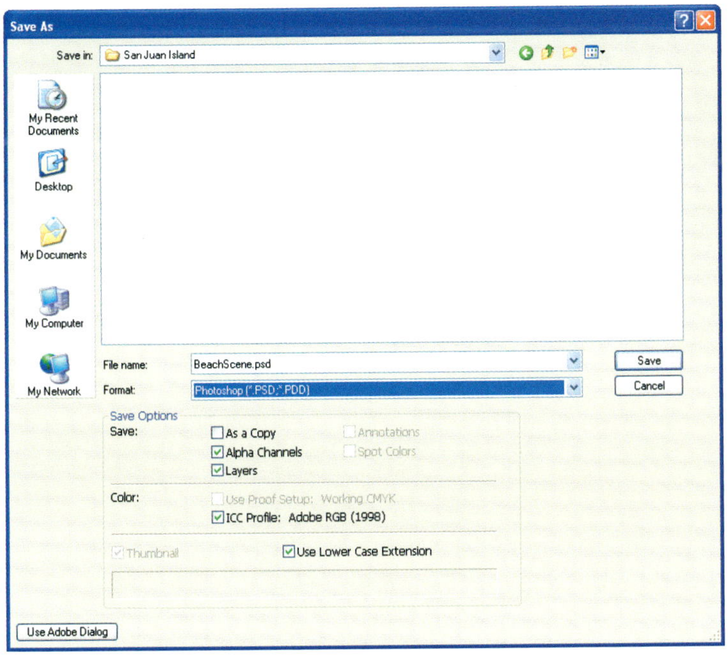

Figure 12.3 The Save As dialog box allows you to select the location, filename, and file format to use when saving your master image file.

Note: Deciding which folder to place the image in is your first step in keeping your images organized. I recommend saving all image files in a single primary folder, using subfolders within that main folder to organize images into categories that are appropriate for your type of photography and suit your method for staying organized.

The next step is to provide a name for the image file. It is important to select a useful name so you'll be able to easily identify the image later. In fact, I recommend utilizing the filename as another method for staying organized. By naming your image files with useful names, you can search for filenames or otherwise keep them organized. You can even use names that allow you—within reason—to know what the contents of the image are without even opening the file.

It is important to get organized early with your filenames. I recommend finding a system that works for you to organize and categorize your images, and that enables you to search for filenames by doing a rudimentary keyword search. However, I also recommend incorporating serial numbers as part of your file-naming system so you can have a collection of images saved with the same basic name but a unique number to identify each.

Note: It can be very helpful to retain the source filename as part of the filename for the master image file, so that if you ever need to go back to the original capture you'll know what filename to find.

With the location and filename established, the only other major option you need to select is the file format in which you'd like to save the image file. The file format can be selected from the Format dropdown (Figure 12.4). Although many options are available on this list, you really need to choose between only the Photoshop PSD and TIFF file formats.

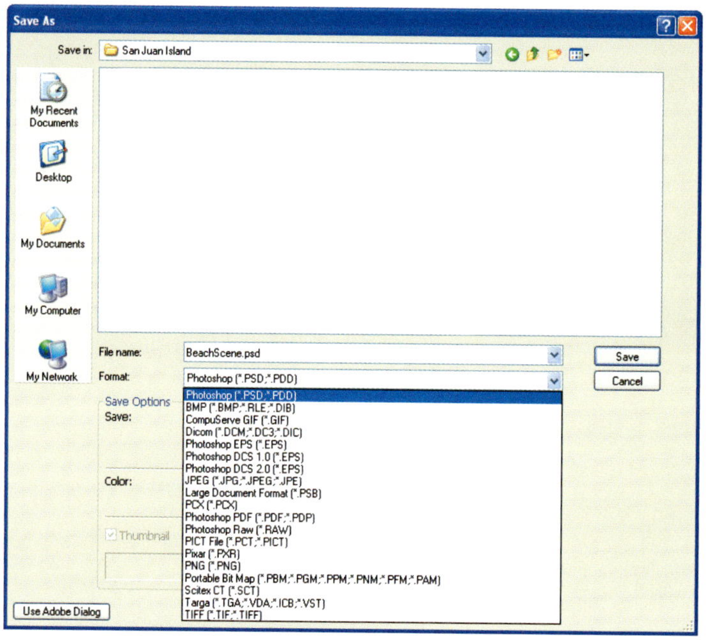

Figure 12.4 Although many options are available when saving your image files, the only two you really need to consider are Photoshop PSD and TIFF.

Photoshop PSD

The Photoshop PSD file format is well suited to saving your master image files. Because it is the native file format in Photoshop, you can trust that it will preserve all of the adjustment layers, image layers, and saved selections. All of these features are supported for both 8-bit and 16-bit files, so you can feel totally confident that everything you've done to your image can be preserved in the master image file you save.

The Photoshop PSD format utilizes lossless compression, which means the file data is stored efficiently without changing any pixel values. This helps to reduce the overall file size, while not risking your image data.

To save the master image file in the Photoshop PSD file format, select Photoshop PSD from the Format dropdown and click Save; the image will be saved in the location and with the filename you've specified.

Note: After you've saved the image once (which should really be done early in the workflow process), you should update the saved file on a regular basis. Every time you make a significant adjustment, choose File > Save or press Ctrl/Command+S to save the file with updates.

TIFF

The Tagged Image File Format (TIFF) has gone through various iterations, and the latest versions of Photoshop support the saving of multiple image and adjustment layers in the TIFF format. For all intents and purposes, I consider TIFF to be equal to PSD in terms of the features supported. In other words, anything you do to your image, including all of the techniques covered in this book, are equally supported by PSD and TIFF.

To save an image in the TIFF format, simply select TIFF from the Format dropdown in the Save As dialog box and click Save. When you do so, an additional TIFF Options dialog box will be presented, providing special options unique to the TIFF format (Figure 12.5).

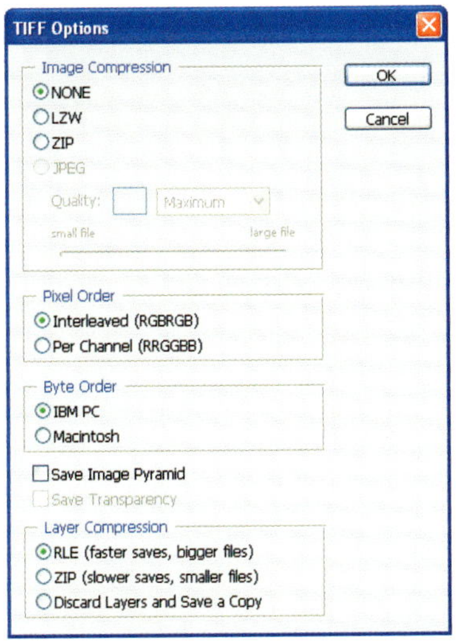

Figure 12.5 As you are saving an image in the TIFF file format, a TIFF Options dialog box will allow you to set compression and byte order options before the image is actually saved.

The first section of the TIFF Options dialog box allows you to select the Image Compression setting to be used. The None option will not apply any compression to the image, resulting in a relatively large file size. The LZW option applies the Lempel-Ziv-Welch compression algorithm (named after the three people who developed it) to the file but doesn't compress image data. In other words, this provides lossless compression that will reduce the file size without any effect on image quality. The ZIP option also provides lossless compression and often results in file sizes that are slightly smaller than when LZW is used.

Both LZW and ZIP will reduce the file size, but there is a compatibility concern with both of them. Not all software that can read TIFF files supports LZW or ZIP compression. LZW has broader support than ZIP compression, but both have limited support. However, because you aren't likely to send your master image files to others, you could certainly take advantage of either of these options for your own purposes. My preference is for LZW compression because it has broader support among image-editing software.

The Pixel Order option allows you to determine in which order the pixel values will be recorded in the image file. The options are Interleaved or Per Channel. In prior versions of Photoshop, only the interleaved option was available. The Per Channel option offers the potential to improve the read and write speed of the file, as well as to provide better compression, so I would recommend using this option.

The next section in the TIFF Options dialog box allows you to determine whether the IBM PC or Macintosh byte order should be used. In theory, this allows you to choose between compatibility on a Windows or Macintosh PC. However, the term *IBM PC* as a generic description of the Windows platform hints at this being a dated setting. Both platforms are perfectly capable of reading files with either byte order set, so it isn't critical which one you choose. I would simply choose the byte order option appropriate to your platform, but there's no need to be concerned about additional compatibility issues related to this setting.

Finally, the Layer Compression setting allows you to determine how layers should be saved. The RLE option applies run-length encoding as a compression algorithm to the layers in the file. This reduces the overall file size somewhat and processes quickly. This is the option I prefer because of its speed. The ZIP option applies different compression, which yields smaller file sizes but takes longer to process. The differences aren't generally significant, so I prefer to stick with RLE. The "Discard" option will cause the image to be saved as a flattened version without any layers. This is helpful if you're saving a second copy of your image file to send to someone else, but is obviously detrimental to the master image concept and shouldn't be used for your main image file.

After you've established the appropriate settings in the TIFF Options dialog box, simply click OK, and the image will be saved.

Choosing between PSD and TIFF

As you've probably gathered, there are only minor differences between the PSD and TIFF file formats, which often leads to confusion when trying to decide which format to use. Quite honestly, you could use either format without any problems; both support all the features that are important to you in saving a master image file.

The primary difference between the two comes down to compression. Although the Photoshop PSD file format does utilize some lossless compression, it isn't as powerful as the LZW or ZIP compression available with TIFF files. Therefore, in most cases the TIFF file with LZW or ZIP compression will be smaller than the same layered file saved as a PSD.

So, if file size is an important consideration, I would opt for the TIFF file format with LZW compression. However, I utilize the PSD file format for my master image files. The reason is one of organization. Although the PSD files are slightly larger than they would be if I saved them as TIFF files with LZW compression, I gain a slight organizational benefit by saving all my master image files in PSD.

The reason for this is that I'm accustomed to thinking of TIFF images as images without layers, because it used to be impossible to save TIFF files with layers intact. Therefore, I save my master image files as PSD files and save any copies of the images made for other purposes (such as for publication in a book or magazine) as TIFF files without layers. By using this system, I can look at a list of files on my hard drive and know which are master image files and which are copies for other purposes.

This is a minor consideration, but I find it helps me. You'll have your own priorities and can make your own decision now that you have a better understanding of the issues involved with each file format.

Note: After you've safely saved your master images, you've completed the full workflow. Of course, it is also critical that you back up those important master image files, preferably in a different physical location than your primary storage.

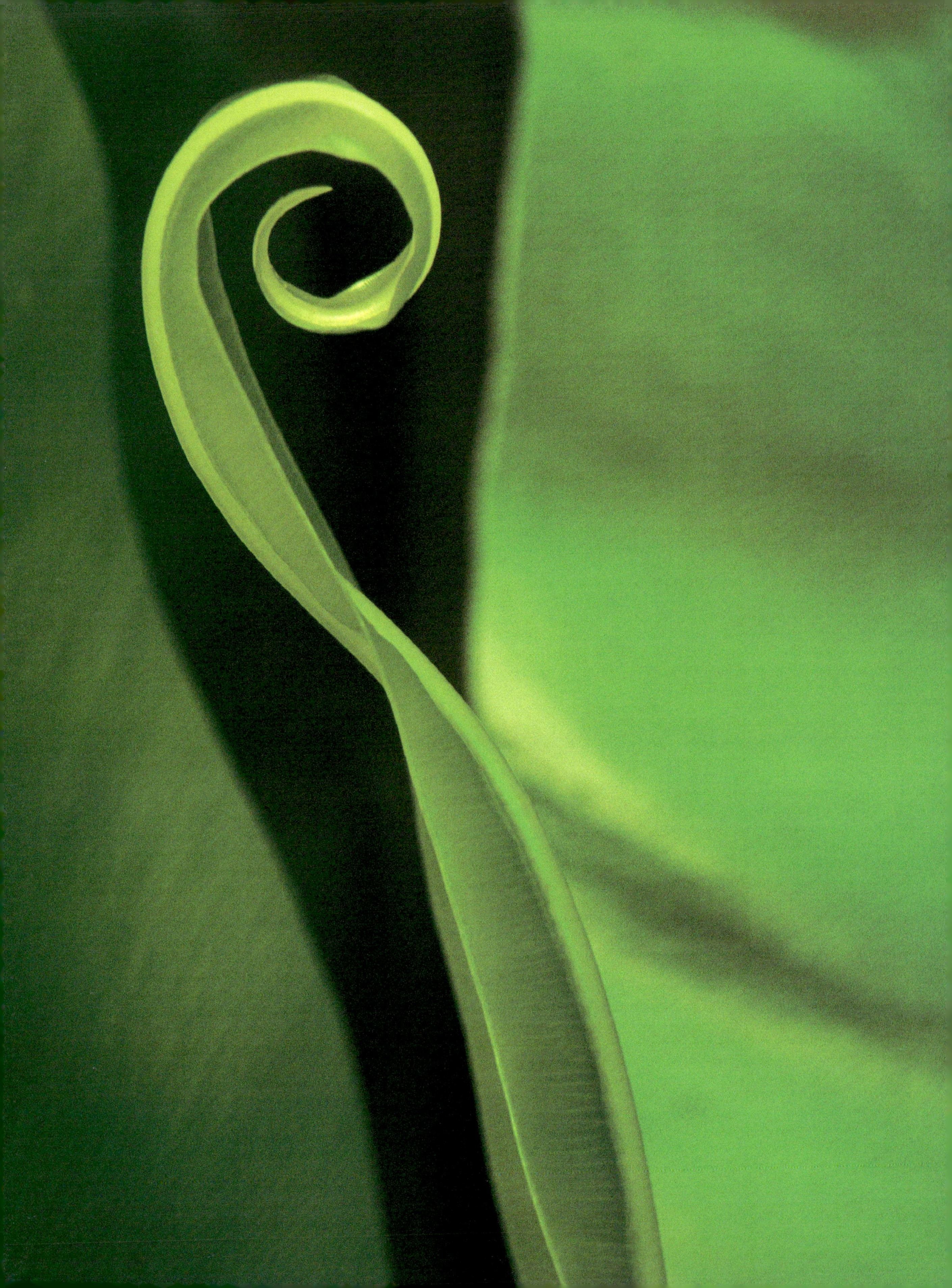

Workflow Automation

After you've mastered a workflow for your digital images, producing exactly the desired results with optimal quality, you'll probably start thinking about finding ways to automate tasks that you perform repeatedly. Any task—or even a set of tasks—that you need to perform on multiple images is a candidate for workflow automation, especially if it involves steps that don't require any decision-making on your part. This chapter will show you ways to achieve the benefits of automation in Photoshop.

13

Chapter Contents

Image Processor
Actions
Batch Processing
Droplets

Image Processor

One of the easiest ways to process a series of images is to use the Image Processor. Its primary function is to enable you to convert images to a different file format (for example, saving your master PSD files as JPEG images for use on a website) and resize the images in the process. You can also apply actions (discussed later in this chapter) to the images being processed with the Image Processor, making it even more powerful.

The first thing I generally do before using the Image Processor is to copy the images I want to work with into a new working folder. This allows me to work on the specific images I want even if they come from a variety of different folders. You can launch the Image Processor by selecting File > Scripts > Image Processor from the menu, which will bring up the Image Processor dialog box (Figure 13.1).

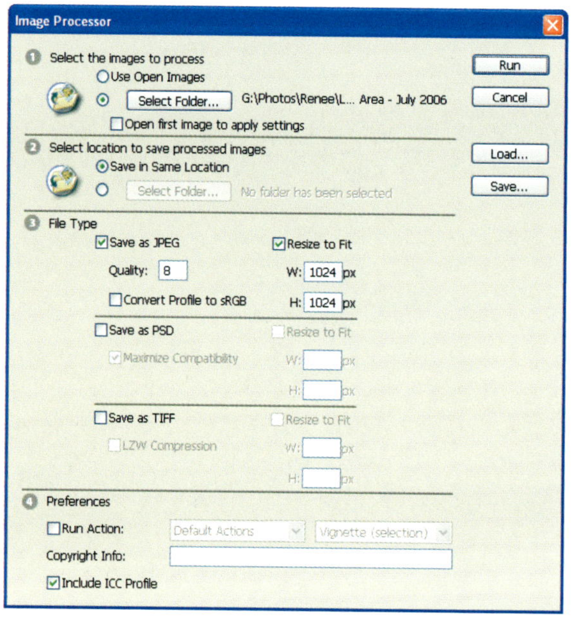

Figure 13.1 The Image Processor dialog box provides a variety of controls that enable you to easily process a large number of images.

The first section of the Image Processor dialog box allows you to select which images should be processed. If you have images already opened in Photoshop, the Use Open Images option will be available. This will cause the processing to apply only to the images currently open in Photoshop. Because I'm generally working with a folder of images to be processed, I normally use the second option associated with the Select Folder button. Click that button to select the folder containing the images you want to process. Below the Select Folder button is a checkbox labeled "Open first image to apply settings." Select this checkbox if you are processing a set of RAW images and want to have the same settings applied to all (which is really only useful if all of the images to be processed were captured under nearly identical conditions). This will cause the first image to be opened before processing so you can apply settings that will then be used for all images being processed.

The second section allows you to designate where you want the images created by the Image Processor to be saved. Because the Image Processor will automatically create subfolders for each file type it creates, I normally use the Save In Same Location option. However, if you prefer to have all images saved in a different location, you can select the second option and click the Select Folder button to select (or create) a folder where you want the resulting images saved.

The third section is the key to the Image Processor. Here you can specify which file types you would like to create from your source images. Options are available for JPEG, PSD, and TIFF. You can select the checkbox for the file type you want the images saved as, and multiple options can be selected. All three options include a Resize To Fit checkbox. When selected, this will enable Width and Height boxes that allow you to enter values in pixels to have the images resized during processing. This is particularly helpful for images you need to resize for the Web or e-mail.

Note: If you want to resize images so horizontal and vertical images are the same size on the longer dimension (for example, horizontals are 1,000 pixels wide and verticals are 1,000 pixels tall) simply enter the value you want to use for the long side into both Width and Height boxes, and all images will be constrained to this square boundary to produce the desired result.

The JPEG section also includes a Quality setting, which is the same as that found in the JPEG Options dialog box when you save a JPEG image. I recommend a setting of 8 when you want to minimize file size while still maintaining good quality, and 12 when quality is your primary concern. There is also a checkbox to Convert Profile to sRGB. I recommend using this option whenever you are preparing images as JPEG to be displayed by a monitor or digital projector (which is the most common reason for creating JPEGs). This will help ensure the most accurate results possible based on the default behavior of these display devices and the color gamut they are generally able to display.

The PSD section includes a Maximize Compatibility that is the same setting normally available when you are saving files in the PSD file format. Using this option (which was discussed in Chapter 12, "Saving Files") will cause a full-resolution composite version of your image to be stored in the file when it is saved. This will significantly increase the file size, but it also provides some potential advantages. I generally do not use this option because I prefer to keep the file sizes smaller, and I don't often need to share PSD files with others who are using different versions of Photoshop.

The TIFF section includes a LZW Compression checkbox. This provides one of the compression options (the most popular option) normally found in the TIFF Options dialog box when you are saving a file as a TIFF. The LZW compression is lossless, meaning it will reduce the file size through storage efficiencies not image compression that will degrade quality. I generally don't use this option if I am sending files to others, unless I know they'll be using Photoshop (or another application that supports LZW compression) to view or open the files.

The final section of the Image Processor dialog box provides some preferences that allow you to change how the images are processed. The first option is a checkbox called Run Action. As the name implies, this will cause the selected action (you can choose the set and action from the dropdowns to the right of the checkbox) for each image as it is processed. For example, if you have an action that will produce a sepia tone version of the image, you could run it on the images being processed so all of them have a sepia tone appearance in addition to the other changes being applied by the Image Processor. You'll learn how to create actions later in this chapter.

The Copyright Info field allows you to enter text that will be added to the metadata for all processed images. Simply enter the text you would like to have applied. This is a good option to take advantage of if you'll be sending your files to others.

The final checkbox allows you to Include ICC Profile. In general, I recommend using this option to help ensure the most accurate color results for any recipient of your images. The only reason I would not select this checkbox is if you are preparing images for online viewing and want to keep the file size to a minimum (embedding an ICC profile does cause the file size to increase).

With all of the settings established, click the Run button to start processing. Photoshop will then open and process each of the images you specified. The resulting images will be placed in the folder indicated in your settings, with subfolders created for each image file type (for example, a JPEG folder for the JPEG images).

Batch RAW Conversion

In Chapter 3, "RAW Conversion," I promised I would present a method for batch processing RAW files using the Image Processor. First, I have to remind you that I don't normally recommend converting RAW images in batch because each image deserves individual treatment during the conversion process. However, when you simply want to process a group of RAW images quickly for a purpose that doesn't require optimal quality, this method can be helpful.

If you want to apply some basic adjustments to your images in the RAW conversion process, you'll need to take care of that first. You can open individual RAW captures, make adjustments in the Camera Raw dialog box, and then click Done, and the RAW conversion settings will be updated without opening the image. You can also apply RAW settings from one image to others (for example, when they were all shot under similar conditions) by applying settings to one of the images in the group and copying them to other images. To do so, apply adjustments in Camera Raw to the first image and click Done, right-click on that image in Bridge, and select Develop Settings > Copy Settings from the popup menu (or choose Edit > Develop Settings > Copy Camera Raw Settings from the menu in Bridge). Select all of the other images you'd like to apply the same settings to and right-click, and then choose Develop Settings > Paste Settings from the popup menu (or choose Edit > Develop Settings > Paste Settings from the menu in Bridge).

If all of the images you'll be converting will benefit from the same adjustments in Camera Raw (this isn't likely to be the case unless the images were captured under nearly identical conditions), you can skip the above adjustments and go directly to the Image Processor. Simply select the

continues

"Open first image to apply settings" checkbox and when you start the processing, the first image will be opened for you to adjust, with those settings then applied to all images being processed.

You can then use the Image Processor as discussed in this section to convert the RAW captures and save them in another file format. I recommend using the option to save the files in the PSD format because that is the file format I prefer for my master image files. This will produce images that are ready for the full optimization process. Of course, if you're simply converting these RAW captures so you can quickly post them to a website or otherwise share them, you may want to save them as JPEG images with the Image Processor instead. Of course, the Image Processor actually offers the ability to save files in multiple types at once, so you could also select multiple options if needed.

Actions

Actions in Photoshop provide a way to record steps as you perform them, and then replay those steps to apply the same changes to one or more images in an automated fashion. This allows you to quickly apply a complex series of steps to an individual image, or to apply tasks to a large number of images.

By using actions, you can greatly improve your workflow efficiency. For example, you could create an action to create smaller versions of your master image files for display on a website (Figure 13.2). Performing the same steps manually on a large number of images would be inefficient and time-consuming.

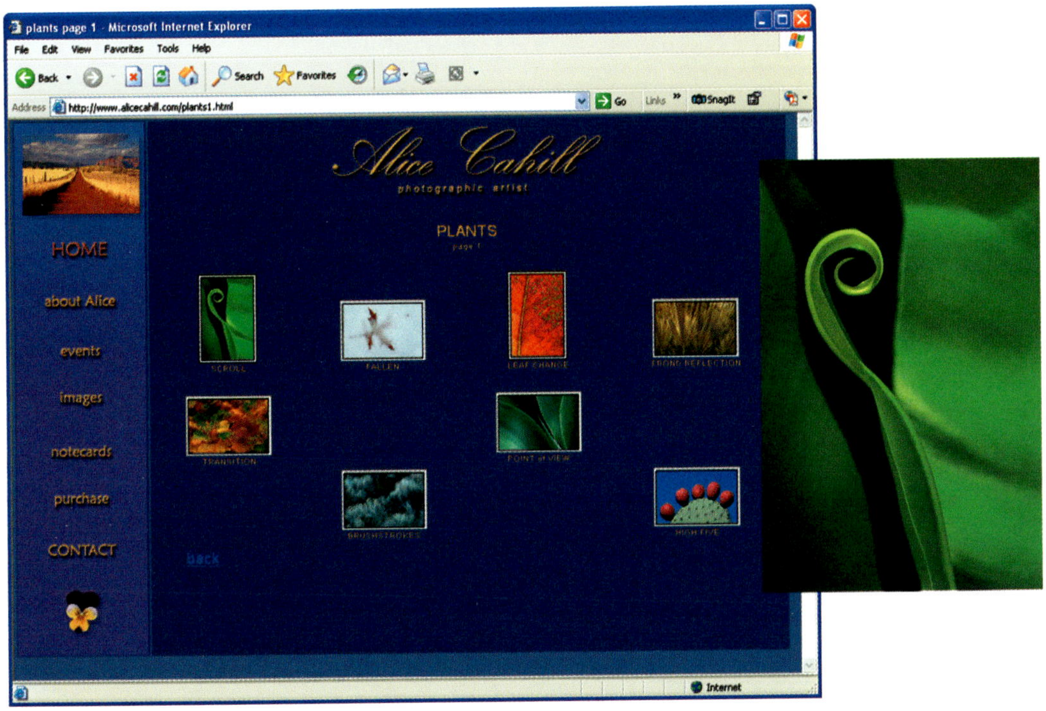

Figure 13.2 Preparing a group of images for display on a website is a perfect use of actions. (Photos by Alice Cahill, www.alicecahill.com)

Recording Actions

Managing your actions in Photoshop is handled through the Actions palette, so the first step is to make sure the Actions palette is visible. If it isn't, choose Window > Actions from the menu.

Note: To help you get started using actions, several are available for download from my website, www.timgrey.com. They can be found by following the link to this book from the Books page.

The Actions palette organizes your actions into sets (Figure 13.3). The Default Actions set contains the actions included with Photoshop. I recommend creating your own sets to keep your actions organized.

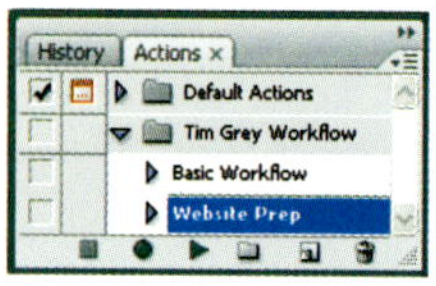

Figure 13.3 The Actions palette allows you to organize your actions into sets based on logical categories.

To create a new set, click the Create New Set button on the Actions palette. Enter a name for the new set and click OK (Figure 13.4).

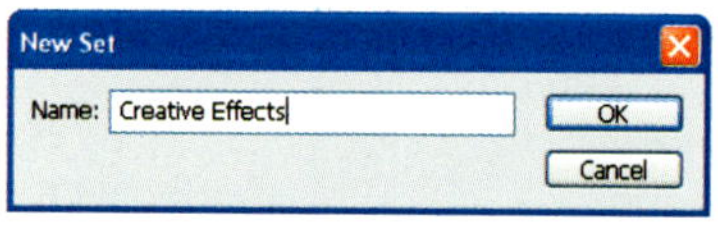

Figure 13.4 Creating a new actions set

You can use individual sets to hold various categories of actions, making it easier to stay organized and find the appropriate action when you need it. For example, I create sets for Output Preparation, Workflow Automation, and Creative Effects. These are just a few examples, and you'll certainly want to define your own categories based on the way you work and the tasks you want to automate within your workflow.

After you've created a set to contain your new action (or selected an existing set you'd like the action placed in), you're ready to begin the recording process. Make sure the set you want to place the new action into is selected on the Actions palette, and then click the Create New Action button to bring up the New Action dialog box (Figure 13.5).

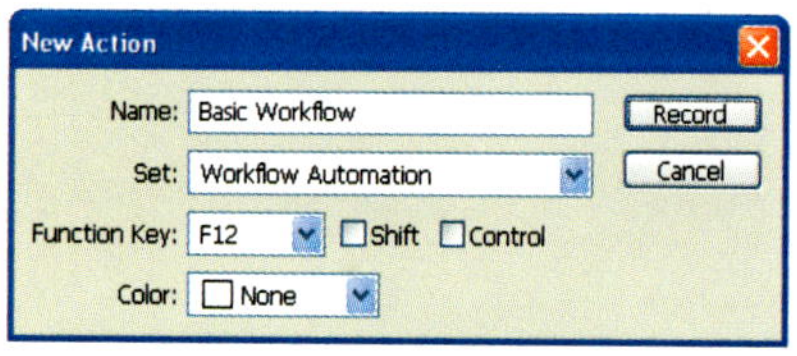

Figure 13.5 The New Action dialog box allows you to set the attributes of your new action, including the name and function key to be used for quick access.

Enter a name for the new action. This is the name that will appear on the Actions palette, so it is best to use a name that describes the result you'll achieve with the action. For example, if you're creating an action to process a series of images for display on a website, you might call the action *Website Prep*. The set that was active when you clicked the Create New Action button will be selected in the New Action dialog box by default, but if you selected the wrong set, you can choose the correct one from the dropdown list.

The Function Key settings allow you to assign a keyboard shortcut to the new action. Start by selecting one of the function keys from the dropdown list. You can also add modifier keys to this new keyboard shortcut by selecting the Shift and/or Control/ Command checkboxes. These options will determine the keyboard combination that can be used to immediately invoke a particular action on the current image.

Note: If you're using function keys for your actions, I recommend including the shortcut key in the name of the action so you can see the shortcut on the Actions palette for quick reference.

The Color option in the New Action dialog box allows you to specify a color for the action, but this color is visible only when you set the Actions palette to Button mode (Figure 13.6). Normally, the actions are displayed in a list under each set on the Actions palette. However, you can switch to Button mode by selecting that option from the palette menu. When you do so, each action will be displayed as an individual button with the color that was assigned to it, and each action can be run by simply clicking its button. I generally don't use Button mode, so I don't assign colors to my actions. However, if you prefer to work with the Actions palette in Button mode, you can use this facility to color-code your actions into categories to make it easier to find the right action when you need it.

Note: If you configure the Actions palette in Button mode, you'll lose the organizational benefit of having individual actions contained in sets.

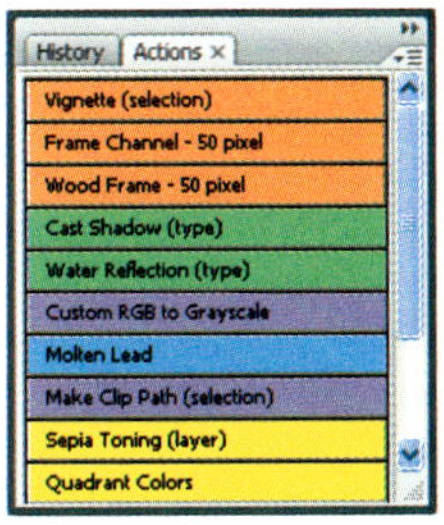

Figure 13.6 If you use Button mode for the Actions palette, the color property you assign in the New Action dialog box will be the color of the action's button.

Note: If you are creating an action that you'll typically apply to a single image, start recording the action with an image already open so that a File > Open step won't be included in your action.

When you click Record, the recording of your new action begins. Keep in mind that Photoshop is registering the *results* of each step you perform, rather than recording what you do in real time. Therefore, you can take your time thinking about each step and deciding upon the best settings without worrying about the speed of playback for your action later. The action will always run as quickly as possible.

Note: Before you start performing the action steps, spend some time thinking about exactly what steps you want to include and in what order. It might even be helpful to write a list of steps you can review before getting started to make sure you include every necessary step and that they are performed in the correct order.

When recording the action, simply perform the steps you want to include in the action. Be sure to perform the steps in the order you want them repeated when you play the action for a given image. You can revise the settings as much as you like during the process of recording the action; Photoshop will save only the final result of each step.

Note: I recommend creating a working copy of the image you are using to record your action so you don't accidentally save your master image file after making modifications.

If you'll be running an action on a large group of images, I strongly recommend saving the resulting image and closing the file as the last steps of the action. This will ensure the results are saved properly and that each processed image is closed so memory consumption doesn't become a problem. When you are finished performing all the steps you'd like to include in the action, click the Stop Recording button ■ on the Actions palette. The action will be ready for you to use, contained in the selected set on the palette.

Note: Although actions offer a powerful way to automate many tasks in Photoshop, they don't provide an ideal solution for tasks that relate to specific positions within an image, because positions that are possible for one image may not be an option for another, and all coordinates relate to the top-left corner. For example, placing text in the bottom-right corner via an action wouldn't work well because those coordinates would be different for images with different pixel dimensions.

Revising Actions

At times you'll discover that an action includes steps you don't want to have included or that steps you want to include were left out. Fortunately, resolving these issues is easy.

To remove a step from an action, first expand the action display (if it isn't already) by clicking the arrow button to the left of the action name. This will show you all of the steps included in that action. Select the step you want to remove and click the Trash icon on the Actions palette. You can also drag individual steps to the Trash. This will remove that step from the action without affecting any of the other steps.

If you need to insert a step in an action, make sure the list of steps in the action is expanded on the Actions palette and select the step located *before* the position where you want to insert the new step (or steps). Then click the Record button on the Actions palette to resume recording at that point in the action. Any new steps you perform will be inserted into the action. When you're finished performing the steps you want to insert, click the Stop Recording button on the Actions palette.

Although the whole idea of creating actions is to automate certain tasks as much as possible, at times you will want an action to stop and allow you to adjust the settings. By default, an action will simply play back the steps you performed with the same settings, and you'll never see any dialog boxes during playback. If you'd like to see a dialog box for a particular step so you can adjust the settings as needed, click in the empty box to the left of that step in the palette. This will place a small icon in the box, indicating that the dialog box for that step will be displayed. The settings recorded as part of the action will be the default settings for the dialog box, but you can revise them during playback if desired. When you click OK in the dialog box during playback, the action will continue from that point. You can choose to enable the dialog box for as many steps in the action as possible, but keep in mind that this reduces the automated benefit of using actions, so you should use this option only when you really need to customize settings for a particular step.

It can also be helpful to insert messages into your actions to remind you of what should be done at a particular step. For example, I've created workflow actions (available on my website at www.timgrey.com) that automate the task of processing an image in a typical workflow. For users just starting with the workflow, I created a version of this action that includes messages at each step reminding the user of what should be done with the dialog boxes that follow each message (Figure 13.7).

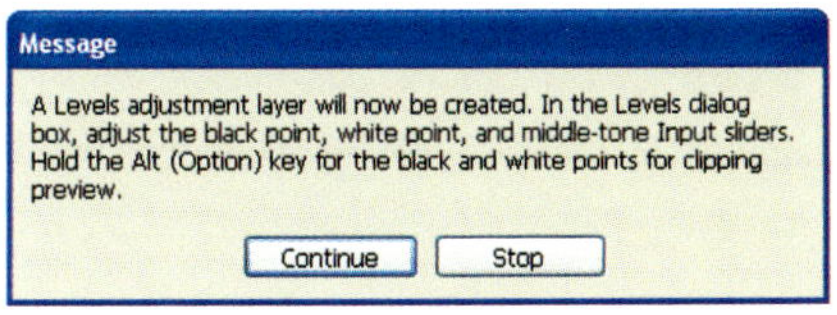

Figure 13.7 Inserting a stop into an action is a good way to remind yourself of what steps need to be taken at a particular point in the action.

These messages are created by adding a stop to the action after you have recorded it. To add a stop, first select the step in the action *before* the position where you want the stop to be added. Then select Insert Stop from the Actions palette menu (Figure 13.8). The Record Stop dialog box will appear, dominated by a Message text box, where you can type the message you'd like to be displayed at this point in the action (Figure 13.9). Enter the message exactly as you'd like it to appear in the dialog box that will display when the action is played back.

Note: Stops can also be added while the action is being recorded in the same way as described earlier in this chapter, but I tend to add the stops after recording so I can focus on the actual tasks I'm trying to perform during that process.

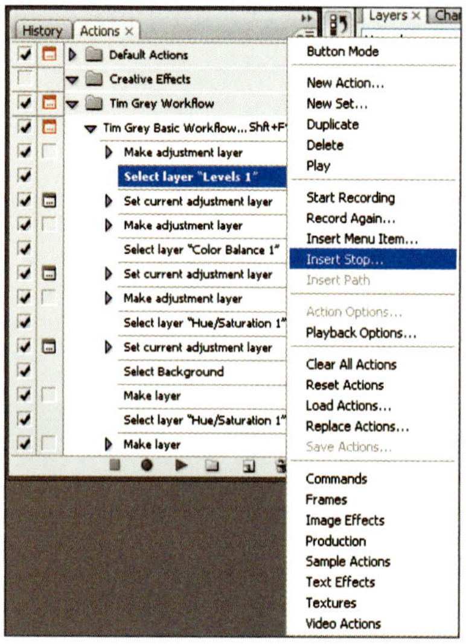

Figure 13.8 To insert a stop into an action, select the step before the position where you want the stop to be added and select Insert Stop from the palette menu.

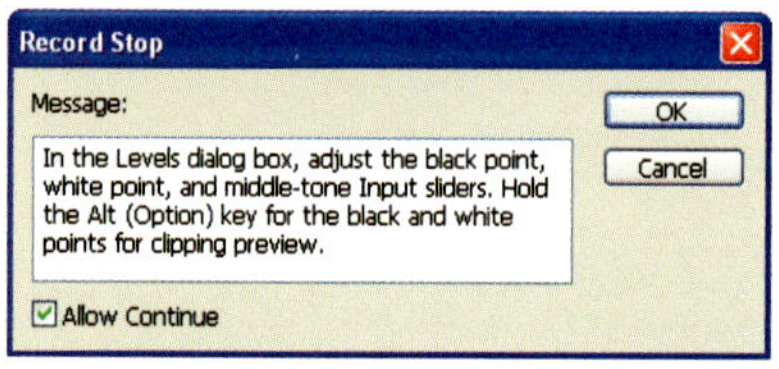

Figure 13.9 In the Record Stop dialog box, type the text you'd like to have displayed when the stop occurs in the action and select the Allow Continue checkbox.

By default, the action will stop at this point (thus the name *stop*), which means steps after the stop will not be performed. To get the behavior you're looking for, which is to simply pause to remind the user of something, be sure to select the Allow Continue checkbox. This will ensure that both Continue and Stop buttons are included on the message box that will be displayed at this point when the action is played.

Playing Actions

You can play back a recorded action at any time to apply the steps included in that action to a given image. This would most often be done when you have an image open and you want to apply the steps to that image.

There are a couple of ways you can play an action to apply its steps to the currently active image. One method is to select the action on the Actions palette and click the Play button ▶, or if you're in Button mode, simply click the name of the action. If you assigned a keyboard shortcut to the action when it was created, you can press that shortcut key to run the action.

Note: If you forgot to assign a keyboard shortcut to an action or don't remember what it is, you can select Action Options from the side menu on the Actions palette to open the Action Options dialog box, which contains the same settings as the New Action dialog box.

An Action in Action

To give you a better sense of how this whole process works, here are the steps you could use to create a simple action to prepare images from your master image files (PSD files with layers) for use in a digital slideshow, assuming a digital projector with a 1024×768 display resolution:

1. Open one of your master image files that contains multiple layers.
2. Create a working copy of this image by choosing Image > Duplicate from the menu and clicking OK in the Duplicate Image dialog box.
3. Close the original master image file, keeping only the working copy open.
4. On the Actions palette, select an appropriate action set folder, or create a new one by clicking the Create New Set button.
5. Click the Create New Action button and enter a name for your new action, such as *Digital Slideshow Prep.* Select a function key from the dropdown if you'd like to be able to run this action by pressing a button. Click Record to start recording the action.
6. Choose Layer > Flatten Image from the menu to flatten the layers in this image.
7. Choose File > Automate > Fit Image from the menu, enter **1024** for Width and **768** for Height, and click OK.
8. Choose Edit > Convert To Profile from the menu, select sRGB from the Profile dropdown list, and click OK. This will help ensure the best color possible for slideshow applications that aren't color managed.
9. Click the Stop Recording button on the Actions palette to stop recording this action.

This action can be run on any image you'd like to prepare for a digital slideshow. As discussed in the next section, you could also batch process a group of images with this action for even greater automation. If you will batch process images with this action, add as a last step saving the image as a JPEG file.

Batch Processing

The ability to apply actions to a group—or *batch*—of images all at once provides one of the greatest potential benefits of actions. The basic concept is that you can perform a task once during the process of recording an action, and then with complete automation apply that action to a folder full of images.

First, of course, you need to create an action that will be appropriate for applying to a large number of images. As part of the process of creating such an action, I recommend including steps to open the image, save the image, and close the image. This will make applying the action more efficient, which you'll see as you explore the options.

With the action created, choose File > Automate > Batch from the menu. This will bring up the Batch dialog box, which includes all the options you need for applying an action to a group of images (Figure 13.10). The Batch dialog box is divided into parts that are described throughout the rest of this section.

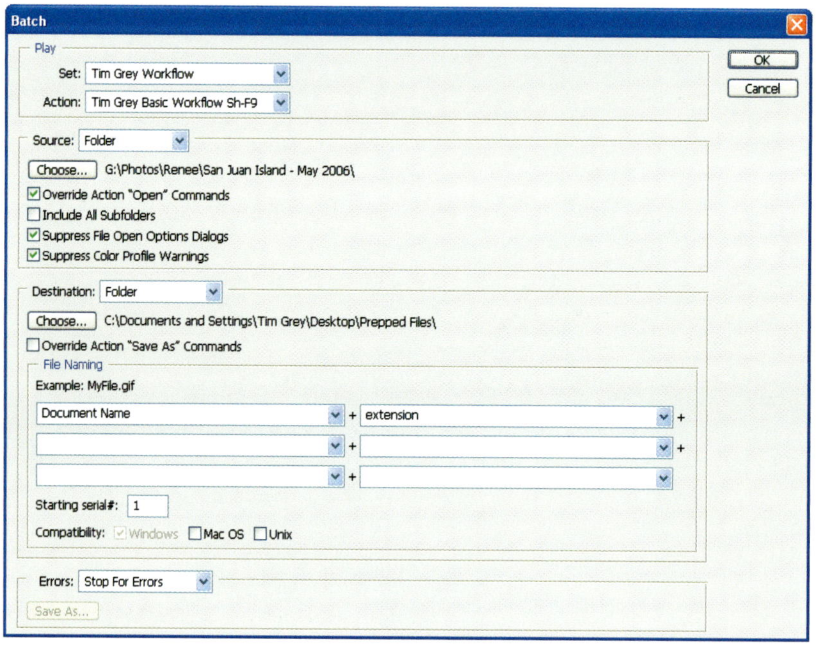

Figure 13.10 The Batch dialog box allows you to establish settings for running an action on a large group of images automatically.

Play Settings

The Play section of the Batch dialog box allows you to select the action you would like to run, by selecting the set that contains the action and then selecting the specific action to use. Both of these options will be selected automatically for you based on the action that is selected on the Actions palette when you select the Batch command from the menu, but you can always change the action here if necessary.

Source Settings

The Source section allows you to specify the source of images to be processed as well as set some options for how those images should be handled.

The Source dropdown list at the top of this section allows you to select Folder, Import, Opened Files, or Bridge. I normally use the Folder option, which allows you to process all images in a particular folder. If you select the Folder option, be sure to click the Choose button and specify the folder that contains the images you'd like to process. The Import option allows you to process images from a PDF document, scanner, or digital camera. For a typical workflow this wouldn't provide a significant benefit, but it would certainly be possible to use this capability to automatically download and process images from a digital camera. The Opened Files option will apply the selected action to all images that are currently open in Photoshop. Finally, the Bridge option will apply the action to the images that are currently selected in Bridge.

Note: You can also apply an action to multiple files by first selecting them in Bridge and then choosing Tools > Photoshop > Batch from the menu in Bridge.

The checkboxes that provide additional options in the Source section of the Batch dialog box are a common source of confusion because of the way they need to be used to get the desired behavior.

The Override Action "Open" Commands checkbox determines whether any steps in the action that would open a file are going to be overridden by the action during batch processing. If you select this checkbox, no files will be opened unless there is an open step in the action for it to override. In other words, if you don't have an open step, there's no command to override, and so no opening is performed at all (making the action useless). This checkbox is helpful when you've recorded an action that will open specific files, and you now want to run that action on different files. In most cases, you should not select this checkbox, especially if you have open commands within the action that do need to run during the processing of the action.

The Include All Subfolders checkbox, as its name indicates, determines whether folders inside the selected folder will be checked for images to process with the action. If you select this box, all images inside all folders within the folder you selected for processing will be processed with the action.

The Suppress File Open Options Dialogs checkbox is especially helpful for processing RAW files. Selecting this checkbox will cause any dialog boxes that appear when you open an image to be suppressed. As you've no doubt noticed, for most file types no dialog box appears when you open the file—the image simply opens. RAW files are a notable exception. If you want to process such files—or any other file format that causes a dialog box to appear, such as a PDF—you can select this box. In the case of RAW files, the images will then be converted based on the stored settings for each image (see the earlier sidebar "Batch RAW Conversion" for more information).

Finally, the Suppress Color Profile Warnings checkbox allows you to disable any missing profile or profile mismatch dialog boxes that could otherwise pause an action in the middle of a process, requiring user intervention. However, note that this option won't disable the alert message that appears when you have already disabled these dialog boxes in Color Settings. These alert messages can be disabled upon their first display by selecting the Don't Show Again checkbox.

Note: I recommend selecting both of the Suppress checkboxes to take full advantage of a completely automated batch processing of an action.

Destination Settings

The Destination section allows you to specify what should be done with the images when the action has finished processing them. Although several options exist, my recommendation is to always use the Folder option.

Note: Regardless of the Destination settings you're using, I recommend including a way for the images to be closed when the action completes (either by selecting the Save And Close setting or by including a File > Close step in your action) so excessive memory isn't consumed by leaving a large number of images open in Photoshop.

Selecting None will cause nothing special to be done with your files when the action completes. Although this may seem like a silly option, it provides the ability to let your action handle all of the file management chores. The only time I use this option is when I'm processing a set of duplicate image files and want to simply save them and then close the images. More often, I'm creating a separate version of images for a specific purpose, and so I want to utilize different output options. If you are using the None option, be sure you have both a Save As and a Close step in your action.

The Save And Close option will, as the name indicates, save the image with changes based on the steps performed by the action and then close the image. This is similar to the results of selecting None, except that the saving and closing of the images is done automatically without steps in the action to perform those tasks. I don't recommend using this option under most circumstances because it will replace the original files with the changed version, which causes you to risk replacing master image files with altered (and potentially damaged to some extent) versions.

As I said, the Folder option is the one I recommend using for most actions. It allows you to indicate a specific location where you would like to save the images after they are processed by the action. After selecting this option, click the Choose button to select the folder where you'd like the images to be placed, using a location that is different from the source folder for the images.

I also recommend selecting the Override Action "Save As" Commands checkbox, although you need to be aware of a catch. In order for this setting to work properly, you must have a Save As step as part of your action. It may seem pointless to have this Save As step if you're just going to override it, but doing so allows you to establish file settings that will be used even though the override option is selected. For example, if you've created an action to prepare images for posting on a website, you could include a Save As step that saves the files as a JPEG at a Quality setting of 8. When you override this setting, the actual location and filename will be overridden during the batch processing, but the file type and attributes will be preserved. Therefore, in this case you'd still be saving JPEG files at a Quality setting of 8, but you'd be saving them in the specified location with the opportunity to change the filename.

The File Naming section provides the opportunity to specify filenames if you are using the Folder option. The name is established with a series of combination dropdown boxes. You can either type a value or choose a preset value from the dropdown. For example, if you wanted your files to have a structure such as `Music0001.jpg`, you could type **Music** into the first field, select 4 Digit Serial Number from the second dropdown, and Extension from the third. You could create much more complicated filename formats if desired by choosing any combination of options or typing custom values in any field. Note that the preset fields are *case-indicative,* meaning the way the option is formatted tells you how the result will be formatted. For example, "DOCUMENT NAME" will result in the original filename being used with all-caps, and "document name" will result in the original filename being used with all lowercase.

Below the series of dropdown controls is a Starting Serial# text box, where you can type a numeric value for the serial number used in destination filenames. This setting is applicable only if you've included one of the serial number options from the dropdowns. You can set this to any value that is within the range of the number of digits you've included, which is helpful if you are adding to an existing library of processed images.

Finally, the Compatibility option allows you to select for which operating system you want to ensure file-naming compatibility. If you know what platform the final images are going to be used on, you should select the appropriate option.

Error Handling

The final section in the Batch dialog box allows you to specify how errors should be handled. The only options are Stop For Errors and Log Errors To File. My feeling is that if an error occurs in an action, one (or more) of the steps you wanted to apply to the image couldn't be completed, and you should know about that and deal with it immediately. Therefore, I recommend using the Stop For Errors option. If an error occurs, the action will stop processing where it left off, and you can proceed from there.

Of course, if you're processing a large number of images and don't want to interrupt that process, you may want to use the Log Errors To File option and then check the log file for any problems after the batch processing is complete. If so, you'll need to click the Save As button after choosing Log Errors To File to specify where the log file should be saved.

Process the Batch

After you've established all the settings for processing a group of images, you can simply click OK and the process will begin. Provided there aren't any errors, each image to be processed based on the Source settings will be processed with the action you specified, with the resulting images created (or updated) based on the Destination settings. The result is an incredibly flexible way to automate repetitive tasks on one image or hundreds of images.

Droplets

Actions allow you to process images individually or by batch within Photoshop, but you can also create *droplets* so you can perform the same tasks on an individual image (or folder full of images) by simply dragging them onto an icon outside of Photoshop from your operating system's file system.

The first step is to create a droplet. To do so, choose File > Automate > Create Droplet from the menu. This will bring up a dialog box that is virtually identical to the Batch dialog box discussed earlier, except that there's no Source section and there is a Save Droplet In section (Figure 13.11).

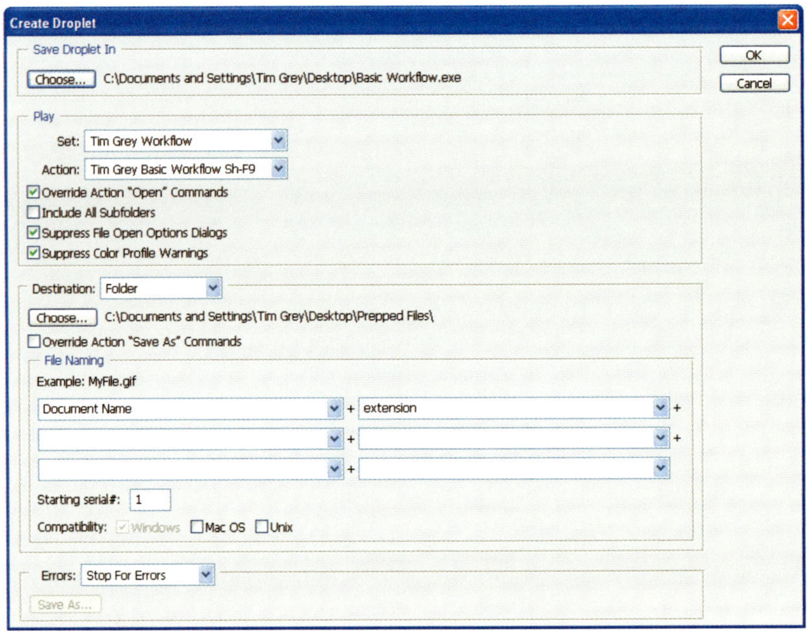

Figure 13.11 The Create Droplet dialog box allows you to turn an action into a droplet onto which you can drag and drop images.

Click the Choose button and specify the location and filename for the droplet. For maximum accessibility, I recommend saving the droplet on your desktop with a name that defines the task to be performed by the associated action. Set the rest of the options in the Create Droplet dialog box exactly as you would for the Batch dialog box, selecting the action to be played (and related options), the Destination settings, and how you want errors handled. Click OK, and the droplet will be saved based on your settings.

To use the droplet, simply drag any image file (or folder containing image files) onto the droplet icon (Figure 13.12). Photoshop will automatically launch if it isn't already running, and the action will be run on the image(s) based on the settings you used when creating the droplet.

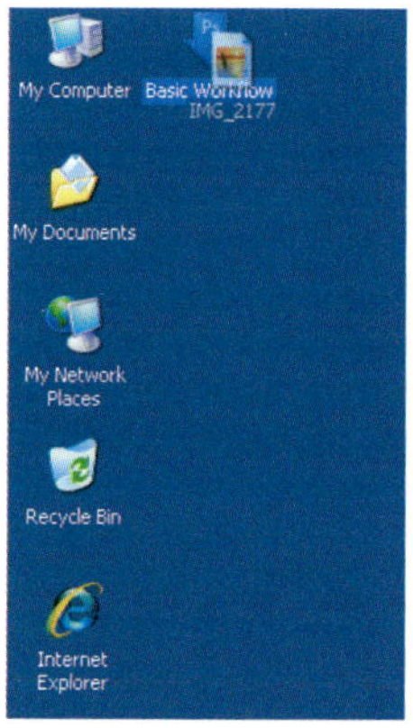

Figure 13.12 To apply an action to an image from a droplet, simply drag and drop the image file onto the droplet. Photoshop will launch automatically and process the image with the associated action.

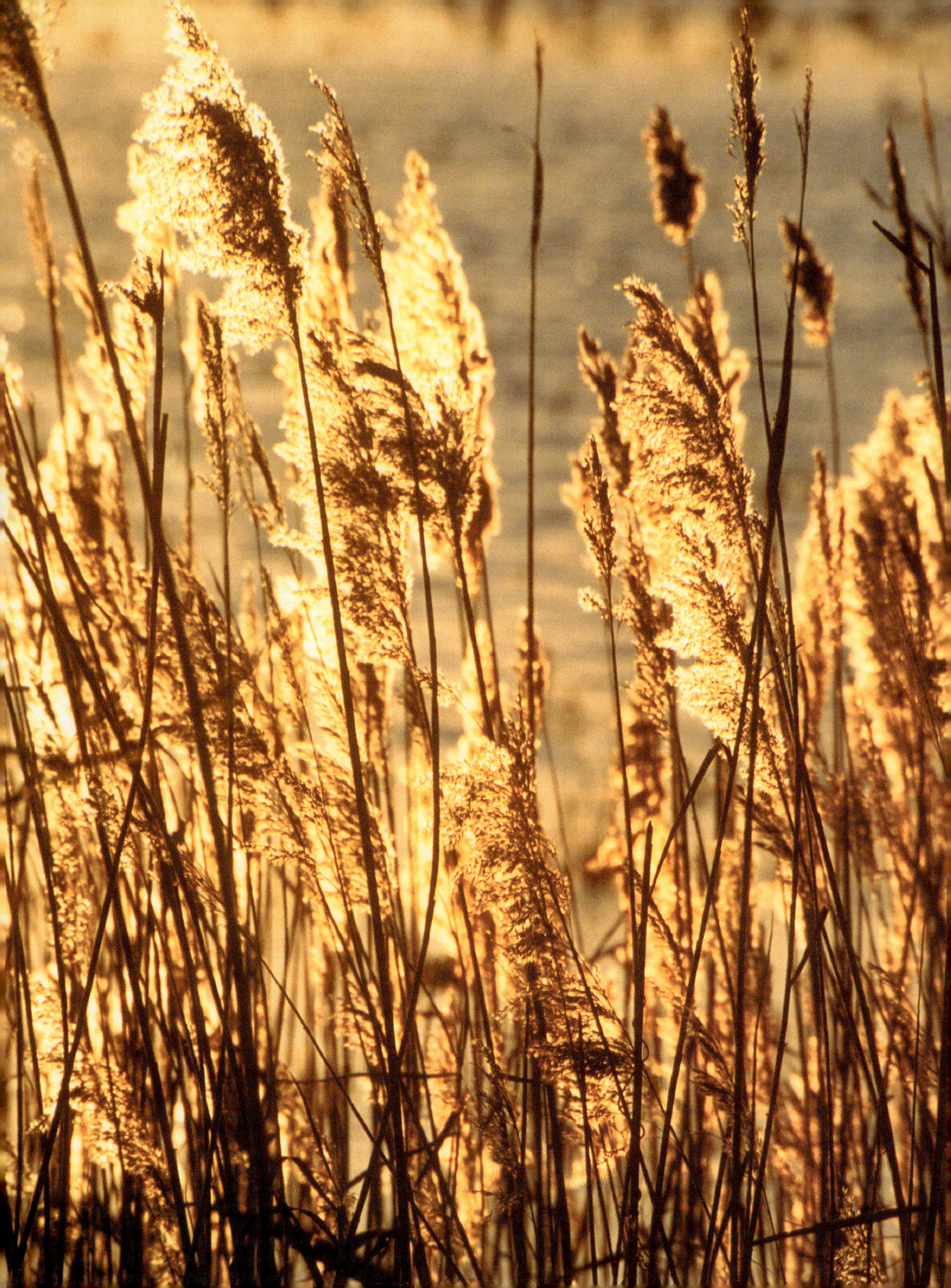

14 Output Processing

The ultimate goal for most photographers putting an image through the paces of an optimization workflow, as presented through the chapters of this book, is to prepare an image to share with others. That generally means producing output in some form, most commonly as a print. To preserve the work you've put into the original image and to ensure the best output quality possible, following an output processing workflow is important.

Chapter Contents

Output Workflow

The output workflow I recommend is a process that helps ensure you don't lose any information in your master image file (Figure 14.1). Throughout this book I've demonstrated methods of working with your images in Photoshop that not only preserve the original information contained in your image in the form of the Background image layer, but also preserve in discrete packets all of the adjustments you've made to the image in the form of adjustment layers and additional image layers (Figure 14.2).

When producing output from your images, you will need to perform tasks that will destroy some of the information in your image. Therefore, a workflow that insulates you from the risk of permanently losing that information is important.

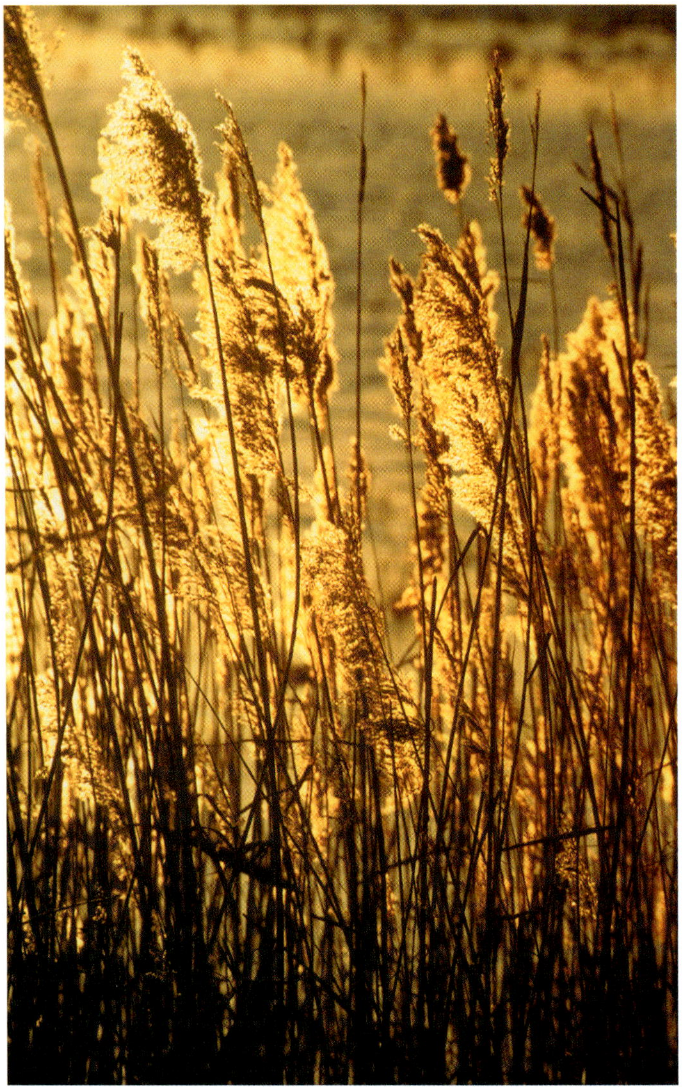

Figure 14.1 When you've put the effort into optimizing your image to produce exactly the result you intended, preserving that information in a master image file is important. (Photo by Gabby Salazar, www.gabbysalazar.com)

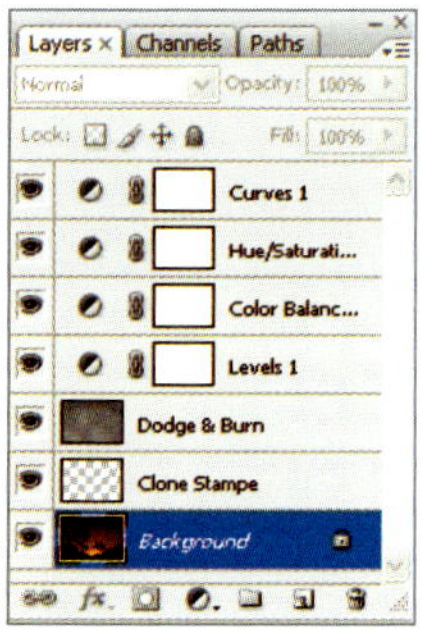

Figure 14.2 The master image file preserves the original image by maintaining a Background image layer that isn't modified and other layers that perform the actual adjustments.

Preserve the Master Image

The first step in preparing your image for output is making sure you've preserved the information contained in that image file. As discussed in Chapter 12, "Saving Files," when you have completed the process of optimizing your image by using the workflow techniques discussed in this book, it is important to save the file with all layers included in that file. This file, typically saved as either a Photoshop PSD or TIFF file, becomes your master image file (Figure 14.3). It contains both your original capture information and all information about the adjustments you've made to improve the image. It is critical that this information be preserved to provide you with maximum quality and flexibility later should you choose to revise your adjustments.

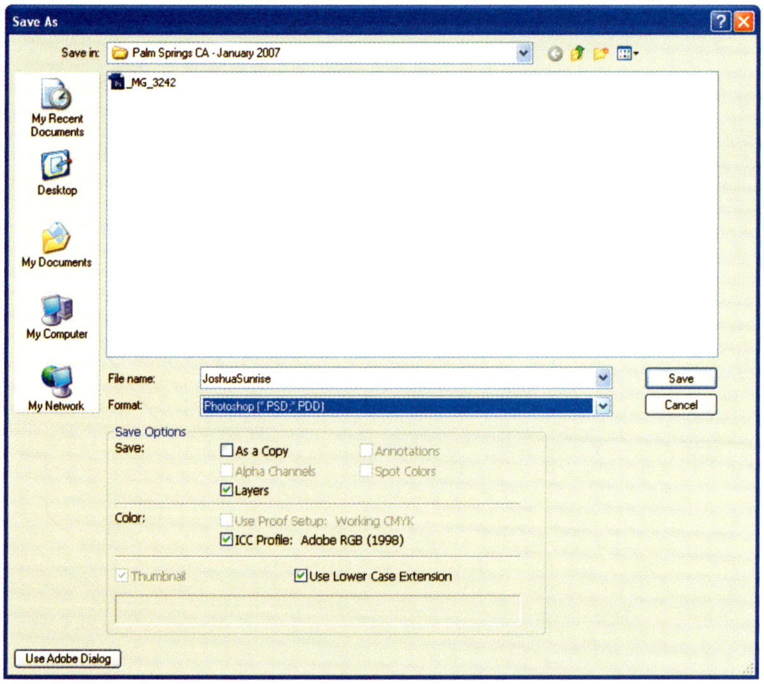

Figure 14.3 Saving your master image file as either a Photoshop PSD or TIFF image ensures you'll maintain all layers used to optimize the image.

Before you move on to preparing an image for output, be sure you have indeed saved the master image file. If you make any changes to this master image file, be sure to save it again so you don't lose those changes.

Note: Saving your master image file is important for obvious reasons, but it is also important that you back up your essential files. I recommend the use of external hard drives for this purpose, because they provide a fast, convenient, and scalable backup solution. However, any system that works for you is good, as long as you're safely backing up your images.

Process a Working Copy

With the peace of mind that comes from knowing your master image has been saved, you're ready to start processing your image to produce the intended output. This involves a series of steps that will prepare the image to be printed or displayed in the final form you have planned. By processing a working copy of the image, you'll be able to work without any concern that you'll harm your master image file.

Open the master image file for the photo you want to prepare for output, and you're ready to get started with the output preparation workflow.

Duplicate Image

The first step in processing your image safely is to create a working copy of the image. To do so, choose Image > Duplicate. The Duplicate Image dialog box will be displayed, allowing you to enter a name for the new image document (Figure 14.4). The name in the text box will simply be the name of the document you are duplicating with the word *copy* appended to it. You can enter a different name if you like, which will become the filename if you save this duplicate image. This can be helpful if you plan to save a copy of the processed image (as I'll discuss later in this chapter), but otherwise you can just accept the default name.

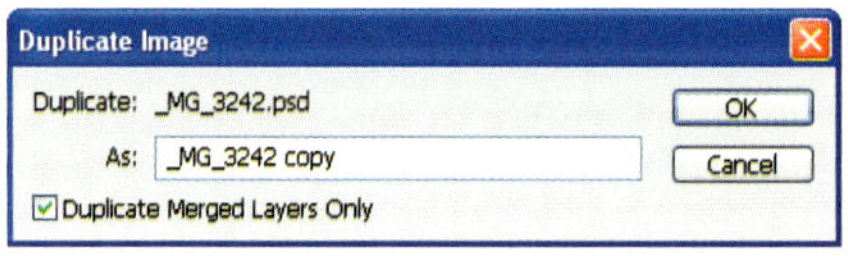

Figure 14.4 Using the Duplicate command allows you to create a working copy of your image, so you can work without worrying about accidentally replacing your master image file with a degraded version.

The Duplicate Image dialog box also contains a checkbox labeled Duplicate Merged Layers Only. This checkbox will be enabled only if the image you're duplicating contains multiple layers. If you select this checkbox, the duplicate image will be a flattened version of the original image, which is convenient because it allows you to skip the next step in the process. After you click OK to create the working copy of your image file, you can close the original master image.

Note: You can bypass the Duplicate Image dialog box by holding the Alt/Option key as you choose Image > Duplicate from the menu. The image will be duplicated with the default name and without flattening the layers.

Flatten Image

If you didn't flatten the working copy of your image in the process of creating the duplicate copy, I recommend flattening at this point. Generally speaking, it isn't necessary to flatten the image before printing it or saving it for other output. For example, you can most certainly send an image with many layers to your printer, because Photoshop will send the data based on the final appearance, so no problems are created for the printer.

However, as I said, I do recommend flattening the image at this point. You can feel perfectly comfortable doing so because you've already saved your master image file and are now processing a working copy of that image. There are also some benefits to flattening the file now. For one thing, flattening the file reduces the memory footprint and processing time required for the image. This is generally a small benefit, but it can be significant for large images. Another benefit has to do with sharpening. For most output methods you'll want to sharpen the image. Sharpening, as with any filter, can be applied to only one image layer at a time. If you have additional layers for cloning, compositing, or other purposes, you'd need to sharpen each of those layers individually. By flattening the image, you need to sharpen only once.

If you didn't already flatten the image during the Duplicate Image step, you can do so now by choosing Layer > Flatten Image from the menu, or by choosing Flatten Image from the palette menu on the Layers palette. All layers will be merged into a single layer, preserving the appearance of your image (Figure 14.5).

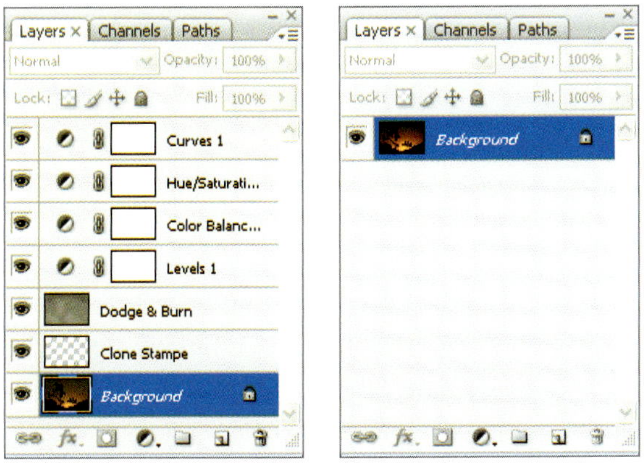

Figure 14.5 When you flatten an image, all layers from the original are merged into a single layer while maintaining the appearance of the image.

Image Size

Chances are the native size of your image doesn't match the final output size you're targeting, so you'll need to resize it. This requires setting the resolution for both the final output and the actual output size. To change the size of the image, choose Image > Image Size (Image > Resize > Image Size in Photoshop Elements), which will bring up the Image Size dialog box (Figure 14.6).

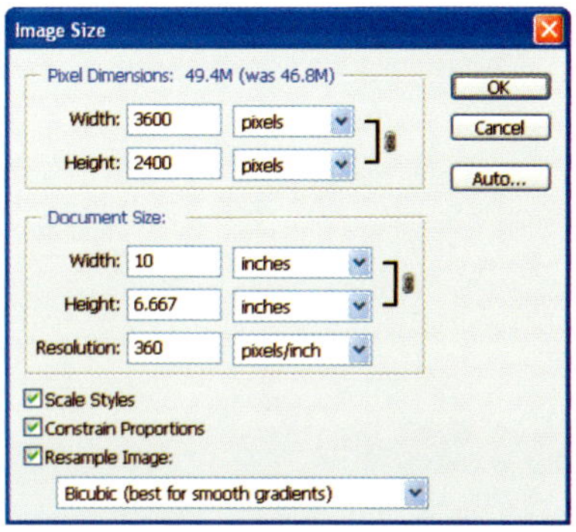

Figure 14.6 The Image Size dialog box allows you to resize the image to exactly the output size you need.

Note: If you need to crop your image to achieve a specific size, you can use the Crop tool with settings established for Width, Height, and Resolution on the Options bar to crop and resize in a single step.

Although you would typically start at the top of a dialog box and work your way down, in the case of Image Size I think it makes more sense to start at the bottom and work your way up. At the bottom, be sure the Resample Image checkbox is selected. The dropdown list to the right provides options for the algorithm to use for interpolating the data in your image. Bicubic is the sort of "all-purpose" best option and the one I generally recommend. If you're creating a particularly large enlargement from your original, the Bicubic Smoother option is a good choice. I don't like using Bicubic Sharper, which is designed to maintain sharpness when reducing the size of an image. I'd rather use Bicubic and apply my own sharpening later in that situation. The other two options provided, Nearest Neighbor and Bilinear, are not appropriate for producing high-quality photographic output and should not be used.

The Constrain Proportions checkbox should always be selected, in my opinion. Doing so ensures you'll maintain the aspect ratio for the image. If you clear this checkbox, it is possible to stretch the image in one direction or the other. Although this isn't a problem when done to a very small degree, it can produce a distorted result if taken too far, and I recommend eliminating the possibility altogether by keeping the checkbox selected.

The Scale Styles checkbox determines whether layer styles will be scaled when you resize the image or kept at their same size. This isn't an issue at this point because you have already flattened the image. However, if you were resizing an unflattened image, keep this checkbox selected because you generally want to scale any layer styles along with the image.

The Resolution box in the Document Size section of the Image Size dialog box determines how the pixels will be distributed when the image is output, and it plays a role in determining the number of pixels required in the final image. This number is irrelevant for digital display (monitor and digital projector, for example). However, because some applications that you may import your images into do indeed look at this number, I recommend setting it to about 96 dpi for those situations. For printing, it will depend on the output method being used, but 300 dpi is a good standard value.

Note: If you're working with film scans, it is particularly important to keep an eye on the Resolution setting. If you've scanned at 4,000 dpi, you don't want to resize to a 20″×30″ print without changing the resolution to a more appropriate value, or you'll produce an absolutely huge file that will take forever to resize and likely crash your computer.

The next step is to set the actual output size. For printed images, this should be done in the Document Size section, setting either the Width or the Height. You can change the unit of measure with the dropdown to the right. If you have the Constrain Proportions checkbox selected (as I recommend), then you can set one and the other will adjust automatically. I recommend sizing the image to fit the paper you'll print to, although obviously in some situations you'll need to set a more specific output size.

Note: When you make adjustments in Image Size that affect the pixel dimensions of the image, the current size is displayed after the Pixel Dimensions label, and the starting size is shown in parentheses.

For images that will be displayed digitally on a monitor or digital projector, the size should be adjusted by using the Width or Height text boxes in the Pixel Dimensions section. This allows you to set the specific pixel sizing for your intended purpose. For a digital slideshow, for example, you might set these dimensions to fit within the resolution of your digital projector. For a website, you might set them to a standard output size you deem appropriate for your specific site design.

Note: For more discussion of preparing your images for all types of output, see my book *Photo Finish* (Sybex, 2004), coauthored with Jon Canfield.

After you've established the sizing parameters in the Image Size dialog box, click OK and the image will be resized accordingly.

Unsharp Mask

Virtually all images that are being prepared for output in any form need to be sharpened to some degree in order to optimize their appearance and compensate for the loss of sharpness that occurs at the time of output. The only exceptions are images that don't contain any real detail you want to enhance. However, this is generally a rare exception, so you can assume that all images need to be sharpened.

Note: It is important to apply sharpening after you have resized the image, so the effect will be optimized for the actual pixel dimensions and won't be altered by subsequent resizing.

To apply sharpening, choose Filter > Sharpen > Unsharp Mask from the menu. This will bring up the Unsharp Mask dialog box, which allows you to adjust three values for modifying the sharpening effect: Amount, Radius, and Threshold (Figure 14.7).

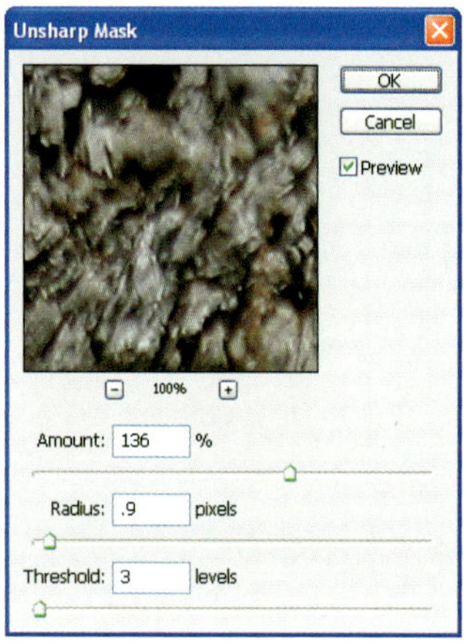

Figure 14.7 The Unsharp Mask dialog box allows you to adjust the sharpening effect by specifying values for Amount, Radius, and Threshold.

Unsharp Mask operates by enhancing contrast along the edges of objects within your image. In other words, it enhances contrast where contrast already exists. Adjusting the controls in the Unsharp Mask dialog box allows you to change how this contrast enhancement is applied.

The Amount setting determines the extent to which contrast is enhanced along edges. You can think of this as an intensity control. The higher the setting, the more intense the edge contrast will be in your image. As a general rule, I work in a range from about 100% to 300% for Amount.

The Radius setting allows you to determine the size of the area to be affected by the boost in contrast along edges. For images with high detail, you'd generally want to have the impact affect only a small area for each edge, so work in a range of around 0.4 to 1.0 pixels. For images with low detail, a setting of between 2.0 and 3.0 is probably best. When in doubt, work in a range from about 1.0 to 1.5.

The Threshold setting provides something of a "damage control" function. It determines how much contrast must exist between two pixels for them to be considered as defining an edge. With a minimum Threshold setting of 0, virtually all pixels will be affected by sharpening. As you increase the value, fewer areas will be sharpened because they must exhibit a certain amount of contrast before sharpening will be applied. This enables you to maintain smooth textures in areas of the image where that is important.

For high-detail images, you'll generally want to use a very low Threshold setting, between 0 and 4. For images with areas of smooth texture that you want to preserve, a setting of between 8 and 12 is probably appropriate.

It is important that you evaluate the effect of Unsharp Mask on a 100% preview of your image. However, I don't zoom in to a 100% scale on the image itself when using Unsharp Mask. I find it much more convenient to resize the image to fit the screen (by pressing Ctrl/Command+0) so I can see all of it at once. Then I use the full image to decide where I want to look, clicking on that spot with the mouse. The preview within the Unsharp Mask dialog box defaults to a 100% scale, so I can use that to evaluate the actual effect. In addition, you can click and hold your mouse on the preview image in the Unsharp Mask dialog box to see the "before" version and release the mouse button to see the "after" version again. By using this method, I can quickly click on various areas of the image to preview the effect in key areas (Figure 14.8).

After you've established your settings for Unsharp Mask, click OK and the effect will be applied.

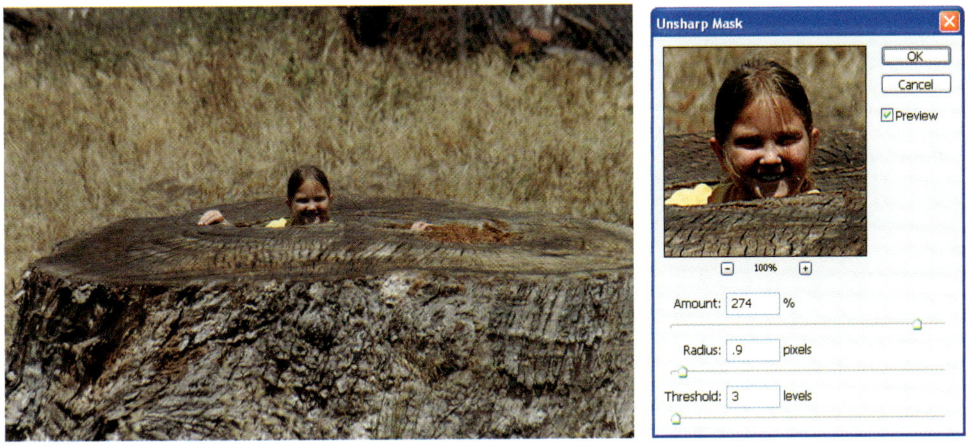

Figure 14.8 By keeping the image sized to fit your display, but the preview in Unsharp Mask set to 100%, you can easily navigate around your image and check the effect of your sharpening settings on various areas.

Note: I've written an e-book specifically on the subject of sharpening. *Photoshop Sharpening* is available for purchase and download as a PDF from www.sybex.com.

Image Output

The image is now prepared for final output. If you are preparing the image for a digital slideshow or web display, you can simply save the file. If, however, you are going to print the image, this is the time to do so, making sure to use the appropriate settings for your printer. By using the workflow presented in this chapter to prepare your image, you can rest assured that the master image file is safely protected and that the quality of the final print will be the best possible.

Note: For more details on sending your prepared image to the printer with all appropriate settings to ensure accurate results, see my book *Color Confidence* (Sybex, second edition 2006).

Smart Sharpen

Photoshop includes several options for sharpening besides Unsharp Mask, and the Smart Sharpen filter is a good alternative. I prefer not to use it because it doesn't offer a Threshold setting for reducing sharpening in smooth areas. However, it does include options for mitigating sharpening in shadow and highlight areas in your image (among a few other benefits), which can be a helpful feature.

If you'd like to try Smart Sharpen, you can get started by selecting Filter > Sharpen > Smart Sharpen from the menu. Set the option to Advanced so you can see all of the available controls, and select the More Accurate checkbox so the preview will better reflect the final result (although this will also slow down the update for the preview, especially on large images).

The Amount and Radius controls behave as they do in Unsharp Mask (with some differences in the effect due to the use of different algorithms). The Remove dropdown allows you to select between Gaussian Blur, Lens Blur, and Motion Blur. I generally use Lens Blur, unless I am in fact trying to compensate for some minor motion blur in the image. In the case of motion blur, you'll also be able to adjust the Angle setting to define which direction the motion is going within the image.

The Shadow and Highlight tabs each include the same controls. Fade Amount allows you to reduce the amount of sharpening applied to the darkest or lightest areas of the image, depending on which tab you're working on. The Tonal Width control allows you to adjust the range of values to be included in the range to be affected. In other words, how bright can an area be and still be included as a shadow area, and how dark can an area be and still be considered a highlight area? The Radius setting controls how far out from the shadow areas the reduction in sharpening should extend.

Save a Copy

Naturally, if you're preparing an image for use in another software application, such as when you're building a web page or producing a digital slideshow, you'll need to save a copy of the file. To do so, simply choose File > Save As from the menu, specify a location, filename, and file format, and click Save. For these types of usage, it is generally most appropriate to save the file in a JPEG format, with the Quality setting based on the priority between quality and file size (for example, file size is more important on the Web, whereas quality is a higher priority for digital slideshows).

Note: If you are preparing your image for digital display, such as on a monitor or digital projector, and the application used to present that image doesn't support color management, it is a good idea to convert the image to the sRGB color space before saving a copy of the image.

If you've prepared the image for printed output, saving a copy of the result is optional because you already have the master image file saved. That master image file should be the starting point for any future output, so the only real reason to save a copy of the final file is if you think you'll be printing that image repeatedly at the same size. Then you can simply open the prepared version and print it rather than going through the full output processing workflow each time you want to make a print at that size. The decision then is a matter of how often you'll print the file at that size and, therefore, how important it is to consume additional hard-disk space with an additional file.

If you do choose to save a copy of the file for print purposes, I would recommend saving the file in either the TIFF or Photoshop PSD format. For this purpose, I prefer to use the TIFF format because I'll know which are my master image files (which I save in Photoshop PSD format) and which are my copies for printing (which I save in TIFF). Either format is fine, though, so whatever you prefer will do the job.

Appendix

A Sample Workflow Checklist

The chapters of this book presented a logical workflow for optimizing your images. However, because the chapters offer considerable detail about how to perform each step, I am providing this basic checklist for use as you develop your own workflow. Think of this as a way to remind yourself of the order in which I recommend performing the steps of an image-optimization workflow, and use it as a guide for developing a workflow that works best for you. I'm also including a reference to the chapter that contains details on performing each step.

Sorting

- Download your images from your digital camera or memory card (Chapter 2).
- Use the Light Table workspace in Bridge to quickly review thumbnails and discard the obviously unacceptable images (Chapter 2).
- Use the Horizontal Filmstrip or Vertical Filmstrip workspace in Bridge to review your images more closely, discarding those that do not seem to be worth keeping and identifying images that are your favorites (Chapter 2).
- Evaluate your favorite images with great scrutiny to make sure they are worth the effort of a complete image-optimization workflow (Chapter 2).

Initial Image Preparation

- Convert RAW captures into image files with Adobe Camera Raw so you can optimize them in Photoshop (Chapter 3).
- Perform basic rotation to place the image in the proper orientation (Chapter 4).
- Perform basic cropping and rotation to eliminate unwanted pixels around the periphery of the image and to fix the horizon if crooked (Chapter 4).

Basic Optimization

- Perform a basic tonal adjustment by using Levels to set the black point, white point, and middle-tone values (Chapter 5).
- Perform a basic color balance adjustment to deal with any color cast in the image (Chapter 5).
- Perform a saturation adjustment with Hue/Saturation (Chapter 5).
- Clean up dust, scratches, and other blemishes by using the Clone Stamp, Spot Healing Brush, Healing Brush, and Patch tools (Chapter 6).

Advanced Adjustments

- Perform advanced tonal adjustments by using Curves, a dodge and burn layer, and blending modes on separate layers (Chapter 7).
- Perform color adjustments targeted to specific color values by using Hue/Saturation and Selective Color (Chapter 8).
- Perform targeted color fixes and saturation painting (Chapter 8).
- Create and save selections that isolate areas that will require targeted adjustments (Chapter 9).
- Make targeted adjustments to specific areas of your images by both creating selections and painting on masks (Chapter 10).
- Perform any creative adjustments you'd like (Chapter 11).

Workflow Wrap-Up

- Decide on a file-naming and organization plan regarding file location (Chapter 12).
- Save your master image file, preferably in the PSD file format (Chapter 12).
- Find ways to automate tasks that you are performing repeatedly in your workflow so you can work more efficiently (Chapter 13).
- Prepare your master image files for output so they can be shared with others (Chapter 14).

Index

Note to the Reader: Throughout this index **boldfaced** page numbers indicate primary discussions of a topic. *Italicized* page numbers indicate illustrations.

A

B

C

D

E

F

G

H

I

J

O

P

Q

R

S

T

U

V

W

Y

Z